FREUD,
PSYCHOANALYSIS,
SOCIAL THEORY

SUNY series in Social and Political Thought
Kenneth Baynes, editor

FREUD, PSYCHOANALYSIS, SOCIAL THEORY

The Unfulfilled Promise

FRED WEINSTEIN

State University
of New York
Press

Published by
State University of New York Press, Albany

© 2001 State University of New York

Production by Susan Geraghty
Marketing by Patrick Durocher

Printed in the United States of America

For information, address State University of New York Press,
90 State Street, Suite 700, Albany, NY 12207

Library of Congress Cataloging-in-Publication Data

Weinstein, Fred, 1931–
    Freud, psychoanalysis, social theory : the unfulfilled promise / Fred Weinstein.
        p. cm. — (SUNY series in social and political thought)
    Includes bibliographical references and index.
    ISBN 0-7914-4841-X (alk. paper) — ISBN 0-7914-4842-8 (pbk. : alk. paper)
        1. Social sciences and psychoanalysis. 2. Freud, Sigmund, 1856–1939. I. Title. II.
Series.

BF175.4.S65 W45 2001
150.19'52—dc21
                                                                    00-029138

10 9 8 7 6 5 4 3 2 1

For Joan,
the Children,
and the Grandchildren

CONTENTS

PREFACE

The history of psychoanalysis is always interesting, but never more so than when it is approached critically by psychoanalysts themselves. There is no aspect of psychoanalysis, and certainly no aspect of Freud's work, that has not been examined and rejected by any number of psychoanalysts, and I am not referring just to such obvious examples as Alfred Adler, C. G. Jung, John Bowlby, or Heinz Kohut. The critical spirit within psychoanalysis is far more widespread than that. I will focus on this aspect of the subject with particular reference to affective and cognitive issues; the structures of inference that provide no means for discriminating better from worse among an ever increasing number of competing perspectives; the implications of a lingering sense of regret among a number of psychoanalysts for Freud's abandonment of the "seduction theory" (actually a series of speculative propositions on the effects of sexually traumatic experience that preceded Freud's focus on intrapsychic reality, or what he considered to be psychoanalysis proper); and an enduring sense of crisis promoted in large part by the fragmentation of the discipline that these and still other issues have fostered.

I have chosen to focus on these problematic issues within psychoanalysis because, apart from being interesting in their own right, they also serve to underscore some important, perhaps unexpected, similarities between psychoanalysis and the social and behavioral sciences. I refer to the structures of inference of these disciplines, particularly where larger issues of cultural significance are concerned, to their fragmentation, and to the sense of crisis all of them have experienced over the past several decades on the testimony of concerned professionals themselves. In these terms, the gap between psychoanalysis and the social and behavioral sciences is not as great as many would like to think, given the constant criticism of psychoanalysis as singularly deficient. I will explore these issues in order to clarify what it will take to move all the different disciplines beyond the current impasse.

One aspect of this problem merits further comment. The attempts to redress the situation within the social and behavioral sciences by allowing method to dictate approach in the quest for predictive precision, distancing them thereby from the failed regulative constructs of earlier generations of theorists, have proved especially disappointing to those who, like Jerome Bruner or Richard Sennett, believe that their disciplines, psychology and sociology, should still be participating in the kind of cultural conversation once associated with systematic contributions to social theory. Bruner has noted that the devotion to "methodolatry" among academic psychologists has succeeded mostly in driving their audience away,[1] while Sennett has objected to the "dumbed down"condition of academic sociology that, because of its focus on small, quantifiable studies, has become "a refuge for the academically challenged."[2] It is worth considering the circumstances in which the situation in the social sciences might change.

One other general point merits comment as well: the extensive discussion of psychoanalytic theory obliges me to emphasize the distinction between critical appraisals of Freud and the sport of Freud bashing. I treat Freud and psychoanalysis critically, largely by reference to commentaries already available in the psychoanalytic literature itself. But for a very good reason, best revealed in recent work on mind and society by such professionals as Jerome Bruner and Joseph LeDoux, Freud bashing is pointless. That is, although Bruner and LeDoux cannot agree with Freud, their treatment of him is restrained, even generous, because they are only too aware of how little they actually know about mind and the relationship of mind to society, and how hard won any knowledge they do have really is.[3] Their approach to Freud's work is the only sensible one to take.

The uncertain state of theory in all the disciplines suggests that the important questions worth addressing now are, how did the different disciplines get to this point, and where do they go from here? These are difficult questions because, as Lewis Thomas noted of the study of social relationships, "Our behavior towards each other is the strangest, most unpredictable, and almost entirely unaccountable of all the phenomena with which we are obliged to live."[4] But it is necessary nevertheless to continue to address them.

Academic work directed to such complex questions is above all a cooperative enterprise, and I must once again acknowledge my indebtedness and thank all the friends and colleagues who helped me complete this project. I refer particularly to Gerald M. Platt whose contributions, as always, added significantly to the quality of what I have done. Naomi Rosenthal and William R. Taylor also read the book and made many valuable suggestions, as indeed they have also done before. I greatly appreciated as well the enthusiastic support of Kenneth Baynes, the editor of the series in social and political theory in which this book appears.

In addition, now that I am close to retirement, I want to take this opportunity to thank all my colleagues in the History Department at Stony Brook for their many kindnesses. But I especially want to thank a number of former graduate students for their effort, support, and friendship over many years, including Mel Albin, Joyce Antler, Seth Armus, Dominick Cavallo, Ann Geneva, Jane Gover, Peter Dobkin Hall, Katy Stewart, Robert Thomas, and Mitchell Thomashow. I also want to acknowledge my gratitude to Dan Omel, whom I taught as an undergraduate student at Stony Brook. Dan generously initiated a fund in my name that will provide a substantial award each year to a graduate student who, according to the judgment of an academic committee established for the purpose, has written the best chapter in a dissertation.

For convenience' sake, I provide a list of short titles to designate works that are most often cited:

SE   *The Standard Edition of the Complete Psychological Works of Sigmund Freud*, 24 volumes, translated by James Strachey (London: The Hogarth Press, 1953–1974).

Letters   *The Complete Letters of Sigmund Freud to Wilhelm Fliess, 1887–1904*, trans. and ed. Jeffrey Moussaieff Masson (Cambridge, Mass.: Harvard University Press, 1985).

IJPA   *The International Journal of Psychoanalysis*

IRPA   *The International Review of Psychoanalysis*

Ps St Chi *The Psychoanalytic Study of the Child*

JAPA   *The Journal of the American Psychoanalytic Association*

INTRODUCTION

The highly visible critiques of psychoanalysis by Frederick Crews, Adolf Grünbaum, Jeffrey Masson, Frank Sulloway, Peter Swales, Richard Webster, and others, have adversely affected the public's perception of the discipline.[1] But the sense of drift and crisis so pronounced within psychoanalysis is not so much a result of what these critics have done as it is of what psychoanalysts themselves have done over a period of time. Psychoanalysts are well aware that psychoanalysis has "lost its place as a body of knowledge and source of hypotheses after much of its early contributions found their way into the main body of psychiatry and psychology and the accretion of new knowledge slackened and stalled."[2] But they are also aware that the weaknesses in psychoanalytic theory and their critical examinations of theory are as responsible as anything else for this outcome.[3]

Few psychoanalysts have imagined that they could challenge Freud's work with the intention of supplanting it in a larger systematic sense. The names of the few who have attempted it are well and widely known: Alfred Adler, John Bowlby, Erik Erikson, W. R. D. Fairbairn, Sandor Ferenczi, Erich Fromm, Karen Horney, C. G. Jung, Heinz Kohut, Jacques Lacan, Melanie Klein, Otto Rank, Wilhelm Reich, Harry Stack Sullivan, D. W. Winnicott, and perhaps some notable others. Rather, psychoanalytic workers typically take a more modest approach, examining discrete elements or components of drive theory, object relations theory, structural theory, developmental theory, clinical theory, affect theory, identification, internalization, repression, transference and countertransference, and so on. It is in this context, especially in monographs and in the journal literature, that the extent to which psychoanalysts have themselves taken the discipline apart is best revealed. Thus while it is true that psychoanalysts have been too sectarian in outlook and too ready to bestow an inappropriate degree of loyalty on authoritative figures, and while it is also true that what started as theoretical "scaffolding" became, inappropriately, matters of doctrine and belief, they have taken on the critical task and challenged especially Freud's work in every dimension.[4]

I will examine here the consequences of these developments in the history and theories of psychoanalysis. This history—of the theories that

1

Freud had considered and then rejected, or adumbrated and then ignored; of the observations made by psychoanalysts in the course of struggles over clinical and theoretical issues; of the notable failures, evasions, and silences, particularly the long-term reluctance of psychoanalysts to assimilate their own data to the problems of theory and practice; and of the perspectives that still retain heuristic value, including, for example, the importance of wishful or fantasy thinking[5]—presents us with an especially favorable field for exploration of Freud's paramount interest, cultural analysis and interpretation.

Thus in the first of four chapters on psychoanalysis, I will explore some themes that Freud could have systematically pursued more than he did, notably loss, which is related in both biographical and larger theoretical terms to the long-term absence of a theory of affects in psychoanalysis.[6]* This absence, which successive generations of psychoanalysts have pondered and puzzled over, facilitated Freud's development of psychoanalytic theory in some terms even as it crucially thwarted development in other terms.[7] The effects of this extraordinary circumstance, commented on by any number of psychoanalysts, have persisted to this day, hampering the development of psychoanalysis and the social psychologies informed by it.[8] The generations that followed Freud were quick to note the lack of an affect theory but very slow to do anything about it, and especially slow to address Freud's relationship to it. This observation will enable me to focus on the relationship of loss in Freud's biography to the absent affect theory, as well as on the subsequent effects of this absence on the profession, and on issues of ideology and authority within it.

In the second chapter, I will reconsider the biographical significance of some of Freud's other preoccupations, for example, his childhood poverty, his resentment of his father who was unable to prepare him for the tasks he undertook, and then, too, his comments on how far he had come in spite of his background. It is necessary to emphasize, in other words, just how important the concept of agency is for understanding Freud, who was bereft of the resources he needed to pursue the kind of career he was interested in and angry on that account. In the matter of a career he was on his own, and his vulnerability, along with his exceptional capacities, fostered his ability to invent and reinvent versions of himself and his project. I will argue that there is no way to explain Freud's career or his innovative capacities in the ontogenetic terms he

---

* For analytic purposes, psychoanalysts and other researchers may make distinctions among affects, emotions, feelings, moods, etc. However, psychoanalysts may also use the terms "affects" and "emotions" interchangeably, and this is the practice I will follow here. See note 6.

preferred.[9] The emphasis in this chapter on agency and cognitive capacities complements the emphasis in the first chapter on loss, affect, ideology, and authority, all important elements for an alternative approach to what Freud considered to be the paramount task, cultural analysis.

One crucial aspect of such a prospective approach that must be mentioned at the outset is the diminished importance of the notion of unconscious mental activity or motivation to any social theory, or any conception of the ways that mind and society are related, on any level beyond biography. This conclusion is obligated by the idiosyncratic and discontinuous resolutions to personal conflict as revealed by clinical practice, and also by the continuing, seemingly unending, proliferation of perspectives that the concept of unconscious motivation has fostered, with no ability to discriminate better from worse among them by reference to evidence.[10] As psychoanalysts have themselves pointed out many times, there is no interpretation of theirs that cannot be substituted for by another one using the same evidence.[11]

In the third chapter I will account for the failure of psychoanalysts to deliver on the promise of an independent, viable psychoanalytic theory of culture, ascribing this failure in part to the absence of theories of emotion and cognition as discussed in the first two chapters, and in part to the observation just referred to, the idiosyncratic contents of dynamic conflict, and the discontinuities of life as people have reported them. But I will also discuss in this context the problem of agency, that is, the capacity of people to interpret the significance of events in terms of their own interests, needs, and expectations and to act on these interpretations.

The reference to agency is not meant to suggest free will, but rather that however determined behavior may be, people must still act in a variety of historical and social contexts or locations, and it is the difficulties involved in deciding about their own prospects and choices that complicate their lives, as well as the systematic observation of their lives. People are not merely the passive recipients of heteronomous moralities, they are not just trapped in structures, nor do they simply reproduce internalized behaviors.[12] Rather, they have the ability to act in ways they determine for themselves, to scan the environment and establish a basis for decisions about their problems and conflicts consistent with their interests and moral inclinations, particularly by inventing and reinventing versions of their lives and experiences. Freud of course was more or less aware of some of these issues, noting at one point, for example, that recollections of experience are not veridical, they are constructed in light of immediate exigencies. However, he could not for various reasons accommodate his awareness to the kind of theory he intended to develop, and he never adequately or systematically pursued the issues.[13]

In addition, I will emphasize in the context of the declining influence of psychoanalysis on cultural analysis the advice to colleagues of such knowledgeable psychoanalysts as Robert Wallerstein and Joseph Sandler to focus attention on clinical rather than cultural concerns. The reason for this advice is not, as radical critics have long claimed, that psychoanalysts are hopelessly enmeshed in bourgeois ideology and intent on betraying Freud's critical vision. The reason is that they have been unable to solve basic problems even at the clinical level, let alone provide anyone with concrete solutions to larger cultural problems. There seems little choice for most psychoanalysts now but to retreat from Freud's sense that psychoanalysis could prove "indispensable to all the sciences which are concerned with the evolution of human civilization and its major institutions such as art, religion, and the social order."[14]

In the fourth chapter I will explain two of the more notable results of the situation I have outlined. One is the fragmentation of psychoanalysis, the constant proliferation of psychoanalytic perspectives. Freud tried to bridge the gap between structure and cultural imagination, but he could not do it in his own terms, freeing (or compelling) those who followed to invent a remarkable variety of other terms. Having developed a clinical situation in which individuals were invited to enter a less inhibited imaginative world, Freud discovered just how idiosyncratic motivation and dynamic conflict are even at the level of the unconscious. So he invented a still "deeper" archaic unconscious to smooth out the differences in an attempt to make cultural interpretation consistently possible. Psychoanalysts found that maneuver unacceptable, and they proceeded to invent a succession of competing terms of their own. My intention here is to demonstrate how persistent, pervasive, and, under current conditions, irreversible, this fragmentation is.

The second result involves another long standing if largely implicit tendency among a number of psychoanalysts to express regret for Freud's abandonment of "the seduction theory" on behalf of what he considered psychoanalysis proper. The earlier version, whatever purpose it may have served for him,[15] involved cultural and historical themes that he gave up, including threatened or actual experiences of loss or the significance to people of the absence or failure of authoritative individuals and ideals at crucial moments, and the theoretical importance of affects in this context.[16] I will also argue that when it comes to social or cultural theory, Freud was doing better before the "breakthrough" than after. There are psychoanalysts who often hint at this and regardless of what Freud himself thought, this move was and still is a problematic one for many of them. As Martin S. Bergmann has recently written, "The question of the role of reality and particularly traumatic reality versus wish-fulfillment fantasy has remained with us ever since."[17]

Psychoanalysis, then, has had an enormous cultural impact on the strength of an inferential logic that is not warranted by clinical data, presumably the basis on which psychoanalytic cultural speculations rest. The problem for Freud in this context, considering especially his cultural interests, was that no matter how regular mental processes may be, the reasons people give for their behavior in the clinical setting are idiosyncratic, anomalous, and accidental.[18] Freud was determined to find a basis for making universally valid causal statements that would allow the widest scope for thinking theoretically about cultural problems. But the problematic relationship between clinical outcomes and theoretical vantage points as underscored by psychoanalysts after Freud, in fact, the break between outcomes and vantage points, along with a persistent emphasis on clinical results,[19] means that psychoanalysts can effectively deal only with the idiosyncratic and discontinuous outcomes that are the reported results of therapy. In clinical experience there is no warrant for the kinds of cultural interpretation that Freud offered or that are often derived from the work of such authors as Melanie Klein, Jacques Lacan, or Herbert Marcuse.

It may be objected that other sciences, biology for example, also treat idiosyncratic subjects (i.e., apply general theoretical principles to unique instances). But this is no argument for psychoanalysis in terms of its singular utility for social or cultural theory. As Richard Lewontin has pointed out, in comparison with a discipline that seeks to interpret human behavior, the task of the molecular biologist, for a number of reasons, is trivial.[20] Moreover, because the structures of inference that guide psychoanalytic clinical practice provide no basis for explaining more complex social behavior, and there is no other source of data apart from what more systematic ties to academic psychology and neuroscience might at some point be able to provide, it is difficult to see where adequate data might come from.[21] Constructing an inferential framework for reasonably connecting external events to a group's subjective sense of them therefore requires extra-analytic propositions. However, Freud was determined to avoid such a situation at all costs, and the other authors mentioned here have not provided any such propositions.

Sometimes an attempt is made to bolster the position of psychoanalysis by offering the supplementary argument that symbols constitute an independent confirming source of Freud's assumptions, a "'second and independent factor' in dream interpretation, a factor that also often plays a crucial role in the interpretation of neurotic symptoms, parapraxes, literary works, and so on." But this argument cannot be sustained: symbols do not have a fixed and single meaning to people.[22] Freud's opinion on this subject of extraclinical confirmation of psychoanalytic propositions changed over time, as it did on many subjects. He claimed in "Leonardo da Vinci and a Memory of His Childhood" that "according to the usual way in which language makes use of substitutes, the vulture's 'coda' cannot possibly signify anything other than a male genital, a penis." He also indicated in "The Introductory Lectures" that as knowledge of dream symbolism increased it would be possible to dispense with the dreamer's associations.[23] But that expectation was never realized, and Freud ultimately concluded that psychoanalysis is a communicative discipline rooted in the therapeutic encounter: if people do not say, the psychoanalyst cannot know. There is no way to infer from everyday speech in the absence of a subject's associations the unconscious significance of any statement.[24] As Freud later explained to André Breton on the subject of dreams, "a mere collection of dreams without the dreamers' associations, without the knowledge of the circumstances in which they occurred, tells me nothing, and I can hardly imagine what it could tell anyone."[25]

It is also worth noting that the cultural theories focused on identity issues vital to groups hitherto largely excluded from decision-making processes, especially those informed by versions of psychoanalysis, have only reproduced the failed inferential logic of the earlier constructs. This is particularly true of Lacan's work, which has found favor especially among cultural and literary theorists. Lacan has been praised by different psychoanalysts for his contributions to psychoanalysis, referring especially to the significance of his emphasis on language and culture as opposed to the traditional emphasis on human instinct and drive.[26] But Lacan has also been justly criticized on a number of grounds, in the most interesting way for our purposes by his countryman, André Green. Green objected to the absence of an affect theory in Lacan, his refusal to grant the problem of affects the conceptual status it merits. Psychoanalysts, other than Lacanians, deem the emotional contents of patients' expressions crucial to the clinical enterprise, and Green was particularly discouraged by his inability to connect Lacan's theories to practice in this context. But if it is difficult to conceive of a clinical theory in the absence of some conceptual orientation to affects, it is even more difficult to conceive of a cultural theory absent such an orientation.[27] In short, there is no better basis for Lacan's inferential judgments in terms of cultural theory than there is for anyone else's.[28]

Thus it is fair to say that the examination of identity issues over the past decades has raised interesting questions and led to important changes in historical interest and perspective. But it is also fair to say that there has been a notable lack of restraint in the interpretive claims made especially for psychoanalytically informed theories of sexuality, gender, and race that, moreover, continue to be produced and amplified as ideological requirements dictate.[29] The cultural theorists have changed the focus and the language of debate but they have not solved any of the interpretive problems.

I cannot emphasize too strongly that these comments are not about the end stage of an accumulation of knowledge that has illuminated the ways in which events, perceptions, and feelings are related, at which point one is logically prevented from making claims for absolute knowledge on the grounds that a hypothesis can only be negated, it can never be proved. This is not about ultimate statements on causality or about the last things theorists do not know; it is about the first things they do not know. This is also not about recent changes in the scientific worldview, which have affected psychoanalysis as they have other disciplines.[30] Rather, this is about the virtual absence of any knowledge of the ways in which social relationships and events affect perception and feeling, or the ways in which people construct interpretations of relationships and events, given the variety of social locations they inhabit, or the material interests, moral perspectives, and wishful expectations they express. Interpretive statements, regardless of vantage point or discipline, are therefore based on intuitive leaps and are not assessable except by the current viewpoints of the different disciplines, all of which are problematic by their own standards of self-appraisal.

It is insufficiently recognized just how far different social psychologies and other relevant disciplines are from being able to justify or support the kind of interpretive statements that routinely appear in both academic and popular publications. There is no body of work that can adequately describe in affective and cognitive terms how information about the self, others, and the social world is developed, processed, evaluated, and elaborated; how information gets represented in memory and how memory is used to make decisions or to interact with others in a cultural context; or how mental representations influence cognitive structures of belief, knowledge, inference, and evaluative judgment or affect the social behavior of people. Most of the research devoted to social memory, for example, has focused on a dyadic context, the perceiver and one partner, still at a one-dimensional level of conversational interactions focused on attitude, or on aggression, or on morale, and so on. Researchers have only recently turned to questions of how choices, judgments, inferences, and decisions are derived from cognitive representations, or how constructed cognitive representations are actually used. But little work has been done, particularly by social psychologists, on how the cognitive system affects or relates to subjective states (moods, emotions) in terms of social behavior.

Put the other way, despite the many successes of cognitive science in understanding how the unconscious processing of information works, and how judgments about beliefs, attitudes, behavior, and other aspects of mental functioning are arrived at,[31] an enormous amount of work remains to be done in the areas of language, memory, cognition, affect, and the relationship of these phenomena to the social world before any significant conclusion about the social world can be justified by reference to evidence. Psychologists still do not have a model of memory, especially long-term memory, and its relationship to the judgment of events, or one that can otherwise relate the cognitive and emotional responses to complex social experience.[32] There are interesting studies of potentially larger significance, particularly of unconscious processing, and the construction of memories. But they are still remote from the world of interests and moral perspectives and the kinds of social movements and conflicts that historians, for example, are interested in.[33]

The reluctance to recognize this crucial absence of knowledge is itself a cultural problem, revealing of the need people have for the closure provided by the different interpretive languages. The situation, however, has allowed one assumption in particular to persist against the knowledge we do possess: no matter how heterogeneous any population is or how diverse or confused the response of any population may have been to events, there is at bottom a single explanation that ties these responses together, an underlying unity of motive that observers can identify even if participants were unaware of it at the time. This assumption undergirded the regulative constructs of the classical theorists of the nineteenth century, particularly those of Marx and Freud, and though most would agree that these constructs have failed from the standpoint of their originators, the particular focal point of that failure, the assumed unity of motive through a population, still orients the way people think about the social world.

It is perhaps easiest to identify the influence of these inferential strategies as they appear in the popular press, where impressionistic interpretations of the behavior of masses of people are dressed up by academic commentators and other experts who provide an appropriately recondite language, conveying thereby a much greater sense of knowledge-in-hand than can possibly be the case. Thus a psychiatrist explained in The New York Times that the millions of people who enjoy eating at America's fabled diners do so because the diners induce "a pleasant melancholia, a dreamlike state, evocative of memory and loss."[34] A social scientist explained in the same venue that the resurgence of interest in magic is a logical response to contemporary life: "Magic . . . is a way for an industrial society to recreate a sense of danger without experiencing real danger, and a way of creating the imponderable in full knowledge that a simple gimmick is at work. It is a clear reach into the anthropological past."[35] Or again, a critic explained that the appeal of horror shows "is directly related to the country's economic woes and fears about a failing safety net and a changing world, a state of affairs remarkably similar to the mood that prevailed in the 1930's, the decade that witnessed the birth of the modern horror film."[36] Similarly, we read that the Japanese will no longer produce Godzilla films because "Japan is now an assertive economic superpower, sure of its ability to shape world events, rather than a powerless country struggling, through fantasy, to overcome the threats it perceives. . . . Japan . . . no longer needs an ambiguous, amphibious monster to stand up for its interests."[37]

Never mind how quickly events undercut these interpretive conclusions; after all, accurate observation was never the point, and of course the process continues. How is it, the newspaper headline asks, that "The Once-Lowly Canvas Sneaker Is Pedestrian No More?" The answer is, "We didn't become the leisure society. . . . People's lives are too job-oriented. But sneakers make us look leisured. They offer a rebellion against the sedentary life."[38] And one last example: "The possibility of being observed in the act of sensual enjoyment is what gives a crowded department store or restaurant its special charge and Ms. Wilson . . . does justice to this theme. She points out that what women experience in such places fuels the anti-urbanism of moralists determined to sequester in suburban villas any dangerous outbreak of female sexuality."[39] The unity of motive among a necessarily heterogeneous population is taken for granted; no evidence is reported and none is required in the popular context in which these statements appeared, which is just as well because no evidence is available. Sometimes it is not even clear what would constitute evidence.

These inferential interpretive statements about the puzzling behaviors of people and their everyday lives are not based on experimental, longitudinal, or clinical studies, nor can anyone claim that the authors made any attempt to locate sources of bias and error and correct for them. They offer no solutions to the problems of theory or history, in other words, they merely illuminate them. These statements, and all interpretive statements that purport to account for instances of conflict or cooperation, the elevation or suppression of people in terms of class, gender, ethnicity, or race, the persistent power of authoritative figures in all spheres of life, and so on, typically assume not only what they have to prove, they assume what they cannot prove, the underlying unity of motive, the homogeneity of reasons and intentions through a population. Clinical psychoanalysis, rooted in the most intense scrutiny of motives, reasons, and intentions, persistently demonstrates just how idiosyncratic personal conflict is, raising questions even at this level about how people are related in a social sense to each other.

As things now stand, what is important about the interpretive assessments of historians, social scientists, journalists, and others is not "footnoteable"—there will not be any confirming evidence because there is, except in a still trivial sense, no knowledge of how mind and society are related to each other or to the way that people perceive and respond to events. It must be emphasized, therefore, that if psychoanalysts could not find a way to confirm the interpretive logic Freud had invented, the other social sciences, history included, fared no better, regardless of the terms employed. Whatever the objections to psychoanalysis, authors in all disciplines employ a similar inferential logic on every occasion that requires an interpretive judgment. Freud was not the only one who promoted this familiar logic, though he, more than anyone else, taught people how to think in these terms, that is, how to make sense of people's behavior by inventing reasons for it that they have not expressed and are not themselves aware of. The content of this inferential logic is not necessarily Freudian, but the form typically is, and the form retains its persuasiveness because where people are concerned, as Freud knew, the first act is not to reproduce life but to imagine the reproduction of life, and achieving closure in the imaginative sphere still depends in no small measure upon the kind of logic he provided.[40] This is the point at which all the disciplines have proved vulnerable to the unresolved problems that pushed psychoanalysis off its preferred cultural ground. The interpretive judgments of social scientists on cultural issues are qualitatively no different from or better than those that appear in the popular press or in the psychoanalytic journals, for they are based on the same logic, the same form of argument, and the same assumed underlying unity of motive as we have just seen. These comments underscore the impoverished state of available theoretical languages in psychoanalysis and the social sciences alike, and account for the persistent search for new languages and for the seemingly excessive reliance on the authoritative figures who provide them.

This is what we learn from knowledgeable in-house critics of the social sciences. In 1964, Peter Berger published his influential *Invitation to Sociology*. But in 1992, Berger published a paper entitled "Sociology: A Disinvitation?" in which he underscored the problematic situation of sociology, ascribing the often remarked contemporary crisis to "parochialism, triviality, rationalism, and ideology." Each one is crippling, Berger noted, but "[t]heir combination has been deadly."[41] The following year, Irving Louis Horowitz addressed "the decomposition of sociology" in similar terms, a great discipline undermined by ideological commitments that have turned it sour.[42] And the year after that, sociologist Stephen Cole edited a volume on the crisis in sociology, abstracting the following factors from the various papers published therein: "the absence of theory that can be utilized in empirical research, the fact that theory development seems to follow fads rather than make progress as in the natural sciences, the lack of cognitive consensus in the discipline, the emphasis on methodology as opposed to findings, the interference of political ideology with cognitive development, and the failure of the products of the discipline to be relevant for solving social problems in the society."[43]

To be sure, these commentaries reflect a bitter disappointment with the identity politics and theories characteristic of recent times, but they are also on the mark apart from all that, given especially the current pre-occupation within the social and behavioral sciences on problems amenable to quantitative analysis. Indeed, there is not a discipline devoted to social or cultural studies that has not been subjected to a sim-ilarly acute critical appraisal and has not witnessed a radical dampening of ambitions as a result. The scope and expectations of anthropology have been significantly reduced as revealed in the reflections of Clifford Geertz.[44] B. F. Skinner drew attention just over a decade ago to the fact that very little agreement exists about the principal achievements of psy-chology, and he noted that when ten psychologists were asked to name the most important discoveries made during a fifteen-year period, no two of them could agree.[45] Psychiatrists have "been unable to define mental health or mental illness or to create a reliable classification scheme of its 'illnesses.'"[46] In addition, psychiatrists do not yet have a measure that will allow them to predict who will or will not be violent that is even crudely accurate, while "quantitative measurements of crim-inal behavior are notoriously imprecise."[47] The diminishing (at least for now) crime rate represents "a humbling time for all crime analysts. . . . It is a puzzlement."[48] "The truth about alcoholism, violence, and divorce is that we don't know the truth. There are no positive claims about their causes that can be made with any honest conviction."[49] Demographic projections, which would seem to be a fairly straightforward matter, are also notoriously unreliable.[50]

The situation I have described even extends to economics, the most highly regarded of all the social science disciplines. I cannot be specific here about the problems of economics, which have lately become public in a way they never have before.[51] But it is worth noting that in an attempt to restore a sense of realism about the discipline, both Paul Krugman (MIT) and Greg Mankiw (Harvard) have recently described economics as a "primitive science," Krugman offering as a useful paral-lel for the sake of defining how primitive, "medicine at the turn of the century."[52] In fact, economists are as remote from answering fundamen-tal questions as workers in any of the other disciplines, and for quite similar reasons. As Richard Thaler put it, "We just don't understand the social psychology of financial markets."[53]

The upshot of these reflections is that economists have been compelled by experience to become as alert to the significance of anomalous or contradictory data as workers in other disciplines, they are as likely to draw contradictory conclusions from the same data, and these conclusions are as readily contaminated in an ideological sense as the conclusions in any of the other disciplines.[54] Hence the observation of Jon Elster, a prominent rational choice theorist, that "the social sciences are light years away from the stage at which it will be possible to formulate general-law-like regularities about human behavior."[55]

In a concluding chapter, then, I will draw attention by reference to concrete historical examples to the kind of empirical problems that undermined the regulative constructs in psychoanalysis, the social sciences, and history alike. The classical theorists wanted to get around the confusion of everyday events by imputing motivational unity to people. They believed that social scientists would finally be able to specify the sources of this unity in a precise way, while historians oriented themselves to the social sciences on the strength of this belief. But people do not live their lives in terms attributed to them by theorists, and social scientists have not been able to find the kind of invariant rule they have been looking for; on the contrary, they just make trouble for themselves by continuing to look for it.

These problems, phrased in terms appropriate to the cultural or social level of activity, include the heterogeneity of populations, the discontinuity of events, and human agency. For our purposes, we may think of the heterogeneity problem as a spatial metaphor, referring both to the effects of objective (demographic or structural) heterogeneity that derive from the multiple social locations people inhabit (class, gender, age, race, religion, ethnicity, region, language); and from the effects of subjective or interpretive heterogeneity that derive from the different perspectives and beliefs available as public culture to people in any of these contexts.[56] In brief, the different material interests, moral perspectives, and wishful strivings people have, and the variety of social locations they inhabit, become so many occasions for the expression of subjective intentions and aspirations, with often unanticipated results.

We may then think of discontinuity as a temporal metaphor focused on contemporary or historical personal and social breaks that occur to people over the short or long run, in the course of a day, a month, a year, and so on. And we may think of agency as an active process of constructing versions of events in terms of the narratives, authoritative leaders, and concrete objects that are available in all societies in different ways (such as property, money, codified learning, sacred or other communal sites, weapons) as adaptive means people employ to help make sense of social life in the face of the heterogeneous and discontinuous conditions referred to.[57]

This adaptive capacity by itself may never allow the social sciences to become predictive to any precise degree at any level beyond a relatively simple numerate one. This capacity also makes it difficult to explain retrospectively how heterogeneously motivated populations succeeded in becoming attached to each other and to the symbols and goals they shared. In this paradoxical way, the people who provide theorists with the best data they have for assessing the significance of events by reporting on their own mental states turn out also to be the greatest obstacle to theory. As Lewontin pointed out, how sad is the situation of those observers "whose objects of study have consciousness and who depend on the objects themselves to report on their own state."[58]

It is not surprising, given the complexity of the problems, that some "postmodern" critics have proven to be effectively skeptical of the prospects for psychoanalysis, the social sciences, and history. Sometimes it seems as if every literate individual must by now be familiar with Friedrich Nietzsche's critical observations of the need people have for closure, or his belief that the tendency to form categories, concepts, and lawlike generalities is not to be understood as a way of perceiving the true world but as a compulsion to adapt ourselves to a world in which closure and thus existence are made possible. Postmodern critics have made so much of this insight that it too has become the stuff of everyday journalism: "The world itself, knowable only through imprecise perceptions, is a tissue of uncertainties, ambiguities, fictions masquerading as facts and facts as tenuous as clouds. Life today resembles a fictional paradigm more and more."[59]

If it is important to refute this bleak view and to recover the position of the different disciplines, continuing to look for some underlying or unconscious unity of motive, that is, marching backwards into the future, is not the way to go about it. It is necessary rather to change the approach to theory, or to devise a strategy sufficient to the complexities of mental processes, including obligated forms of nonrational behavior, emotional and cognitive capacities, and agency, in terms of the variety of motives for behavior[60] and the multiple social locations people occupy. In the last chapter I will indicate briefly the form such an approach might take, focusing on these and a number of other issues already referred to, including ideology and authority. However, because of the different complexities already described, it is important always to keep in mind Paul Feyerabend's admonition not to think of theory "as a well defined entity that says exactly what difficulties will make it disappear," but as "a vague promise whose meaning is constantly being changed and refined by the difficulties one decides to accept."[61]

CHAPTER 1

Loss and Affect in Psychoanalysis

There are at least five fundamental approaches to questions of motivation and behavior in psychoanalysis: sexuality, aggression, narcissism, attachment/loss, and adaptation. These five approaches can be viewed more or less consistently in terms of drives or object relations, each set of terms deploying a different developmental scheme. And they can also be viewed from three different vantage points: people as pleasure seeking, as object seeking, or as meaning seeking.

It is not hard to imagine that a potentially large number of clinical, theoretical, and political perspectives might follow from such variety, and of course this is what happened. Given Freud's initial emphasis on sexuality, and the routine identification of Freud and classical psychoanalysis with this approach, it should be noted that Anna Freud had later concluded that "aggressive material abounds in child analysis . . . it is undeniable that, against previous expectations, aggression looms larger than sex in child analysis."[1] This and other assessments of the importance of aggression have occasioned an independent vantage point on cultural and historical events, both in Freud's instinctual terms and in terms of aggression as a derived phenomenon (frustration/aggression).[2] That is, a number of psychoanalysts have questioned Freud's assumption that aggression is a primary, nonerotic drive, including John Bowlby, Erik Erikson, Erich Fromm, Otto Kernberg, Heinz Kohut, and still others.[3]

In addition, Herbert Marcuse, anxious for people to escape from a culture based "on toil, domination, and renunciation," focused attention on narcissism, which, he declared in an elaborate fantasy improvisation, "survives not only as a neurotic symptom but also as a constitutive element in the construction of the reality coexisting with the mature reality ego."[4] Christopher Lasch, two decades later, in no mood any longer to celebrate the possibility of a "non-repressive erotic attitude towards reality," described what he referred to as the "new narcissist," haunted not by guilt but by anxiety, the final degraded product of bourgeois individualism.[5]

Then, too, the psychoanalytic emphasis on attachment and loss, referring to perceived experiences of abandonment or betrayal by parents, siblings, and other loved individuals,[6] but also in a larger sense to the failure of institutions and authoritative figures to sustain valued moral or ideological perspectives, has also provided an important basis for assessing the impact of crucial cultural and historical events.[7] To be sure, individuals can absorb significant instances of personal loss because societies provide all kinds of ritual supports to help them through the mourning experience. But the loss of valued, or even just familiar, perspectives and leaders is not so easily prepared for from the standpoint of conscious expectations. No social organization is in the business of preparing its citizens for its demise, or instructing them in the possibility that the codes, rules, norms, values, standards, and expectations characteristic of the society may at some point be rendered ineffective or dysfunctional by social change.[8] People do not routinely imagine that the cultural "background of safety" they take for granted as they pursue the routine tasks of everyday life will one day (or even, as in recent history, quickly) disappear. Individuals may have trouble with sexuality, but societies typically have sexuality under control. Individuals have less personal trouble with experiences of loss, but it is far more problematic for societies.

Threatened or actual experience of loss, conceived either as the failure of a system or, given social change over time, the absence of an appropriate alternative to it, accounts for the impact of major historical events in better ways than either libidinal ties or the pursuit of common interests and common work can. It is important to emphasize that Freud's observation that people become emotionally (libidinally) bound to the societies they live in because common work and common interests are not sufficient to the task, mistakenly diminished the theoretical importance of work and interests.[9] But so too did those who focused on interests mistakenly diminish the cultural importance of emotional and moral commitments. Threatened or actual social change that undermines the standards and expectations of a society, and that people have trouble absorbing because it evokes memories of separation, abandonment, deprivation, betrayal, neglect, and injustice, affects their emotional and moral commitments, their sense of adequacy, and their ability to continue to define themselves as worthy, admirable, and good. People must be able to organize experience using the language and perspectives they have learned, primarily from authoritative individuals; the inability to do so as a result of social change fosters activity aimed at repairing the loss.[10]

As for the related theme of adaptation, Michael Franz Basch and others have noted that with the publication of *Inhibitions, Symptoms, and Anxiety*, affects had become for Freud a means of communication in the interest of adaptation, rather than an indicator of discharge, and that, most important in terms of what followed in cognitive psychology, affects must be viewed as a cognitive contribution to adaptation and not as the antithesis of cognitive processes.[11] In this psychoanalytic context, people are capable of modifying their environment, "and these modifications frequently carry with them the need to adapt to new changed conditions and the solution of sometimes new and unsuspected problems. The modifications . . . refer not only to the physical conditions of . . .[our] milieu . . . but to those in our social, political, philosophical, and even religious systems."[12] Indeed, psychoanalysts' rules for accepting patients are predicated on the adaptive capacity of people to alter the conditions of their lives. Emphasizing the long-standing importance of this theme in psychoanalysis, Peter Loewenberg pointed to C. G. Jung's focus "on adjustment and adaptation a quarter of a century prior to" the appearance of well-known works by Anna Freud (1936) and Heinz Hartmann (1939).[13]

Little wonder that André Green facetiously asked whether sexuality has anything to do with psychoanalysis.[14] From the standpoint of systematic social or cultural theory, as distinct from individual biography, the answer is, not much. Freud's initial belief that the problems of social psychology could prove soluble on the basis of a single concrete point, man's relation to his father, is the least interesting and important of the different psychoanalytically informed perspectives. By contrast, there are reasons to select from among the many different ones the concepts of loss and adaptation as a basis for the continued elaboration of social or cultural theory. Aggression and narcissism are easily subsumed by these concepts, which have in any event achieved a distinctive place within and beyond psychoanalysis.[15] Moreover, loss and adaptation have a particular salience in terms of Freud's life and work, as Peter Homans, Didier Anzieu, Max Schur, and others have argued.[16]

In the larger cultural terms, in addition to the authors who have linked the origins and impact of psychoanalysis itself to cultural discontinuities experienced as loss and treated as the occasion for adaptive change (Peter Homans and Philip Rieff among them),[17] it is important to recall Bruce Mazlish's account of the emergence of sociology in the nineteenth century, and Robert Jay Lifton's account of the appearance of "Protean man," both of which are also linked to experiences of loss and adaptation.[18] Consider, too, John Bowlby's biography of Charles Darwin, with its only-to-be-expected emphasis on loss and mourning,[19] as well as Bowlby's foreword to David Aberbach's book *Surviving Trauma*, subtitled *Loss, Literature, and Psychoanalysis*.[20] In fact, there are a number of recent biographies of Emily Dickenson, Nathaniel Hawthorne, Charles Ives, and Edgar Allan Poe in which the theme of loss figures significantly or is perceived as crucial to the life and art.[21] It is not surprising that a critic would ask whether "all the best poems [are] about loss?"[22]

Didier Anzieu and Homans have claimed that in Freud's case especially it was the experience of loss and the adaptive search for restitution that sparked the creative crisis that led to Freud's recovery as defined by the abandonment of the seduction theory and the emergence of psychoanalysis proper.[23] Anzieu referred to the death of Freud's father, his newly achieved consciousness of hostile and jealous feelings, and his recognition of the source of these feelings as a result of his self-analysis. This emphasis on loss is hardly surprising considering that Freud made persistent and recurrent personal as well as theoretical statements on its significance, which had in any event long since been elaborated by psychoanalysts as an independent vantage point.[24]

The difference between this emphasis and Freud's on the sensual and sexual lives of people based on his elaboration of a hitherto hidden world, an unconscious fantasy world driven by life lived in the body and the demands made by the body on the mind, involving caretaking parents and jealous, competitive children in a wishful drama centered on rivalrous love and murderous fantasies, is crucial for understanding Freud's biography and the theory he developed. For Freud's actions and statements, especially in *The Studies on Hysteria*, the correspondence with Fliess, and often *The Interpretation of Dreams*, too, underscored the contingent quality of life and the impact of recurring and traumatic experiences of separation, abandonment, betrayal, and loss. By contrast the theoretical breakthrough that made him famous underscored the fixed, structured, recurrent, and sexualized quality of life. Freud's emphasis served him well and he spent the rest of his life working out the implications as best he could. But the experience of loss is by far the dominant experience in his life as he reported it, referring not only to the death of his father, but to the death of his brother Julius,[25] the disappearance of his nanny, the disappearance of his mother due to her pregnancies and illnesses, the loss of his stepbrothers and their children who emigrated to England, his loss of place as the family moved from Freiberg to Vienna, all of which he described in letters to Fliess and elsewhere. From the standpoint of systematic theory, this story, which is as familiar to students and observers of psychoanalysis as the story of Little Red Riding Hood, deserves pride of place, as Anzieu, Homans, and many others have already noted.[26]

Indeed, the logic of Freud's argument that childhood seductions are not initially traumatic but become so only later, in the light of subsequent experience that the grown child can comprehend, referred to as "deferred action," or as the "retranscription of memory," is more parsimoniously employed in terms of Freud's reported experiences of loss than sexuality.[27] The choice Freud made had to do, in part, with his understanding of how to constitute a science, his search for universals, and his need to reject for these purposes apparently random and accidental experiences, not with the specific weight of his own reported experiences. But in part, it also had to do with some personal reluctance—hence failure—to perceive the universal significance of separation and loss, some connection that Freud failed to make that he was able to rationalize on the grounds of theoretical indifference to accidental and random events, although as he later explained in *Inhibitions, Symptoms, and Anxiety*, there is nothing random about experiences of separation, and death obviously is as universal as sexuality.[28]

In retrospect it is not hard to see how he could have failed to pursue this track more systematically, given his own criteria for the unobserved effects of symptomatic conflict on intellectual endeavor. His own reported experiences, which he relied upon constantly to provide insights, the reported experiences of his patients, in addition to his awareness of a variety of affecting social conflicts, all suggested the paramount importance of loss. Freud must also have been aware, as William J. McGrath has explained, of the "two-ego psychology" of his teacher, Theodor Meynert, in which "trauma played a much more basic role. The example central to both Schopenhauer and Meynert involved the trauma of loss, the death of a loved one, and its impact on rational functioning."[29]

The importance of the problem of separation and loss to Freud is underscored by his letters of October 3–4 and October 15, 1897, to Fliess.[30] These letters encompass what Freud then recalled or reconstructed of the deeply affecting experiences of loss in his early life. He had lost his nanny who was so dear to him that he recalled her as the one who had provided him "at such an early age with the means for living and going on living." She had been arrested for stealing from the family and sent to prison. He had lost his brother Julius who died in infancy, and whose presence on his own testimony he had greeted with hostility and jealousy. He had lost privileged access to his mother in the wake of that and many subsequent births. Indeed, he described an occasionally recurrent memory in which, as a young child, he was crying in despair over the disappearance of his mother. His twenty-year-older stepbrother, Philipp, he recalled, had unlocked a wardrobe for him, and when he did not find his mother there either he cried even harder. This behavior had puzzled him, but in retrospect he decided that he had asked his brother to do this. "When I missed my mother, I was afraid she had vanished from me, just as the old woman had a short time before. So I must have heard that the old woman had been locked up and therefore must have believed that my mother had been locked up too—or rather, had been 'boxed up' [eingekastelt]—for my brother Philipp, who is now sixty-three years old, to this very day is still fond of such puns. The fact that I turned to him in particular proves that I was well aware of his share in the disappearance of the nurse." How very much like this episode is the reaction to separation Freud later depicted in *Inhibitions, Symptoms, and Anxiety*: "This anxiety has all the appearance of being an expression of the child's feeling at its wits' end, as though in its still very undeveloped state it did not know how better to cope with its cathexis of longing. Here anxiety appears as a reaction to the felt loss of the object."[31]

There were other affecting instances of loss, of his birthplace, as the family moved from Freiberg to Vienna;[32] of family members, as his step-brothers Philipp and Emanuel with their wives and children, especially his nephew John and niece Pauline, subsequently moved to Manchester, England. He also commented to Fliess on his travel phobia. As Max Schur noted, "The affect which comes through most prominently in these constructions is the desperate fear of losing the mother, something now generally subsumed under the term 'separation anxiety.'"[33]

Of course, Freud, ever focused on sexuality, also related to Fliess that between the age of two and two and a half, "my libido toward *matrem* was awakened, namely, on the occasion of a journey with her from Leipzig to Vienna, during which we must have spent the night together and there must have been an opportunity of seeing her *nudam*." But the emotional impact of the experiences of loss, the cumulative effect on him as he related them, outweighed his oedipal striving, and despite the justifications Freud offered for his emphasis on sexuality and the importance of his work in these terms to the wider culture, there are two good reasons for concluding that he had evaded in a systematic sense the significance of these experiences of loss, as a result of symptomatic conflict.

First is the recognized importance of the concept of loss within psychoanalysis. Scott Dowling, for example, has explained, contradicting Freud's chosen emphasis, that there are actually two interrelated sources of wishful thinking, drive expression at different levels of development, and, implicitly acknowledging that psychoanalysis lost a lot when Freud gave up the seduction theory, traumatic experiences of helplessness in the face of abandonment, separation, and loss.[34] It is important to note, too, Harry T. Hardin's depiction of the series of misfortunes Freud had described to Fliess as screen memories, particularly the loss of his nanny, and his recollection of the trip with his mother, when he thought he might have seen her nude. It was not two years later that Freud explained in his paper on screen memories that we may not have memories at all from our childhood but only memories relating to (or about) our childhood. Such memories are not accurately recalled, they are reconstructed, in this case as a way of masking painful affects.[35] Later, Freud referred to the therapeutic task, descriptively speaking, as filling in the gaps in memory, as if the recollections of past events could be veridical.[36] But by any contemporary standard of research in the field of memory, the earlier position was the correct one.

Second, then, is the absence for the longest time of a theory of affects or emotions and its subordination within the body of theory, despite the widespread and certain understanding of its importance. As Edith Jacobson pointed out, "The affects are . . . responsible for the fact that in human beings the emotional life maintains an independent existence, not only alongside of but also apart from reasonable thought and action. What turns us into human beings is, indeed, the organization not only of our thought processes, but also of a wide range of feelings, of complex emotional attitudes and affective states unknown to the animal."[37]

This absence, which has always puzzled and concerned psychoanalysts, followed upon Freud's abandonment of the seduction theory in 1897. Both of these concepts, loss and affect, have substantial histories within psychoanalysis. But before we examine them further, it is useful, by way of establishing Freud's perspectives on loss and affect and the place he assigned them in his overall system, to recall his observation that at and after the stage of system-building, "two sets of reasons can be assigned for every psychical event that is consciously judged—one set belonging to the system and the other set real but unconscious."[38]

Margaret Mahler's observations on "separation-individuation" are as a good place as any to begin to examine the experience of loss. According to Mahler, "This growing away process is . . . a lifelong mourning process. *Inherent in every new step of independent functioning is a minimal threat of object loss.*"[39] Mahler's suggestion was subsequently developed by Paul Ricoeur, who, recalling Freud's definition of character as a precipitate of abandoned object-cathexes, pointed to the inevitable work of mourning that "brings absence into the very makeup of the ego."[40] Joseph Sandler emphasized these same issues, noting that the fantasies that arise because of external events, insults, threats to self-esteem, and so on, form a large part of our mental life. Sexual and aggressive drives provide highly important motives, "but so do threats to our feelings of safety (to the 'integrity of the ego'), injuries to our self-esteem, feelings of guilt and shame, and threats from the real ('external') world. Above all, *anxieties* of all sorts provide motives which are of central clinical significance."[41] Hence "the pain of *loss* will evoke wishes to restore the relation to the lost object in some way," because of the need to recover a sense of well-being and security.[42] John Bowlby had noted much earlier that a number of Freud's patients had fallen ill "whilst nursing a sick relative. Now investigation has shown that the illness or death of a near relative is an exceedingly common precipitating factor in both psychoneuroses and functional psychoses.[43] Marion Milner, too, referred to the dread of loss and abandonment as central to her daily work with patients.[44]

In the same vein, Erikson ascribed the creative capacity to the sense of loss in early childhood, referring to the anxiety that arises with awareness of separation from one's mother, the feeling of mistrust of the world that follows from the perception of the absence or loss of a loving parent: "The late adolescent crisis, in addition to anticipating the more mature crises, can at the same time hark back to the very earliest crisis of life—trust or mistrust in existence as such. This concentration in the cataclysm of the adolescent identity crisis of both first and later crises in the human life may well explain why religiously and artistically creative men often seem to be suffering from a barely compensated psychosis, and yet later prove superhumanly gifted in conveying a total meaning for man's life."[45] Albert Solnit, referring also to Anna Freud's work, also compared this developmental task of adolescents to the process of mourning: "[T]he relinquishment of the dormant oedipal longings that are reawakened for this formative developmental separation is perceived as a painful, haunting loss."[46] Peter Blos had also written that "such sensitization to special danger situations of a permanent traumatic valence are to be found . . . in object loss, passive dependency, loss of control, decline of self-esteem."[47] Hans Loewald had earlier observed that what the ego defends itself against primarily is the loss of reality, the sense of integration with the world (referred to by Winnicott as "the unthinkable anxiety").[48] Linda Joan Kaplan also wrote that all behavior can be construed in psychoanalytic terms "as an attempt to prevent losses of objects and to regulate some fundamental susceptibility to depression (loss)."[49] There are many other works that emphasize the primacy of loss in psychoanalysis.

The discrepancy between Freud's version and those of Anzieu, Homans, or Erikson, of Freud's creative experience following the death of his father is therefore readily resolved in favor of the latter three. As Anzieu wrote, "The survivor can, through a process of revival, master both the conflict of ambivalence towards the image of his father and the dependence or counter-dependence that goes with authority, and thereby, if he has the makings of a creator, cease to consider himself solely as someone's child and assert himself as the father of his own works. . . . In other words, the work you are about to create takes the place of the loved and lost object that created you."[50]

Of course, Freud also wrote about loss and the regulation and control (or the failure to control) experiences of loss, in *Mourning and Melancholia* and *Inhibitions, Symptoms, and Anxiety*, and in many other texts as well. In 1923, Freud explained that when the ego is overwhelmingly threatened by real dangers beyond any capacity for response, "[It] sees itself deserted by all the forces of protection and lets itself die. Here, moreover, is once again the same situation as that which underlay the first great anxiety-state of birth and the infantile anxiety of longing for an absent person—the anxiety of separation from the protecting mother."[51] In this same text, Freud also described the ego as "a precipitate of abandoned object-cathexes," a passively experienced mode of mastering situations of loss. It was on this basis that Ricoeur later claimed that "the lost object and the substitute object are the constant theme of psychoanalysis." Ricoeur noted—in language reminiscent of Mahler's depiction of development as "a lifelong mourning process"—that Freud's reference to abandoned object choices not only implicates the work of mourning, but it is impossible "to separate the ego's coherence and structural autonomy from the work of mourning without also abandoning the peculiar field of speech in which psychoanalysis operates."[52]

Freud often returned to the related theme of separation anxiety. In perhaps the most famous instance, he described his grandson Ernst Halberstadt's game with his reel and string, throwing the reel and retrieving it, making it disappear and reappear, which was also about learning to master situations of separation and loss.[53] Further, Freud pointed out, in *Mourning and Melancholia*, that the loss of more remote and abstract cultural relationships to traditional authorities, ideals, and symbols, can evoke the same range of responses and needs as personal experiences of loss.[54] Freud had referred to this kind of cultural experience both earlier[55] and later.[56] But it is especially useful to recall that according to Freud, Moses, an Egyptian of unknown but probably aristocratic origins, following the death of Akhenaten and the abolition of his monotheistic religion in Egypt, driven by "disappointment and loneliness," turned to the Hebrew people "and with them sought compensation for his losses. He chose them as his people and tried to realize his ideals in them."[57] Freud could have related his statements in *Moses and Monotheism* about "[w]hat the real nature of a tradition resides in, and what its special power rests on," and about the singular contributions to "world history of individual great men," as readily to loss and reparation as to the oedipal terms he preferred.[58]

Freud had also written about the mastery of separation or loss and reparation in his often discussed "Non vixit" dream (*The Interpretation of Dreams*),[59] although he did not think of it in such terms, at least in part because he had raised other important issues as well. Significantly, however, three of the characters that appear in the dream, people Freud admired or was close to, were dead: Ernst Brücke, Ernst Fleischl-Marxow, and Joseph Paneth. The fourth, Freud's great friend Fliess, was very ill at the time, and Freud's thoughts about him were hostile as well. Freud described the figures he had conjured in his dream as "revenants," apparitions or ghosts, a series of reincarnations of his childhood friend, his nephew John, who, as noted earlier, had moved with his family to Manchester. Freud was pleased to emphasize that all the figures were removable anytime he wished it.[60] "It was therefore also a source of satisfaction to me that I had always been able to find successive substitutes for that figure [John]; and I felt I should be able to find a substitute for the friend whom I was now on the point of losing [Fliess]: no one was irreplaceable."[61] This was evidently a comforting thought at the time, though in the end it proved not to be a true one.

But however often Freud returned to the subject of loss, he wanted to deal—apart from some notable, anomalous exceptions—with only one kind of wishfulness or fantasy related to drive expression at different levels of development, ignoring in a systematic sense another kind revealed in the dream resulting from traumatic experiences of helplessness in the face of abandonment, isolation, loss, and separation. All this raises interesting questions about the gaps in Freud's self-analysis, some of which have already been addressed by various scholars and psychoanalysts.[62] Freud had trouble coping with the introspective examination of his own experiences of abandonment, isolation, loss, and separation, as reflected in the way he treated the role of his mother in his life, the role of mothers and women in his elaboration of psychoanalytic theory, his relationship to Fliess, and, too, the way he treated the affect theory with which psychoanalysis began.[63]

Freud's attempted self-analysis may have been as heroic as Ernest Jones, Kurt Eissler, and others have claimed.[64] But just as there are limits to sexual experience for any individual in any relationship no matter how passionate, so too there are limits to self-exploration and self-analysis, as Ferenczi (as well as Nietzsche, Kafka, and some others) had also explained. Freud, who did more than anyone to undermine and otherwise challenge commonsense versions of the world, who was arguably without peer as a non-commonsensical thinker, pointed out on the subject of limits that if any individual had the chance actually to experience all the sexual fantasies that his or her mind could conjure, the result would not be a great sense of pleasure, it would be a great sense of panic. By the same token, if one had access to every memory and could recall every incident that affected one's life, the result would be disorientation, not enlightenment.

The familiar quip that one never tells everything to one's accoun-

tant, lawyer, or therapist implies a conscious withholding of information. But there is also knowledge that is not under conscious control,
that in Freud's terms remains repressed.[65] (As Freud would have
explained, the knowledge that is repressed and that accounts for the
experience of panic in the example above is that parental figures stand
behind all the fantasized sexual encounters, hence the counterintuitive,
paradoxical response.) What then emerges from Freud's own reporting
in the correspondence with Fliess, the dream book, and other papers in
which he explored experiences from his own self-analysis, is that the
sexual phenomena he believed to be universal and that he predicated his
work on were not as compelling in his own life as the experiences of loss,
separation, and abandonment (or absence perceived as abandonment),
and the emotional effects of such experiences. What psychoanalysts
themselves have described as the "limits," "blind-spots," and "resistances" of Freud's self-analysis reveal above all is that he could never get
his mind around the problem of loss and emotional responses to loss, he
could not make the connections in this and related areas—affects and
countertransference—[66] that would have enabled him to treat these subjects systematically, in addition to maternal figures, women in a larger
cultural sense, and the reasons for his persistent falling out with close
friends. Making these connections would have required him to subordinate the point of view on drives and sexuality he had worked so hard to
establish, although this has happened anyway, as we can see.[67]

Freud understood that his self-analysis was incomplete—he explained
to Fliess at one point that "[t]rue self-analysis is impossible; otherwise
there would be no [neurotic] illness."[68] Later (1911) he explained to his
friend Ludwig Binswanger that he is sometimes assailed by dissatisfaction
with the progress of psychoanalysis and there arise in him some slight
doubts about the future. "The truth is, there is nothing for which man's
capabilities are less suited than psychoanalysis."[69] And some months after
that, he wrote to James Jackson Putnam that "[s]elf-analysis is a never
ending process that must be continued indefinitely," noting how each
renewed attempt brings its own surprises.[70] In 1935, Freud had also written that the danger of incompleteness is particularly great in self-analysis
because one is too soon satisfied with a part explanation that perhaps
masks something that is more important.[71] He also referred famously to
psychoanalysis as the third of those impossible professions, after education and government, "in which one can be sure beforehand of achieving
unsatisfying results."[72] The impossibility of bringing under conscious control all the personal anxieties and conflicts of his life, at which I am willing to believe he worked harder and longer than anyone else, had more to
do with his judgment of the limits of his own insight than the problems
presented for psychoanalysis by his patients.

C. G.Jung pointed out to Freud the dilemma for psychoanalysis of gaps in his self-analysis, and so later would Ferenczi.[73] Jung reminded Freud that their analysis came to an end because Freud worried that continued analysis would compomise his authority, a statement that is believable enough under the circumstances.[74] Any psychoanalyst would recognize Freud's exceptional claim instantly as resistance and would so name it if anyone else had made it. Toward the end of his life, Ferenczi was more critical, perceiving and complaining with some bitterness that Freud wanted to play at being the "unmoved mover," although he remained too close to Freud to see the problem in any terms but Freud's: Freud "founded the theory of the parricidal Oedipus, but obviously applied only to others, not to himself. Hence the fear of allowing himself to be analyzed. . . . In his conduct Fr[eud] . . . wants to ignore the traumatic moment of his own castration in childhood; he is the only one who does not have to be analyzed."[75]

On the one hand Freud wanted to be ruthlessly honest about his project and he therefore made the statement to Fliess and others about the impossibility of self-analysis. On the other hand, he was inclined to wishful omnipotence, and he did often act or write as if he could have brought everything under control in his self-analysis, or, having failed to do so, act as if in all logic he should nevertheless be entitled to persist as an exception to his own rules. He noted of Leonardo da Vinci that "[t]here is no one so great that it would be a disgrace for him to be subject to the laws that govern normal and pathological activity with equal severity."[76] But Freud tended to treat himself as an exception, and there was for the longest time an unfortunate tendency in the psychoanalytic literature to indulge him in this conceit, a bad sign for the effective elaboration of theory.

Thus Freud wrote remarkable things about experiences of traumatic helplessness and about separation and loss. He kept returning to these themes in his work, he made cryptic or difficult-to-place comments about them—referring to separation anxiety once as occupying a unique place in the mental economy, having claimed that missing someone who is loved and longed for is "the key to an understanding of anxiety."[77] The early work, particularly the *Studies on Hysteria*, is replete with significant instances of loss, as John Bowlby had also pointed out. Frau Emmy von N., just to recall one instance, was one of fourteen siblings, only four of whom survived; her husband was dead, and she was depressed, pain wracked, and suffering with insomnia. She explained to Freud that she was easily frightened because of her childhood experiences, which she related to him: "First when I was five years old . . . my brothers and sisters often threw dead animals at me. . . . Then I was frightened again when I was seven and I unexpectedly saw my sister in her coffin; and again when I was eight and my brother terrified me so often by dressing up in sheets like a ghost; and again when I was nine and I saw my aunt in her coffin and her jaw suddenly dropped."[78]

In terms of actual reporting in the *Studies on Hysteria*, as distinct from Freud's inferential and, in retrospect, unwarranted judgments about sexuality and sexual abuse in that text, the themes of loss, absence, failure, and betrayal, of violent attacks on personal integrity and self-esteem and other themes mentioned earlier by Ricoeur, Sandler, Hardin, Blos, and so many others outweigh the theme of sexuality.[79]

Freud also reported on many occasions that he, personally, had the least tolerance of all for experiences of abandonment and separation. It is obvious that Freud was alarmed by unaccountable silences in the course of his correspondence with Fliess: "I am tossing *The Psychopathology of Everyday Life* aside to answer you immediately, now that your last letter has finally broken the alarming silence."[80] Freud wrote to Fliess in 1895, "Demon, Why don't you write? How are you? Don't you care at all anymore what I'm doing?"[81] Freud had earlier written to his betrothed, Martha Bernays, summing up the ways in which his life had progressed to that point, concluding with this thought: "I have remained in good health and done nothing dishonorable; even though I have remained poor, those things which means something to me have become available, and I feel safe from the worst fate, that of being abandoned."[82] Later, on a solitary trip to England, Freud wrote as well that "this is my last attempt to enjoy freedom alone. Last year in Rome it was already hardly bearable."[83] (It is interesting, too, that Freud did not attend his mother's funeral, which, as Hardin notes, "makes no manifest sense.")[84]

The problem was that Freud could not integrate the experience of loss in his imagination and give it—except at different moments and in unexpected ways—the emphasis it deserved in terms of his own life's experiences and the experiences of many of his patients, not to speak of experiences in the wider world.[85] It was perhaps unavoidable, considering both Freud's desire to found this science and the kind of choices this might involve, and also the limits of imagination in this sphere of life, that Freud would have spared himself yet more difficult periods of self-examination. The problems of loss and of affective responses to loss were on his mind and they stayed on his mind, but they never achieved the status implied in his letters to Fliess, in such earlier work as the *Studies on Hysteria*, and in Schur's informed judgment.

Even more interesting, then, considering everything that Freud said about emotional life, the emotional turmoil of his own life, and the long-term therapeutic experience of all psychoanalysts with the emotional life of patients, is the other point referred to, the absence in psychoanalysis of a theory of affects. The compulsion to repeat is nowhere more evident as symptomatic expression than in the persistent if puzzled commentaries by psychoanalysts on the absence of a theory of emotions and the inability of the profession effectively to address the anomaly or to develop such a theory, which continued more or less through to the last decade.

In his "Autobiographical Study" (1925), Freud explained how impressed he was by the fact that Anna O. had been relieved of her symptoms after having been encouraged "to express in words the affective phantasy by which she was at the moment dominated."[86] As early as 1893 Freud pointed out that individual susceptibility determined how any individual might deal with the affects associated with traumatic experience, fright, shame, anxiety, pain.[87] Freud's earliest reference to "the process of censorship" is in connection with "affects of shame, of self-reproach, of psychical pain," or the sense of being harmed.[88] Indeed, Israel Rosenfeld noted that recent discoveries in neuroscience were foreshadowed long ago "when Freud noted the fundamental role of emotion in all recollection. His theory may well have provided a more complete understanding of the limbic system and its role in brain function in general than do many of the piecemeal neuroanatomical studies being published today."[89]

Thus Freud often referred to the significance of affective expression in the *Studies on Hysteria*, he wrote an important section on "Affects in Dreams" in *The Interpretation of Dreams*, which includes especially his discussion of the "Non vixit" dream.[90] He wrote to Fliess in November 1899, "A riddle is lurking in the region of affects,"[91] and he observed many times that the opposition to psychoanalysis stemmed from emotional rather than intellectual sources. He also noted at one point that all mental states are to some degree affective, stating even more emphatically at a later point that "[b]iological necessity demands that a situation of danger should have an affective signal."[92] Freud also wrote that "to suppress the development of affect is the true aim of repression," and again, famously, in "Jensen's *Gradiva*" (1907): "We remain on the surface so long as we treat only of memories and ideas. What is alone of value in mental life is, rather, the feelings. All psychic forces are significant only through their aptitude to arouse emotions. Ideas are repressed only because they are bound up with releases of emotions, which are not to come about; it would be more correct to say that repression deals with the emotions, but these are comprehensible to us only in their tie-up with ideas."[93] If Freud believed all this to be true, what happened to the affect theory with which psychoanalysis began?

Given the obvious depth of feeling that threatened or actual separation and loss could arouse in him, given his own reported experiences and those of his patients,[94] given that so many subsequent and important psychoanalytic developmental theories emphasize separation and loss, and given, finally, that vital aspects of the classical sociological theories—including especially theories of Marx, Weber, Durkheim, and Tönnies—were all in their different ways theories of loss, it is important to reconsider the implications of the conclusion that Freud reported in that same letter to Fliess of October 15, in which he had recounted so many of his experiences of loss: "A single idea of general value dawned on me. I have found, in my own case too, [the phenomenon of] being in love with my mother and jealous of my father, and I now consider it a universal event in early childhood."[95] One would have to be in love with Freud's work—in the technical sense of being unable to render a critical assessment—to accept this concatenation of ideas without comment, for in terms of what psychoanalysts routinely regard as data, where Freud is personally concerned, the experience of loss far outweighed the experience of sexuality.

Freud made a decision to focus on what later became the drive theory and the developmental phases culminating in the Oedipus complex, but he would not focus on traumatic experience, the kind that he wrote about at length in his earlier work, and with great feeling in the correspondence with Fliess, involving abandonment, loss, separation, and sometimes a sense of helplessness in the face of events. At the same time, he would also diminish the significance of affect theory, even when he had moved on from his notion of affect as discharge (affective expression is related to drive tension, affects arise as safety valves and indicators of drive tension) to affect as communication.[96] In this context, we may assume that Freud's reluctance to address the problem of affects with the gravity it merited was in no small measure autobiographical in content. It was also the source of a fundamental error, as confirmed in both the psychoanalytic[97] and the neuroscientific literature.[98]

It would be difficult to exaggerate the obstacles the problem of affects presents to any researcher. But on his own testimony, Freud was dealing constantly with patients' feelings, even if his earlier discharge model hardly did justice to his own experience. We may recall that in the *Studies on Hysteria*, Breuer and Freud were focused on an "events and affects" psychology. They claimed there "that external events determine the pathology of hysteria to an extent far greater than is known and recognized." In addition, they claimed that each individual hysterical symptom immediately and permanently disappeared when "*we had succeeded in bringing clearly to light the memory of the event by which it was provoked and in arousing its accompanying affect, and when the patient had described that event in the greatest possible detail and had put the affect into words.*" They also described the cultural content involved in traumatic experience, the processes by which it achieved a symptomatic effect and by which the effect was resolved, pointing out in particular that recollection without affect almost invariably produced no result.[99]

The concept of affect as it appears in *Studies on Hysteria* was hardly adequate to the theoretical task, but regardless of how affect is conceived, it is impossible to miss the compelling clinical experience of it. Thus when Freud abandoned this version of his psychology, rooted in what he thought of as the accidental, the contingent, and the historical, on behalf of his universal propositions, he crucially compromised also the continued systematic study of affects. [100]

This reluctance to address the problem of affects is reflected most obviously in the kind of emotional control Freud recommended to therapists as the correct practice, based on his own experience. It is quite well understood that "[a]t no time . . . did Freud lose sight of or minimize the importance of the affective relationship between the patient and the analyst."[101] Still, Freud emphasized that "[a]fter forty-one years of medical activity, my self-knowledge tells me that I have never really been a doctor in the proper sense. . . . I have no knowledge of having had any craving in my early childhood to help suffering humanity. I scarcely think, however, that my lack of a genuine medical temperament has done much damage to my patients. For it is not greatly to the advantage of patients if their doctor's therapeutic interest has too marked an emotional emphasis. They are best helped if he carries out his task coolly and keeping as closely as possible to the [his] rules."[102] Freud did not always abide by his own technical recommendations for abstinence, and there are reports of Freud's humaneness in the analytic situation; his recommended posture did not preclude warmth and spontaneity.[103] Nevertheless, Freud acted with respect to the emerging profession as if the integration and control of impulse and emotional constraint within each analyst, or among less disciplined or experienced analysts, was problematic, so that segregated and elevated authoritative teachers had to become institutionally responsible for training focused on emotional constraint, with all the problems that this has entailed. To preclude contamination he insisted upon everyone else maintaining emotional distance, whether he always did so or not.

The technical recommendation of abstinence, however he handled it in specific instances, allowed Freud to manage the constant engagement with and separation from people in intense emotional circumstances. This was the condition that enabled him to proceed at all. But even as it allowed Freud to see some things, it prevented him from seeing others. Freud's organization of therapy, his technical recommendation of neutrality, which allows patients to express love, anger, disappointment, fear, and so on, may have been restitutive, adaptive, and functional, but it was also symptomatic. Freud had observed in one of his papers on technique, having explained that the psychoanalyst had to learn to attune his unconscious mind to his patient's, that the psychoanalyst could not as a result "tolerate any resistances in himself which hold back from consciousness what has been perceived by his unconscious" because "he would introduce into the analysis a new species of selection and distortion."[104] This is an impossible standard, and Freud himself failed to manage it.

The technical principles of abstinence and neutrality that guided Freud's recommendations to the profession, including his reluctance to discuss the problem of countertransference, are significantly related to his experiences as reported in the well-known "Fragment of an Analysis of a Case of Hysteria," the Dora case, which, although it was completed in 1901, was not published until 1905. It is important to recall here what Freud wrote in "Remembering, Repeating, and Working Through" (1914): "The patient does not *remember* anything of what he has forgotten and repressed, but *acts* it out. He reproduces it not as a memory but as an action; he *repeats* it, without, of course, knowing that he is repeating it. For instance, the patient does not say that he remembers that he used to be defiant and critical towards his parents' authority; instead, he behaves in that way to the doctor."[105] A lot of what Freud wrote was autobiographical, and whether Freud was aware of it or not, in this instance we can say that it is as if, considering Dora's unanticipated departure, the timing of which took Freud by surprise and disturbed him, Freud's response reflected his inability to remember the significance of separation and abandonment to him.[106] The possibility of doing analysis depended upon his ability to keep emotional expression and the impact of separation under control. Dora reinforced the tendency in Freud to suppress and subordinate the problem of emotions, as reflected in his treatment of countertransference as a problem.[107]

In any event, once Freud had made the decision to elevate drive theory and subordinate traumatic experience, which was easy enough for him to rationalize, an inhibiting tendency took over, a result of the need to focus his attention and concentrate, which was bound to limit the perception and organization of contradictory or emotionally difficult data, even as his ability to think about his decision was enhanced because his attention was so acutely focused. This process allowed him the freedom to attack the problems of sexuality and development, which could easily have appeared insurmountable not only in their inherent difficulty but especially in the social impact they might have. Freud after all stirred emotions then and later; in his own terms he saw himself "bringing the plague."[108] But he could not then absorb or use all the information he had, he could not let in everything that he knew; some information and his earlier perceptions of some problems he suppressed, subordinated, or just lost. For the reasons I have noted, he could not keep drive theory and affect theory together, and to the enduring perplexity of generations of psychoanalysts, affect theory in a systematic sense dropped away from his scientific vision. At the same time, Freud could only have done the work that he did by narrowing the possibilities in terms of his scientific interests and by focusing complete attention on, even by exaggerating and overevaluating the significance of, his theories of development and conflict.

It is important to emphasize that Freud was not only responsible for the development of the theory and the elaboration of practice, but in his own mind he had also taken on as a sacrifice what Colin Murray Parkes referred to as "the worry work," the anticipation of future struggles rendered inevitable by the content of the work.[109] By taking on himself the risks, he also claimed for himself the right to map out any future his work might have. There were, thereafter, many things that Freud could not see or take fully into account, and the problems of loss and affect were paramount among them. As Freud explained, one of the ways of managing the subordination of affect is to disavow or otherwise fail to make the connection between one's own conflicts and the importance of affective responses.[110] In addition, as psychoanalysts also explain, resistance to regression can be a dangerous thing, and while Freud prided himself on being able to overcome such resistance, he was not always up to it, and he could not discriminate and identify all the instances when he was not. Or as Freud wrote to one of his correspondents, Frederick van Eeden, psychoanalysis teaches us "that our intellect is really a feeble and dependent thing, a plaything and tool of our instincts and affects, and that we are all compelled to behave cleverly or stupidly according to the commands of our [emotional] attitudes and internal resistances."[111]

In the story Freud told about Dora, he wrote that "[h]e that has eyes to see and ears to hear may convince himself that no mortal can keep a secret. If his lips are silent, he chatters with his finger-tips; betrayal oozes out of him at every pore. And thus the task of making conscious the most hidden recesses of the mind is . . . quite possible to accomplish."[112] To live consistently in Freud's world of symptomatic expression, of evasion, suppression, and repression, of resistance to knowledge or an emotional incapacity to tolerate certain kinds of knowledge, the compulsion to repeat, to act out rather than remember, to reveal oneself in the manner Freud described rather than confront issues, to get close to the significance of conflicts and then pull back before their biographical depth is revealed, Freud's own capacity for evasion, suppression, and repression must be acknowledged.

Thus, as Max Schur explained, Freud did not mention his brother Julius in his analysis of the "Non vixit" dream discussed earlier, although as Schur notes there were clear reasons for doing so.[113] In fact, although Freud had himself explained to Fliess the importance to him of Julius's death—which has even been referred to in the psychoanalytic literature as the most important event of Freud's life—his brother is never mentioned in *The Interpretation of Dreams*.[114] Consider, too, that when Freud wrote these passages in *The Interpretation of Dreams* he believed that anxiety was a result of the repression of libidinous wishes that then only achieve affective expression as anxiety. But Freud later reversed that logic in the text on anxiety already referred to (*Inhibitions, Symptoms, and Anxiety*). There Freud explained that anxiety leads to repression as a way of mastering or avoiding threatening experience, and not, as he had explained it earlier, the other way around. Freud wrote that "to interpret and report one's dreams demands a high degree of self-discipline,"[115] but as he also wrote, no one gets it all under control, and in his own terms he was more concealing than revealing. Freud never did explain how this important correction of the significance of anxiety affected the dream book (or the self-analysis, for that matter).

Freud's recording of the "Non vixit" dream demonstrates how arbitrary it was of him to claim that endogenous fantasy is more important than traumatic experience as a source of mental activity. Indeed, a number of psychoanalysts have recently taken Freud and subsequent generations of psychoanalysts to task for having failed to treat traumatic experience adequately, affirming yet again the observations of many earlier critics, notably Sandor Ferenczi.[116] If the dream can be said to have a central theme, it is separation and loss and what Sandler referred to as representational congruity, not the vicissitudes of drive expression. This is clear from what is missing from the dream or from the thoughts that caused Freud to be apprehensive about it, beginning with the failure to observe and systematically integrate the issue of separation and loss, but including also the absence of references to Freud's dead brother Julius, the past and prospective loss of friends (for example, Breuer, Fliess), and the expression of anxiety that remains unexplained in the light of the subsequently revised theory of anxiety.

Freud's insistence on doing things his way, his desire to maintain control, to define problems and options in a narrower way than has appeared appropriate to psychoanalysts for some time, his successful penetration of the world's imagination, his ability to define primacies in terms of sexuality and aggression, his call to a public that was forced to acknowledge their own suppression of such important human motives, all these things worked to deflect attention, to keep suppressed or under control the significance of loss and emotional responses to loss and the kind of theory that might be elaborated in these terms. Or as the psychoanalyst Aaron Karush put it, "That Freud accomplished so much with the libido theory, despite its limitations, remains a major miracle."[117]

There are two further points I want to make in this context. The first involves the technical reason for insisting upon interpreting the significance of any event from both the side of the participants and of the observer.[118] That is, ignoring or bypassing the observations and judgments of the participants when the knowledge of mind and the relationship of mind to society is so slight and problematic is to ignore the best source of evidence for confirmation of one's interpretive conclusions about particular actions. Christopher Lasch, a very astute critic and observer, dismissed this objection because it rendered virtually all conclusions about important issues problematic: "It is not difficult to see that this type of reasoning can be used to refute almost any critical judgment on human actions. Only if the participants themselves agree that they are engaged . . . [in whatever behavior is at issue] can the sociologist describe their actions as such!"[119] However, given the current situation of the social sciences, this is almost without exception the case—but only almost. There may be occasions when judgments become possible in the absence of confirming statements from the subject, especially when blatant contradictions or obvious gaps in logic are sufficient to compromise a well-defended position. The absence of a theory of affects in Freud's psychoanalysis, considering everything Freud wrote about it, is such an occasion.

And second, this is not a question of whether or not Freud moved psychoanalysis in the right direction, particularly with respect to cultural analysis; many psychoanalysts—let alone many observers beyond psychoanalysis—have already affirmed that he did not.[120] This is rather a question of whether or not he provided a theoretically effective direction in the cultural terms he insisted were his paramount interest. The answer is he did not, for an effective theory in cultural terms would have required a primary focus on the social world and the integration of cognitive and affective experience in this context, and Freud did not provide that.

AFFECT

The problems of loss, affect, and the relationship of affect to cognition were subordinated or suppressed by Freud, and for a number of personal, social, and cultural reasons, the question of affect continued to be by subsequent generations of psychoanalysts. In the long run, however, while Freud's original emphasis turned out not to be so significant with respect to loss because psychoanalysts did a lot to repair this deficiency, it remained very significant with respect to affect, on the testimony of generations of psychoanalysts themselves. The difficulty is that loss, affect, and cognition taken together in a social context suggest the possibility of a more relevant and interesting approach to social psychology and history than Freud's original terms do, or, for that matter, the terms of any number of other approaches to social psychology. But the empirical obstacles that thwarted the earlier psychoanalytically informed social psychologies (for example, Erikson's or Parsons's), or any of the other interpretive or "soft" social psychologies, persist and still need to be overcome, to begin with by examining the relationship of threatened or actual experiences of loss to emotional responses and to the ways that these responses affect the cognitive capacities of people and their ability to adapt to changing circumstances.

Psychoanalysts as well as cognitive and neuropsychologists have more recently tried to demonstrate the importance of the connection of affect to cognition even if no one has any substantial sense yet of how the process works.[121] The common impression is that there is more research and more of a developed and useful literature on these subjects than in fact there is. We can find some interesting statements on the subject in the psychoanalytic literature, for example, "affect is a form of thinking, knowing, planning, communicating, and relating. It does the same psychic work as what we are used to calling cognition."[122] And cognitive psychologists have claimed as well "that our ways of knowing the world are intrinsically bound up with our ways of feeling or, indeed, our moral and aesthetic evaluations . . . [C]ognitive theories assume that certain attitudes, beliefs, or patterns of information are more central or self-oriented than others and are more likely to evoke complex affective responses."[123] But as researchers themselves are the first to admit, knowledge of these problems is still best described as inchoate.

Freud's reluctance to deal systematically with loss and emotional responses to loss provides the basis for understanding how emotional ties affected cognitive capacities in the history of psychoanalysis itself. For of all the areas in which the persisting emotional attachment of generations of psychoanalysts to the founder fostered ideological conclusions, the fate of affect theory is the most interesting.[124] Psychoanalysts too often proved willing to go along with Freud's wish to be treated as an exception to his own rules, or to describe Freud's difficulties in intellectual rather than symptomatic terms, or otherwise to express a desire to protect the profession and the community at the cost of maintaining cognitive discipline.[125]

These observations are consistent with what an "outside" observer might conclude but they are also consistent with the conclusion of many participants as well. For a significant number of them have understood that the absence of a systematic theory of affects undermined the possibility of achieving effective theory both in the sense of adequately connecting theory to practice and in the sense of being able to address larger cultural issues, given the knowledge and the epistemic conceptions they themselves had of people, their attributes and conflicts. At the same time, however, they proved unable to do much about it until recently. The complexities that arise from this contradiction, and from the contradictory practice of continuing to elevate and segregate the authoritative founder despite an acute awareness of the problematic nature of his achievement, provide us with an opportunity to observe the ways in which leadership, ideology, affect, and cognition are related in this situation.

The customary approach to the absence of a systematic theory of affects in psychoanalysis is to stress the difficulty of this "ineffable subject," perhaps repeating Freud's assertion from *Civilization and Its Discontents*, "It is not easy to deal scientifically with feelings."[126] By the same token, psychoanalysts might also claim that "people are not the final authorities on their own affective states."[127] But if Freud appears reluctant to deal with feelings and he writes, by way of explanation, that feelings are hard to deal with scientifically, or if he insists that he is capable of a certain kind of emotional control, or claims that he never experienced a certain kind of emotional state, his responses are typically treated as if he could have been the final arbiter of his own affective states. Then, too, Freud's approach to affects is likely to be treated as the consciously considered result of the kinds of patients Freud saw or of the contemporary understanding of medicine.

It is becoming more routine for psychoanalysts to point out Freud's oversights, for example, that he had incorporated a bias into his "core model technique" that led to "a disproportionate emphasis on the interpretive aspects with a relative de-emphasis of the participatory dimensions of the process," a reminder that considerations of Freud's self-analysis should include "the neglected, hidden experiential [emotionally charged] aspects which occurred in his relationship with Fliess."[128] But psychoanalysts are still inclined to explain, as Arnold Modell did, that Freud had more or less neglected the communicative function of affect, because "the first patients studied by Freud were hysterics who, as a group, tended to be hypercommunicative."[129] According to Willard Gaylin, "The neglect of emotion was almost inevitable, given the nineteenth century model of medicine from which it emerged. This neglect was further enhanced with the development of the libido theory and its enchantment with the primitive nineteenth century concept of energy."[130] Frank M. Lachmann and Robert D. Stolorow also noted that "[t]he roots of this felt inadequacy can be found in the intellectual history of psychoanalytic affect theory, in Freud's choice of an economic or drive-discharge model for affect expression."[131] Henry Krystal in turn explained that Freud's view of emotions "simply reflected the physiological and psychiatric attitude of his age. It was burdened with the mind-body schism, and with a mechanistic attitude toward the body processes. The tendency to think of mental function as a reflex arc produced an inclination to consider emotions as discharge phenomena. . . . Freud's absorption with the idea that emotions were discharge phenomena made it impossible for him to consider emotions as unconscious, even when he found clinical evidence of such forces as the unconscious sense of guilt."[132] And Joseph M. Jones wrote that "[a]s Freud worked out the details of his metapsychological theories, one effect was to partially strip affects of their process role. Recognizing that Freud's covert philosophical agenda stripped affects of their process role can be the Rosetta stone for understanding why psychoanalysis does not yet have a satisfactory theory of affects."[133]

It is statements like these, reflecting the reluctance of psychoanalysts to make Freud a subject of his own theory, that frustrate readers of the literature and could even provoke them to say rudely unprofessional things like, "Hey you guys, knock it off." Freud's failure to address this question was overdetermined—how, by any psychoanalytic standard, could it not have been? In Freud's own terms, ideation, symptomatic or otherwise, has various (id, ego, superego) determinants, and it is the psychoanalyst's task to sort out the relationships among them. What happened to the principle of multiple functions, the primacy of unconscious motivation, or the possibility of symptomatic expression? After all, these are statements from professionals who in virtually all other circumstances would quickly explain that "[d]isavowal or denial as originally described by Freud involves, not an absence or distortion of actual perception, but rather a failure to fully appreciate the significance or implication of what is perceived;"[134] or who would argue that "the adaptive function of denial is the avoidance of painful affects evoked by percepts which arouse signal anxiety basically related to the continuum of threats encountered by the developing ego," including superego disapproval and the loss of self-esteem.[135] Just try to imagine the circumstances in which Freud, who admonished colleagues never to underestimate the significance of small signs, would have been content with an intellectual interpretation of the failure to make the connections in as significant an instance as this one![136]

In her admirable book, *Psychoanalytic Theories of Affect*, Ruth Stein describes the affects as "one of the most difficult, problematic, and haunting areas in psychoanalysis."[137] We can certainly understand that affects are difficult and problematic; indeed, Michael Franz Basch has argued that psychoanalysts will never be able to produce a *psychoanalytic* theory of affect at all.[138] In any event, as Charles Brenner has pointed out, "each affect is unique for each individual. Each person's affective life is his own and is never identical with that of another, since each person's wishes, memories, perceptions, fears, and expectations are never identical with those of another."[139] As in all other instances, the idiosyncratic responses make systematic cultural theory difficult and problematic.

But why "haunting," especially when there is not another word in Stein's book that harks back to or explains the reference? The answer is that however much Freud in one way or another acknowledged the importance of the problem, he could not cope with it introspectively in relation to experiences of loss, separation, and abandonment, as a crucial part of the task of his ongoing self-analysis, and therefore as a crucial task for psychoanalysis. Freud was unable effectively to address this problem in a systematic way, and his failure to do so proved costly.[140]

The problem of the emotions has haunted psychoanalysis because there are many psychoanalysts who know or sense that this is the case. Whatever the conflicts stirred up particularly by Freud's resolution of the problems he faced in October 1897 and later, when he launched and elaborated the drive theory—distinguished especially, and ironically, by the theory of repression—his inability to cope systematically with affects, which then dropped out of psychoanalysis as a compelling theoretical problem, was indicative of them. If, as Sandler wrote in the foreword to Stein's book, "[t]he role of affects is becoming increasingly important in psychoanalytic theory;" and if, as Charles Spezzano has claimed, "[a]ffect theory is increasingly recognized as the most likely candidate to bridge the gap between clinical theory and general theory in psychoanalysis," Freud's single-minded focus on drive theory interfered with the project in a very fundamental way.[141] But attempting to redress what is widely perceived within psychoanalysis to be a serious imbalance turned out to be another matter altogether.

Thus despite the decisive importance of experiences with emotional expression among all analysts and despite the presumed relationship of emotional to cognitive capacities, "[a]ffect theory in general has found but a belated and tenuous footing amidst the instinctual drives and psychic structures of our model, and analysts have had to be guided by observations and theories outside their orbit."[142] Ethel Spector Person has claimed that Freud was reluctant to tackle the emotions, and most of the speculations about "this glaring omission," as John Munder Ross has noted, center on Freud's biography. But equally important is the relationship of cognitive mastery to affective commitment in terms of authoritative leadership and ideology. Hence the important question raised by Ross: why have psychoanalysts "so persistently, perhaps phobically, avoided confronting the passions, at once sensual and spiritual, expressed in adult sex and love?" In short, "why the enduring reluctance of analysts after him?"[143]

Psychoanalysts are well aware that the absence of a systematic theory of affects constitutes a remarkable omission and that it compromised the effectiveness of theory and practice. Indeed, Adrian Applegarth wrote at one point that the lack of an affect theory represents one of the worst failures of psychoanalysis, while Adam Limentani wondered how psychoanalysts could have allowed this to happen, considering that "[t]he success and failure of an analysis could in fact be said to rest on the degree of affective change which takes place during its course."[144]

It is interesting to note how long-standing and widespread this concern over the absence of an affect theory is, how little has been done about it, and how often psychoanalysts have addressed the fact. In 1937, Marjorie Brierly pointed out that apart from Freud's work on anxiety, and some contemporary studies on pity and jealousy, very little attention had been paid in theory to affects, although, as she noted, affects had never lost their importance in practice. "Indeed, patients themselves leave us in no doubt here. With few exceptions, they one and all complain of some disorder of feeling and tend to estimate their own progress by changes in their feelings and in their ability to cope with them. In practice we find our way only by following the Ariadne thread of transference affect, and go astray if we lose contact with this. It is time that we restored affects to a place in theory more consonant with their importance in practice."[145] Thirty years later, Leo Rangell wrote that "affects, the original center, in giving way to subsequent developments have become wrongly, 'the forgotten man.' In spite of their ubiquity clinically, [the affects] have in a sense been bypassed, or at least minimized out of proportion, and receive a good deal less of systematic attention than they deserve in our total theoretical metapsychological system."[146] Later still, In 1974, Rangell recalled during a panel discussion on affects that "in 1952 he had served as a Reporter at the first panel on affects of this [American Psychoanalytic] Association, when David Rapaport and Edith Jacobson had presented their now classic papers, and where there had been a lively division of opinion over whether a psychoanalytic theory of affects yet existed." Rangell went on to state that now (1974) there is still absent "a complete psychoanalytic formulation regarding affects." [147] Rangell also recalled an observation of Edith Jacobson's, reminiscent of Brierly's observation, "that affect theory has been a late comer in psychoanalysis, secondary to drive theory, and that this is paradoxical inasmuch as the central concern of the analyst is understanding *emotional* illness."[148]

Actually, Jacobson (in 1971), acknowledging the importance of *Inhibitions, Symptoms, and Anxiety*, particularly in terms of Freud's emphasis "on the causal role of reality events in the formation of mental life" that had "once again focused attention on the role played by reality in emotional reaction patterns," wrote that "[w]hen we search for further analytic papers on the subject [of affects] . . . we are amazed to find how few analysts have dared to tackle this challenging but intricate problem." Jacobson had a lot more to say on the subject, pointing out that Freud's emphasis on anxiety as the key affect may have been at the expense of a general theory of affects that throughout the history of psychoanalysis has remained relatively impoverished.[149] Jacobson then emphasized "the need for a consistent affect theory," arguing that "[i]n fact, the development of the psychoanalytic drive theory appears to have halted our efforts to form equally clear theoretical concepts of the affects and their relations to the psychic drives."[150]

Examples are no proof, but it is important to convey the sense of dismay among psychoanalysts that the problem of affects has evoked. Fifty years after Brierly's statement, William Meissner noted that the psychoanalytic psychology of affective experience remains to be written, and such comments persisted through to the 1990s.[151] There are in fact many, many such comments, the references for which I will provide below. I do not want to tax the readers' patience with a further succession of quotes, but I also do not want this problem, unique in the history of psychoanalysis and revealing in a number of interesting ways, to be subjected to any retrospective reconstructions.[152] If we consider that the psychoanalytic project has even been defined as "the recognition of affects," or that "[t]he transference neurosis does not develop in an emotionally empty space, [i]t can only develop in a space saturated with affects," or that ultimately "it is always the feeling state, existing in the present or anticipated, which is the criterion upon which the ego bases its adaptive maneuvers," or that "the ultimate guiding or regulatory principle in adaptation from a psychological point of view relates to feeling states of one form or another,"[153] or that, "[i]t must be recognized that emotional requirements can, and do, become as imperative as instinctual needs and pressures,"[154] we can see why so many psychoanalysts have pondered the obviously disturbing question of why a psychoanalytic psychology of affects had not long since been systematically addressed within the profession.

The significance of Freud's failure and the failure of psychoanalysts subsequently to address a theory of emotions is assessable in this context, and we can return now to the question raised earlier by John

Munder Ross: even if Freud's cognitive capacities were affected by his personal experiences, hampering the development of theory in this way, "why the enduring reluctance of analysts after him?"[155]

To begin with, it often happens for various reasons that a theoretical problem fails to command an expected degree of systematic interest within a scientific discourse. One reason is that the direction of theory development in a particular domain promises no ready solutions because the problems are too complex to address systematically under current or forseeable circumstances. A second is that a problem appears to be subordinate to other problems that by common agreement more immediately merit focused attention. A third is that possible solutions to the problem appear inconsistent with or contradictory of current practice or belief, particularly as authoritative figures have defined them; or they appear otherwise anomalous in ways that seem to threaten the boundaries of a particular domain and therefore too difficult to absorb or to deal with.

Freud wanted to emphasize the first two reasons for the absence of an affect theory, saying that it was too difficult to address and that working out the vicissitudes of drive theory was more important.[156] But this answer is unsatisfactory: everything Freud addressed was difficult, including the drives. As he noted, "in no region of psychology were we groping more in the dark," and again, "The theory of instincts is so to say our mythology. Instincts are mythical entities, magnificent in their indefiniteness. In our work we cannot for a moment disregard them, yet we are never sure that we are seeing them clearly."[157] Moreover, it has been argued for some time now that as a theoretical problem affect is not inferior to drives, and many psychoanalysts have done so. Thus it is the third reason, the threat to boundaries and the relationship to an authoritative figure and to the culture of psychoanalysis, that needs to be examined.

The most obvious point to make, then, is that affects are decisively present not only in the therapeutic situation but in the social world too, as is readily evident to any observer. Reactions to events do not depend solely upon people's cognition of them but include also how they feel about their own ability to cope with events, or with an adverse or challenging reality. Responses occur not only in terms of a judgment of the significance of what has transpired, but also in terms of feelings about it. How an individual reacts, whether with anxiety, alarm, sadness, disappointment, elation, euphoria, anger, hope, disgust, and so on, depends upon that individual's biography. Breuer and Freud made some of these points in the *Studies on Hysteria* with respect to individual behavior. But in addition to their observations is the further cultural one that individuals are situated in an intersubjective field beyond immediate relationships, both in their own minds and in practice to all kinds of social and cultural figures, symbols, standards, and objects. This is one reason why authoritative leadership remains important in all societies: by vigorously promoting particular solutions to conflict, leaders directly address the challenging aspects of reality, and insofar as their own feelings are effectively channeled, they seem able to restore a sense of order to life. In this way authoritative leaders channel the emotional responses of others.[158] This is also why it is important to focus on both the integrative and the disruptive potential of emotions.[159]

Hence the significance of emotional appeals to patriotic virtue, to national, racial, or religious pride (or bigotry), which take concrete forms in parades and rallies, or the emotional outpourings of crowds of people that are evident to everyone. The public manipulations and expressions of hatred, rage, revenge, love, pride, loyalty, and hope, the declarations of moral superiority, the longing for great deeds, and the realization of great expectations are hard to ignore and hard to miss wherever they occur. Consider only the decade of the 1960s in the United States, the civil rights movement, the stirrings of the feminist movement, the youth movement, the electric effects of Martin Luther King's appeals for justice, rock and roll, free-speech rallies, antiwar rallies, the responses to the Kennedy and King assassinations, and the drug culture. Consider as well the embarrassment of modernization theory (characterized in part by a distinction between the affective responses of people in traditional cultures and the affectively neutral responses of people in modern ones) by the legitimation in the 1960s of affective expression in everyday life, contrary to the expectations of Marx, Weber, and other theorists for the increasing rationalization of everyday life.

However, such *cultural* expressions of emotion, or the interplay between social events and emotional responses, were for the longest time outside the domain, "the motherland," of psychoanalysis as Freud and analysts after him conceived it.[160] Freud was interested in intrapsychic reality and conflict and the ways that such conflict shaped and otherwise achieved expression in cultural life; and he was determined to protect the "distinctive identity of psychoanalysis" by insisting upon the primacy of drive activity.[161] For this allowed psychoanalysis to make a primary contribution to the study of culture, and justified its remaining independent of and not subordinate to other disciplines, a goal that Freud referred to in his *New Introductory Lectures*.[162] The proper tools for exploring unconscious, dynamic conflict were drive theory, resistance, repression, and other symptomatic signs of conflict, and the different vantage points of the psychoanalytic metapsychology[163] that, in developmental and particularly in oedipal terms, suggested a unified, universal perspective on cultural practice.[164] He never excluded traumatic experience from consideration but, as with the war neuroses, he worked hard to bring everything back to his own chosen ground.[165]

Freud did not worry too much about the integration in theory of immediate social conflict and other "external" issues because he had concluded that systematic social relationships mirrored intrapsychic ones and it was possible to understand their significance by understanding that. As for affects, as long as Freud maintained a rigorous therapeutic stance in his treatment of patients, which he thought provided the best means of demonstrating the importance of the drives and their vicissitudes, he could acknowledge the patients' emotional expressions but hold systematic commentary on their subordinate significance in abeyance, and he could forbear commenting on his own. And as long as he perceived external or social events as accidental and contingent, he could continue to justify this approach because he already had a more inclusive one, paramount in its significance, based on the phylogenetic propositions.

I want to emphasize that Freud often commented anomalously on the ways that cultures shape individual responses, and he continued to refer to traumatic experience after his abandonment of the seduction theory. He wrote "that the prescribed course of development can be disturbed and altered in each individual by recent external influences," and he addressed traumatic wartime experience, the war neuroses, in these terms.[166] In addition, he related the rise of neurosis to the decline of religion on several occasions, referring as well to a possible connection between neurosis and social and class origins. He also pointed to the real frustrations and misfortunes of life "from which arise deprivation of love, poverty, family quarrels, ill-judged choice of a partner in marriage, unfavourable social circumstances, and the strictness of the ethical standards to whose pressure the individual is subject."[167] And he warned as well of underestimating the influence of social customs that propel women into passive relationships.[168] One can easily find many more such statements.

The problem is that Freud did not know how to integrate such observations in systematic theory, so while one can always find them in his writings and correspondence, they tend to drop out of sight in any systematic sense. It was a lot easier for him to claim in object relational terms that individual psychology is social psychology than it was to demonstrate the process by which it becomes so. He tried, and others tried after him, but they could not make good on the claim.

In any event, he did not want to deal with accidental factors, illness, fatigue, traumatic experiences, and frustrations of all sorts, and in the famous cultural texts he referred to idiosyncratic instances as rarely as he could.[169] He much preferred to think about the developmental primacy of the Oedipus complex, with its various transformations and resolutions; and he tried as hard as he could to wish an "archaic heritage" into existence because he insisted that, theoretically speaking, he needed it. He stressed the unities imposed by an archaic unconscious, trying to close the gap between the results of therapy and the effects of life in the everyday world by unwarranted phylogenetic inferences because he understood that once the unique and particular aspects of history and culture were allowed to become decisive, psychoanalysis could never play the preeminent role he intended for it, or become the kind of natural science he meant it to become. As he wrote in *Moses and Monotheism*, "Granted that at the time we have no stronger evidence for the presence of memory-traces in the archaic heritage than the residual phenomena of the work of analysis which call for a phylogenetic derivation, yet this evidence seems to us strong enough to postulate that such is the fact. If it is not so, we shall not advance a step further along the path we entered on, either in analysis or in group psychology."[170] If all he really could count on as a result of psychoanalytic endeavor were the idiosyncratic outcomes of therapy, even if he could in each case have systematically described the process that accounted for the outcome, generating thereby a developmental psychology of individuals, he would not have despised the achievement, but he would also have been very dissatisfied with its limitations.

By contrast, the closer one gets to the kind of reality issues that follow from the rejection of the phylogenetic propositions, or to an appreciation of the systematic importance of social or cultural events, and especially of the way that affective expression is connected to such events, as Jacobson pointed out, the more difficult it is to maintain the independence of psychoanalysis and claim an original, unique, and primary contribution. And this is precisely what happened to mainstream psychoanalysts in terms of cultural analysis: unable to accept Freud's version of the "archaic heritage," they distanced themselves from it, while maintaining that "the realm of 'unconscious intrapsychic conflicts' qualifies unequivocally to be at [the] . . . core of universal and persistent psychoanalytic interest."[171] Psychoanalysts continued to insist, in other words, that "[t]he psychoanalytic domain is the intrapsychic,"[172] that the intrapsychic is "rock bottom."[173] But this meant staying aloof from those who, like Erikson, promoted a more systematic sociological perspective;[174] and it meant holding off systematic consideration of affects, which are much more evidently tied to social relationships and immediate events.

Psychoanalysts sometimes saw the dilemma, but the situation changed for the profession in terms of affect theory only after "social constructivist" or "relational" models of therapy challenged the traditional hierarchical arrangements and the emphasis on drives;[175] countertransference, referring to the psychoanalyst's own emotional state, was systematically addressed in this relational context in the 1980s;[176] and psychoanalysts began to look for alternative approaches (for example, in academic psychology) to problems of affect and cognition, which became necessary because of the impoverished state of psychoanalytic contributions.[177]

It is important to emphasize—and psychoanalysts have themselves made this point—that when the approach to clinical practice takes on a more social character, the familiar hierarchical (medical) relationship of analyst to patient no longer obtains, and transference becomes "a joint production of the analyst and the patient," as it does in "social-constructivist" or "relational" models, it follows that "the concept of intrapsychic process is essentially jettisoned."[178] As Freud understood, once that happens, psychoanalysis must lose the distinctive role in cultural analysis he had envisioned for it, because there is no way to surmount for larger purposes the idiosyncratic and discontinuous outcomes of therapy. Psychoanalysis must then become dependent upon sociological or anthropological perspectives to make sense of cultural events, an outcome Freud was determined to avoid and one he never wanted to see.

It is important to emphasize, then, as Edith Jacobson had done harking back to Freud's earliest work, that "[t]o a greater or lesser extent, every affect involves an emotional response to reality."[179] This is evidently the case in a clinical context, but it is particularly the case in respect of Freud's paramount interest, the cultural context. Thus, avoiding the systematic study of affects, and especially the cultural or social implications of affective expression that figure crucially in both clinical and cultural realms, was a way of protecting the intrapsychic domain (hence the special mission) of psychoanalysis; it was a way of protecting the perspectives of the founder; and it was a way of protecting the hierarchical structure of the clinical situation itself.

Among other things, if the cultural world is allowed to intrude in the clinical situation, it is only a question of time before the material interests and moral orientations of the psychoanalyst must also intrude. Psychoanalysts historically have contrasted their rationality to the irrationality of the patient, as if the third possibility, nonrational (or moral) perspectives, do not enter into it. Even now, when psychoanalysts more readily acknowledge that they do not have a privileged perspective on truth, as "dialogue and intersubjectivity" move closer to the center of psychoanalytic interest, it is still as if the solutions arrived at between patient and therapist did not have a problematically moral dimension.[180] As long as the focus is on intrapsychic reality (Freud's "one person psychology") or on a narrow understanding of intersubjective relatedness (a "two person psychology"), the pretense that the therapist is not also the representative of a moral or political order can be maintained. Once the conception of the cultural world is appropriately broadened, it is much more difficult to maintain.

The systematic study of affects in the wider world had other troubling implications stemming from the variety of idiosyncratic emotional responses to accidental and contingent events and their discontinuous character over time. One can always defend the primacy of intrapsychic conflict by claiming that an unconscious oedipal or preoedipal fantasy is constant over time, a function of universal developmental processes. But there is no way that one can make that kind of claim for emotional responses to changing real circumstances, and explaining them in systematic terms requires extra-analytic propositions, once again challenging the boundaries of the psychoanalytic domain.

Let me clarify this by example. More than thirty years ago, psychoanalyst Dale Meers spent three years doing therapeutic counseling in the ghetto neighborhoods of Washington, D.C. Meers described his experience, declaring that he was "stunned" by the ghetto child's exposure to "physical and emotional trauma," to physical assaults, not excluding assaults on small children, and to shootings, knifings, murders, drunkenness, and rape. Meers was also impressed by the ghetto child's resilience, "his adaptation without readily observable, external evidence of neurotic symptomatology." Meers was all but shouting at his psychoanalytic colleagues that there was no way to understand the lives of ghetto children in primarily intrapsychic terms or apart from the damaging and dangerous environment in which they were compelled to live. "Like the primary process mentation of the artist, the instinctual openness of the ghetto child can appear (socially) deviant yet be adaptive without necessarily deriving from intrapsychic conflict." In addition, "[d]epressive affects, the most dramatic and pervasive emotional attitudes in evidence, could have had neurotic or psychotic origins, yet such affects may simply be direct consequences of grief or fatigue that result from reality stresses of an unkind fate."[181] (As for the moral dilemma for psychoanalysts once the social world is allowed in, how could any psychoanalyst morally justify the consequences of treating children only to send them back to an environment they believed caused the problem in the first place?)

Norman Zinberg was also forced to consider the importance of the wider culture in his investigation of drug use among American soldiers in Vietnam. Zinberg explained that it was a misconception to imagine a one-to-one relationship between personality maladjustment and drug use. He professed to be surprised by the persistent emphasis on the personality of the drug user "when there is growing evidence of the power of the social setting to sustain controlled use of a powerful drug among many different personality types."[182] Denying the Army's early claim that only those who had been heavy drug users before military service became addicted, and emphasizing the heterogeneous composition of the relevant population, Zinberg concluded that "[t]he determining factor in their heroin use had been the intolerable setting of Vietnam." Once the soldiers returned to familiar surroundings, neither the power of the drug nor a susceptible personality proved to be decisive in keeping them drug dependent.[183]

However, there is no way to address the implied questions (how external social events can compel such affective responses, or how apparently deviant behavior can derive from social, not intrapsychic, conflict), at any level beyond the individual, without introducing a series of hypotheses that are outside the traditional psychoanalytic domain, thereby raising questions about the primary and unique role of psychoanalysis. Given the community's history of keeping psychoanalysis segregated from and elevated above other disciplines, at least until recently,[184] and given the observation that real, immediate social conflict can compel affective responses and deviant but nevertheless adaptive behavior, the best way to cope with the affective (and moral) implications is not to allow these issues to enter the theoretical discourse in the first place.

There is no doubt that psychoanalysts had kept their discipline segregated from the systematic analysis of the cultural and social world, and at great cost to the profession, too, at least in this society, because by continuing to insist on the primacy of intrapsychic conflict and failing to attend to real social pressures and conflicts, they lost the interest and attention of succeeding generations of students. Apart from the efforts of certain feminist and radical theorists, they have fairly well managed to remove themselves from the larger cultural picture. To be sure, psychoanalysts refer to the social or cultural world all the time, but they are very reluctant to do much about it,[185] and if it were not for the efforts of a handful of interested scholars, Peter Loewenberg, Peter Gay, Paul Roazen, Robert Jay Lifton, and some notable others, they could hardly be said to have done anything at all. Erikson long ago berated psychoanalysts for their ambiguous and half-hearted attempts to address the problem.[186] Holt, too, urged psychoanalysts to move beyond their preoccupation with intrapsychic reality and to take seriously the role of environmental threats and opportunities in the lives of people.[187] Still, in its first quarter-century, the *Journal of the American Psychoanalytic Association* published on group psychology or group phenomena the results of one panel discussion (1958), one book essay (1966), and one paper (1975).[188] Even as late as 1994, psychoanalysts were still commenting on how little has been written on the role of external reality in neurotic conflict and its effect on psychoanalytic technique.[189]

It is tempting to say, in response to the question Ross raised, that psychoanalysts evaded the issue of affect theory not only as Freud did, but because Freud did; indeed, Charles Brenner said just that.[190] In general it can be argued that anything Freud did not authorize as a problem proved difficult to establish as a problem afterwards, particularly among "mainstream" or orthodox psychoanalysts.[191] But this would not entirely encompass the situation I have outlined.[192] Freud established the domain, and generations of psychoanalysts defended it, but not just out of loyalty to him.[193] That is, trying to recover the position affect theory originally held would not only have challenged the primacy of the intrapsychic, but it would also have encouraged different inconvenient challenges to the domain in addition to the moral issue, for example, a renewed emphasis on traumatic experience, or a reexamination of Ferenczi's clinical contributions, two problems Freud had hoped psychoanalysts would never have to deal with again.[194] Of course, in the end they did have to deal with these problems, and others, too, including the profession's treatment of Erikson.[195] This is particuarly interesting because among the different reasons that psychoanalysts were reluctant to integrate the cultural or social world in their work, their lack of conceptual experience with it figures prominently. If Erikson could have said that he did not have "the knowledge necessary to approach in any systematic fashion the relationship between ego qualities, social institutions, and historical eras," what could the medically trained professionals of the American Psychoanalytic Association have said?[196]

There are several additional reasons for the failure to deal systematically with affect theory that also underscore the relationship of emotion to cognition in terms of authoritative leadership and the cultural uses of psychoanalysis in the service of the profession and the community. First among them is Freud's conception of psychoanalysis as a natural science, and what this entails for the accumulation and analysis of data,[197] particularly in terms of the emotion-laden environment in which observation occurs.[198] It can easily be argued that therapeutic work is best accomplished in the absence of emotion, and this posture is consistent with the image and myth of the scientist generally, as one who is involved in a value neutral, objective exploration for truth. This important cultural standard has proven to be as compelling in psychoanalysis as it has in any other field that defines itself as scientific.[199]

Moreover, the requirements or expectations of training in this context means that the suppression and repression of affective experience and conflict could rather easily be justified as indispensable to correct practice. Hence, the wish or capacity to respond emotionally was trained out of candidates by a profession that, following Freud's recommendations, valued highly this kind of self-control and treated the suppression of affect as evidence of a capacity for reasoned self-discipline. In his lectures to candidates at the Washington Psychoanalytic Institute, 1941–1942, Robert Waelder explained that the analyst is "not supposed to react emotionally, but analytically." To indulge an emotional response would permit the patient to enjoy his triumph and make the analysis more difficult. "Be careful not to let yourself be provoked to do or to say anything unanalytic, to get angry, to respond with emotions," because patients will try to seduce the analyst to emotional responses.[200]

As a subsidiary feature of this position, it is important to consider, again, at least in this society, the extent to which the cultural climate also allowed the profession to recruit among individuals who suffered from dampened affect (or among whom dampened affect had become an integral part of character). This is an empirical question that is necessary to raise because Waelder's position was and is so valuable both to the training analyst and to the candidate that the problem might well not have been recognized or analyzed for, contributing in this way to the failure to develop an affect theory. As Maxwell Gitelson observed more than forty years ago on the subject of training, an observation that is particularly compelling in terms of affective expression or the absence thereof, "The very fact that in the narcissistic neurosis the ego maintains its capacity to perceive and to deal 'adaptively' with external reality makes it possible for the intra-psychic conflict to be laid out on the framework presented by the environment, and to follow there a course which has the aspects of 'normality.'"[201] This is an interesting instance in which a psychoanalyst acknowledged that social factors can support what would be considered a neurotic trend, rendering it difficult to observe because society has a use for it.[202]

Thus, while psychoanalysts were well aware of the significance of having failed to develop an affect theory, their efforts to redress the situation bear little relationship to their sense of its significance. This persistent and puzzling behavior may be construed as the participants' confirmation of an observer's assessment of the failure of the profession to have developed a systematic theory of affects. Moreover, it is important to emphasize how the training process itself had affected the ability of psychoanalysts to address the problem, whether this was a matter of loyalty to the figure and memory of Freud, or to the profession, or to a culturally valued conception of how scientific endeavor ought to be conducted, or whether it was perhaps a means of deferring to teachers or of defending oneself in a therapeutic situation in which seductions and verbal assaults of one kind or another occur constantly. Considering that

Freud had offered the dissolution of the transference relationship as a guarantee of liberation from the oppressiveness of the past, we might ask, considering the fate of affect theory, just how effective the process of liberation actually is.

At the same time, the therapeutic situation is often too difficult for analysts to cope with emotionally in any other way, which accounts as well for the treatment historically of countertransference as a problem.[203] The intensity and emotional dangers of the therapeutic relationship have often been commented on in different ways and contexts, beginning with Freud who explained that the emotional distance (*Gefühlskälte*) of the psychoanalyst creates the best conditions for both parties: "for the doctor a desirable protection for his own emotional life and for the patient the greatest amount of help that we can give him today."[204] But consider the following statements as well: "interpretations are often made by the analyst in order to deny the anxiety aroused in him by the fact that the situation is unknown to him, and correspondingly dangerous."[205] "Considering the large number of patients seen by a psychoanalyst in the course of a day, it is to be expected that he will have to do something in order to somewhat insulate himself. Some therapists are more successful than others in handling the impact on themselves of their patient's emotional response to the psychoanalytic process, and are therefore able to avoid losing touch with the analysands even when their direct emotional involvement in the relationship is at a low point."[206]

With respect to the therapeutic situation itself, those who consider the affectively neutral posture indispensable, as Freud urged, have no trouble rationalizing it. If, as Wilfred Bion contended, analysts require a disciplined denial of memory and desire, then those who either suffer from dampened affect or are willing and able to suppress affective expression as a sign of scientific commitment or even as a sign of loyalty to the profession and to teachers have the advantage. Or as E. Victor Wolfenstein put it, psychoanalysis "awakens memories and desires, recreates the pain of what did happen and what didn't happen, renews hope and also disappointment. To tolerate the pain of the patient's awakening, and to open a space for it in his or her own mental life, the analyst must cover his or her feelings 'in forgetful snow,' put them to sleep. S/he must undergo what amounts to an emotional death."[207] By the same token, critics and participants—like Ferenczi, but many others as well—have often been dismayed by this posture. As Ernest Becker once wrote, "The emotional impoverishment of psychoanalysis must extend also to many analysts themselves and to psychiatrists who come under its ideology. This fact helps to explain the terrible deadness of emotion that one experiences in psychiatric settings, the heavy weight of the character armor erected against the world."[208]

Interest in affect theory among psychoanalysts has of course picked up considerably, as we can see from the recent books by Stein, Spezzano, Jones, Shapiro and Emde, and by a variety of papers on the subject; and it has picked up beyond psychoanalysis, too, in a number of other disciplines.[209] This change I ascribe first to the legitimation of affective expression in everyday life so characteristic of the 1960s, and so contrary to the expectations of such observers as Marx and Weber. I also ascribe it to generational factors within psychoanalysis itself. Donald Spence has stated that Freud's self-analysis, as the foundational myth of psychoanalysis, remains segregated from criticism, immunized from any attack. But however true this may once have been it is no longer true, as we can see from the many instances I have cited.[210] And it is no longer true either for the systematic study of affects. One of the important aspects of this factor is the need of psychoanalysts to anchor their own efforts empirically and experimentally by connecting with different branches of academic cognitive and developmental psychology and to neuroscience. Finally, I link it to the inability to continue to tolerate this perplexing theoretical anomaly that was interfering with both clinical and cultural observation. Such a long-standing and outstanding mismatch between perception and conception would become, finally, as difficult for psychoanalysts to maintain as it would be for anyone else.

CHAPTER 2

Cognitive Issues in Psychoanalysis

In an often-quoted letter of September 21, 1897, Freud confided to Fliess that he no longer believed in his seduction theory, which, as he noted, Fliess had himself found credible.[1] Freud suggested to Fliess a number of compelling reasons for this change: he had not been able to bring a single analysis to a successful conclusion; people who for a time had been the most involved in the process unexpectedly left; the absence of any completely successful cases that he had been counting on and the possibility of explaining partial successes in other ways; and surprisingly, "in all cases, the *father*, not excluding my own, had to be accused of being perverse—the realization of the unexpected frequency of hysteria, with precisely the same conditions prevailing in each, whereas surely such widespread perversions against children are not very probable." There followed another much-quoted letter of October 15, 1897, in which, having explained to Fliess that his self-analysis was the most essential thing going for him at the time, Freud dramatically related the series of traumatic childhood experiences of loss and abandonment already referred to, adding further that he had discovered the one idea that he considered to be of universal value, a phenomenon of early childhood, love of one's mother and rivalrous jealousy of one's father. Hence, he concluded, "the gripping power of *Oedipus Rex* . . . the Greek legend seizes upon a compulsion which everyone recognizes because he senses its existence within himself. Everyone in the audience was once a budding Oedipus in fantasy and each recoils in horror from the dream fulfillment here transplanted into reality, with the full quantity of repression which separates his infantile state from his present one."[2]

This thought can be as wrong as one likes, but it is not trivial, having affected a number of different disciplines and having proved instrumental in changing the outlook of the twentieth century. But how did Freud manage to switch so fast out of one systematic way of thinking to which he had been committed and about which he had made significant public statements, and into a different one that turned out to have greater force and magnitude, with a high degree of confidence in his judgment and, considering the pressures he was under, a tolerable degree of strain? Freud had obviously been mulling things over for some time.

But it is one thing to mull over the significance of different puzzling contents; it is quite another to define, abstract, and elaborate a pattern from among different contents and then set about to explain both content and process in masterful prose over a relatively short period of time.

Thus even if we take seriously Freud's fluctuating and uncertain sense of the value of his work over a period of time,[3] or his expressed uncertainty about "matters concerning fathers" in his letter to Fliess of April 28, 1897,[4] or again, Ernst Kris's and Didier Anzieu's observations that Freud had already begun to herald the subsequent "breakthrough" by referring to impulses rather than memories (letter of May 2, 1897) and wishes rather than acts (letter of May 31, 1897), that is still only five months from one major statement of Freud's to another.[5] Even if we go back to the letter of February 11, 1897, in which he explained to Fliess that the frequency of the sexual abuse of children in hysteria, including his father's abuse of his brother and sisters, was making him wonder, that is still not a long time considering the complexity and the impact of what followed.

A lot of speculative effort has gone into Freud's decision to abandon the seduction theory[6] in favor of endopsychic fantasy and drive theory, mostly involving Freud's evasions of some harsh truth about himself, his father, his mother, or his early family life with them and his step brothers.[7] But I do not find these arguments persuasive because they do not integrate any positive motive for the extraordinary work that Freud accomplished. The process cannot be understood only in the defensive terms that so many authors have suggested.[8] For an initiative as powerful as Freud's version of psychoanalysis, the defensive response to a traumatic or threatening experience cannot by itself serve as an explanation. There must have been a significant sense of cognitive mastery that derived from his ability to move concepts and information around in novel ways, and from his capacity for invention and reinvention, which fitted well with cultural expectations. Assuming that Erikson also had Freud in mind when he referred to religiously and artistically creative people who often seem to be suffering from "a barely compensated psychosis," Freud's capacity for coping at this level with the contingencies of life cannot be taken for granted.[9]

What Freud did, after all, required pulling together a great deal of information and a variety of ideas and concepts that were then crystallized into a highly elaborate, complex, and unexpected developmental, clinical, and cultural theory. Thanks to the research of a number of scholars, we now know more precisely what this entailed.[10] Moreover, it is important to recall that Freud had written to Fliess on October 11, 1899, that "[a] theory of sexuality may be the immediate successor to the dream book," indicating that he had to a significant extent established in his own mind the foundations of what he conceived of as psychoanalysis proper in just under two years.[11] Emphasizing the defensive aspects of his effort against the cognitive mastery he displayed over such a short period of time misses a significant point. Hence the merit of Frank Sulloway's judgment that Freud's self-analysis could not have played as decisive a role as routinely claimed, and his observation that "[t]he decision to abandon the seduction theory was the culmination of a long conceptual transformation, influenced much more by Fliess and by the inherent flaws of the seduction theory itself than by self-analysis."[12] Freud had a great many ideas in mind that he was able to synthesize quickly, facilitating the choices he finally made.

Insisting on the cognitive and adaptive dimensions of the enterprise adds balance to any judgment of its merits, particularly in the sense that changes occurring in the process of analysis—of self or other—"require a far more complex cognitive model" than the one Freud had provided or that is available even now in psychoanalysis.[13] Freud assumed that his thinking had unconscious sources, but what that means is not as self-evident as Freud thought it was, so that the absence of such a model must raise questions about Freud's version of his life and work.

Still, the accomplishment was remarkable. In the estimation of Masson, who can hardly be described as a friendly or neutral critic, "The new world that opened up to Freud with this 'discovery' was a remarkable one and permitted him to make a large number of genuine discoveries that have retained their value over the years: the sexual and emotional passions of childhood, the reality of the unconscious, the nature of transference and resistance, repression, unconscious fantasies, the power of unconscious emotions, a need to repeat early sorrows, and so on."[14] Sulloway, a stern and more capable critic than Masson, also wrote that Freud's work from *The Interpretation of Dreams* (1900) to *Three Essays on the Theory of Sexuality* (1905) "constitute a magnificent achievement, which certainly places Freud among the most creative scientific minds of all time."[15] I suppose even a genius needs luck, but having made his choice, Freud was able to work it out so fast, and with such results, that it must have taken a lot more than luck (or fear) for him to be able to do it.

The progress of this extraordinary development can be followed in the correspondence with Fliess. In the letter of May 2, 1897, he reported to his friend that since their recent meeting together he had been "in a continual euphoria . . . working like a young man," consolidating his acquisitions, becoming more certain of his insight into the structure of hysteria. Freud, convinced as he often was that he was on the verge of a significant breakthrough, then continued in his inimitable way to explain systematically the differences among hysteria, obsessional neurosis, and paranoia. He thought that his conclusions represented a great advance in insight.[16] On May 25th he explained the architecture of hysteria to Fliess, as well as the formation of fantasies and the relationship of fantasy to memory; and on May 31, he announced that he would shortly uncover the source of morality, adding that "the whole matter is still growing in my expectation and gives me the greatest pleasure."[17] Later, in a letter of August 14, 1897—following a number of letters in which he reported "fathomless and bottomless laziness, intellectual stagnation,"[18] and having only very recently and with great confidence laid out the prospects for the solution of the most difficult problems—he reported being tormented by grave doubts about his theory of the neuroses. He also reported that the chief patient currently preoccupying him was himself as he pursued his self-analysis, which, he said, was more difficult than any other, although he did note that he was making progress with the psychology, which was too difficult to describe.[19] Then, on September 21, he announced to Fliess that he was abandoning the seduction hypothesis, and on October 15 he explained that the seductions he claimed his patients had reported had never occurred, they were memories of wish-fulfilling endopsychic fantasies. He then went on to offer his initial explanation of the universality of oedipal jealousy and rivalry.[20]

Freud had great expectations for his earlier project and had even spoken of it in terms of "absolute certainty," comparing its importance, in a famous phrase of his, to the discovery of the source of the Nile.[21] But he managed quickly to modify his views without ever modifying his wishes, preserving his grand ambition and his scientific aim, an idealized enterprise that was highly valued in the culture, shaped by cognitive processes but also by personal wishes and conflicts, in ways that we still do not understand. Freud was not able at the time to confess his error (which he did not admit publicly until 1905),[22] or face his critics: in the letter to Fliess announcing his abandonment of the seduction theory he explained that he was not about to broadcast his error to the world.[23] He referred ironically to his loss, but he did not stop to mourn it, and he did not much look back.[24]

The promise of a new conception would prove in his own mind and, he hoped, in Fliess's, sufficient to elevate him to the status he was seeking as a world-class discoverer, a compensating fantasy of recovery and conciliation with scientific ideals and revered and respected teachers of science like Brücke and Charcot. As he explained to Fliess, in spite of the apparent setback he was not depressed, confused, or exhausted. It was strange, too, he wrote, "that no feeling of shame appeared . . . but in your eyes and my own, I have more the feeling of a victory than a defeat."[25] The positive impetus for the way he felt was his sense of intellectual capacity and possibility—the dream book, in which he had so much invested, was still secure. As he wrote there, waking or conscious thought follows the same pattern as the process of secondary revision in organizing the content of dreams: "It is in the nature of our waking thought to establish order in material of that kind, to set up relations in it and to make it conform to our expectation of an intelligible whole." This is what he shortly proved able to do to his own satisfaction; he found the pattern he was looking for, and he was able to replace what he considered to be a failed theoretical perspective with a better one.[26]

But there was also a negative impetus: Freud understood that people who manage to establish a sense of order in this way often make mistakes, even strange ones, maintaining order at the expense of truth. It is customary to refer to the life crisis that Freud experienced in the 1890s, centered particularly on the death of his father and his wavering faith in his project that made him doubt his future prospects, but such crises ordinarily lead to a diminished rather than an enhanced capacity for focused thinking. Freud was able to cope with such a dilemma, struggle against pessimism and disillusionment, against the desire to abandon the work, and against the feeling that everything might in the end come to nothing, by finding the pattern he was looking for and by suppressing the costs. Despite the assurances of Max Schur and others that Freud at this point, had "achieved an inner independence," having "solved one of the great riddles of nature," it is important to emphasize not only what Freud's effort reveals about the capacity for change in everyday life, but also the costs, the things that got lost in the transition, like the affect theory.

Freud was obviously aware of this cognitive side of the matter and he referred to it repeatedly: "I cannot convey to you any idea of the intellectual beauty of this work"; "Since I have been studying the unconscious, I have become so interesting to myself." He observed the workings of his own mind: "I am gripped and pulled through ancient times in quick association of thoughts; my moods change like the landscapes seen by a traveler from a train." There are days when he drags himself around "because I have understood nothing of the dream, of the fantasy, of the mood of the day; and then again days when a flash of lightning illuminates the interrelations and lets me understand the past as preparation for the present." And one thought in particular that he repeated, often in different ways: he wrote to Fliess on May 31, 1897, "[h]erewith a few scraps washed ashore by the last thrust. I am noting them down for you alone and hope you will keep them for me. I add nothing by way of apology or explanation: I know these are only premonitions, but something has come of everything of that sort; I have had to take back only bits of wisdom I wanted to add to the Pcs. [preconscious system].

Another presentiment tells me, as though I already knew—but I know nothing at all—that I shall very soon uncover the source of morality. Thus, the whole matter is still growing in my expectation and gives me the greatest pleasure." And again: "Every now and then ideas dart through my head which promise to realize everything, apparently connecting the normal and the pathological, the sexual and the psychological problem, and then they are gone again and I make no effort to hold onto them because I indeed know that neither their disappearance nor their appearance in consciousness is the real expression of their fate."[27] Or: "This morning I had a pleasant feeling, as if I had succeeded in something important. But I don't know what it might be . . . . I am telling you all that has happened because feelings of this sort after a time usually prove to have been right."[28] Freud claimed that there was nothing deliberate about the process and that he had found his way out by "renouncing all conscious mental activity so as to grope blindly among my riddles." He said that he did not actually know what he was doing nor could he give an account of it.[29] There are many more such statements.[30]

That is, Freud made a special effort to let his thoughts wander in the spirit of the proverb, "If you don't know where you're going any road will get you there." Freud on his own testimony often did not know where he was going, although he was confident that everything was connected and bound to feed back into the work. As he had written earlier, "It may be asserted that every single reminiscence which emerges during an analysis of this kind has significance. An intrusion of *irrelevant* mnemic images . . . in fact never occurs."[31]

At the same time, however, he learned that the kind of intensely focused narrowing of attention that the work required may lead to insight in some instances, but it may also lead to the failure of insight in others. In *The Interpretation of Dreams* he reported on an error he had made in recording a dream he had related to Fliess on March 15, 1897: "It is astonishing to observe the way in which my memory—*my waking memory*—was narrowed at this point, for the purpose of the analysis"; and this was not the only such error.[32] He noted to Fliess in addition that while he felt that he could get everything he needed from his own head, the most disagreeable part of his self-analysis was "the moods, which often completely hide reality."[33] Much later he wrote to Lou Andreas-Salomé, "I know that in writing I have to blind myself artificially in order to focus all the light on one dark spot, renouncing cohesion, harmony, rhetoric and everything which you call symbolic, frightened as I am by the experience that any such claim or expectation involves the danger of distorting the matter under investigation, even though it may embellish it. . . . I cannot always follow you, for my eyes, adapted as they are to the dark, probably can't stand strong light or an extensive range of vision."[34] Hence, he also wrote to Felix Deutsch that he could adapt himself to any kind of reality, and even endure uncertainty in the face of reality—"but being left alone with my subjective insecurity, without the fulcrum or pillar of the *Ananke*, the inexorable, unavoidable necessity, I had to fall prey to the miserable cowardice of a human being and had to become an unworthy spectacle for others."[35] Freud also explained that in any event he found it difficult to follow the thoughts of others, and he could only make connections by following his own complicated path.[36]

Given particularly his own testimony that he lost control in a relatively unconflicted instance of dream analysis, and he also sometimes lost sight of different possibilities because he needed to narrow his focus in order to sharpen it, it is necessary to ask what else might he have lost control over that he was not able to observe? Freud had written to Fliess about the perils of self-analysis, about "first fright and discord. Many a sad secret of life is here followed back to its first roots; many a pride and privilege are made aware of their humble origins." And shortly after, "I can analyze myself only with the help of knowledge obtained objectively (like an outsider). True self-analysis is impossible; otherwise there would be no [neurotic] illness."[37] Analytic treatment, as he once put it, does not recognize any right of asylum, but every patient, himself therefore included, is bound to reserve "some region or other so as to prevent treatment from having access to it."[38]

Freud had a strong sense that fantasy thinking is one kind of thinking that, along with other kinds, undergirds the cognitive capacity of people; such thinking involves wishfulness in ways that can lead to distortions of one sort or another but also to the solution of complex problems. He claimed that "the motive force of fantasies is unsatisfied wishes, and every single fantasy is the fulfillment of a wish, a correction of unsatisfying reality." He later recognized this statement was insufficient to an appreciation of the extent of unconscious mental activity, but it can nevertheless refer to all sorts of high-level theoretical and scientific problems, as well as to all sorts of impulsive striving or everyday familial and personal problems.[39]

Freud had convinced himself that he basically understood how mind works. He did not as a result devote much time to examining his conviction that mental life is ordered, nor to the question of how the compelling need to see things as patterned led him to find a pattern. He was not curious about the randomness, or the apparent lack of connectedness at the surface of his own thinking, which he assumed was related to unconscious processes that would somehow guarantee an outcome. He wrote to Ferenczi at a later point about how "two days earlier suddenly an eruption of ideas had appeared . . . after a long pause and of such significant content that it was at first as though I had been blinded." Freud explained that the significance of the thoughts, which had to do with nothing less than the metapsychology of consciousness, eluded him. When he returned to the problem two days later, "the rude awakening came. The thing resisted any depiction, and presented such frightful gaps and difficulties that I broke off."[40] But he was not interested enough in the process that underlay the experience he had described to address the implicit puzzle in a systematic way: why the initial sense of conviction and why upon reflection the loss of it? He worked tirelessly to promote the results of his work because he trusted the process, but he never really had a good idea of what it entailed.

Freud only briefly touched in different ways on the subject of cognitive processes; he ascribed Leonardo's mastery, for example, to a special disposition, "the rarest and most perfect," in which "the libido evades the fate of repression by being sublimated from the very beginning into curiosity and by becoming attached to the powerful instinct for research as a reinforcement."[41] Freud was able to develop this kind of thought subsequently in structural terms by providing ego with "neutralized energy," a position further amplified by the ego psychologists who were more emphatic about the human capacity to bring the world under control.[42] But Freud had other interests and he was not prepared to engage the implications of where his ego psychology was headed, that is, in the direction of mastery and adaptation.[43] Indeed, Robert Waelder reported that in response to a discussion of the implications of the ego psychology, Freud said that he felt "like the skipper of a barge who had always hugged the coast, who now learned that others, more adventurous, had set out for the open sea. He wished them well, but he could no longer participate in their endeavor."[44]

Freud's thoughts on the mind's workings are mostly related to his belief that the unconscious harbors some of the qualities of genius— knows all, sees all, and will tell all if approached in the right frame of mind. Although authors like Jones and Eissler have been more than a little smarmy about his self-analysis,[45] it really is interesting that he was not afraid to pursue his thoughts as most people are, particularly random sexual or hostile thoughts, as if such thoughts might actually define their character. Needless to say, the fear inhibits their ability to think and provides a cultural role for artists, clergy, and professional therapists who do this kind of thinking for them.

But he was moving too fast and was compelled to suppress too much to appreciate sufficiently the significance of the detours, the manner in which fantasy thinking acquires a particular content but is also constrained or is then related to realistic thinking in terms of what is ultimately conceivable for the individual and his or her society. As I have noted, this would have required a far more complex cognitive theory than he could have imagined.[46] The persistent wishfulness revealed by Freud's own correspondence provides a case in point, particularly a letter to Fliess in which he asked whether one day there might be a marble tablet erected in his honor at the Bellevue villa where "on July 24, 1895, the secret of the dream revealed itself to Dr. Sigm. Freud."[47] It is easy to demonstrate that Freud spoke with a sense of conviction even in instances when he turned out in his own mind to have been dead wrong. Fueled by his extraordinary ambition, he often claimed to have managed some great achievement only to turn around and admit that things had gone awry.[48] There was the wish to succeed that undergirded both the seduction theory and the subsequent wish-fulfilling fantasy theory. There were, as well, fantasies of grandiose expectations, of discovery, of being the one to reveal the secrets of nature to a breathless world, of fame and wealth based on the certainty that existed in his mind that he could specify all the connections between mind and society both in terms of process (how one thing gets connected to another thing to produce an effect), and content (where all the ideas that guide and orient people in their lives come from).

But Freud was no more interested at that point in pursuing the cognitive implications of fantasy thinking, or a cognitive or learning theory, than he was in pursuing an affect theory or the only apparently random and accidental instances of loss and deprivation he had also reported.[49] He was also not interested in or able to observe his own role as the provider of a legitimating orientation in the culture that both heralded and called for changes in sexual, familial, and other cultural practices. There were certain connections he was not interested in making and other connections he was not able to make, a situation that, when we consider the fate of affect theory in psychoanalysis, underscores the glibness of Schur's (and Eissler's) assessments of the degree of independence of mind that Freud had achieved.[50]

It pays to examine here a statement of Lou Andreas-Salomé's to Freud on the subject of such connections. His trusted friend once wrote to him in a dutiful, deferential, respectful, but also optimistic manner, quite opposed to Freud's familiar perspective, that "[w]hat particularly fascinated *me* in your present view of things [a reference to Freud's work on *Moses and Monotheism*] is a specific characteristic of the 'return of the repressed,' namely the way in which noble and precious elements return despite long intermixture with every conceivable kind of material. . . . Hitherto we have usually understood the term 'return of the repressed' in the context of neurotic processes: all kinds of material which had been wrongly repressed afflicted the neurotic mysteriously with phantoms out of the past. . . . But in this case we are presented with examples of the survival of the most triumphant vital elements of the past as the truest possession in the present, despite all the destructive elements and counter-forces they have endured."[51] Freud, not surprisingly in her case, let her get away with this statement, although he could not have approved of it.

Still, Andreas-Salomé's statement is interesting for the question it raised: what precisely was she referring to? She was clearly not referring to preconscious mental activity, which is under the control of secondary processes. She was referring to primary process activity, the "dynamic unconscious"—in structural terms, the id—as a source of structured, imaginative thinking. In other words, her conception of unconscious mental activity as a source of creative thinking, though hardly adequate to such a complex issue, is still an interesting one, considering Freud's demonstrated capacity for using his self-analysis in the systematic elaboration of theoretical perspectives, and his references to the id as a seething cauldron, absent structure.

Freud wrote in *The Ego and the Id* that the superego arises from an identification with the father taken as a model, and that "[a]s a child grows up, the role of the father is carried on by teachers and others in authority." Their injunctions and prohibitions remain powerful and continue, in the form of conscience, to exercise the moral censorship. "Social feelings rest on identifications with other people, on the basis of having the same ego ideal."[52] He also wrote later, in *Inhibitions, Symptoms, and Anxiety*, that "[j]ust as the father has become depersonalized in the shape of the superego, so has the fear of castration at his hands become transformed into an undefined social or moral anxiety." The ego escapes this anxiety by living up to the internalized injunctions and if it cannot do so, "it is at once overtaken by an extremely distressing feeling of discomfort which may be regarded as an equivalent of anxiety and which the patients themselves liken to anxiety."[53]

But how exactly do these notions of superego as internalized parental authority, or as the impersonal, abstract representative of social authorities and ideals, square with Freud's self-image as a radical thinker whose fate it was "to disturb the sleep of mankind," whose work was bound to revolutionize the world, who saw himself as "bringing the plague," fundamentally altering cultural understandings and behavior that might be difficult for people to manage, on the basis of his discoveries of unconscious, hitherto repressed ideas? Freud was certain that Jews were bound to be offended by his conception of Moses as an Egyptian but he went ahead with his project anyway. He thought of his work as distressing to people but necessary for them to understand, and he thought and wrote of himself constantly as defiant and oppositional, ready to stand by himself against the world, as a marginal individual who, by virtue of his Jewish past, was released from conformist cultural commitments and enabled thereby to take an independent stance against the world, developing and promoting the most radical kinds of cultural critique.[54] At the same time, how does Andreas-Salomé's statement square with Freud's assumptions about moral orientations and transgression?

Freud had begun to elaborate especially the moral elements of a social psychology in his paper "On Narcissism," moving from the individual's ego ideal to the group's. He noted that individuals unwilling to forego the narcissistic perfection of childhood, but disturbed by the admonitions of others and by the awakening of their own critical judgment, can seek to recover that perfection in the new form of an ego ideal. "The ego ideal opens up an important avenue for the understanding of group psychology. In addition to its individual side, this ideal has a social side; it is also the common ideal of a family, a class or a nation."[55] But his depiction of this ideal or his elaboration of the concept of internalized morality, which formed the basis subsequently of the unsustainable sociologies of Talcott Parsons and Erik Erikson, does not describe his own behavior (nor Erikson's, for that matter). Unlike other great figures who acted in the past as ideal representatives of prevailing standards, Freud had every intention of supplanting prevailing standards that he thought were deficient, hypocritical, and even, because of people's fears and the enduring ignorance of their own motives, dangerous. Freud's depiction of internalized morality is therefore problematic also with regard to anyone else who might have shared important elements of his kind of cultural experience, for example, the children of immigrant families who had to fit themselves into and gain a measure of control over a strange, hostile, unaccommodating world.

In fact, Freud was a provocative and challenging figure who would have felt that he had betrayed his calling had he conceded anything to social feelings resting on identifications with other people, except perhaps other equally radical or dedicated scientific workers. He specifically said that although people wanted him to make such concessions he could not oblige them, whatever the costs. He would rather wait things out, for he was confident that his work would be vindicated in the end. Hence his well-known comment, "He who knows how to wait need make no concessions." The last thing in the world people wanted to contend with, on Freud's own understanding of the matter, was his conception of their inner life. Freud was convinced that society would not grant authority to psychoanalysis because it was too revealing of internal conflict and too critical of different social practices that cause such conflict. "Just as we make an individual our enemy by uncovering what is

repressed in him, so society cannot respond with sympathy to a relent-
less exposure of its injurious effects and deficiencies. Because we destroy
illusions, we are accused of endangering ideals."[56]

This is the point of underscoring Andreas-Salomé's observation:
Freud could not account for his own remarkable ability to recover from
his initial failure—and the other perceived failures and shortcomings of
his life—in the terms he preferred. The image he projected in the passages I have referred to was adequate to a conception of stability, not to
a conception of the kinds of change he was capable of implementing or
intending to promote. Moreover, Freud considered that people cope
passively with experience, and if they have a capacity for active mastery
it is a matter of unconsciously reproducing in attentuated versions experiences they had earlier suffered through passively. Freud had also begun
to consider, in his late reassessment of anxiety, the possibility that people do respond actively to immediate situations, but again unconsciously, on the basis of an internalized "signal" in terms of flight or
fight. The kind of elaboration that Andreas-Salomé offered, however, is
quite different and much more consistent with larger historical experiences, including Freud's own. This capacity she referred to, which suggests that life is more discontinuous and situational than Freud wanted
to acknowledge, is indispensable to all people and certainly to all
marginal people for whom the kind of internalizations Freud described
in The Ego and the Id could prove costly, fixing their behavior in ways
that could only hamper development and change.

Freud emphasized sexuality, while other psychoanalysts, Anzieu
and Erikson among them, emphasized loss and adaptation (or restitution). He emphasized fixity of character, whereas they emphasized
change and the capacity for reconstruction. To protect the integrity of
the theory of sexuality he was developing, Freud asserted that this
capacity for change is rare. But while there are few people indeed who
can work at Freud's level, the cognitive/affective capacity for change,
reconstruction, or reinvention is not rare. Anzieu wrote of Freud, in
terms that are more widely applicable than the particular occasion, that
his first misfortune, "premature exile at the age of about three and a
half . . . turned out in fact to be yet another boon: a person creates not
by continuing to mourn for what he has lost, and what he knows to be
irretrievable, but by replacing it with a work of the kind that enables
him, in the process of constructing it, to reconstruct himself."[57]

Freud was able to pursue the elaboration of certain thoughts, compensated by pleasurable fantasies of having realized the fondest wishes
of his dazzled and admiring parents, siblings, and friends, remaining
connected to revered teachers, and securing the future for himself and
his family. But he did so at the cost of forfeiting his ability to acknowl-

edge the importance of other thoughts, or more accurately, his ability to continue to make certain connections having to do most importantly with traumatic experiences of separation and loss, the role of the social world and of the authoritative individuals in it, affective responses to traumatic experience, the cognitive dimensions of recovery, and, in interesting ways, countertransference.[58] Having worked through different potentially damaging and depressing experiences in 1896–1897 (the death of his father, the feelings he experienced in the process of recalling the death of his brother, Julius, his awareness of and his need to accommodate the shortcomings of his friend Fliess, the need to abandon the seduction theory to which he had been emotionally committed, certain lingering fears and phobias, mainly that he would not succeed, but including also his travel phobia), Freud was able to remain excited, exhilarated, and elated about the prospects of a much more significant breakthrough.[59] He then felt better prepared to bring the world into line with his thinking about the vicissitudes of sexuality, combining a sense of high hope for scientific progress with a withering appraisal of the human condition. Freud was able to rationalize and justify his position by intensely focusing on the problem of endopsychic fantasy that he had only begun to explore and that he would spend the rest of his life exploring.

But again, there were the costs: certain things were suppressed or fell out of awareness,[60] primarily, in the systematic theoretical sense that was his paramount interest, the larger human significance of his experiences of separation and loss, and the larger significance as well of a theory of affects and the relationship of affect to cognition. As Freud noted in *The Interpretation of Dreams*, whatever interrupts the progress of analytic work constitutes resistance, and Freud's resistance proved costly to psychoanalysis.[61] Freud prided himself on his emotional restraint and personal discipline, but that was not an entirely straightforward, uncomplicated, or self-evident result of his self-analysis. As the subsequent history of psychoanalysis and the testimony of dozens of psychoanalysts reveal, the conflicts provoked by those experiences impinged upon and hampered the development of psychoanalytic theory and practice, and of other disciplines as well.

Critic and author Margo Jefferson recently described Oscar Wilde as "still the supreme genius of self-invention." At its best, she went on to note, self-invention "is the redesigning of cultural conventions and expectations in order to perceive oneself and the world in new ways and to new ends. At its worst, it is an erasing or suppressing of all those things in order to enhance one's status in the world."[62] If these are indeed the criteria of self-invention, Freud is a much better candidate than Wilde for being its supreme genius. Indeed, the paramount significance of the correspondence with Fliess, his self-analysis, and the *Interpretation of Dreams* is that in the course of all this effort and turmoil Freud reinvented himself as he also invented a conception of life, a product of cognitive and affective processes that he was not able to engage but that, in a cultural sense, have proved more important than his conception of human sexuality as defined by the oedipal project.

Consider the many statements Freud made, especially in *The Interpretation of Dreams*, on the subject of the reinvention of self, in the sense that what he reported, by any contemporary standard, were reconstructions of memories and not veridical recollections. Harking back to the dream of the botanical monograph, Freud wrote that "[t]he thoughts corresponding to it consisted of a passionately agitated plea on behalf of my liberty to act as I chose to act and govern my life as seemed right to me and me alone."[63] "Once again, the dream, like the first one we analyzed—the dream of Irma's injection—turns out to have been in the nature of a self-justification, a plea on behalf of my own rights." This dream, Freud continued, had still other significance. "What it meant was: 'After all, I'm the man who wrote the valuable and memorable paper (on cocaine),' just as in the earlier dream I had said on my behalf: 'I'm a conscientious and hard-working student.' In both cases what I was insisting was: 'I may allow myself to do this.'"[64]

Freud insisted on emphasizing his independence from authority, the importance of his work, his willingness to engage the problems it presented, and his novel contributions. The theme of Freud's story was focused on his determination to get out of his parents' world and terminate as many of the dependent relationships imposed by it as he could. "The dream thought, however, which was operating behind all this ran as follows: 'It is absurd to be proud of one's ancestry; it is better to be an ancestor oneself.'"[65] "The scene was a concise but entirely adequate representation of a conditional sentence in the dream thoughts, which ran in full: 'If only I had been the second generation, the son of a professor or Hofrat, I should certainly have *got on faster*.' In the dream I made my father into a Hofrat and Professor."[66] Who better than Freud to have conceived the idea of the family romance, or to have made transparent the fantasy that the parents one actually knows are not one's real parents, who were princely or in any case much grander and more elevated. Freud, in a well-known statement, referred to himself as a conquistador. How exactly does Jacob Freud fit into the parental background of a conquistador, even in fantasy, considering especially that if Freud had worked over and through any relationship at all, stripping away its mystery and surmounting its conflicts, it was this one. As he wrote in *The Interpretation of Dreams*, "From here my thoughts went on to the subject of the names of my own children. I had insisted on their names being chosen, not according to the fashion of the moment, but in memory of people I have been fond of. Their names [of his revered teachers, for example, Ernst Brücke and Jean-Martin Charcot, and of Oliver Cromwell] made the children into *revenants*. And after all, I reflected, was not having children our only path to immortality?" On the one hand, naming children in the tradition of his parents, that is, after the revered dead as a way of maintaining the continuity of generations, was not just "the fashion of the moment." And on the other hand, anyone who could write as he did to his friend Fliess, "I have the distinct feeling that I have touched upon one of the great secrets of nature," has already found another, perhaps even more desirable path to immortality than his children.[67]

Of course, Freud's self-conception as a world-renowned scientist was elaborated in a series of autobiographical statements on his progress through life, in terms of his own interpretations of the sources of his own behavior. However, these autobiographical versions have been challenged, as has his interpretation of the dynamic sources of his work. There is more than one psychoanalytic interpretation of Freud's work and life, and still others beyond psychoanalysis. All this is by way of noting that the fashioning of an identity on the basis of claimed self-knowledge leading to a career and a life that no one among the people he grew up with could have prospectively imagined entails a process of reinvention of self. Freud was able to use some of his experiences to accomplish this but not all, and he made decisions about what he would tell of his story and what he would not. We know that he was able to resolve various conflicts in the course of writing *The Interpretation of Dreams* in a way that enabled him to devote his life to his work. But we also know that some things eluded him; there were some connections he was unable to make.

Freud had provided a version of psychoanalysis in which childhood sexual or sensual experiences are determinative. There is a characteristic look to this version, already well explained in *The Interpretation of Dreams*: "In my experience . . . the chief part in the mental lives of all children who later become psychoneurotics is played by their parents. Being in love with the one parent and hating the other are among the essential constituents of the stock of psychical impulses which is formed at that time and which is of such importance in determining the symptoms of later neurosis." Freud went on to note that neurotics do not differ sharply in this respect from other people who remain normal; and also to relate the legend of King Oedipus, "a legend whose profound and universal power to move can only be understood if the hypothesis I have put forward in regard to the psychology of children has an equally universal validity." As the poet unravels the past and brings to light the guilt of Oedipus, "he is at the same time compelling us to recognize our own inner minds, in which those same impulses, though suppressed, are still to be found."[68] Freud retained this perspective and the theoretical and therapeutic strategy it suggested, with modifications, to the end.

This particular view of Freud's is the familiar one but as always in psychoanalysis it is not the only one, and for some psychoanalysts, not even the most important one. Peter Blos pointed out some time ago as a matter "generally accepted" among psychoanalysts that "prelatency disturbances are unreliable predictive indicators of the nature and severity of an adult illness." Blos referred in his paper as well to Anna Freud's initially "disappointing discovery" that "there is no certainty that a particular type of infantile neurosis will prove to be the forerunner of the same type of adult neurosis. On the contrary, there is much clinical evidence which points in the opposite direction." Blos also emphasized the unpredictability of accidental circumstances and the capacity of people to alter their behavior in the face of such circumstances, "despite the existence of a neurotic potential, whenever the growing individual is able to draw on constitutional resources, object relations, and environmental conditions so as to work out a serviceable adaptation to life."[69] Still others have argued that "the psychological complexities perceived in the adult cannot be explained adequately by a straightforward extrapolation from childhood development."[70] This perspective, moreover, is consistent with the results reported in the sociological and anthropological literature.[71] By contrast, although the traditional perspective on the determinative influence of childhood experience is obviously crucial to the psychoanalytic project, psychoanalysts themselves have not yet developed the kind of longitudinal data that could confirm or refute it.[72]

In other words, there are or could be relationships between social structure and personality not mediated by the family or by mental representations of childhood figures.[73] John Bowlby had made a similar claim, noting that "[i]t is therefore absurd to conceive of a patient in terms of any one condition. He must be thought of as *an individual of certain potentialities, a unity of which the particular traits and symptoms shown at any one moment are but fleeting expressions.*"[74] Moreover, it is also important to emphasize, as Andreas-Salomé did, that this is as true of focused, adaptive behavior as it is of neurotic behavior, a conclusion that serves as a suitable context for recalling Erikson's warning against "a habit of thinking which reduces every human situation to an analogy with an earlier one, and most of all to that earliest, simplest, and most infantile precursor which is assumed to be its 'origin?'"[75]

Although many psychoanalysts understand that this is true of Freud's life and work, they do not always know quite how it fits in, or they are reluctant to follow observers like Blos who nevertheless insist that people are capable of significant change as they respond adaptively to changed circumstances.[76] At the same time, however, the integration in psychoanalysis of theories of narcissism and object relations has at least made it easier to acknowledge the possibility of individual change (and discontinuity), more rarely for ordinary people (though Erikson was prepared to make this argument), more typically for truly exceptional people. As Eva Rosenfeld wrote, "A genius finds his family from among heroes,"[77] and discussions of Freud's creative capacities ordinarily occur in the context of these exceptional others.

Thus, in his depiction of Freud's increasing awareness of the need to break with his friend Fliess, having worked out in his mind the inhibiting or destructive uses to which such a friendship might be put, Erikson wrote that "Freud had now to become his own father, and, as it were, the father of a people of his own."[78] To readers familiar especially with the literature of psychoanalysis, a number of people are alluded to in this passage other than Freud and Fliess. Erikson himself made the connection to Moses, for example: "Calling himself a 'shabby old Jew' ('*Israelit*' is the German word, with a stronger connotation of geographic displacement), he speaks with the words of a latter-day Moses: 'It will be a fitting punishment for me that none of the unexplored regions of the mind in which I have been the first mortal to set foot will ever bear my name or submit to my laws.'"[79] It is important to recall, however, that Moses did not rebel against his father, as Freud related the story; rather he had lost his fatherland because others had rebelled against the restrictions of his Pharaoh's monotheistic religion. Moses then also had to become his own father as well as the father of a people he made into an instrument of his own calling.[80] In *Moses and Monotheism*, Freud defined a hero as "someone who has had the courage to rebel against his father and has in the end victoriously overcome him."[81] But, as Erikson indicates, that does not apply to Freud, nor, given Freud's explanation of the origins of Moses as a leader, does it apply to Moses. There is of course an oedipal rebellion in the story, and Freud, as the founder of psychoanalysis, could easily identify with the slain Moses, done in, as he imagined it in the story, by his followers, the Hebrews. But this is not the paramount source of the identification of Freud with Moses that often appears in the literature. This identification is based rather on the sense that emerges from different statements Freud had made about being able to stand alone, or to take an oppositional stance against the "compact majority."[82] In other words, such individuals do not experience development in the same way as either normal or neurotic individuals do, and the idea of describing them in terms of the conventional oedipal notion of rivalry with a feared and envied father seems more than inappropriate.

Then, too, Freud had written many years earlier of Leonardo da Vinci, "All his instincts, those of tenderness, gratitude, lustfulness, defiance and independence, find satisfaction in the single wish *to be his own father*." Leonardo, his father absent, was never involved at the crucial point in his development in a triangular situation. "In most other human beings—no less today than in primeval times—the need for support from an authority of some sort is so compelling that their world begins to totter if that authority is threatened." But Leonardo was able to dispense with that support because he had learned early in life to do without his father. "When anyone has, like Leonardo, escaped being intimidated by his father during his early childhood, and has in his researches cast away the fetters of authority, it would be in the sharpest contradiction to our expectation if we found that he had remained a believer and had been unable to escape from dogmatic religion."[83] Freud does also refer to Leonardo's oedipal conflicts, but not centrally, reflecting more his desire to reassert the primacy of the Oedipus complex than his sense of what was most important about Leonardo's creative capacities.[84]

Moreover, Freud resembles Leonardo in this respect, even if his father was present and there was an oedipal tale to tell. "It is, in fact, rather probable," Erikson wrote, "that uncommon men of outstanding gifts experience filial conflicts with such inescapable intensity because they sense in themselves already in early childhood some kind of originality that seems to point beyond a mere competition with the personal father's accomplishments." Theirs is also an early conscience development, Erikson continued, "which makes them feel (and appear) old while still young and maybe even older in single-mindedness than their conformist parents, who, in turn, may treat them somehow as their potential redeemers. Thus, they grow up almost with an obligation (beset with guilt) to surpass and originate at all costs."[85]

There are others who figure in Erikson's statement still somewhat hidden in the shadows. Some years before Erikson wrote the passages I quoted, Jeanne Lampl-De Groot, a psychoanalyst who had been trained by Freud, who remained close to the Freud family, eventually taking her place as one of Freud's adopted daughters,[86] wrote: "Most children of parents who demand complete obedience and conformity do not acquire a nonconforming superego. Only exceptionally strong and gifted children can sometimes succeed in building up norms of their own which deviate from those of their parents. An impressive example of this is . . . Michelangelo. . . . It is interesting to note that Michelangelo's nonconformism led to a full unfolding of his forcefully driving talent and to his becoming one of the greatest sculptors of the Renaissance. He nevertheless paid for his disobedience to his father with a strong inner struggle and guilt feelings that forced him to live in poverty in order to meet the financial demands of his family."[87]

Not only is the figure of Michelangelo—who did not on this view subordinate himself to his father's morality—as familiar in the work and thought of Freud as Moses and Leonardo, but it is hardly conceivable that Lampl-de Groot's observation is only about Michelangelo and not in some part about Freud. (In fact, it is commonplace in the literature to underscore Freud's identification with all these exceptional individuals, Moses, Leonardo, and Michelangelo.)[88] Freud was special on this view because his rebellion is not well described as an indispensable and routine feature of the succession of generations, even when the outcome may be deemed "normal," rather than neurotic.[89] Nor is it well described in the later structural terms, in the sense that Freud's career would not have been possible if he had taken his father's ego interests and superego standards as a model.[90] Indeed, if Freud's is a life for our time, in Peter Gay's phrase, it is because his life contradicts his theories about ontogenetic fixity of character and the repetitive quality of life. Freud is modern not only because he changed speech and focused people's attention on the workings of the mind and on sexuality and aggression in ways that no one else had or could, but also because he shared a capacity with the others just mentioned, and with a lot of others besides, of being able to invent or reinvent a novel and challenging version of himself, whatever the costs. I have already indicated that the question with which we began, about Freud's ability to switch quickly out of one way of thinking and into another, thereby reinventing a version of himself and his work, was better addressed by Andreas-Salomé than by Freud, but is still too difficult to answer in any decisive way because we lack adequate knowledge of how cognitive processes work. But what we do know is that Freud's accomplishment had a lot to do with cognitive and adaptive processes in more complicated ways than he could have guessed, and this includes a capacity for change.[91]

Every social change or radical contribution to the reorientation of the way the world thinks and acts entails this kind of independence of the past, of the "internalizations" that Freud otherwise conceived of as the building blocks of character. It entails a cognitive and emotional capacity to bring together different forms of knowledge and to scan the environment for further cues and clues, as a means of constructing alternative ways to proceed. The ability to think in novel combinations that might well transgress inherited standards is the hallmark of exceptional individuals who do not experience their effort as transgression, or if they do, they are either not worried about it, or they are prepared to pay the costs because the costs of not making the effort seem to them higher still. Thus, trying to infer Freud's career from his childhood experiences in the developmental terms he preferred quickly becomes an empty exercise. To state it in the most definite way, Freud's career cannot be inferred from his childhood relationships, insofar as these are known.

It should be noted that Erikson, who also had to construct a novel version of himself, who had in a sense also to become his own father and find a people, an audience, worthy of his unique talents, figures in his statements about those exceptional individuals who become fathers to themselves, that is, invent versions of themselves. The principal difference this makes here is that with respect to oedipal dynamics there would be five immediate exceptions to Freud's "universal" rule rather than four. This points in a dramatic way to a universal rule different from the one Freud was anxious to establish, the rule of the exception, which has now become operative: if one exception can be found, more than one can be found, as demonstrated in this case.

Moreover, the rule of the exception makes it difficult to argue that people are essentially products of endogenous fantasies, psychobiological forces, linguistic structures, or cultural stories, absent a coherent self or core, or that their behavior is determined (rather than affected) by internalized images and standards. For if this were true, how could anyone have given up the first stories that ever got told? How did any subsequent story prevail and why was that one supplanted by still other ones, or why do people take sides for and against any of these stories in unexpected ways? This perspective is always undermined by any of the kinds of cultural or value change that have occurred over time. For even if we can imagine an idiosyncratic individual elaborating a novel and radically transgressing perspective, what mobilization can this individual hope to achieve if all the other individuals he can appeal to are "never anything other than a certain specification of the collective history of his group or class," a "structural variant" of all other "group or class habitus," or if people are manipulated or indoctrinated "down to their very instincts," or are affected by a "depth of the preconditioning" that shapes the "instinctual drives and aspirations of the individuals and obscures the difference between true and false consciousness."[92]

The notions of discontinuity of development and of the cognitively empowered capacity of individuals to escape from the past in terms of the invention or reinvention of self obviously undermine the theoretical intentions of Freud's phylogenetic and ontogenetic schemes—as they undermine all logically similar positions of the sort just noted—pointing away from the kind of universally inclusive conclusions he wanted to draw from his understanding of oedipal conflict.

In fact, considering the famous innovators referred to above, it bears emphasizing that any combination of possibilities—strong father, weak father, present father, absent father—can produce any result, running the gamut of ego interests and superego traits (integrative, disintegrative, harsh, punitive, tolerant, accepting). If any result can emerge from any possible familial configuration, *and* if therapeutic results are as idiosyncratic as Freud and any number of other psychoanalysts have explained, then one must assert the primacy of history and culture with respect to individual development, while viewing individual behavior as contingent, anomalous, situational, and potentially adaptive to changing social circumstances.[93]

Hence the usefulness of Freud's early concept of *Nachträglichkeit*, which ought to be viewed in terms of the capacity of people for active adaptations to or constructions of reality.[94] Freud wanted to explain with the concept of *Nachträglichkeit* that memories of sexual seduction can become traumatic after the event, in relation to subsequent events, that experiences that could not have been assimilated or rendered coherent when they initially occurred can be retranscribed in the context of later experience. "As you know," he wrote to Fliess, "I am working on the assumption that our psychic mechanism has come into being by a process of stratification: the material present in the form of memory traces being subjected from time to time to a *rearrangement* in accordance with fresh circumstances—to a *retranscription*."[95] In this context, Freud added that "[e]verything goes back to the reproduction of scenes. Some can be obtained directly, others always by way of fantasies set up in front of them. The fantasies stem from things that have been *heard* but understood *subsequently*. . . . They are protective structures, sublimations of the facts, embellishments of them." And again, "Fantasies simultaneously serve the tendency toward refining the memories, toward sublimating them. They are manufactured by means of things that are *heard*, and utilized *subsequently*."[96]

These remarks are consistent with the observation that the behavior of people is not as ontogenetically fixed as Freud needed it to be once he abandoned the seduction theory in favor of the drive theory and, regardless of Freud's emphases, they have significant cognitive implications for adaptive behavior.[97] The implication is that Freud's conception of "deferred action" (or the "retranscription of memory"), which he wanted to apply to sexually traumatic situations, as readily accounts not only for the ways in which people manage troubling experiences, but also for the ways in which they manage novel, adapative thinking, and recognize things about the culture that allow the thinking, however challenging and provocative it may be, to be integrated in the larger world and not dismissed out of hand as deviant, criminal, or sick.

Freud lived with and was animated by expectations of great achievement. As he wrote to Fliess, "There is something odd in the disproportion between one's own estimate of one's intellectual work and other people's."[98] But Freud had the sense of being able to see through the secrets of nature, solving particularly complicated riddles, identifying nature's laws in the process, however difficult this might prove to be.[99] This as much as anything accounts for his sense of conviction and imbued him with the desire to bring the world into line with his wishes, reflected in his apparently deliberate and disarming frankness, which lent his work a note of authenticity, as it also changed the nature of discourse in the twentieth century.[100] His sense of conviction proved also to be the spur to his extraordinary reliance on his intuition, which justified in his mind running ahead of established evidence. As Freud noted to and about his friend Fliess, "One cannot do without people who have the courage to think new things before they are in a position to demonstrate them."[101] It was also the spur to his productivity, his capacity for organization and manipulation, and his willingness to engage the struggle.

But as with all contribution, there was the other conflicted, more problematic side: if all morality begins in hypocrisy, as Ferenczi asserted, so too, it has been said, does all sublimation.[102] Always striving for a more realistic sense of life, Freud himself suggested how instructive it would be for people "to get to know the much trampled soil from which our virtues proudly spring."[103] But there were obviously limits to what it was that he could know (or be willing to acknowledge) of the source of his particular virtues.

Just as the concept of loss has a certain priority in the contemporary literature, so too do the themes of cognition, emotion, and memory, directed especially to the understanding of the need and capacity of people to reconstruct versions of themselves and reinvent versions of life. The sense that Freud's creativity was somehow related to painful experiences of loss is a strong one, though that still leaves us with the questions of how the experience is transmuted and turned to gain and what the costs were, keeping in mind the history of affect theory in psychoanalysis and the observations of Edith Jacobson and others on the subject.[104]

Still, whatever the process, whatever the source of the content, and however the impact is accounted for, it is clear that people have a capacity for change, for reconstructing versions of life based on cognitive capacity and adaptive mastery, even if that means inventing a version of life more conformable with self-estimation. They are not so bound by internalizations or by underlying structural factors that they cannot change their behavior and situation. For if they were bound in these terms, how could so many people have found their way to psychoanalysis and reoriented their beliefs and their lives in terms of the criteria Freud had provided? As Peter Fonagy has explained, "Psychoanalysis is more than the creation of a narrative, it is the active construction of a new way of experiencing self with others."[105] Moreover, psychoanalysis is not the only culturally available technique for achieving such an outcome. Of course, how (in the sense of process) people are able to scan the environment and attempt to resolve their conflicts by adopting and acting on the mandates of one or another novel perspective is still an open question. But there is no question that it happens.

Sexuality and aggression are powerful motives, as Freud explained. But they are not the only motives, and in addressing the more limited question of Freud's biography we should keep in mind a variety of other motives that Holt, Sandler, and others have explained are not reasonably reduced to sexuality and aggression, including "dependence, self-esteem, curiosity, and group belongingness."[106] We should also keep in mind this admonition from a contemporary psychoanalyst to her colleagues: "In our search for what is hidden, we may skip over much that is apparent, and which (if attended) can lead us farther, and far less inferentially, to what indeed had been buried, to pathways that had been unconscious."[107]

Indeed, part of the difficulty of understanding the extent to which Freud deployed his remarkable cognitive capacities to reinvent himself and versions of his life, stems from his own single-minded preference for endopsychic explanations, particularly the genetic component of them, from the authoritative force of his conclusions, and generally from the traditional kinds of psychoanalytic propositions that, as many have by now suggested, are inadequate to an explanation of this kind of accomplishment.[108] There was a lot more involved than Freud was able to acknowledge in a systematic sense, including the cultural effects on one's mental outlook and interests of such social issues as ethnicity and poverty that, because people are obliged to live in the world and not just in their bodies, also become part of the bedrock.

It is important to understand, too, that Freud was a theoretical bulldog. (As Winston Churchill explained of the stubborn streak in English character, bulldogs are built so that they can sink their teeth into an opponent and hang on while continuing to breathe.) He made a point of saying that he would not give up the vital elements of his theory "except under irresistible compulsion,"[109] and he tried as hard as he could to maintain intact what he considered to be his highly innovative, radical, and fundamentally world-changing system, often painting himself into contradictory corners in the attempt to do so. He was also not above manipulating data to bolster the system.[110]

However, as I noted earlier, Freud did at various points acknowledge that social and cultural contexts can be a source of conflict and change. And of all the statements Freud made on the subject, one in particular is worth noting here. In a letter to Ferenczi, Freud explained about traumatic wartime experience (noting that it was probably only a dream formation) that "[i]t has to do with a conflict over two ego ideals," the one people are accustomed to and the one forced on them by the war. "The latter rests totally on fresh object relations (superiors, comrades) and should thus be likened to an object cathexis, a so to speak not ego syntonic object choice." This, Freud concluded, leads to "a *new ego*" and causes conflict within the ego, as distinct from a conflict between ego and libido.[111] The statement is interesting because it states clearly, if anomalously, that conflicts emerge from real contacts and relationships, that current conditions can compel unexpected outcomes, and that life is more situational and discontinuous than he otherwise wanted to acknowledge.[112] And this is the way the effects of certain of Freud's experiences, especially his poverty and marginality, should be understood.

Anzieu's suggestion of cognitively disciplined reconstruction of life and thought is vital here, but he is too sanguine in his sense of the ease with which this got accomplished in Freud's life. In Vienna, Anzieu noted, Freud became an educated, cultured, scientifically ambitious individual, having "learned to write a language that existed in two forms of characters . . . a language of reference by which his parents set great store, and a code that arranged, but did not destroy, previously existing structures." This is a generous but contradictory assessment of the situation: there was no way that Freud could have accomplished as much as he did without surmounting or destroying existing structures and, as often happens with Freud, he did in a random way emphasize this possibility, in this case to Marie Bonaparte: "All activities that rearrange or effect changes are to a certain extent destructive and thus redirect a portion of the instinct [for destruction] from its original destructive goal."[113]

Thus Freud "studied classics with great success. He attended one of the oldest universities in the world, where he acquired scientific exactitude and encountered—then repudiated—all the teachers that he needed to admire, imitate and reject. . . . In other words, Vienna was an ideal medium for his conquering identifications."[114] But it was never easy for him to get that far out in front, less in the sense of feeling guilty for any oedipal rivalry than in the sense of feeling guilty because he found it so hard to excuse his parents for not having made things easier for him. Freud constantly mulled over the costs to him of his familial past and there are wishful aspects of Freud's biography focused on the grievous inadequacies of his parents and his desire for a different or better past.

Writing to his friend Eduard Silberstein Freud described the mother of his friend Emil Fluss, a cultured woman—which on everyone's testimony Freud's mother was not—with a wide breadth of knowledge, the kind of woman who banishes conflict and overcomes deficiencies, who encourages, enhances, supports, elevates her children in ways that Freud's mother could not do. "Other mothers—and why hide the fact that ours are among them; we shall not love them any the less for it— only look after the physical needs of their sons. Their spiritual development has been taken out of their hands. . . . Frau Fluss knows no sphere that is beyond her influence."[115]

Then too Freud wrote to Emil Fluss (September 18, 1872), describing an overheard conversation on the train home from his visit: "Now this Jew talked the same way as I had heard thousands of others talk before, even in Freiberg. His face seemed familiar—he was typical. . . . I have had enough of this lot. In the course of the conversation I learned that Madame Jewess and family hailed from Meseritch: the proper compost-heap for this sort of weed."[116] Freud made other equally contemptuous statements on the subject which have been well and widely reported.[117] The extent among assimilated Jews in Germany and Austria of this attitude toward the East European, Yiddish-speaking past as reflected in bitter commentaries, conversions, repudiations of conversions, and suicide, is legendary. Recall son Martin's description of his grandmother: "A typical Polish Jewess, with all the shortcomings that that implies. She was certainly not what we would call a 'lady.'"[118] Breuer also commented in like fashion,[119] as did many other of Freud's contemporaries.[120] Freud famously described his train trip with his mother as a young child on the way from Freiberg to Leipzig, and he saw her, as he described it to Fliess, "nudam." I suppose on this trip Amalia Freud had the occasion to speak to her son, but what language was she speaking to him in? He does not say, although Theodore Reik, who knew Freud for many years, claimed that she spoke to him in Galician Yiddish.[121] Freud's choice of a Latin expression here is usually treated as a way of distancing himself from sexually compelling memories of his mother, but he was distancing himself from more than that.

Freud had on different occasions expressed his desire to be independent, to be able to do things for himself as he wanted to do them. Recall the statement from his "Botanical Monograph" dream: "The thoughts corresponding to it consisted of a passionately agitated plea on behalf of my liberty to act as I chose to act and to govern my life as seemed right to me and me alone." Commenting yet again on the manifest content, the indifferent quality of the dream, Freud wrote that he was reminded "of the peace that has descended upon a battlefield strewn with corpses; no trace is left of the struggle which raged over it."[122] This expression is also usually taken to have oedipal significance, but as a letter he wrote to Martha after their engagement in August 1882 indicates, this was perhaps not the most interesting thing about it. Freud here declared a compelling desire to move to England, which, as he explains it, not only offers a chance for independence but in a cultural sense is about as far removed from the Jewish-Austrian life that formed him as anything could be: "I am aching for independence, so as to follow my own wishes. The thought of England surges up before me. . . . If we possibly can, let us seek a home where human worth is more respected."[123]

This was a wish he had expressed on different occasions earlier, following his visit to his half-brother Emmanuel in England, 1875. To his friend Silberstein he wrote (September 9, 1875): "As for England itself, I . . . can say straight out that I would sooner live there than here. . . . Many peculiarities of the English character and country that other continentals might find intolerable agree very well with my own nature."[124] And then later, in *The Psychopathology of Everyday Life*, he referred back to this experience again. As William McGrath explained it, "Since Emmanuel Freud's branch of the family, in contrast to the Viennese Freud's, enjoyed a substantial degree of material prosperity as well as the absence of any significant anti-Semitic pressure, Freud's wish implicitly criticized his father for his failure to provide these desirable conditions."[125]

This sounds like a version of the "family romance" as Freud later explained it, the believable wish to be other than, better than, different from what one is, to be gone somewhere else, to get "free from the parents of whom he now has a low opinion and of replacing them by others, who, as a rule, are of higher social standing."[126] The wish to join those Protestant Englishmen, which he repeated on several occasions, removes him, even if it is only a wish, from the world in which he grew up. Freud wanted to be out of his situation, to reinvent his life, to be in a better place with different, loftier values, and separate especially from the residual influences of East European Jewish culture.

This is not just about oedipal conflict or symptomatic expression, or about the persistence of authoritative prohibitions, or about wishes and fantasies displaced from the past and acted out in the present. On the contrary, as Freud pointed out, under the influence of rivalry and disappointment in real life, the child begins to detach himself from his parents and to adopt a critical attitude toward his father, with whom he grows dissatisfied.[127] And while the past retains a hold so that no one can live entirely in the present, there are primacies and therefore also opportunities for surmounting personal and cultural constraints, however they may be understood. For if Freud had succeeded in Vienna as an accountant or haberdasher instead of as a pioneering psychoanalyst, the familiar claim for the oedipal roots of success could have also been made, so that this element of a complex relationship is hardly sufficient to account for the exceptional result.

The wish Freud expressed to be elsewhere represents something different, a potential he had for changing his life, a compelling, cognitively and emotionally focused interest in and capacity for inventing a sense of himself that was different from what one would otherwise have thought possible, suggesting a capacity for becoming more independent of the past than he for the most part ever suggested was possible in theory or allowed his audience to imagine in practice. Freud redirected his wish and capacity for adventure, exploration, innovation, to be and to make something new and unexpected out of himself, providing by his example and his work eloquent testimony to the potential for change all people harbor and for the heterogeneity of experience and the discontinuities of life that were possible in that community, or in any other one. It is clear from Freud's autobiographical statements that there are things he did not want to talk about for various reasons, and other things that he could not have talked about, or that he plainly made up, involving loss, separation, the cognitive implications of the retranscription of memory for the reinvention of one's life, and the emotional costs entailed in the process. On Freud's view of the matter, he had taken all the risks entailed in the development and promotion of psychoanalysis, so it is not surprising that he should want to tell the story in his own way, revealing thereby his intense narcissistic self-regard, which included of course the need to ensure the future of his work.[128]

All this brings us to Freud's own reported experience once again, specifically to the experience he described in the paper he wrote in honor of Romain Rolland, "A Disturbance of Memory on the Acropolis (1936)." Freud described here an experience of derealization attendant upon an unexpected opportunity to fulfill a long-held wish of his to visit Athens and to see the great monuments he had read about as a child. He was traveling with his younger brother, Alexander, they were compelled to change their original travel plans, a business acquaintance of Alexander's in Trieste suggested as an alternative a trip to Greece; the opportunity was there, and the trip was easily scheduled. However, Freud observed, "As we walked away from this visit, we were both in remarkably depressed spirits." Freud explained that the possibility of ever making such a trip, that he should ever get the chance travel so far, "go such a long way," had seemed remote, a sense that was linked to his family's limitations and poverty, that is, to the failure of his father. "My longing to travel was no doubt also the expression of a wish to escape from that pressure, like the force which drives so many adolescent children to run away from home. I had long seen clearly that a great part of the pleasure of travel lies in the fulfillment of these early wishes . . . rooted . . . in dissatisfaction with home and family." Thus, he wrote, he might have turned to his brother that day on the Acropolis and said, "Do you still remember how, when we were young, we used day after day to walk along the same streets on our way to school, and how every Sunday we used to go to the Prater . . . ? And now, here we are in Athens, and standing on the Acropolis! We really *have* gone a long way!"

Writing in 1936, having two decades before publicly explained that when it came to disturbing the world's peace he ranked the significance of his own work with that of Copernicus and Darwin, what did Freud mean by "we," what was the point of including his brother in his sense of having gone so much farther than his father's personal, financial, and cultural circumstances would in logic have permitted? Those impoverished familial circumstances and the resentment they bred were obviously still very much on his mind. In any event, Freud did not mean by including his brother just to make a polite but empty gesture as a part of the remembrance of the event.

What Freud meant is related to how Freud felt about his father, his family, and his life. As Freud pointed out, the child has to make discoveries that undermine his original high opinion of his father. He finds that the father is no longer the mightiest, wisest, and richest of beings, and he learns how to estimate his place in society. Then as a rule he makes him pay dearly for the disappointment he has caused. Freud went on to note that everything that is hopeful as well as everything that is unwelcome in the new generation is determined by this detachment from the father.[129]

One important incident that very much affected the way he felt about his father Freud related in *The Interpretation of Dreams*, this time in connection with his wish to visit Rome, the prospect of which had always made him anxious. He was then working through the phobic significance of Rome as part of his self-analysis, as well as being affected by the increasingly strident contemporary anti-Semitic movement: At that point he recalled a story his father had told him on one of their walks, when he was ten or twelve years old, about the cruel treatment of Jews that had affected him deeply. "'When I was a young man, I went for a walk one Saturday in the streets of your birthplace [Freiberg, in Moravia]; I was well dressed, and had a new cap on my head. A Christian came up to me and with a single blow knocked off my cap into the mud and shouted: 'Jew! Get off the pavement!' 'And what did you do?' I asked. 'I went into the roadway and picked up my cap,' was his quiet reply." Freud was disappointed in his father's conduct but he was able to repair the situation by imagining a more heroic outcome, a content, which, as he noted, remained in his imagination as one of his favorite fantasies.[130]

But the other factors that deeply affected Freud and that were mentioned in this paper were equally important, in the first place his poverty. In order to make his way through the University and then through medical school, Freud had to borrow (he was also given outright) significant amounts of money.[131] His benefactors included his former Hebrew teacher, Samuel Hammerschlag, certain of his wealthier and generous colleagues at Brücke's Institute, two individuals in particular who had featured earlier in the "Non vixit" dream, Joseph Paneth and Ernst Fleischl-Marxow, and other friends as well, but especially Breuer. Freud had written the *Studies in Hysteria* with Breuer, whom he always acknowledged as one of the founders of psychoanalysis, but with whom he had then fallen out. Both Paneth, who had set aside money for Freud's use so that he could visit and ultimately marry Martha (the Bernays family having moved in the course of events to Hamburg), and Fleischl-Marxow, had died before Freud could pay them back.

From Freud's point of view, however, the worst situation of all involved Breuer, to whom Freud was the most indebted by far. As Freud remarked in one of his recorded dreams, "The first sentences of the dream alluded under a transparent disguise to the fact that for some time this colleague [Breuer] had taken over the duties which my father could no longer fulfill . . . and that, when our relations began to be less friendly, I became involved in the same kind of emotional conflict which, when a misunderstanding arises between a father and a son, is inevitably produced owing to the position occupied by the father." In this dream in which he had made his father into a Hofrat and professor, Freud explained that the most blatant and disturbing absurdity in the dream resided "in its treatment of the date 1851, which seemed to me not to differ from 1856, *just as though a difference of five years was of no significance whatever.* But this last was precisely what the dreamthoughts sought to express." That is, four or five years was the length of time that Breuer had helped support him; it was also the length of time he had made Martha Bernays wait until they could be married.[132]

The effects of the obstacles and disabilities of poverty and cultural background, particularly the anger and sense of injustice Freud felt with regard to his father, whose failure and ignorance of how people moved ahead in the society put him at the mercy of such relationships as the one with Breuer, remained with him from beginning to end.[133] As he wrote to Ferenczi in July of 1913, in connection with the breakdown of his relationship with Jung, "I had intended to thank Jung for the feeling that the children are being taken care of [a reference to the future of psychoanalysis, but to the point], which a Jewish father needs as a matter of life and death."[134] One might well ask, considering what Freud wanted to do with his life and what he needed actually to do it, how his own father had measured up to this standard.

He had explained earlier in a letter to Martha that when he had to borrow money or was just given money outright, he at first felt "very ashamed," although he came to accept "the idea of being indebted to good men and those of our faith without the feeling of personal obligation."[135] He wrote to Fliess that "[m]oney is laughing gas for me. I know from my youth that once the wild horses of the pampas have been lassoed, they retain a certain anxiousness for life. Thus I came to know the helplessness of poverty and continually fear it."[136] Lamenting the need to reject the seduction theory for which he had had such high hopes, Freud wrote in his letter to Fliess, "The expectation of eternal fame was so beautiful, as was that of certain wealth, complete independence, travels, and lifting the children above the severe worries that robbed me of my youth."[137] He returned often in the correspondence to the subject of his poverty, one of the important contents of a "big dream" that Fliess had urged him to drop from his dream book; and shortly thereafter again: "Robert is quite right; he suspects that money is a means of unchaining slaves; that one obtains freedom in exchange for money, as one otherwise sacrifices freedom for money."[138] And later again: "My [railroad] phobia . . . was a fantasy of impoverishment, or rather a hunger-phobia, determined by my infantile greediness and evoked by my wife's lack of a dowry (of which I am so proud)."[139] When he was courting, he wrote to Martha (1882) that fortune's manner of rewarding or ignoring merit is capricious and unjust, that is, so many others have money and they have none. "Oh, my darling Marty, how poor we are! Suppose we were to tell the world we are planning to share life and they were to ask us: what is your dowry?—Nothing but our love for each other."[140] But the lack of a dowry, as we see, acquired greater significance later. As Freud explained to Jung, he had established his practice in 1886, thinking only of a two-month trial period and of emigrating to America with his fiancée had it proved a failure. "You see, we both of us had nothing, or more precisely, I had a large and impoverished family and she a small inheritance of roughly 3,000 fl. from her uncle Jacob. . . . But unfortunately things went so well in Vienna that I decided to stay on, and we were married in the autumn of the same year."[141] As he explained to Karl Abraham, reflecting on the hardships imposed later by the war, he had always feared impotence and penury and he was now approaching both.[142]

Freud made many other comments on this painful subject—his choice of career path, at Brücke's urging, was different from the one he wanted to follow, and was also determined by his impoverished circumstances. As he explained in his autobiography, "The turning point came in 1882 when my teacher, for whom I had the highest possible esteem, corrected my father's generous improvidence by strongly advising me, in view of my bad financial position, to abandon my theoretical career. I followed his advice."[143] Thus he began to study nervous diseases because there were few specialists in that field, which meant, among other things, as he characteristically expressed it, that "one was forced to be one's own teacher."[144] The facts of his enforced dependence on Breuer, for advice as well money, and on the financial resources of so many of his friends and colleagues, persistently invaded his thoughts.[145]

Even more important, however, were the cultural circumstances of Freud's father as he described them to Rolland, for these circumstances, above all, indicate just how bereft of familial support and how much on his own Freud really was, that is, just how much his life was his own invention. Freud's father had understandably left the choice of career to his son; indeed, he had to make this choice himself, for there was no part of his career and professional world or those of his brother, who became an expert on tariffs and trade, that Freud's father could have assisted with.[146] This was the sense in which Freud had used the plural pronoun and included his brother in his experience. There was nothing Freud's father could have told either of his sons about making their way in the world in which they had chosen to work and live, there was and there could have been no guidance in the matter of a career, no instruction on how careers were made, no explanations, no advice, no direction, no example, no understanding of where anything was or how anything in the world Freud or his brother wanted to inhabit was acquired or occurred. Sigmund and Alexander Freud were as much on their own in life, as far as their careers and families were concerned, as they were standing there by themselves on the Acropolis. It is not hard to understand Freud's statement in his "Revolutionary" dream that "[i]t is absurd to be proud of one's ancestry; it is better to be an ancestor oneself."[147] That was Freud's experience and his fate. What is the difference between a tailor and a psychoanalyst, goes a Jewish joke? One generation is the answer; but do not ask the tailor how he thought the psychoanalyst made it through college and medical or graduate school, or, having made it through, what the psychoanalyst actually thinks or does for a living.[148]

Thomas Carlyle once said that he stood upon his father as upon a rock, a statement that seems to substantiate the kind of cultural transmission from father to son that Freud had suggested with his notion of identification. But that statement reflects rather a cultural convention of the time. Carlyle's life was his own invention, a version rendered legitimate by the contemporary society, which even then allowed a variety of ways of expressing patterns of behavior. English character in Carlyle's day was as diverse and idiosyncratic as the English devotion to eccentricity or the subsequent history of psychoanalysis would have allowed us to predict. It would not be difficult to specify instances of this kind of experience, but the point is that if Freud had stood upon his father in the way that Carlyle had boasted, using his father's standards and expectations as a fixed model for his own life, he would have ended up at best as an educated merchant, quite possibly in England. What all this implies, as different authors have explained it, is the elaboration of legitimated cultural practices based on an increasingly monetized economy in an increasingly literate world, which expanded the sense of being able to refashion or reconstruct versions of self and world.[149]

What Freud was relating to Rolland, then, was the manner of his self-invention: he had named himself (literally, as he adopted the name Sigmund; he had also named his brother)—and he had made himself. Freud was a self-proclaimed conquistador, a self-declared, self-nominated genius whose work he had himself compared to the work of Copernicus and Darwin. He believed himself to be a world-class figure long before the world actually granted him that status. In short, he had invented himself, as much as he had invented a profession and a point of view: his life was his own construction, he was on his own and, as it were, he was his own father, not as repetition, in the manner he preferred to think about these things, but as an independent actor, the author of his own life's adventure. There may have been a real state in the past that provoked a sense of longing, a desire to reestablish a connection that could be enjoyed permanently on the basis of exceptional worthiness, or some such similar fantasy. But as Freud had come to understand with respect to Fliess, dwelling on such a fantasy can inhibit the ability to work, and it must be suppressed.

Indeed, what could happen when a marginal family's standards and expectations fall far short of those established and available in the wider society, particularly when the opportunity exists to realize and enhance larger scientific and professional standards? In a letter to Martha in April of 1885, Freud wrote that he had just made life difficult for his biographers, having destroyed all his diaries, letters, scientific notes and manuscripts of the past fourteen years. All of his old friendships and associations passed before him and were given the *coup de grâce*. All of his earlier thoughts and feelings about the world in general, and about himself in particular were declared unworthy of survival. "Everything, moreover, that lies beyond the great turning point in my life, beyond our love and my choice of profession, died long ago and must not be deprived of a worthy funeral."[150]

To be sure, Freud was able to be so bold because he had found someone to love who would also love him and be devoted to his care. Those who had earlier devoted themselves to his care were no longer sufficient for his mature self-regard, and Martha too at some point would also prove insufficient to this task. But Freud was always able to find others, including Fliess, Martha's sister, Minna Bernays, and his daughter Anna, with whom he had established a unique relationship that, insofar as it included his therapeutic relationship to her, was as novel as anything else he did (and, by any psychoanalytic standard, damaging to her well-being).[151] But it is important not to lose sight of the fact that the larger experiences of reappraisal and change that he reported were connected to his rich imaginative and cognitive capacities as well as to his marginal status, so that when he said he was cutting loose from the past he meant that he could in fact do it.

However, for an individual like Freud, given his self-perception as being uniquely responsible for a fundamental turn in cultural sensibilities, one that was likely to provoke hostility and resentment, the process of reinvention requires in a metaphorical sense, as Erikson had suggested, the death of parents, in Freud's terms particularly, the death of the father, as the representative of an old order. Self-proclaimed radicals like Martin Luther or Marx become the parents of their parents as they become teachers to the world, and Freud was prepared, not to say determined, to become such a figure. In any event there was no sense in which Jacob Freud could have retained superordinate status in reality or in fantasy once Freud had launched his project. Hence Freud's comments on "the final episode" of his "Revolutionary Dream," in which the roles of father and son got reversed: "The older man (clearly my father, since his blindness in one eye referred to his unilateral glaucoma) was now micturating in front of me, just as I had in front of him in my childhood. In the reference to his glaucoma I was reminding him of the cocaine which had helped him in the operation, as though I had in that way kept my promise. Moreover, I was making fun of him; I had to hand him the urinal because he was blind, and I reveled in allusions to my discoveries in connection with the theory of hysteria, of which I felt so proud."[152]

Freud's theory of course was intended to revolutionize the cultural world, to separate it irrevocably from the past, so that Freud, whose father died as he was working his way through the changes that made him one of the cultural icons of the century, lost his father twice as it were, in fact and as metaphor, a shared fate of many Jews who wanted to participate in and contribute to the larger society. The definition of a hero that Freud offered in *Moses and Monotheism*—"one who has had the courage to rebel against his father and has in the end victoriously overcome him"—makes no sense except in terms of having overcome his father's world.[153] As Hannah Arendt explained, this kind of experience was common for Jews trying to make their way in the different secular Western societies. And a number of authors have pointed out that psychoanalysis ironically provided these and other harried people making their way in a potentially chaotic world with one of the integrative languages they could and did use to construct versions of their experiences and lives, regardless of their familial, religious, ethnic, or national background.[154]

In the preface to the second edition of *The Interpretation of Dreams*, Freud wrote that the book, apart from being the founding document of psychoanalysis, had a further subjective significance for him personally, which he had grasped only after he had completed it: "It was, I found, a portion of my own self-analysis, my reaction to my father's death—that is to say, to the most important event, the most poignant loss, of a man's life."[155] Freud had written at the time to Fliess, "By one of those dark pathways behind the official consciousness the old man's death has affected me deeply. I valued him highly, understood him very well, and with his peculiar mixture of deep wisdom and fantastic light-heartedness he had a significant effect on my life. By the time he died, his life had long been over. But in [my] inner self the whole past has been reawakened by this event. I now feel quite uprooted."[156] This was one of the costs of continuing to do the work he wanted to do, which required him to separate from his father's world. But as Freud would have readily acknowledged, the costs are not the most important thing about the ability to do this kind of work, or to change the conditions of one's life.

Thus Freud had written in the paper he dedicated to Rolland explaining his experience of derealization: "It must be that a sense of guilt was attached to the satisfaction in having got so far: there was something about it that was wrong, that was from earliest times forbidden. It was something to do with a child's criticism of his father, with the undervaluation which took the place of the overvaluation of earlier childhood. It seems as though the essence of success was to have got further than one's father, and as though to excel one's father were still something forbidden." But, Freud added, "there was a special factor present in our particular case. The very theme of Athens and the Acropolis in itself contained evidence of the sons' superiority. Our father had been in business, he had had no secondary education, and Athens could not have meant much to him. Thus, what interfered with our enjoyment of the journey was a feeling of *piety*."[157] Erikson had admonished his readers not to confuse Freud's experience with the ordinary circumstances of an oedipal conflict, and rightly so, for something much more profound had occurred, something that explains Freud's acute sense of loss upon the death of his father and the feelings of poignancy and piety that he expressed earlier and later.[158] The cost of Freud's achievement was the progressive and inevitable death of his father's world, the termination of connections with it, as the people and things in it became ever more irrelevant and remote.

In what was at the time an utterly unexpected statement, the psychoanalyst M. Masud R. Khan wrote a few years ago that by adopting a new style and scope of clinical work with a particular patient, he was freeing himself of "the rigid Yiddish shackles of the so-called psychoanalysis. I say 'Yiddish' because psychoanalysis, for better and worse, is not only Judaic in its inherited traditions, but also Yiddish and Jewish. The three are quite distinct in my experience. Even though only two Jewesses played an important role in my education (Melanie Klein for a short while, and Anna Freud mutatively and for much longer), the impact of the Judaic-Yiddish-Jewish bias of psychoanalysis was neither small nor slight on me."[159] Apart from the vehemence of the statement, it is the reference to the Yiddish past that is unexpected. For when authors refer to the roots of psychoanalysis in terms of Freud's background, they tend to identify some element of the Jewish tradition deemed to be more appropriate to the dignity of psychoanalysis, which is then related to things judaic, rabbinic, hebraic, talmudic, cabalistic. "Freud's early intellectual development was shaped by his absorption of the cultural world view, the ethical and historical perspective, of an integrationist German/Jewish tradition in which the distinctive contributions of Jewish culture (especially the Old Testament) to the universal humanistic ethos of western culture were stressed and Jewish theology and ethics were reinterpreted through the neoclassical humanist and idealist categories of German poets and philosophers of the late eighteenth and early nineteenth centuries."[160]

Rarely, in short, is the force that animated psychoanalysis related to things Yiddish, although his mother spoke Yiddish to him in some form, a source of enduring influence in conventional psychoanalytic terms.[161] Indeed, authors quoting Freud's correspondence with Fliess sometimes edit out the Yiddish words he used, even though some portion of the fundamental sensibility of Freud's version of psychoanalysis is redolent of the life of Yiddish-speaking Central and East European Jews. The story Freud's father had told him about being pushed into the gutter by a hostile gentile, which is perhaps the best known of all of Freud's stories and appears in virtually all biographies, is Yiddish in its sensibility, redolent of the familiar expression "people don't live, people don't die, people just suffer." I don't know whether Freud ever heard this expression, but we can recognize the spirit of it in his ironic comment that the best he could do for people is to turn hysterical misery into everyday unhappiness; in his aphoristic statement that people don't live life, they hold out against it; and in his persistent view that human happiness is not part of the ground plan. Rather, people must learn to tolerate the burdens of life, which is unrelentingly harsh and will never be otherwise.[162]

But even stranger is Khan's connection of the Yiddish influence to psychoanalytic practice, which in Freud's insistence upon abstinence, neutrality, and emotional distance, at least in his published advice to other psychoanalysts whom he did not trust necessarily to be as disciplined as he was, is specifically divorced from that influence. Khan's own notion of practice and his critique of psychoanalytic practice resembles Ferenczi's, who was angrily critical of Freud's understanding of how treatment should proceed. Ferenczi, who was experimenting with therapeutic practice, particularly with the mutual analysis of patient and analyst, complained of Freud's approach "becoming more and more impersonal (levitating like some kind of divinity above the poor patient, reduced to the status of a mere child, unsuspecting that a large share of what is described as transference is artificially provoked by this kind of behavior), [allowing one to postulate] that transference is created by the patient."[163] Khan also wrote that "[i]t is my experience that letting myself be known to my patients, in a certain measure, 'neutralises' the situation in a positive way; whereas the assumed anonymity of most analysts can provoke unnecessary infantile attachments and attitudes in the patient which analysts then interpret as the patient's transference. And whereas my clinical approach creates its own demands for both analyst and patient, it also facilitates that mutual sharing which is fundamental to my way of working."[164]

Freud, however, rejected this approach, at least in his essays on technique, as contaminated by sentimental and sexually intrusive striving, favoring his publicly expressed commitment to a disciplined, controlled, and emotionally austere approach that he could claim was clinically correct and scientific, and one that he would never have thought about in a cultural sense as Yiddish.[165] Marcuse noted that "Freud was cold, hard, destructive, and pessimistic," but that—at least the cold and hard part—harks back to Freud's longing to be an Englishman, to live more like the *goyim*, as he once jokingly wrote to Martha, not to his Eastern European Jewish background.[166] As Freud explained to the American psychiatrist Joseph Wortis, then a patient of his, "I personally do not see anything wrong in mixed marriages if both parties are suited to each other, though I must say that the chances for success seem greater in a Jewish marriage: family life is closer and warmer and devotion is much more common."[167] Jewish parents of East European background, exploring the other side of Freud's comments and referring specifically to his mother, may have been domineering, manipulative, suspicious, pessimistic, and hard to put up with, but the environment was not cold in the sense Marcuse intended.[168] If anything, it is the approach to therapy of Ferenczi and Khan that recalls the Yiddish-speaking cultural environment, not the one that Freud had promoted.

Thus, Freud never repudiated his Jewish past; indeed, his son, Martin, related the family stories of Freud as a fierce defender of the tradition, quoting liberally from Freud's explanation of himself to members of B'nai B'rith.[169] Still, there are many different Jewish traditions and the one Freud was instrumental in promoting was the secular, intellectual one devoted to the "great riddles of life,"[170] to the great questions of the time that Jewish scholars and authors addressed as profoundly and with as great an effect as any others in the modern world: what is the nature of mind, what is the nature of social order, what is the nature of the universe.

Freud's ideals, the goals of his life, were those of his teachers, Brücke, Charcot, and others, the people he named his children after by way of memorializing them, not those of his father. Naming is very important among East European Jews, and even those who have abandoned the religion are likely still to maintain the link with the generations by naming children after deceased grandparents and parents. But Freud rejected this tradition, memorializing rather those people from whom he wishfully desired confirmation of his excellence and from whom he realistically could have gotten it, thereby evoking a state the ego requires to make it ideal and therefore lovable—to use his own structural terms. The familial past no longer figured for him in this and in other connections. Indeed, his teachers and the ideals he adopted from the wider culture, specifically the culture of science and learning, made up for the perceived failure of his family, restoring to him a sense of the capacity for special deeds, which served to orient him to the future and instilled in him the desire to move toward it.

CHAPTER 3

Obstacles to Theory and Practice in Psychoanalysis

Theorists have long been frustrated by their inability to explain satisfactorily the relationship of mind to society and the ways that emotional and cognitive processes fit in. An interlocutor once asked Erikson, "But how do an individual's inner perceptions get influenced by his material surroundings? To what extent are basic human drives derived *from* material conditions and to what extent are they changed *by* material conditions?" Erikson replied, "A good question. Yes, indeed, if I could only answer *that* one."[1] Clifford Geertz pointed out more than thirty years ago that "[t]here is a good deal of talk about emotions 'finding a symbolic outlet' or 'becoming attached to appropriate symbols'—but very little idea of how the trick is really done."[2] And while everyone would agree that knowledge of these processes is indispensable to systematic cultural theory in psychoanalytic or in any other terms, everyone would also agree that not enough has changed since these statements were made to warrant correcting them.

Still, despite the evident difficulties, it is important to continue to explore these problems of theory, keeping in mind Feyerabend's comments on the subject, and keeping in mind as well that there is no developed cognitive-affective-evaluative scheme that can satisfactorily account for the way that people assess their sense of self as integrated and continuous, their ability to manage everyday interests, expectations, and needs, the ways they are actually related to others, and why these relationships change over time.[3]

In this context, however, it is useful to suppose that there is an information-seeking process bound up with feelings about and moral valuations of people, codes, rules, and objects as they are related to work, family, religion, class, gender, ethnicity, and the like, and related as well to opportunities and future prospects and to wishes and fears about being able to continue to function. It is also useful to suppose that people need constantly to confirm the connection between perception and conception, prompted by the need to preserve a sense of society as a "background of safety" in which they can continue to act as workers, parents, citizens, believers, and in still other ways of interest to them. Real events that threaten the ability to preserve this sense of society, economic downturns, wars, revolts, disruptive cultural changes of all kinds, then compel an assessment of one's sense of adequacy or one's capacity to cope with them and a search for the personal and social means of bringing them under control. For all manner of cultural experience suggests to people that if such events are not controlled, emotional responses—anger, anxiety, despair, apathy—will become more global and less focused and threaten finally the hold on reality.[4]

These suppositions then obligate the study of emotions as connected to cognition and action, and despite the ways in which psychoanalysis and other disciplines have fallen short,[5] there are still useful suggestions in the literature, and we can begin to approach the problem on this basis, initially by treating emotions as a form of meaning that has two aspects relevant to social order: "they 'say' something about our organismic state (i.e., they meter its moment-to-moment readiness), and they 'say' something about the environment."[6] Emotions, then, serve as the primary basis for integrating individuals into social arrangements, in the sense that they are the basis for indicating to individuals that they are being rewarded or sanctioned, that they are members of a community in good standing or bad, that actions are consonant with standards and expectations, and so on.

Standards for material and moral achievement and for the gratification of wishes are thus constrained by emotionally bound evaluative definitions of legitimate behavior and by culturally consistent responses to perceived transgressions. Of course, in small ways the received culture is being transgressed all the time, as people interpret codes in the light of situational and temporal exigencies, and variations in expected patterns do occur. But most of these variations appear routine or at least non-threatening and are tolerated. At the same time every society retains the right to define behavior as sick, criminal, or deviant, and even those who are able to suppress emotional expression and who apparently "feel nothing" learn to abide by the emotional significance of events for others, lest they be judged criminal or deviant after all.[7]

The underlying assumptions in social as well as individual terms are that every relationship has an emotional component; that positive and negative feelings are invested in self and others; and that while at any given time these emotional components are available as part of a pattern of behavior they are also subject to change. In addition, emotional commitments to mental representations of people and things are based on real experiences in two culturally legitimate public spheres, self-interested material activity and moral activity, in terms of shifting primacies and priorities, depending upon the situations that people are called upon to face. Specifically, notions of self-interested behavior cast in terms of safe and dangerous, or in terms of advantage or disadvantage, are distinct from self-interested notions cast in terms of good and evil, as are the kinds of emotional and wishful expression involved in each, though societies value and use each.

In this context, the variety of emotions (love, hate, euphoria, anger, altruism, envy, satisfaction, disappointment, and so on) are controlled and channeled by cultural standards, authoritative leaders, and continued or prospective access to the consolations of status and to those concrete objects (money, property, sacred sites and texts, weapons) that allow for an ongoing sense of adequacy and stability. In addition, this integrated focus on the ways that cognitive, moral, and wishful perspectives are related to emotional commitments is meant to suggest that it may not even be possible to perceive individual or group interests in the absence of a moral perspective or have feelings or fantasize about them in this context.

Thus a number of psychologists have explained that emotions, cognition, and action cannot be considered in isolation, but must be considered as aspects of a larger integrated cultural system.[8] As Piaget noted, "affective states that have no cognitive elements are never seen, nor are behaviors found that are wholly cognitive."[9] Moreover, "[e]motion is not usefully isolated from the knowledge of the situation that arouses it. Cognition is not a pure form of knowledge to which emotion is added."[10] Cognitive psychologists claim as well that our ways of knowing the world are intrinsically bound up not only with our ways of feeling, but also with our moral and aesthetic valuations.[11]

One important work on these subjects, interesting for what it says but also for indicating the still empirically tenuous basis for saying anything, is Antonio Damasio's *Descartes' Error*.[12] Damasio, who claims that feelings have "a truly privileged status," and whose own sense of the matter is that *"feelings are just as cognitive as any other perceptual image,"* refers to Freud only briefly, to psychoanalysis hardly at all, and he takes cognitive psychologists to task for having failed to acknowledge the importance of emotions in any overall conception of the mind because, as he notes, emotions are considered elusive entities unfit to share the stage with the tangible contents of the thoughts they nonetheless qualify. "The terms reasoning and deciding also usually imply that the decider possesses some logical strategy for producing valid inferences . . . and that the support processes required for reasoning are in place. Among the latter, attention and working memory are usually mentioned, but not a whisper is ever heard about emotion or feeling, and next to nothing is ever heard about the mechanism by which a diverse repertoire of options is generated for selection."[13] By contrast,

Damasio explains the process that allows him to suggest a partnership "between so-called cognitive processes and processes usually called 'emotional,'" all of which bear some relationship to external circumstances.[14]

It is reasonable to suggest, in other words, that the emotional significance of thought and action, an important aspect of the self-evaluative capacity to judge the adequacy of thought and action, develops in a social context. Emotions may arise from within but the mind cannot be isolated from its environment: emotional expression must be learned as a communicative system, just as language is learned, from interpersonal and other environmental interactions. Moreover, the cognitive discipline we take for granted in the culture, or the rationality we take for granted as a technique of environmental control, is part of a moral order to which people are emotionally committed. Thus, emotional responses, however idiosyncratic they may be, are linked imaginatively to some valuation process, and in that way exist as the basis of exchange and integration at the social level.[15] People have emotionally bound obligations to adhere to these behaviors as a way of allowing others to interpret action in a positive light. It is in this sense that emotions become the basis for integrating individuals into social organization and for constraining behavior, for defining behavior as moral, and for providing effective control over behavior regulated more by moral authority than by external coercion.

Hence the difficulty of imagining a theory of culture or of the ways in which people are related to culture in the absence of theories of emotion and cognition, and in the absence, too, of a strategy sufficient to encompass the different motivational systems suggested by the variety of psychoanalytic perspectives described earlier (including, on one view, attachment/ affiliation; sensual/sexual pleasure; self-preservative; competence/mastery; competitive/territorial).[16] For if we consider that the best way to start any cultural analysis is with the dominant material and moral conceptions of life, we must also consider the ways that people pursue their concrete interests, moral perspectives, and wishful expectations as related to an individual (or private) sphere, referring to the unique mental representations of these conceptions, and to a social (or public) sphere, referring to the latitude of acceptable behaviors in the multiple social locations people inhabit. That is, decisions about behavior occur on the basis of the variety of motivational systems in terms of both individual and social bases for action. It is the unique, idiosyncratic content of individual activity, or of the mental representations of material and moral conceptions, particularly the emotional component of them, and the fact that people inhabit multiple social locations, that account for the fluctuating numbers in social movement participation over time and make a predictive social science the problematic affair that it is.

For these reasons, it is arbitrary to assume retrospectively that there was a specific superordinate cultural source for Freud's initial emphasis on sexuality, which could be perceived as part of a long-standing, determinative discourse that would enable society the better to integrate and manage its citizens. This emphasis of Freud's did not last long enough, too many other versions of psychoanalysis became too quickly available, the body of doctrine was too diverse, Freud's theoretical interests were too contradictory or internally inconsistent, and there were too many knowledgeable critiques of the doctrine, including all the different in-house critiques, to speak with confidence of the possibility of a single perspective like sexuality having a singular significance for society. The other perspectives discussed earlier (aggression, attachment/ loss, narcissism, and adaptation) were already being developed in Freud's lifetime. As Harold Bloom pointed out, "[i]f one of the marks of major literature is its uncanny ability to evolve endlessly diverse readings, then Freud matches nearly any difficult and original writer who has informed our culture in ways that are inescapable."[17]

The point is that people are constantly involved in a sense-making operation, they will adapt for this purpose whatever narrative forms and authoritative sources are available and useful for them, and they will change their commitments to these forms when they deem it necessary. In heterogeneous societies there are bound to be multiple forms, and not just within psychoanalysis or social theory, but within religion, art, or any sphere of life that affords people the possibility for closure. It is the availability of multiple perspectives that allows people to invent and reinvent versions of their lives and world in terms they can justify, just as Freud did with psychoanalysis.

It is important to emphasize, as obvious as it must appear to many, that the concept of culture must not be reified, as if it is or could be a concrete thing existing "out there." There are leading ideas, sacred texts, and authoritative individuals who represent these things to people, but there are no unified enduring structures guiding people to conclusions about what these ideas, texts, and individuals mean to them over time. The stability of culture depends upon general agreement with the ways in which resources and power are distributed; it does not depend upon any unified conception of the material significance or moral appropriateness of the distribution. Societies do the best they can to instill a unified conception of material interests and moral perspectives, through families, schools, churches, different forms of therapeutic interventions, and in still other ways, but their success is always limited. It is therefore best not to think in terms of collective (in the sense of unified) identity, collective memory, unity of motive, fixity of character, "core personality," or continuity of events over time.

It is also best not to think of the familiar sociological categories, class, gender, race, and the like, as the central organizing locations of everyday life, in the conventional sense that they somehow determine or decisively condition behavior. People inhabit a variety of such locations that occupy a space between their unique, idiosyncratic perceptions and striving and the cultural perspectives that guide and orient behavior, and they can act in terms of any one of them. Sociologists have pointed out that contemporary identity movements are heterogeneous in composition, cutting across class, gender, race, and other lines by definition.[18] But the decisive feature of social movements historically, even when they have been rooted in class or gender, is their heterogeneous character. It is not difficult at all to show that middle- and upper-class people were recruited to defend proletarian interests in numbers too great to be accounted for by accident or coincidence, or that men have been mobilized to support the feminist movement and women to oppose it.

Thus rather than assume that mental states and outlook are determined by any particular social location, it makes better sense, even with respect to known statistical tendencies, to assume that decisions are made in a variety of social locations, that they are shaped by the texts, authoritative figures, and objects characteristic of different social locations, and that primacies shift within and among these locations depending upon the specifics of any situation as people are obliged to interpret them. The texts, figures, and objects make effective conveyance of meaning possible, but the interpretations of their significance will vary as interests, expectations, and needs vary. Knowledge and conceptions of social situations may be shared in the sense of agreement as to their importance, but not in the sense that people construe their significance or feel about them in the same way.

Moreover, it is then difficult to claim that people are compelled to view society as hostile to their wishes, expectations, and interests, or that there is the kind of antagonism that Freud assumed between civilization and the aspirations of people, however they are defined. On the contrary, people need to have the sense that society functions for them as a "background of safety" within which they can pursue their own interests, moral perspectives, and wishful aims, a reflection of the desire for order or the need to avoid chaotic conditions. Ironically, the very multiplicity of available perspectives that leads to tensions within society also affords people the opportunity to imagine or rationalize a sense of integration with the social world.

It is easy to see why the absence of theories of emotion and cognition in terms of the effects of external social events on mind accounts in important ways for the diminishing importance of psychoanalysis as a source of cultural interpretation. But there are a number of other reasons for this outcome. Equally important, though perhaps not as immediately obvious, are the reported results of psychoanalytic clinical practice itself, referring to the idiosyncratic outcomes of therapy, the discontinuties of life as revealed by therapy over time, and the capacity of people for active constructions of reality as even many psychoanalysts have now come to conceive it.

One of the fundamental problems for successive generations of psychoanalysts intent on pursuing Freud's cultural interests was their inability to resolve the contradiction between the reported results of clinical practice, the idiosyncratic and discontinuous outcome of individual instances, and the larger interpretive ambitions. In the "postmodern" world, the idiosyncratic quality of behavior is much more readily taken for granted, as it appears, for example, in Eve Sedgwick's *Epistemology of the Closet*.[19] But it is important to underscore the significance of these persistently reported experiences in psychoanalysis. As Leo Rangell once put it, the intrapsychic constellations that may lead to distortion or variation in object relations are myriad, and vary as much as people do. Or as Maxwell Gitelson perceptively noted, "[e]ach case represents a way of life, a method of adaptation which has been compelled by particular deviations in the internal and external environment [sic] which have been impressed upon the whole development of the personality."[20]

In short, the individual conflicts psychoanalysts report on have never pointed to a unified, underlying narrative. On the contrary, "[e]very childhood drive derivative, every wish for drive satisfaction, has to do with a particular person or persons, with particular memories, with a particular form of pleasure, all of which are unique for that child."[21] Harold Blum wrote that "[e]ach patient reacts to the significant real events of life in his own particular fashion, based on his total personality, and some ego-syntonic character patterns may remain distant from transference conflict and analysis."[22] Thus psychoanalysts explain that the confirmation of clinical hypotheses "remains of specific relevance only to any one person,"[23] and that "the efficacy of any kind of psychotherapy is difficult because personality and individual mental illness, constitutional disposition and temperament, resilience, and motivation all differ greatly from one patient to another."[24] Or as Oliver Sacks noted, "[n]o two 'individuals' show identical behavior—and the details of their reachings and learnings cannot be predicted."[25]

I have discussed this before, and I do not want to elaborate it here any further, except to comment on two particular aspects of it. First, it does not matter what the theoretical vantage point or language is, the outcome remains the same: not only do solutions to conflict vary significantly among individuals, but modern societies are so differentiated, complex, and heterogeneous that individuals whose developmental experiences may be similar can nevertheless end up in opposed cultural or political camps. There are too many legitimate institutionalized ways to accommodate the variety of individual resolutions to conflict to imagine a shared motive leading to a unified solution to any conflict. Invoking any structuralist's argument as a way of bypassing the surface tensions by suggesting an underlying (unconscious) unity of motive changes nothing in this regard.

A second and related aspect of the reported results of therapy involves the psychoanalytic discussion of who gets taken by surprise in the clinical setting.[26] If one believes in the unity of unconscious impulse and striving, or in the possibility of a single underlying narrative, then it is the patient who gets taken by surprise—by unexpected outbursts of feeling, slips of the tongue, unbidden thoughts, and so on; the analyst is only hearing what he or she expected to hear, having heard it all before. But if one acknowledges the idiosyncratic and heterogeneous quality of mind, then "[i]t is not just the patient but the analyst too who must be constantly open to surprise."[27] Hence, it is not a question of theoretical orientation or psychoanalytic hypothesis, but rather "the emergence of circumstantial detail, having an astonishing degree of specificity and idiosyncratic nuance. . . . Such details have not previously been remembered by the analysand . . . and almost certainly have not previously been imagined or guessed in advance by the psychoanalyst. A psychoanalysis without surprises cannot properly be termed a psychoanalysis at all."[28]

This point, which has also been made many times before,[29] should be sufficient to put an end to the interminable reworking of especially Freud's case histories, and most especially of Freud's "Fragment of an Analysis of a Case of Hysteria," the Dora case. The idea that anyone can reinterpret a case history like this one, which is based on Freud's own reporting of the matter and is absent the reporting of the subject whose associations alone can confirm or disconfirm a conclusion, implies that there are no surprises in therapy, that the system provides the kind of schematic knowledge that might permit such a reworking, which it absolutely does not in any of its versions.[30]

Freud acknowledged the dilemma of idiosyncratic outcomes virtually from the beginning. In 1894 he wrote to Fliess about the different cases he had found in which anxiety arose from a sexual cause, citing seven different kinds, which seemed "at first to be quite heterogeneous [recht disparat]," and he wondered how all the separate cases could be brought together.[31] As much as he would have avoided the problem, he understood that "[e]ach case must be dealt with individually. Our presentation begins to be conclusive only with the intimate detail,"[32] and the detail is always idiosyncratic. Indeed, the logic of many of the things Freud wrote, particularly *Inhibitions, Symptoms, and Anxiety*,[33] pushed psychoanalysis in the direction of idiosyncratic outcomes, a dilemma that recurred whenever he addressed the issues of sublimation, the overdetermined quality of symptoms and symbols, the repetition compulsion, which ensures that the repressed will return in a manner disguised by displacements, or whenever he considered in any text the relative contributions of constitutional and accidental or environmental factors in the outcome of life.

Thus even if the Oedipus complex is a universal experience, it achieves expression in idiosyncratic ways. The audience may all be captivated by the drama, but they are captivated in their own way and for their own sakes. Freud's patients may all have been involved with him but they were all involved uniquely. The claim that the Oedipus complex is universal does not address the larger problem of the stability or instability of culture, and certainly not in the most immediately obvious and preferred terms, that people and the authority they crave recognize each other because they share similar motives and traits. As Freud understood, this is not what therapeutic results reveal.

Freud constantly returned to this problem, which he explained at length in a letter he wrote to a friendly critic in 1911: "We find in psychoanalysis that we are dealing not with *one* disposition but with an infinite number of dispositions which are developed and fixed by accidental fate. The disposition is so to speak polymorphous." Freud went on to discuss the possibilities of variation in individuals in terms of inherited dispositions or accidental influences that "work here and there so powerfully that they arouse and fix this or that part of the originally dormant disposition."[34] Freud made many more statements on the idiosyncratic outcomes of life,[35] but this one from a paper on clinical technique (1913) is indicative of them all: "The extraordinary diversity of the psychical constellations concerned, the plasticity of all mental processes and the wealth of determining factors oppose any mechanization of the technique."[36] That is, as psychoanalysts well understand, addicts seek out dependent relationships, obsessionals turn life into a succession of empty rituals, depressives seek absolution and/or punishment, sadomasochists seek out tormenting struggles and structure their relationships to extract suffering from them, compulsive individuals defend themsevles by doing and by persistent effort at accomplishment, hysterics by dramatization and symbolization, paranoids by intellectualizing conflict, or by "explanations" of it, and so on.[37]

Freud never could solve the puzzle presented for social order by idiosyncratic outcomes, or account for the discrepancy between individual dynamics and the complexity of more or less stable social organizations. He was confounded by the results of his own specially devised therapeutic arrangement. As Freud understood when he discussed in *Three Contributions to a Theory of Sexuality* the perversions (fetishism and homosexuality) or the neuroses (phobia, obsessive-compulsive disorder, hysteria), or when he discussed the extraordinary diversity of psychical constellations, referring to the different transference and narcissistic neuroses, there is no reason on the face of it why such diverse types should combine in various kinds of unified social structures. These structures in fact share particular features no matter where they appear, but are nevertheless characterized by multiple, competing, and conflicting interests and orientations. The preferred solution to this puzzle in terms he was anxious to promote would have required some notion of a collective archaic unconscious, but even he did not have the courage to suggest that.

Given the dilemma, however, it is not hard to see why Freud nevertheless promoted his phylogenetic propositions virtually from the beginning to the end,[38] to the great distress and even embarrassment of his closest adherents.[39] Indeed, as Max Schur was at pains to disclose, he, Ernst Kris, and Ernest Jones all tried to talk Freud out of his phylogenetic propositions as they appeared in *Moses and Monotheism*, but Freud refused to be budged. Schur ascribed Freud's stubbornness in the matter to unresolved "inner conflicts," while Jones, also referring to his obstinacy in the matter, professed to be baffled by what Freud's decision meant both for his ideas and his personality.[40] Even in his last work he was still claiming, in reference to the child's first erotic attachment to the mother, that the phylogenetic foundation has the upper hand by far over personal accidental experience.[41]

Those for whom these problems matter but who find it impossible to accept Freud's phylogenetic conclusions have tried to move psychoanalysis in a more sociological and historical direction. Schur, for example, wanted to argue on Freud's behalf that he had seen "again and again that virtually no human being failed to encounter in the course of his development the kind of situation which generated typical oedipal conflicts."[42] But the psychosocial, functional, and Marxist standpoints that Erikson, Parsons, Fromm, and others developed, or that Schur alluded to, failed as sociology or social psychology because they also implied a high degree of unity of unconscious motivation and hence of stability or continuity in character and social organization, neither of which can be demonstrated to exist by reference to clinical evidence, ostensibly the paramount source of evidence for psychoanalysts. Their vantage points were too rooted in Freud's assumptions with respect to the dynamic primacy of sexuality and aggression and too focused on guilt and shame or on repression carried out as a function of internalized morality as a way of accounting for stable social behavior.

There are as well more strictly psychoanalytic attempts to straighten Freud out, but everything psychoanalysts have done in this regard only underscores the problem Freud was trying to get around in the first place. That is, as soon as one assumes that relationships structure instinctual life rather than the other way around (Hans Loewald took this approach and others have as well),[43] as soon as the argument is made that "[i]ndividuals are embedded in, and shaped by, their culture and by their moment in history,"[44] we get into the world of accidental experience and heterogeneous response on all levels, as already suggested by the many statements Freud had made. Sandler's belief that a revitalized psychoanalysis must have at its core "the idea of an organized, unconscious, internal world and unconscious, internal, object relationships," underscores the notion that psychoanalysts cannot, on their own intrapsychic ground, get beyond the idiosyncratic and the accidental outcomes of life.[45] Hence Sandler's emphasis on clinical concerns: "What is critical is not what psychoanalytic theory *should be*, but what should be *emphasized* within the whole compass of psychoanalytic thinking. *And what should be emphasized is that which relates to the work we have to do.* This means that for most of us the theory needs to be a clinically, psychopathologically, and technically oriented one, which also includes a central preoccupation, not only with the abnormal but with the normal as well."[46]

Freud could not make good on his goal and promise to specify conditions dependent on absolute time and not on life time. He could not account for the contents of cognitive, moral, or wishful thinking in terms of instinct or drive (or "psychical reality"), because drives are without quality and drive energy cannot by itself create a mental or cognitive content, nor could he reconcile the basic contradiction of his position, idiosyncratic outcomes in the context of recurrent and specific forms of social organization.[47] Thus while social and historical arguments appear in Freud's work in a minor way,[48] essentially, as the cultural texts reveal, he was not interested in unique instances or change over time. But in the end he could not otherwise effectively fashion a solution to his problem.

The problem of idiosyncratic resolutions to conflict that lies behind all of these discussions is compounded by the discontinuity of personal and cultural experience, the second problem that emerged from clinical (and also historical) experience. There are many ways of expressing this notion of discontinuity. On one level, for example, people are arguably "never exactly what they were moments before, and objects are never seen in exactly the same way"; our recollection of things is too dependent on changing contexts so that it may well be necessary for our perception of things to change quickly.[49] Indeed, it was the discontinuity of therapeutic experience in particular that animated André Green's critique of Lacan. Green explained that one cannot infer the continuity of meaning from the recurrent use of language because feelings about the changing situations people face are not constant over time and feelings in this context are impossible to ignore.

But probably the best way to describe discontinuity of personal and cultural experience is in the language of the psychoanalytic structural theory. Thus Roy Schafer, invoking Robert Waelder's "principle of multiple function"[50] observed that "[t]he ideal of efficiency . . . may simultaneously express the superego objective of instinctual renunciation, the ego objectives of successful defense and adaptive cultivation of order, health, success, and attractiveness, and the id objective of satisfying anal-retentive and anal-expulsive tendencies. The ideal of patriotism may express the superego goal of renouncing parricidal impulses, the id goal of passively fusing with and being satisfied by mother and father, and the ego goal of reaction formation against rebelliousness and preserving and enhancing accustomed object ties, values, and modes of work." The ego psychologists Hartmann, Kris, and Loewenstein also wrote that "[t]he same institution may, in some persons, appeal most effectively to their ids; in others, to their superegos; in a third group, it may be used predominantly by their ego interests, etc."[51] Psychoanalysts realize that ideas and events affect all dimensions of personality, that "different kinds of motives and claims go into shaping any significant piece of psychic life—the moral and the judgmental claims of the superego, the realistic assessments of external situations by the ego, and the imperatives of aggressive and sexual demands."[52] There are primacies, but primacies change quickly in dynamic and social terms in the course of an hour or a day, let alone in the course of an ongoing and related series of events or a historical period. The basis for decision-making changes from one situation to the next and varies from one person to the next (and all this still apart from the problem of multiple social locations).[53] As Schafer concluded, "at different times the same ideal may carry different weights of superego, ego, and id meanings."[54]

The answer to the question of why any individual joined this or that movement or group is that in a dynamic sense there is no single answer: in libidinal terms, perhaps because one needed the contact and the sense of belonging and nurturance, or because one felt justified in being hostile and defiant, or because one wanted to show how strong and competitive one is; or in structural terms, because joining provided a way of pursuing material interests, because it was morally appealing, or because it presented a legitimate opportunity for the expression of wishful striving. To invoke an older "constructionist" (or "constructivist") sociological perspective, amply confirmed by clinical, social, and historical experience, behavior is relative in space and emergent in time.[55] Ten people sitting around a table have ten reasons for being there, and the reasons may well not be the same the next time they sit together. This is why Geertz insisted that the problem is not in heads, why the view of culture as gyroscopic rather than causal or motivating is so compelling, even if it too cannot account for the sources of the different cultural contents, why authoritative individuals must still be accorded a vital place in systematic social theory, and why the importance of unconscious motivations to such a theory is radically diminished (because motivations are multiple, idiosyncratic, and discontinuous over time).

The problems for theory revealed by the discontinuities of motive and behavior are underscored particularly by the changing nature of symptoms over time and from place to place. Of course, the extent to which symptoms change and the extent to which psychoanalysts fail to account for the relationship of such change to larger issues of social change, or are obliged merely to speculate on it, is a crucial aspect of the cultural decline of psychoanalysis, but it is one that is readily confirmed by the testimony of innumerable psychoanalysts themselves. Otto Fenichel had addressed the problem of changing symptoms by 1938, but we may recall as well Erikson's statement that identity was as important a concept for his generation as sexuality was for Freud's, and that he came to the identity concept "not by theoretical preoccupation but rather through the expansion of . . . clinical awareness to other fields (social anthropology and comparative education)." Anna Freud, too, at approximately the same time, noted that social change had given rise to changing symptoms, the more lenient child-rearing practices in Western societies accounting "for the fact that the less well defined and fluctuating developmental disorders are on the increase at the expense of the real infantile neurosis which was more frequently recorded and treated by the analytic workers in the past."[56]

The conviction that symptomatic expression (like fantasy expression) changes according to time and place is widespread and often reported by psychoanalysts, particularly because of their experience with narcissistic, psychotic, and borderline patients, as well as with reality factors. Psychoanalysts have reported for a long time that presenting problems have changed over time and from place to place. "No longer are we presented with the florid conversion reactions, fugues, massive amnesias, etc. Today our more sophisticated, urbanized patients complain of chronic maladaptation in living, i.e., in working, loving and playing. The characteristic modes which predetermine these maladaptations have been designated 'character neuroses,' or 'character disorders.'"[57] Arnold H. Modell also noted the "vast differences in those who have sought analytic treatment over the years between the early flamboyant hysteric, who has all but disappeared, and the current group, whose conflicts appear to be chiefly in the area of object relationships." Modell concluded that if such changing patterns reflect broader social processes, "the assumption that one may generalize for the entire species, would no longer be relevant."[58]

There is so much of this kind of reporting that no further elaboration of the point is required.[59] I will cite only two other interesting instances here. Michael Franz Basch has written that no one was "more knowledgeable about, or more sincerely dedicated to Freud's work than Heinz Kohut," and that he, Basch, though an adherent of Kohut's, certainly considers himself a psychoanalyst. The problem is that he no longer sees in his practice the kind of psychoneurotic patient for whom classical or traditional analysis is appropriate. "Some fifteen years or so ago," Basch wrote in 1984, "I did have one case of a psychoneurotic patient of the sort Freud described." Sandler has also written that "[i]n England, where it is well recognized that truly neurotic cases are few and far between and that candidates tend for the most part to be sent cases of character disorder or borderline disturbance, the problem that institutes require control cases be neurotic and develop a transference neurosis, which has to be resolved before the candidate can be given credit for the analysis of the case and allowed to graduate, does not arise."[60]

The idiosyncratic and discontinuous outcomes of clinical practice raise crucial questions about the relationship of mind to society that cannot be addressed in any terms that Freud would have approved. And all this is still apart from a third problem that undermined Freud's expectations for psychoanalysis, the capacity of people for active constructions of reality. Psychoanalytic ego psychologists began to make this kind of argument some time ago; such a possibility was always implicit in the stress within ego psychology on the adaptive capacities of people and on ego autonomy. However, the argument, which has achieved recognizably popular status as it appears routinely in fiction, film, and the popular press, as well as in other abstract psychological and social theories, is currently being more forcefully pursued in psychoanalytic therapy and theory in the light of recent developments in cognitive and developmental psychology and neuroscience, in terms of memory, perception, affect, and the relationship of self to others.[61]

I have already noted Freud's early observation that when memories of childhood events are aroused, they do not emerge in any veridical sense: they are formed at the time, with no concern for historical accuracy.[62] Consistent with Freud's depiction of the construction of memory, Loewald argued in 1955 that "[r]ecollection . . . is not a re-recording but the creation of something new."[63] The following year, Kris, too, emphasized the constructed nature of memories of childhood events.[64] Holt then subsequently discussed the image of Man "as an *active, responsible agent*," who can respond appropriately to the things that happen in the world, referring to David Rapaport's and Hartmann's conception of autonomous ego capacities that actively resist causal pressures stemming from both the environment and from internal impulses. This is contrasted with Freud's familiar conception of the passive ego menaced by dangers from every side.[65] Humberto Nagera claimed that the development of new ego apparatuses in the light of changed conditions is a never-ending process, that people are capable of modifying their environment and also of adapting to new and unsuspected problems resulting from the modifications, and that in the course of civilization the human species has developed a number of "functional structures" that were required to deal with changed conditions.[66] Gilbert Rose, too, explained that "perception and memory do not merely record reality, but *actively* construct it. Perception is not a unitary event which is given, but a cognitive experience abstracted from a framework of contexts. Our sense organs select forms out of William James's 'big blooming, buzzing confusion' of stimuli."[67] Consistent with this perspective, Jay Greenberg, in his revision of Freud's dual drive theory, offered effectance and safety drives as an alternative to sexuality and aggression, stating that "the feeling state that is the aim of effectance is characterized by a sense of self-sufficiency, autonomy, and individuation."[68]

The argument that people are capable of active constructions of reality is now even more focused.[69] This argument, which gives people far more latitude to correct experience than Freud typically allowed, particularly in his genetic, dynamic, and structural schemes, reflects a number of contemporary conditions, not least economic conditions. But of particular interest to us at this point are tendencies current in clinical practice. To put it briefly, the therapist is not the only one who can promote change in a patient; whether the issue is insight based on interpretation or a narrative that two partners can agree upon, the result of clinical practice is structural change and the reinvention of an individual.[70]

In addition, this notion of experiences that are not passively recorded as individual memory traces, "but are actively integrated into a constantly changing structure,"[71] has led to different understandings of how therapy works that are often indebted to the kind of "constructionist" sociology referred to earlier. On this view, the subjective accounts patients construct of their past are characterized by the contingency and ambiguity of "emergent personal meaning"; they are not fixed once and for all in childhood, they are the result of a process of negotiation between therapist and patient.[72] In this interactive, interpersonal encounter, meaning is not just discovered, it is created.[73] *"The representation is thus an active construction—in truth a creation—that embodies the event's meaning to the subject."*[74] Indeed, as one professional explained to a lay audience, "Insufficiently trained therapists may fail to take into account the complexity of the intermingling of fantasy and memory and the way the human mind actively constructs rather than passively registers perception."[75]

There are variations on this perspective that more emphatically stress the elements of therapy that conduce to "secondary socialization" or resocialization, with reference to Peter Berger and Thomas Luckmann's *The Social Construction of Reality*. On this view, therapy is not so much about recovering experiences and working through their emotional significance in the sense that they are effectively recalled and imaginatively absorbed. Rather, it is about active agents working together to reinvent a sense of self.[76] It does not matter, moreover, whether there are grounds for validating an interpretation or not; there are always other possible interpretations of experience, and the feelings about as well as the interpretations of the significance of experience will change over time.

It is important to emphasize, however, that if appropriate narratives are constructed, if "truth," or a moment of understanding, is something that is negotiated between patient and analyst, emerging in the course of their activity together in such a way that "there is a change in both,"[77] if people are being resocialized or living through an experience of "secondary socialization," if there is no interpretation offered in a clinical setting that cannot be substituted for by another one, if therapy is not a matter of historical reconstruction or if recall is a matter of active construction rather than discovery, if psychic reality as an articulation between internal and external realities is under permanent construction,[78] if "in the analytic situation, both analyst and analysand are continuously constructing their individually experienced situations,"[79] then the debate between the older drive-positivist and the more recent relational-constructionist camps within psychoanalysis becomes moot in terms of the real effects of therapy.[80] For something novel emerges from the encounter between patient and therapist regardless of the therapist's perspective, in the sense that in either case the relationship fosters the reinvention, not merely the recovery, of a sense of self. To the extent that it works at all, this is what happens.

Put another way, psychoanalysis is one of a number of culturally available techniques, including the constant availability of multiple cultural perspectives, the presence of authoritative figures in all domains, and the proliferation of novel perspectives and figures, that facilitate the process of invention and reinvention of self. Hence the widespread contemporary interest in the capacity of people to invent versions of the world, or to invent and reinvent versions of themselves, responding actively in this way to changed circumstances when they need to, in terms of the different social locations they occupy. As Roy Schafer has explained, even the experiences reported by an introspecting subject require "an actively introspecting subject, an agent engaging in a particular set of actions."[81]

Of course this notion of agency, or of the capacity of people actively to construct versions of reality, has a distinguished academic provenience.[82] It is linked, for example, to Suzanne K. Langer's and Robert White's observations that the active construction of versions of events is an essential feature of mind, as behavior is not only activated by peremptory impulses but also by the need to maintain contact with others and with an agreed-upon conception of reality. It is also linked to the various notions of adaptive behavior referred to earlier, to the notion that culture acts gyroscopically, not causally, to orient a heterogeneous population to a common goal, and to cognitive conceptions of the ways in which information, including emotional responses to events, is received, coded, and used, so that people can regulate their interactions with the social world without getting hurt.

But more recently this perspective has been amplified in psychoanalytic discourse as well, with a degree of legitimacy never accorded particularly to the earlier work of Robert White. I refer to Arnold Modell's extended discussion of Freud's concept of *Nachträglichkeit*, which he, following other psychoanalytic discussions of the inadequacy of Strachey's translation of the concept as "deferred action," refers to as the "retranscription of memory."[83] Modell claimed that "*the ego can constantly remodel memory in accordance with current and immediate experience.*" Modell added, quoting from Israel Rosenfeld's discussion of recent neuroscientific investigations, that "[e]ach person . . . is unique: his or her perceptions are to some degree creations, and his or her memories are part of an ongoing process of imagination. . . . Human intelligence is not just knowing more, but reworking, recategorizing, and thus generalizing information in new and surprising ways."[84] Donald Spence, too, has written that more than was realized: "the past is continuously being reconstructed in the analytic process," the analytic situation itself helping to shape what patients remember.[85] Or as Rosenfeld claims, "[m]emories are not fixed but are constantly evolving generalizations—recreations—of the past, which give us a sense of continuity. . . . But continuity is in terms of the present, in our capacity to generalize and to categorize when confronted with the new and unexpected."[86] Memories, Rosenfeld noted, are generalizations that are constantly being revised, and necessarily so, because there is no memory

without context and the context, the social world, is constantly changing. Daniel Schacter, in his work on memory, cites recent contributions
indicating that "there is no single representation or engram stored in
memory that has a one-to-one relationship with the mental experience
of recollecting one's past. Instead, such experiences are always constructed by combining bits of information from [the different levels] of
autobiographical knowledge." In addition, Schacter notes that like more
mundane memories, "recollections of emotional traumas are constructions, not literal recordings."[87] And Oliver Sacks, in his discussion for a
popular audience of Gerald Edelman's *Bright Air, Brilliant Fire*,
explained that in Edelman's view "[i]t is up to the infant animal, given
its elementary physiological capacities, and given its inborn values, to
create its own categories and to use them to make sense of, to *construct*,
a world—and it is not just a world that the infant constructs, but its *own*
world, a world constituted from the first by personal meaning and reference."[88]

Finally, Sacks, claiming that Freud meant by his concept of
Nachträglichkeit "an imaginative, context dependent [that is, situational and therefore historical] construction or reconstruction," aptly
describes life as "a journey, full of novelty and adventure." Sacks also
referred to Modell's discussion of *Nachträglichkeit* as "the retranscription of memories which had become part of pathological fixations, but
were opened to consciousness, to new contexts and reconstructions, as
a crucial part of the therapeutic process of liberating the patient from
the past, and allowing him to experience and move freely once again."
And all the authors referred to here on the subject of memory, Sacks,
Modell, Rosenfeld, and Schacter, quoted the Cambridge psychologist
Frederic Bartlett (1932): "Remembering is not the re-excitation of innumerable fixed, lifeless and fragmentary traces. It is an imaginative reconstruction or construction, built out of the relation of our attitude toward
a whole mass of organized past reactions or experience."[89]

These processes of invention and reinvention of self in a cultural
context are too complex to be accommodated by any of the familiar psychoanalytic speculations that, as a result of the persistence of the traditional conception of the domain, are not keyed to the way "external
reality is received and organized inside the mind [sic] so as to form cognitive structures based on experience and appropriate for relating to the
external world."[90] That is, as I indicated earlier and as many authors
have explained, "[a]ction required for its explication that it be *situated*,
that it be conceived of as continuous with a cultural world. The realities
that people constructed were *social* realities, negotiated with others, distributed between them."[91]

This refers, among other things, to the orientation of individuals to action in singular historical and cultural contexts and to the cognitive and emotional components of behavior and relationships (including emotional attachments to mental representations of relationships), which also vary over time and from place to place. Individuals understand that positive and negative feelings are invested in self and others, and that "bad" behavior may have bad consequences. At the same time, however, there is not just one right way to do things, there are many right ways to do things. There is always some latitude in the interpretation of the norms and values that orient people, so that while all members of a group are involved together in various relationships, there are nevertheless different conceptions of them and different outcomes.[92]

The view of the changeableness of character as a way of coping with changed circumstances implies that people have a degree of cognitive control over symbolic or cultural codes, that emotional attachments to patterns of behavior do not necessarily hinder the capacity to make sense of new types of experience or to bring them under control, that threatening circumstances can be perceived as potential opportunities as well as obstacles, and that there are social techniques facilitating this process even if these may include over a shorter or longer period of time subordination to the claims of an authoritative leader. All these conclusions, of course, are suggestive of the circumstances undergirding the origins of psychoanalysis as a profession. In any case they lead away from the kinds of universally inclusive conclusions Freud and others have wanted to promote.

Moreover, the claim that people can invent and reinvent versions of self is remote even from those psychoanalytic observations that, though they may have challenged the ontogenetic terms of the older orthodoxy, still retain a sense of the grip of internalized images and superego mandates on people, fostering passive responses to the heteronomous demands of the social world. It would not be difficult to convey here the extent to which this claim has penetrated popular imagination and become available in everyday popular expression. However, because the notion is well on the way to becoming as routine as the familiar Freudian developmental schemes had earlier been, I will provide a few indicative examples from both popular and professional publications, keeping in mind that I could reproduce the following statements many times over: "By appropriating a style, an attitude, a look, recycling [of cultural images and themes] focuses on surface appearance. Madonna dons Marilyn Monroesque clothes and strikes Marilyn Monroesque poses, then exchanges them for poses borrowed from Marlene Dietrich, implying . . . that identity is mutable, that labels can be shrugged on and off at will—reasoning oddly echoed by Marion Barry and Oliver North, who similarly suggest that there are second and even third acts in a life, that the past can always be reinvented."[93] Or again, "[r]einventing one-self—it's a very postmodernist notion, perfect for the age of morphing and Madonna."[94] The author of Ralph Ellison's obituary in *The New York Times* selected this passage from *Invisible Man*: "In the South, everyone knew you, but coming north was a jump into the unknown. How many days could you walk the streets of the big city without encountering anyone who knew you, and how many nights? You could actually make yourself anew."[95] Note, too, this comment on the then Congressman Kweisi Mfume: "For in his new life, Frizzell Gray gave himself a new name. In a consummate act of self-reinvention, the father-less child of the streets once known as Pee-Wee became Kweisi Mfume—'the conquering son of kings.'"[96]

Of special interest, however, is Erikson's reference to the United States in 1971 (following Robert Jay Lifton's introduction of the con-cept of "Protean Man")[97] as a "self-made country" in which the "'self-made' ideal and the technocratic vision fused into an idealized image of a man who almost literally made himself, created himself, manufactured himself, invented himself."[98] Lifton, who had long since abandoned the traditional psychoanalytic perspective on character development,[99] later amplified his sense of the ability of people to invent and reinvent ver-sions of themselves, citing various historical influences that have con-tributed to "the protean self."[100] Lifton offered a number of examples in his work, including references to the biographer of William Paley, who saw him "as a man who virtually invented himself, and who 'like many people who invent themselves . . . came to venerate the invention'"; and the novelist Ann Beattie: "All my life I've felt like I was just making things up, improvising as I went along. I don't mean telling lies, I mean inventing a life."[101] We should also note finally this statement of Stephen Greenblatt's from *Renaissance Self-Fashioning*: "Perhaps the simplest observation we can make is that in the sixteenth century there appears to be an increased self-consciousness about the fashioning of human identity as a manipulable artful process."[102]

Of course, popular and professional writers and their audiences are constantly searching for language more consistent with contemporary experience, so that the repeated resort to the language of self-invention can be perceived as yet another ideological gesture. But it also provides in fact a better insight into the way people are related to the social world. What must be stressed here is that there are not likely to have been two different modes of character development, the kind that Freud wrote about and another kind. Put another way, there are not two his-torically successive concepts of development; there is the one, implying that people are and have historically been actively involved in con-structing versions of themselves and the world in ways that are related to the opportunities and orientations available in the larger culture, including all the forms of psychotherapy.

All this has become more publicly evident because of changes in the economy that have compelled observers to make explicit the instability of the work world and to emphasize the prospective need of people to change careers over time, or to reinvent themselves as workers. But it is related also to discussions of agency, to active rather than passive conceptions of the assimilation of experience. It is important to consider as well the "postmodern" emphasis on the heterogeneity of populations and discontinuity of events, including the particularist demands of identity movements, mobilized by groups hitherto excluded from the decision-making processes, with whatever tension and struggle this has entailed. These demands also strongly suggest that people are actively engaged in evaluating their own experiences, and this could not be explained away by the familiar theories based on unity of internalized mandates.[103]

Hence the bind that psychoanalysts in particular have found themselves in as a result of the failure of traditional psychoanalytic theories of character development to account adequately for everyday individual and group experience. Peter Blos observed some years ago that there are at least four such theories of character development: character traits traced to a specific level of drive development or fixation (Freud), character traits that result from the choice of defense mechanisms (Wilhelm Reich), character traits that, following Freud's later notion (in *The Ego and the Id*), are viewed as "the precipitates of abandoned object cathexes," and character traits that emerge from psychosocial development as described by Erikson.[104] However, the emphasis on emergence, and on active construction and reconstruction as a means of coping with everyday experience, suggests that there must be other sources of character formation more consistent with social and historical data.

One is obviously linked to the interventions of leaders in disrupted social situations in the familiar sense associated with Martin Luther, Oliver Cromwell, and Maximilien Robespierre. That is, once people experience the actual or threatened loss of expected behaviors and the explanatory language that justifies them, they will actively search for alternatives and particularly for authoritative figures who can explain the current turmoil, constructing versions of the significance of such leaders for themselves in a manner appropriate to the context in which they appear.[105] We can put to rest the impossible notion that the motives of the followers can be inferred from the motives of leaders, or that knowledge of the leader's biography affords knowledge by definition of the biographies of followers. Motives in this case are as heterogeneous and discontinuous as in all other cases. In this way, social change that renders symbolic or cultural codes ineffective, unavailable, or dysfunctional systematically engenders the redefinition of self and others.[106]

The second, and for the purposes of this discussion more important, source is linked to the impact of changed circumstances that are not necessarily disruptive to society in a revolutionary sense but that do require unfamiliar responses from people faced with unexpected situations, a changed job market or economy, changes in familial arrangements, the need or demand of marginal people to become integrated in the larger society, or an immigrant's need, having moved or been moved to a different society, to reestablish life under radically altered circumstances.[107] People act in terms of a variety of mandates and in the context of many social locations, but they are also engaged in thinking about and interpreting the significance of these mandates and locations and deciding upon primacies among them. This is the sense in which character and relationships are understood as emergent: the codes, rules, ideals, values, and prohibitions that define the relationship of self to others are not a once-and-forever phenomenon in anyone's mind.[108] The relationship between individuals and society is continuously being produced. It is established initially and must be reestablished constantly over time, as people negotiate with themselves and others over the prospects and costs of continuing one or another kind of behavior. Thus to the extent that people must continue to function in the everyday world, they do so through the attachment to traditional ideals or, if the occasion should arise, through the attachment to novel ideals, and they do so through the union with authoritative figures, or through the abandonment of these figures in favor of others who can present themselves as worthy proponents of novel kinds of belief and action.

It is important to emphasize again that the three issues taken together, idiosyncratic resolutions to conflict, discontinuities of behavior over time, and the capacity of people to manage active constructions of reality, diminish the importance to social or cultural theory of what Freud considered his most important contribution to the interpretation of culture, unconscious motivation. Moreover, if we add these problems to the many social locations people are obliged to act in as situations and primacies change over time, it becomes easy to see why reality appears to be in flux (in technical terms why the kinds of numerate data social scientists and historians rely on do not remain constant over time, and why the social sciences have trouble with their predictive capacity).[109]

As far as psychoanalysis is concerned, Freud had it right the first time, in this sense: from a strictly psychoanalytic point of view, and with an eye to keeping psychoanalysis independent of other, related disciplines, either the phylogenetic propositions are retained and general statements are possible, or they are not, and what remains is in the realm of idiosyncratic resolutions of conflict with no wider application than individual psychology, the therapeutic situation, and biography. Schur suggested what most psychoanalysts are inclined to suggest once the phylogenetic propositions are abandoned, that is, to historicize the process, or to make sociological propositions out of psychoanalytic observations of the family and the internalization of character traits and values in the context of the family. But as long as there is no phylogenetic unity of unconscious motivation, and no psychoanalytic way of linking the idiosyncratic results of therapy to wider social contexts of stability and conflict without resort to invented and unverifiable "metaphors," such as the ones provided by Freud, Lacan, Melanie Klein, and others, then all that is left to work with in psychoanalytic terms is either a logically constant proliferation of perspectives serving moral or ideological purposes, produced as needed in response to constantly changing social circumstances, or the results of the therapeutic encounter as described.

We should recall that Erikson had also addressed these issues of discontinuity and the active construction of versions of the world.[110] Discussing the adaptive function of certain adolescent processes, Erikson noted, again as a concession to work of Robert Lifton that preceded his, that the fragmentary conflicts of childhood are revived "for the sake of recombining them actively in a new wholeness of experience."[111] Erikson also referred to "the impossibility of ever achieving an identity as fully formed, as static, as secure, as could be done (or so it now seems) in past periods," suggesting that "identity formation can adapt itself to multiple demands." "While it is true that some basic design is formed in adolescence, such a design need not—and should not—foreclose all variations for once and for all. . . . [I]t is quite possible in principle that rapid changes in technology and culture can count on *some* adaptiveness of identity throughout life."[112]

It is the hesitation implied in the word "some" that is the problem—for the sense of a capacity for active reconstruction, or the sense of a capacity for invention or reinvention of identity that Erikson also wrote about,[113] implies a lot that cannot then be easily accommodated to Erikson's principal notions of identity formation in a familial and communal context. As Erikson explained, "[i]dentity is both an individual and a communal concept because you cannot have a sense of identity—or better, you cannot grow a sense of identity step for step through the life stages—without anchoring it in the group setting."[114] Erikson hesitated, then, because it is difficult in the abstract to envision, given the different assumptions, how a sociology or social theory might emerge from them. Erikson had difficulty reconciling what he obviously realized was possible in terms of character change—given the circumstances of his own life, if nothing else—with the identity and internalization concepts and their familial and communal implications.

Thus, Erikson remains an enigmatic figure in the history of psychoanalysis because he was of two minds on the subject of the changeableness of people in a social context.[115] Sometimes he seemed to be implying no more, really, than the use of character traits at higher or more complex levels of generalization as people move into the adult world of family and work. At other times he suggested much more in a way that is insightfully prescient given recent cultural signs, but that also contradicts his larger sociological and historical ambitions. It has often been said that Erikson's theoretical contributions could not be effectively adapted by others and that he was therefore unable to found a school. One important reason is that his exceptional insight into individual lives, particularly the lives of great individuals, was manifestly inconsistent with the sociology he had in mind to develop.[116] He was never able to square this circle. Neither were any of the other psychoanalytic initiatives, especially those based on the ego psychology, able to do so.

CLINICAL ISSUES

There are of course psychoanalysts and readers of psychoanalysis for whom these issues are not very important. If they think about the problems at all they handle them in one of several ways that avoid recognition of the seriousness with which Freud viewed them and the way that he chose to address them. They may imagine that the contents patients report originate in the pressures of bodily demands on the mind, leading to "a far-reaching attribution of qualities to the drives,"[117] although Freud explained that the drives are without quality and the content must come from some other source.[118] Or they have a commonsense notion of fantasy-thinking as a mode available to individuals who construct unique fantasies peculiar to their own lives; accordingly, Freud "attributed their complaints [the complaints of his patients] to fantasy. . . . Psychoanalysts believe this was the discovery of psychic reality. That is, each of us carries our own version of our history and experiences that are influenced by many factors beyond simple objective reality, including age (and cognitive development), prior experiences and wishes and fears."[119] Or they adopt a third approach, following one of the versions Freud gave of an instruction that appeared to him in a dream he recalled from the night before his father's funeral: "You are requested to close the eyes."[120]

Those for whom these issues are important but who have given up the possibility of a consistent cultural or social theory in psychoanalytic terms, at least for the time being, have offered another solution, an emphasis on clinical rather than cultural concerns.[121] As I noted earlier, radicals have complained for a long time about this emphasis, which they claim is intended to domesticate Freud and make psychoanalysis more palatable to a bourgeois society. Indeed, the emphasis is so pronounced that even psychoanalysts have commented on it. John Gedo noted that American psychoanalysis has become more and more therapeutic in orientation, having largely abandoned Freud's program "of supplying the psychological core for a science of man."[122] Philip Holzman, too, has decried the overwhelming emphasis on therapeutic practice, which he claims has led to the increasing isolation of psychoanalysis from other spheres of critical activity.[123]

However, this narrowed focus cannot be viewed simply as an ideological gesture, or a result of the medicalization of psychoanalysis, or anything like that. Rather, the focus on therapeutic practice has occurred to this extent because there seems at the moment no other effective way for psychoanalysts to proceed. We have already noted Joseph Sandler's insistence on the primacy of clinical concerns. Robert Wallerstein, past president of both the International and the American Psychoanalytic Associations and for more than twenty years American editor or associate editor of the *International Journal of Psychoanalysis*, also advised his colleagues in his plenary address to the International Association (1987), that the only way to keep psychoanalysis from fragmenting beyond repair is for psychoanalysts to surmount decisively the problems presented by "psychoanalytic pluralism," i.e., the ability to make plausible interpretive statements from an ever increasing number of vantage points.[124] And the best way to do this is by concentrating more exclusively on clinical observations and the data of the consulting room, and to concentrate also on "low-level and experience-near" clinical theory, which is all "the theory that psychoanalysis needs and is indeed all the theory that its data can truly sustain and can test." Wallerstein stated that anything beyond this experience-near theory is in the realm of "metaphor," or as historians would rather put it, in the realm of ideology or discourse. Wallerstein concluded with respect to all the different and distinguishing theoretical positions that at this stage of development the large-scale explanatory metaphors remain useful for providing a sense of coherence and closure to the psychological understandings of clinicians and to their psychoanalytic interventions. "They are therefore the metaphors we live by, that are our pluralistic psychoanalytic articles of faith, and that I feel in our current developmental stage to be essentially beyond the realm of empirical study and scientific process."[125]

The significance of Wallerstein's statements and of his and Sandler's references to clinically and technically oriented theory and to therapy are clear enough: they have made explicit the need to retreat from what had once been a more optimistic perspective. These references all but contradict Freud's wish that psychoanalysis not be reduced to a clinical specialty or become "a handmaiden of psychiatry," that the therapeutic aspect of psychoanalysis not become the dominant one, that psychoanalytic effort be directed primarily to cultural analysis and interpretation. Freud stated in his famous defense of lay analysis that he only wanted "to feel assured that the therapy will not destroy the science." Freud later explained that he was not in any event a therapeutic enthusiast.[126] However, Freud's wishes aside, psychoanalysts can no longer be as sanguine about prospects as he was, they are no longer as certain that his discoveries represented a decisive turn in cultural interpretation. On the contrary, Wallerstein and Sandler came to their conclusions because they needed to be realistic about the situation of psychoanalysis and because the best way to handle the weight of disappointed expectations as epitomized in the constant and seemingly unending proliferation of vantage points and the constant infighting among proponents of the different vantage points is to go back to square one, clinical practice, and for the most part stay there.

The title and content of Wallerstein's paper, "One Psychoanalysis or Many?" also recalls the title and content of an earlier paper by another prominent American psychoanalyst, George S. Klein, "Two Theories or One?" Klein referred to the exceptional circumstance that psychoanalysts employ two kinds of theory in their work, the abstract metapsychological theory distinguished by a language of psychic energy and economics, of force, mechanism, discharge, cathexis, drive and drive energy in a state of fusion, diffusion, or neutralization, describing processes of tension and tension reduction in the organism; and the kind of experience-near clinical theory Wallerstein referred to, involving a language of relationships, encounters, conflicts, wishes, crises, dilemmas, and conscious and unconscious fantasies. Klein's point, and Wallerstein's, is that the clinical theory involves narrative contents and meaning, and that there is a language appropriate to this level of theory, including projection, resistance, repression, identification, and the like.[127] Moreover, according to Wallerstein, the clinical practice of psychoanalysts, whatever their larger standpoints may be, is sufficiently alike in terms of clinical theories of defense and anxiety, conflict and compromise, transference and countertransference, to make feasible a concerted effort at scientific endeavor at this level.[128]

However, psychoanalysts themselves have underscored the problematic status of psychoanalysis even at this level and questioned Wallerstein's hopeful depiction of "the common ground of psychoanalysis."[129] As Cecilio Paniagua put it, "[i]f we have common ground how come we do such different things?"[130] On the testimony of psychoanalysts themselves, the manner of conducting analysis is "extremely heterogeneous," as ideal-typical recommendations are ignored or transgressed all the time.[131] Arnold Goldberg has pointed out that there is "a sometimes startling and bewildering array of therapeutic interventions," adding that there is no true way to proceed; the rules of the process, the theory behind it, the type of communicative exchange all may be different from one analyst to the next and even in the practice of any single analyst over time.[132] Sandler explained that psychoanalysts often work with implicit "private theories" that are worth examining for their content but are hard to pin down because those who hold them would just as soon not make them public and suffer the criticisms of colleagues that are bound to follow.[133] Schafer has argued, too, that the key words of clinical practice, transference, analyze, resistance, regression, do not have reliable definitions, they are used in association with too many different developmental perspectives; the same point has been made with respect to the concept of defense.[134] In other words, no one knows for certain even now what actually goes on in anyone's practice.

In addition, the fact that the same case material can be plausibly interpreted in a variety of theoretical terms without being able to discriminate better from worse among them implies that there is as yet no established canon for the interpretation of clinical observations, and no way of assessing the relationship between therapeutic outcomes and the value of the various theoretical terms.[135] "'Clinical experience' is the ultimate court of appeal to most practitioners, but the diversity of opinion among analysts about what comprises their clinical experience, or what their clinical experience teaches them, makes this body of data a controvertible source of confirmation."[136] There is in any event a lack of outcome data, there are problems with longitudinal studies, and there has been a notable neglect of the confirmation problem, while the recommendations for attacking the confirmation problem are not encouraging.[137] Moreover, if any of this comes as a surprise, then it is more a matter of postponed insight, or deferred judgment, or loyalty to a community and to a tradition, or indifference to or a failure to understand the importance of the issues raised by psychoanalytic theory and practice than it is a lack of information.

The focus on clinical theory and on the earlier, minimal criteria Freud had established for psychoanalysis (1914), constitutes one tactical approach to the problems just outlined. Then Freud had insisted only on "the facts of transference and resistance. Any line of investigation which recognizes these two facts and takes them as the starting-point of its work has a right to call itself psycho-analysis, even though it arrives at results other than my own."[138] This earlier perspective of Freud's provides the widest opportunity for integrating the multiple and competing perspectives.[139] This integrative approach emphasizes the creative aspects of the competition among different theories, and, at least in Roy Schafer's version, precludes the prospect of "a single master text for psychoanalysis."[140]

A second approach aims at a theoretical revolution in psychoanalysis as a means of restoring an agreed-upon perspective and resolving, or at least diminishing, the dilemma of a seemingly endless proliferation of perspectives. John Gedo noted in 1979 that piecemeal attempts to hold theory together would no longer be adequate, and Sandler had declared his intention to "stoke the fires of theoretical revolution," starting with the structural theory, a target of many contemporary psychoanalysts.[141] Attempts to revolutionize the theory are a credible response, especially if the primary consideration is the development of cultural rather than clinical perspectives. But because this cannot happen apart from reconsideration of the psychoanalytic domain, which implies a much greater degree of change—for example, in training procedures, and in recruiting among people with broader cultural backgrounds and interests—than psychoanalysts have considered before, the continued proliferation of vantage points is the likeliest outcome.

This is not the place to engage further the question of theory development or the complexities of clinical practice. But it is worth noting that the problems of theory and practice are related within psychoanalysis in the following way. Although everyone would agree that clinical practice is not separate from wider social issues and relationships either in material or moral terms, there has been little systematic effort to examine how this might affect either theory or practice in terms of the practical purposes and the moral consequences of working to reintegrate patients comfortably in their everyday routines. Psychoanalysts have not demonstrated sufficient appreciation of the cultural position of psychoanalysis, either in making plain the point of their integrative task, or in clarifying the extent to which psychoanalytic and other forms of therapy are available as a cultural tool to facilitate the reinvention of self, or the invention of a different version of self, for people who feel the need to change what and where they want to be. On the contrary, psychoanalysts continue to stress intrapsychic reality at the expense of the social world, although in order to return people to everyday life in good order they are obliged to smuggle the social world back in. Indeed, they can hardly function in the absence of some knowledge of this world, for they are themselves obliged to participate in the material and moral conditions of it. Psychoanalysts have noted a split within their own ranks on how to treat questions of the interaction between the everyday relationships and the internal world of their patients. They keep promising to do something to repair the split, but they have never managed to do it. The recent turn to the constructivist clinical perspective and the acknowledgment by psychoanalysts of the importance of academic developmental and cognitive psychology, learning theory, and studies devoted to the relationship of emotion, cognition, and memory have thus far underscored the persistence of the split, rather than serving to repair it.[142]

In any event, the theoretical and practical conceptions of the clinical encounter, which takes place in particular and changeable cultural and historical circumstances with all the interpretive dilemmas implied thereby, must be deficient to the extent that this remains true. It is worth noting in this context Benjamin Spock's concluding comment on his efforts to keep his child-rearing manual up to date in the face of constant social change, and the failure of his advice over so many years to affect social relationships in any direction he wanted to go. After six editions and 43 million copies, Spock offered this "bleak verdict" on his fifty-year effort to orient parents to the task of child-rearing: "I don't see that what I've written has made any difference at all."[143]

CHAPTER 4

The Fragmentation of Psychoanalysis

Despite evident gaps and unresolved questions, Freud was convinced that his work represented a fundamental turning point in the cultural sciences and that after him nothing could be the same again. The inter-related series of hypotheses he had elaborated—psychic determinism, the dynamic unconscious, the pleasure principle, a stage theory of development based on the unfolding of libidinal and aggressive drives that show a capacity for fixation, regression, and sublimation, the systematic depiction of conflicts that all individuals must experience and master culminating in the Oedipus complex, the idea of symptoms as a compromise formation that allows a conflicted life to continue, the ideas of defense, repression, resistance, the division of mental processes into spheres or realms encompassing impulsive striving and moral and cognitive capacities, the metapsychological vantage points to the extent that he had developed them as a guide to assessing the comprehensiveness of any analysis,[1] the therapeutic innovations based on "free association," the role of transference, and the basic cultural proposition, the fundamental antagonism between individuals and social order[2]—the whole he deemed correct in principle needing only to be fleshed out in the details.

In 1981, a year before her death, Anna Freud referred back to a lecture she had delivered fifty years earlier on the psychology of children that had focused on the divisions within the child's personality, the constant clashes among the aims of the pleasure-seeking sexual drive, the reasonable, reality-oriented ego, and the moral trends that are closely tied to the parents' wishes and instructions. In this turmoil of conflicting forces, the child's intellect was described as being merely one of the combatants, constantly threatened with being overwhelmed or at least interfered with by the urgency of feelings, wishes, and anxieties. It was, by 1981, an often-told story, for as she pointed out, "[r]epression of childhood memories, the infantile and sexual phases, castration and Oedipus complex, division of the mental apparatus into id, ego, and superego, defense mechanisms in the service of impulse control have become—if not household words—at least familiar concepts." The only thing that needed to be added was the emphasis on aggression, as opposed to Freud's initial emphasis on sexuality. With the exception of this single observation, the information she had imparted fifty years earlier "still stands as correct."[3]

However, none of this was as straightforward as it was made to appear. Aggression turned out to be a more difficult problem than anyone anticipated. The psychoanalytic ego psychologists in the postwar period had hoped to distinguish a nonerotic aggressive instinct from Freud's notion of a "death instinct" and then elaborate a developmental scheme for aggression equivalent to the one that existed for libido, but they were unable to do so.[4] We have already noted that a number of psychoanalysts had rejected on a variety of grounds Freud's assumption that aggression is a primary, independent, nonerotic instinct. It is equally interesting that aggression is not in any case typically discussed in the literature in its instinctual sense, "but in its affective and behavioral sense (as hostility or rage)."[5]

The variety of competing perspectives in this area is characteristic of psychoanalysis in every area. The gaps in theory, the questions that could not readily be answered about early development or the impact of external events on intrapsychic reality or on the emotional, cognitive, and adaptive capacities of people to cope with these events, fostered the constant proliferation of competing perspectives. There is no theoretical or therapeutic vantage point that has not been contested, no innovation that has not been challenged by further innovation. Indeed, in the same publication that Anna Freud's statements appeared, Leo Rangell complained about the effects of this result on theory and practice: "[Melanie] Klein follows a strict technique, emphasizing an almost exclusive interpretation of transference; Kohut stands for a use of transference permitting idealization and providing empathy presumed to have been deficient before. Kohut downgrades conflict, stresses defects; Klein and Kernberg center on conflicts, differing from each other, and from Freud, as to their contents. Bion's theories [have little] . . . similarity to any of the others. Fairbairn dismisses metapsychology; Kernberg retains it." And, with references also to Jung, Adler, Rank, Horney, Sullivan, Bowlby, Winnicott, and others, Rangell continued on, invoking finally a comment of J. S. Grotstein's on the psychoanalytic "cafeteria of paradigms."[6]

Moreover, this fragmentation of psychoanalysis has occurred even in areas that Freud had considered bedrock in terms of both practice and theory. With respect to practice, there is nothing of Freud's that has not been examined and rejected by one or another group, including even the fundamental rule, not to mention Freud's insistence on the analyst's objectivity and neutrality, or his notion that the lifting of repressions is the paramount goal of therapy.[7] The same is true for theory with respect to the Oedipus complex, the primacy of the father in psychic life, drive theory and psychic conflict, transference, and so on. I will briefly review indicative examples of important critiques of each of these positions by way of demonstrating the extent of the fragmentation:

The Oedipus Complex Contrary to Freud's expectations, the importance of the Oedipus complex has been radically devalued, partly a result of various object relations theories that either, like Melanie Klein's, place the significant conflicts at an earlier period, or like Kohut's, are not rooted primarily in Freud's drive theory,[8] and partly a result of the diminution over time of Freud's unique authority on this subject.[9] Freud wrote in a footnote added in 1920 to the "Three Essays" that "[e]very new arrival on this planet is faced by the task of mastering the Oedipus complex. . . . With the progress of psychoanalytic studies the importance of the Oedipus complex has become more and more clearly evident; its recognition has become the shibboleth that distinguishes the adherents of psycho-analysis from its opponents."[10] Freud wrote further that "I could not name any neurosis in which this [Oedipus] complex is not to be met with." However, as psychoanalysts proved more willing or felt better able to codify their own experiences and observations, explorations of alternatives to Freud's version of the Oedipus complex—the metaphoric significance of the actions of Laius or Jocasta or still other figures for intrapsychic conflict—occurred much more frequently and were justified, as psychoanalysts also insist, by clinical experience.[11]

A number of other recent statements disputing the paramount importance of the Oedipus complex to psychoanalysis are equally indicative of this larger tendency. On one view, Freud's single greatest contribution to the study of the human mind and the interpretation of culture was not the Oedipus complex, but "the method of free association, referred to as 'the fundamental rule.'"[12] Others have claimed that Freud's distinction between primary and secondary processes is a more likely candidate for this distinction.[13]

The Primacy of the Father Freud's well-known statement from *Civilization and Its Discontents*, "I cannot think of any need in childhood as strong as the need for a father's protection," has not been persuasive to psychoanalysts for a long time. In 1951, Bowlby published his monograph *Maternal Care and Mental Health*, demonstrating decisively the extent to which the appreciation of the paramount role of the mother had already grown in the psychoanalytic literature.[14] In 1951, Loewald also pointed out (with reference to the work of Karen Horney), that mother figures can be hostile and punitive as well as nurturant and protective and that father figures are not primarily hostile: the threatening character of the father is secondary, implying as well that reality is as readily conceived of as integrative as it is conceived of as hostile, a point made more or less at the same time by Erikson and later in different terms by Kohut.[15] Emphasizing Freud's reluctance to address this issue in the kind of forthright way Freud always claimed to have pursued, Loewald wrote (1951) that "much in contrast to the proud and rebellious motto of *The Interpretation of Dreams*—'Flectere si nequeo superos, Acheronta Movebo'—here [on the preoedipal mother in *Civilization and Its Discontents*] he exclaims 'Let him rejoice who breathes the rosy light of day,' as against the diver who has to plunge into the depth and darkness of the ocean."[16] Loewald indicated that it was necessary to make a fresh start "and consider again the relationship between child and mother."[17] On this same subject in the following year, in a group of papers devoted to the preoedipal mother, Maxwell Gitelson wrote that pathological development may be established by earlier constellations of factors than the Oedipus complex, "there may be more primitive libidinal positions which may be of central importance," a position already systematically and lengthily discussed in the course of the bitter debates within the British Psycho-analytical Society between Anna Freud and Melanie Klein.[18] It is useful to recall as well Winnicott's introduction of the concept of "transitional objects and transitional phenomena" emphasizing the primacy of mother-child interactions, in 1953.[19]

Drives and Affects   Departing from classical theory, Loewald argued that the first assumption in psychoanalytic psychology is an interactional field, represented in its most primitive form by the infant-mother psychic matrix. "What we call *instincts* in psychoanalysis—libido-aggression, or erotic-destructive, or life and death instincts—do not *ab initio* reside in an already separate psychic unit, the infant (or infant-self)." Loewald argued, in reference to the earliest stages of development, that "*instinct* (or *instinctual drive*) is a term for (interactional) psychic processes occurring in that matrix. . . . The [infant's instinctual] repertoire is by its origins already marked by contributions from the motivational repertoire of the caretakers."[20] In addition, Kernberg has argued that affective states represent the most primitive manifestations of drives and constitute essential links of self and object representations from their origins onward: "My theoretical formulation proposes that affects are the primary motivational system and, internalized or fixated as the frame of internalized object relations, are gradually organized into libidinal and aggressive drives as hierarchically supraordinate motivational systems." This concept, Kernberg says, distinguishes his position from the theories of motivation of other major authors whose work had influenced his own,[21] although "the emphasis on the central clinical position of affects is common to all of us."[22] Sandler in particular had long since substituted affect theory for drive theory as a motivational force.[23] Still other psychoanalysts beyond the group mentioned by Kernberg have also placed "affects in the center of motivational experience," for example, "If primary process means the first information-processing system to come on-line, then affects are our real 'primary process.'"[24]

In this context, consider Freud's famous metaphor of id processes as a chaos, a cauldron full of seething excitations, as distinct from the less dramatic observation that the id must have structure.[25] This notion of a structured id appeared quite early in the literature, Paul Federn having suggested long ago, in response to Freud's idea that the ego is a separated and specially differentiated portion of the id, that "[i]t is rather the reverse: the id is largely a series of repressed or 'lived out' ego states. The ego begins with the start of life."[26] Talcott Parsons, too, made the point in his own sociological terms in 1951: Freud's strongly held views precluded the possibility of extending his analysis from the internalization of moral standards "to the internalization of the cognitive frame of reference for interpersonal relations and for the common system of expressive symbolism; and similarly it prevented him from seeing the extent to which these three elements of the common culture are integrated with each other."[27] It is also worth noting that in this same year, 1951, the theme of the Amsterdam Congress of the International Psychoanalytic Association was "The Mutual Influences of the Ego and the Id."[28] The claim that the id has structure has been made many times and in many contexts since then, most notably by Max Schur, Freud's personal physician as well as an important member of the group of psychoanalysts identified as "mainstream."[29]

The drive theory, in short, proved problematic in too many ways, but especially with respect to explaining how cultural or social theorists can account for the specific contents of belief and behavior. Holt, by way of summing up the effects of various shortcomings, declared that the drive theory "is an anachronism beyond hope of rehabilitation;" consistent with a longstanding distinction between the metapsychological and the clinical theories, Holt proclaimed, "Drive is dead; long live wish!"[30]

Transference and Countertransference   Freud had offered the dissolution of the transference relationship in the course of terminating analysis as the guarantee of liberation from symptoms and the demystification of the world, the process by which psychoanalysts—and all those willing to accept the discipline—can become independent of authoritative figures and the heavy hand of the past.[31] But psychoanalysts have raised serious questions about this notion of Freud's, especially in terms of the training of psychoanalysts, let alone in relation to the routine treatment of patients.[32] It is important to emphasize that psychoanalysts themselves are the severest critics of the training process, having explained many times and in many venues that the unequal relationship imposed by the training analysis precludes the dissolution of the transference, so that inappropriate feelings toward authoritative figures unfortunately persist.[33] Edward Glover wrote a long time ago that "[i]t is scarcely to be expected that a student who has spent some years under the artificial and sometimes hothouse conditions of training analysis and whose professional career depends on overcoming 'resistance' to the satisfaction of his training analyst, can be in a favorable position to defend his scientific integrity against his analyst's theory and practice. And the longer he remains in training analysis, the less likely he is to do so."[34]

But Glover's is only the best known of a number of similar commentaries on the shortcomings of the training process, which are widely recognized in the profession. Adam Limentani wrote that a candidate may undertake the training analysis with a solid idealization of his analyst, based on his familiarity with his analyst's writings and areas of interest. "I am much less confident of our overall capacity to deal with this kind of idealization. . . . The real reckoning comes at the end of the training when a candidate expects that someone is going to find out what he has done with his analysis and this can become highly persecutory. . . . Some other analysands end up by identifying with the aggressors located in the teaching organizations, and not excluding their analysts." Limentani went on to address problems of identification and pseudo-identification, concluding that "[a]nalysts . . . are particularly prone to be taken in by certain models and to incorporate them in a static manner."[35] Otto Kernberg has written as well that too often psychoanalytic education is conducted in an "atmosphere of indoctrination," and not in one of open inquiry. "It is true that their own analyses [the analyses of candidates] are highly contaminated by transferences."[36] Anna Freud had earlier stated that although a candidate in the British school could choose one of three courses of study (Freudian, Kleinian, or a middle or independent group), without fail they chose the course of their own analyst's persuasion. Jacob Arlow pointed out that this was a result of identification, not insight, and, referring to Anna Freud's original statement after some two decades, he noted that "[t]he situation still holds true today."[37] There are many other similar commentaries on the training process, references, for example, to "the resistance inherent in idealization of the training analyst," who is the representative of an institute serving also as administrator and "judge," increasing the likelihood that "he will be cast in the role of the protector, the omniscient or omnipotent one."[38] Or again, "[s]ince his [the candidate's] narcissism has been strengthened from the moment he had been admitted for training, a realistic assessment becomes difficult from the beginning."[39] If this inability to resolve transference relationships occurs so frequently among professionals, how different could the results be among ordinary patients? In fact, as Morris Eagle and others have argued, a training analysis is not essentially different from any other analysis.[40]

There is much more that could be said on the subject of transference, particularly in terms of the psychoanalytic involvement with psychotic, narcissistic, and borderline disorders, despite Freud's insistence that psychoanalytic endeavors be limited to the classical transference neuroses.[41] In addition, though Freud only rarely referred to countertransference, which he thought was not worth examining because it interfered with the course of analysis,[42] Paula Heimann and Frieda Fromm-Reichmann underscored the importance of countertransference in 1950, although the literature on the problem expanded significantly in the 1980s, to much greater effect.[43]

The critical process has never been easy, to be sure. The manifest loyalty to particular perspectives among psychoanalysts, along with hostility to those critical of them, is an old story, and it has been commented on many times.[44] Sandler recalled witnessing "as a very young analyst, a violent argument between two distinguished senior members of the British Psycho-Analytical Society, Willi Hoffer and Michael Balint, over the question of whether or not a state of primary narcissism could be said to exist in the earliest period of life."[45] There have been other, similar reports of angry public disputes between and among psychoanalysts on behalf of one or another perspective.[46] In addition, Peter Loewenberg has noted that the break between Freud and Jung "was largely due to interpersonal dynamics and minimally due to differences in theory."[47] The same things are said of the break between Freud and Ferenczi as well.[48]

There is evident merit to the claim that psychoanalysts have often expressed sectarian habits of thought that contradict the culture of science. This refers especially to a persistent elevation of Freud; one can still find relatively recent statements affirming his unchallenged primacy, confirming his own valuable observation that conscious awareness of a problem does not imply control over it.[49] Adam Limentani, in his presidential address to the International Association (1985), stated that "[t]he haunting thought for most psychoanalysts is: What would Freud have said about this or that?" Given the wide appreciation of Alfred North Whitehead's aphorism, "A science that hesitates to forget its founders is lost," the thought that should haunt is why this was still a question, or why it should have mattered any longer what Freud would have said.[50]

There have been so many changes, the smaller ones more far-reaching in their incremental impact than the larger, more famous (or notorious) ones, that in very immediate or practical ways Freud has less to do with psychoanalysis all the time. Wallerstein had earlier stated that "Sigmund Freud remains our lost object, our unreachable genius, whose passing we have perhaps never properly mourned, at least not in the emotional fullness that leads to intellective accommodation." But Wallerstein also stated that this continuing fantasy presence is the source of feelings among too many psychoanalysts "of a continuing dependency that can both be infantilizing and stultifying."[51]

There are many well-known instances of rough treatment of psychoanalysts who were perceived as contradicting some important idea or other. Ruth Mack Brunswick reported that "[w]hen we attempt to examine the origins and precursors of the oedipus complex, we encounter among analysts an opposition not unlike the earlier opposition of the outside world to the oedipus complex itself." Brunswick claimed that Freud had authorized her pursuit of this theme, but no matter, she was attacked anyway. Phyllis Greenacre reported a similar experience; and many more psychoanalysts have as well.[52] As Holt noted some time ago, "to challenge Freud's theories has usually been responded to with anxiety, as if a sacrilegious outrage were being perpetrated."[53]

One special feature of this contentiousness among psychoanalysts stems from the belief that alternative arguments cannot occur apart from the personal characteristics of those making them. The typical conclusion is that he/she was insufficiently analyzed, which was essentially what Melanie Klein said of Anna Freud, to take one example.[54] Holt reported, too, that when he began his critiques of psychoanalytic theory in the 1960s, his friends and colleagues reacted with such shock and concern that for many years he did not try to publish the particular paper in which he introduced his viewpoint. Even later, when he raised doubts about the usefulness of the metapsychology, "friends would still gently suggest that a piece of unanalyzed negative transference seemed to be bothering me." Acknowledging his respect for the way Sandor Rado had earlier handled this kind of critique even while Freud was still alive, Holt explained that theorizing in the profession "gets bound up with individual ambitions and struggles for recognition, [leading] . . . to polemical attacks and angry defense; often the level of debate sinks beneath the weight of so much emotion and threatened self-esteem."[55]

One approach critical observers have adopted as a means of getting around the problem is to underscore an attachment to Freud even when challenging the most basic of his premises, often implying in addition that if Freud had thought about it more he would have come to the same conclusion. Lacan's claimed connections to Freud even as he shifted the ground have been referred to as peculiar and even as mind-boggling.[56] But Lacan's "return to Freud" is just one more adaptation of an old trick;[57] authors do not return to Freud, they appropriate him for their own purposes. Thus in a chapter entitled "Freud's Alleged Missing Theory," Charles Spezzano explains that with *Inhibitions, Symptoms, and Anxiety* Freud was on the brink "of developing the reading of his theory of affects that I am undertaking here, but he did not read it as radically as I want to read it. . . . My interest here is in traveling the rest of the way with Freud's conscious and unconscious thinking about affects." What follows, of course, is Spezzano's perspective on affects, not Freud's.[58] Herbert Marcuse, too, belabored Ives Hendrick for his suggestion of an "instinct to mastery," declaring as piously as he dared that "[a]s usual, the revision of Freudian theory means a retrogression." At the same time Marcuse argued, contrary to Freud, that "the Oedipus complex, although the primary source and model of neurotic conflicts, is certainly not the central cause of the discontents in civilization, and not the central obstacle for their removal." Marcuse also observed that "[i]t is only beyond this [patriarchal] reality principle that the 'maternal' images of the superego convey promises rather than memory traces— images of a free future rather than a dark past."[59] Freud, who was angered by Wilhelm Reich's utopian radicalism on the one hand, and Melanie Klein's views on the early oedipal complex and its maternal roots on the other, would not have treated Marcuse's radical synthesis any more gently, though one would never get that impression from Marcuse's comments.[60]

Interesting too, particularly in light of the comments of Loewald and other psychoanalysts noted earlier, is Margaret Mahler's statement that she "maintained a rather personal interest in one specific aspect of the rich heritage that Freud bestowed upon us, namely, his emphasis on the fact that lifelong, albeit diminishing, emotional dependence on the mother is a universal truth of human existence."[61] By contrast, Schur wrote that in *The Ego and the Id* (1923), Freud had just begun to recognize the primary role of the mother and the early infant-mother relationship. In *Civilization and Its Discontents*, Freud still claimed that "I cannot think of any need in childhood as strong as the need for a father's protection."[62] Irving Harrison explained that even in the mid-1930s Freud still had not taken the infant's early experiences of its mother fully into account, and he noted that Freud's attachment to the phylogenetic propositions "obscured the mother's crucial role in the personal history of the individual."[63] Roy Schafer has also pointed out that "Freud ignored the individuality of particular mothers and the phenomenology of particular mother-child relationships."[64]

A second approach to the problem is to acknowledge the gravity of challenging received doctrine while expressing the hope that one will be allowed amicably to adopt an independent position. George S. Klein related how an esteemed colleague had more or less accused him of wanting to abandon the drive theory. Of course, having for some time been attached to the value system of mainstream psychoanalysis he recognized the statement as an indictment based on a perceived violation of sacrament, not as an invitation to inquiry. "And in the offing is a gentleman's equivalent of the pyre, perhaps intellectual isolation in the community. So my reflex was a somewhat testy defensiveness, an impulse to cry, 'No, no you misunderstand'—a not untypical plea of the guilty."[65] Kohut responded similarly to a colleague's suggestion that the anxious response of the older group of psychoanalysts to his work was not so much "that we become grownup but that we become different." Kohut began to worry: "Am I the Pied Piper who leads the young away from the solid ground of the object-libidinal aspects of the Oedipus complex? Are preoedipal and narcissistic factors perhaps no more than precursors and trimming . . . ? Does not lie behind the preconscious fear that the younger generation will be 'different' the deeper and more powerful fear of their killing wish for which the narcissistic concern is only cover and disguise?"[66] Pinchas Noy wrote as well: "In the course of a discussion at a psychoanalytic gathering where I raised some of my ideas, one of the discussants stood up and with an accusing finger pointed incisively at me: 'I would like you to tell us frankly whether or not you still believe in the libido.' I was, of course, embarrassed at such an accusation and I stuttered something to justify myself."[67]

If nothing else, these approaches to Freud's work, meant to forestall the reproaches of colleagues, reveal the extent to which change in psychoanalysis was often not so much a matter of observations or experience as it was a matter of authoritative opinion, social location, and loyalty to a community.[68] However, despite the pressures to conform, the process of fragmentation has never been interrupted, and the only way to maintain any semblance of peace in the psychoanalytic community is to ignore the narrower of Freud's conceptions of psychoanalysis focused on the Oedipus complex and the primacy of sexuality and to fall back on Freud's earlier (1914) conception, which is loose enough to absorb the ever increasing variety of perspectives.[69] There never was a period, from the beginning of Freud's systematic development of psychoanalysis on, when fellow analysts were not ready, in one way or another, to tell him or anyone what was what, starting with Alfred Adler's assertion (1909) that "there is more than one way in psychoanalysis."[70]

The discrepancy between the exceptionally high regard in which Freud continues to be held publicly as one of the great cultural innovators of the century, somehow suggesting to critics that psychoanalysts are incapable of seeing through the shortcomings of his efforts, and the way that psychoanalysts have in fact treated his efforts over a long period of time, is remarkable. Indeed, the different psychoanalytic viewpoints are so at odds with his and with each other that it is sometimes hard to imagine that the authors belong to the same profession or share a common background. We may recall that in his famous case study, "The Wolf Man," Freud referred to accidental external factors and systematic factors of heredity or phylogenetic inheritance: "In this respect, heredity triumphed over accidental experience; in man's prehistory it was unquestionably the father who practiced castration as a punishment and who later softened it down into circumcision."[71] But as Anna Freud later explained (1958), "[i]nvestigation into the first year of life and the consequences of the earliest mother-child relationship had revealed that much may be acquired by the infant that had been considered as innate before, thus putting out of action some more of our basic diagnostic categories."[72] Or as Charles Brenner emphatically put it, "The only mental processes that we can observe, the only ones about which we can collect information by the use of psychoanalysis, are ones which have clearly been influenced by experience, ones which have been, in part, molded by observation, by memory, by thought, however primitive; in a word, ones which involve the functioning of the child's ego."[73] In Freud's terms, of course, ego is in the realm of accidental experience, so that Brenner's emphasis undercut Freud's wishes for the primacy of psychoanalysis in cultural analysis.

In the same vein, Melanie Klein had pushed her conception of psychic development and had described in detail the psychic lives of infants to an extent that Freud, on his own behalf and on behalf of Anna Freud, could not accept.[74] Herbert Marcuse, too, noted in a manner Freud would have deemed unacceptable that "Freud's theory is consistently oriented on early infancy—the formative period of the universal fate of the individual. The subsequent mature relations 're-create' the formative ones. The decisive relations are thus those which are the *least* interpersonal."[75] Lacan, W. R. D. Fairbairn, Bowlby, and Winnicott from their different perspectives also refer to the determinative influence of the first year or year and a half of life. But Anna Freud, noting that "a considerable cross-section of the psychoanalytic community today pins their faith on the analysis of the first year of life" in the hope of modifying the impact of earliest experience, warned against the search for single determinants of conflict in progressively earlier stages of life.[76]

Moreover, we could add to the versions of the mental activity of infants provided by Sigmund and Anna Freud, Melanie Klein, Marcuse, Lacan, Fairbairn, Bowlby, and Winnicott, those of the Balints and the

Sandlers, Erikson and Kohut, Bion, Mahler, Daniel Stern, any number of ego psychologists, feminist authors, members of the French psychoanalytic community, and still other members of the Frankfurt school, and even more beyond all of these. There must be fifty such versions, probably more, which mostly puts one in mind of those television commercials in which babies smile and wave their arms a lot, while a remote, unseen voice-over confidently explains the significance of such joyous behavior, an approach encouraged by the fact that babies have never yet reported on their own behalf.[77]

Indeed, if psychoanalysis is part of a confessional discourse that enables society to exercise control over its citizens, it is because psychoanalysis provided a language that allowed people from a host of vantage points to imagine that the surface confusion of everyday life could be brought under control and that people's motives and intentions could be made transparent. Of course Freud emphasized human sexuality as key to understanding cultural conflict, but that emphasis was vigorously challenged from every direction, as I have noted. Kohut focused on unempathic or failed parenting, an unstable sense of self resulting from psychic deficits, emphasizing the presence and threat of tragic man (as distinct from Freud's version of guilty man), signifying that there are behavioral motives not attributable to sexuality and aggression.[78] Holt also stated that "fear, anxiety, dependence, self-esteem, curiousity, and group belongingness (to name only an obvious handful) cannot validly be reduced to sex and aggression and are motivational themes the therapist cannot afford to ignore."[79] George S. Klein noted that "primary danger and profound anxiety are experienced not only in the eruption of drive and in drive conflict, but in conditions in which conception and perception do not fit the environment in a manner that makes action possible or effective."[80]

In Freud's psychosexual terms, the memory of gratification is the origin of all thinking, and people are condemned to obsessive rumination because the path to any sexual fulfillment is blocked from within.[81] In object relational terms, the absence of the object and the search for restitution is the origin of all thinking. On Freud's view man is pleasure seeking; on Harry Guntrip's view, the pursuit of pleasure as Freud understood it was the result of the failure of object relations.[82] Indeed, many of the British psychoanalysts assumed that people were object seeking rather than pleasure seeking and focused on conflicts and dilemmas stemming from experiences of loss and attempts at restitution. Ian Suttie pointed out in 1935 that separation anxiety was displacing sexual traumata in psychoanalytic etiologies.[83] In still other terms, J.-B. Pontalis wrote, too, that on his view "the theme of death is as basic to Freudian psychoanalysis as is the theme of sexuality. I even believe that the latter was largely accorded a more prominent role in order to conceal the former."[84]

The constant proliferation of competing perspectives is the most characteristic feature of psychoanalysis. Hartmann elaborated notions of ego autonomy, but Marjorie Brierly observed, looking back on her days in practice, that she could not "recall coming across any signs of ego autonomy; my patients' egos seemed much more subject to coercion from within and without."[85] Freud treated his grandson's "fort . . . da" game as a compulsion to repeat in the service of mastering an instinctual wish "beyond the pleasure principle." But Ricoeur argued that the kind of symbolism and play manifest by the child repeats unpleasure "not compulsively, but by creating symbolism out of absence," suggesting "mastery over the negative, over absence and loss."[86] Contrary to Freud's emphasis on sexuality, Ethel Spector Person has emphasized "the nonsexual source of love's urgency. . . . Love is, in part, a roundabout quest for perfection, for the restoration of one's lost narcissism."[87] Freud thought of depression in terms of identification, the shadow of the lost object falling upon the ego, the loss of the object becoming transformed into a loss in the ego. Edward Bibring, acknowledging also the work of Sandor Rado, Otto Fenichel, and Edith Jacobson, supplanted Freud's understanding of depression with one of his own, defining depression as "the emotional expression (indication) of a state of helplessness and powerlessness of the ego, irrespective of what may have caused the breakdown of the mechanisms which established . . . self-esteem."[88] Anna Freud's emphasis on aggression corrected her father's emphasis on sexuality, but she retained always the original dual instinct theory (as Kernberg has also).[89] But Jay Greenberg has offered a different dual instinct theory based on concepts of safety and effectance (that is, following suggestions of Sandler and Robert R. White), as distinct from the familiar emphasis on libido and aggression.[90]

Even the dispute between Freud and Sandor Ferenczi over Ferenczi's attempt to correct Freud's therapeutic and theoretical approach, which at one point might well have appeared to have been easily resolved in Freud's favor, is, given "the widening scope" of psychoanalysis, the increasing identification and treatment of psychotic, borderline, and narcissistic disorders, and the adoption of the "constructivist" position by any number of psychoanalysts, far from resolved.[91] Freud wrote in one of his early papers on technique that he could not advise his colleagues "too urgently to mold themselves during psycho-analytic treatment on the surgeon, who puts aside all his feelings, even his human sympathy, and concentrates his mental forces on the single aim of performing the operation as skillfully as possible." But that view was vigorously challenged by Ferenczi, and by Fromm, Kohut, and many others on a variety of grounds.[92]

Anna Freud objected that Kohut's work, because of his particular emphases, could no longer be considered psychoanalytic.[93] But Winnicott offered what should be the last word on this particular subject, affirming that "We are all Freudians," which is true enough if Freud's earlier, less exacting (1914) standard for psychoanalysis is invoked.[94] If we consider the difference between Freud's vision of the mother as the prototype of all later sexual satisfactions and Winnicott's depiction of the mother-infant relationship, the nursing couple, as basic to his notion of asexual, "good-enough" mothering, we can understand the point of Winnicott's statement.[95]

In Freud's mind psychoanalysis supplied the thread that could lead people out of the cultural labyrinth, but given the fragmented situation I have described, it is more appropriate to argue that psychoanalysis leads people into yet other corners of the labyrinth, with all the frustrating debate this entails.[96] Individuals who were believed to have shared a vantage point, or who did share a vantage point, often disagreed with each other in important ways;[97] individuals who may well have been publicly venerated were more often the subject of criticism from within the profession than outsiders realized;[98] psychoanalysts who could have been more critical of Freud and psychoanalysis than they were, chose, for whatever reason, to act with restraint, Erikson, Winnicott, and Michael Balint among them.[99] Between Loewald and Hartmann, Hartmann and Kernberg, Kernberg and Kohut, Kohut and Lacan, Lacan and Winnicott, Winnicott and Anna Freud, Anna Freud and Bowlby, there are no reconciliations. Hence the merit of Gerald Weissmann's general comment on the changing interpretations of disease: "We fail to recognize the tentative narrative myth of 'scientific' explanations at our own risk: they are as transient as the structure of recollection."[100]

Each individual and school I have mentioned (and there are still others I could have mentioned) represents a distinct psychoanalytic vantage point not readily reconciled to the others or, more likely, not reconcilable with the others at all.[101] The tendency to compel compliance and the sense of transgression following from the failure to comply have never completely disappeared. We may judge by the intense self-scrutiny of those who challenged doctrine, in addition to the equally intense and cutting scrutiny of colleagues, just how difficult the process was for different individuals. But the kinds of pressures that were applied never really proved to be effective.[102] On the contrary, psychoanalysts proved better able to adopt conflicting viewpoints, abandon failed ones, or move off in unexpected directions than their critics ordinarily give them credit for.[103]

Attempts were made to ensure that power resided in one place or in one approach to theory, while concessions to Kleinians, for example, or later to other object relations theorists like Bowlby or Winnicott were only grudgingly made.[104] But that world has passed, with respect both to clinical and cultural concerns, because there was no empirical basis for maintaining it, because experiences and interpretations of experience were too varied, particularly between and among different societies, and because there emerged too many independent institutional arrangements capable of sustaining the vantage points of different authoritative figures. The kind of control Freud might once have attempted to impose proved impossible to arrange finally because of the clinical experiences of psychoanalysts in different times and places, but also because of the organizational shape of psychoanalysis. There was no way to control careers by manipulating resources that were managed locally or cutting off access to publication or to an audience.

Thus Sandler outlined a concept of motive force that challenged the primacy of Freud's drive theory to an audience at the New York Psychoanalytic Association in 1964, commenting on the strain produced by "bringing the energy theory into the picture in order to reduce all motivation to drives and drive-derivatives." Sandler suggested, among other things, that sublimation might be better dealt with by "a theory of displacement and affect change rather than [by] one of energy transformation." The discussion that followed, which involved a number of prominent psychoanalytic ego psychologists devoted to drive theory and energy propositions, became "rather heated." "Heinz Hartmann cordially disagreed with our ideas, but Rudolph Loewenstein warned us most emphatically that we were treading an extremely dangerous path that could only result in our ruination. Looking back I can only say that what we had to say at that meeting must have aroused substantial anxiety in our listeners as well, of course, as in ourselves."[105] That never stopped Sandler from pursuing his own course.

What it comes down to is that no theoretical vantage point proved persuasive enough to hold the discipline together, particularly because of the inability to resolve problems stemming from competing developmental, clinical, and cultural theories. Different perspectives were too inferential to be confirmable by data and too varied to be integrated in any unified frame of reference. As a result, there are multiple and diverse theories that remain valid in the fragmented psychoanalytic domain because they have a deductive coherence, because any theory that provides coherence and closure is arguably as good as any other one in the absence of evidence, and because proponents of each of the theories are institutionally protected.

In addition, though a great deal of energy has been expended on discussions of a new translation of Freud's complete works to supplant Strachey's *Standard Edition*, which many deem deficient because it presents Freud's texts as more homogeneous and scientistic than they really are, the effect will be the opposite of the one apparently intended.[106] For the more accurate the translation, the more allusive, ambiguous, metaphoric, and even contradictory Freud appears to be; in a more faithfully rendered translation, the more versions of Freud or of psychoanalysis there will turn out to be. Psychoanalysts, scholars, and other interested observers use the collected works in whatever language they appear in a "transitional" sense, or in an ideological or moral sense, as the occasion for elaborating different versions of the world, and a better translation is not going to interrupt this process.

Whatever one makes of the restrained, tentative, sometimes even devious way that psychoanalysts and others approached the perceived shortcomings of Freud's version of psychoanalysis, there was no way that the succession of observations could have been assimilated in any body of theory that Freud would have approved of. When it comes to the impact of mainstream critiques of theory particularly, the persistence of loyalty to Freud and his authoritative presence is less important than the fact that the changes suggested over a period of time have led to versions of psychoanalysis that would have been unacceptable and even, as with constructivist views of clinical practice, unrecognizable to him.[107] This includes, it should be noted, the integration of important aspects of the work of Adler, Jung, and others that tended to illuminate some perspective that Freud, in the desire to defend his own system, had excluded with unfortunate results, sometimes, as he later realized with respect to aggression, even from his own point of view.[108] One proof of this assertion is the many discrete concepts subsequently borrowed from the "defectors'" and adapted to mainstream theory by psychoanalysts who would likely have taken Freud's side in any of these disputes.[109] In fact, a case can be made for the reintegration within psychoanalysis of Jung and Adler, for as Loewenberg has noted, Jung appears in a 1913 paper of his "as the forerunner of modern psychoanalytic ego psychology with its emphasis on the presenting life crisis, adaptation and adjustment, and the potential for regression in a crisis situation. His position was neither mystical nor racial. There is much in it that would be entirely acceptable to modern psychoanalytic clinicians."[110]

More specifically, what would Freud have made of the many recurrent observations that challenge particularly his cultural interests: the paramount role of the mother, the primacy of the environment over nature, the primacy of language over drive, the notion that the environment can be integrative and nurturant as well as hostile and punitive, that environmental contacts serve to structure the drives (actually wishfulness and not drives, as suggested by the work of Holt, Sandler, and others), the primacy of affect as against drive, the importance of narcissism and of self-esteem in relation to the social world, and the paramount importance to the project of what the psychoanalysts refer to as object loss broadly conceived, a possibility that Freud had adumbrated in *Mourning and Melancholia* and in other works but that has been extensively elaborated since then.[111] Just think for a moment about Sandler's suggestion to consider "'the child within' rather than the id as the source of peremptory conflictual impulses," which may but need not refer to sexual or aggressive impulses. Freud's point about mind and self was that sexuality and aggression are the most important features of life, particularly of communal life, and potentially the most destructive features of it. The point of this post-Freudian psychoanalysis is that the viability of object relationships is the most important feature of life, particularly communal life, and the absence, failure, or perceived transgression of hitherto cherished standpoints is potentially the most destructive feature of it. Sandler claims that "the basic core of agreement within psychoanalytic thinking is substantial," but this is a political statement meant to encourage continued dialogue. It is not even true with respect to Sandler's specific context, "the practical tasks of the analyst."[112]

This is to say, far from being the authoritatively controlled and easily managed discipline that critics have often claimed it to be, psychoanalysis is and has always been anarchic in its tendencies, resembling too much its clinical subject, the idiosyncratic individual. As Freud's correspondence reveals, he came to regret the energy he had to expend keeping people and things together, and in fact he could not do it.[113] For not only was Freud's version of psychoanalysis insufficient to encompass the theory and practice of the famous "defectors," it was insufficient to the theory and practice of his close adherents as well.[114] Sandler has noted that while psychoanalytic theory is not fully integrated and complete, "it has a solid central core based on Freud's ideas."[115] But psychoanalysis in this respect resembles carbon more than diamond; it is easier to claim a core than it is to identify one.[116]

ANOTHER LOOK AT THE SEDUCTION THEORY

Among the many competing perspectives that have emerged there is one in particular that I want to draw attention to because it reveals the extent to which psychoanalysts have been able to challenge Freud's version of psychoanalysis, particularly in terms of the impact of the social world on people, the rather masked or hidden way in which this often occurs, and also the limitations on cultural analysis inherent in any psychoanalytic perspective. I refer to a continuing interest in (or a reluctance to let go of) Freud's original seduction theory (or theories), or more accurately, his original "events and affects" (or cognitive/affective) approach to theory, which keeps pushing its way back to the surface.[117] We should recall Anna Freud's admonition to look at the useful things that psychoanalysis has lost historically in the development of theory, by way of emphasizing that the approach undergirding the successive versions of the seduction theory that Freud had struggled with before his "breakthrough" may include such things.[118]

The point is that Freud's earlier depiction of traumatic events has sociological implications in terms of the different affective and cognitive responses to these events. Freud's "events and affects" logic turned up again in *Inhibitions, Symptoms, and Anxiety*, in Anna Freud's gloss on it (*The Ego and the Mechanisms of Defense*, 1936), and in the work of Ernst Kris, Joseph Sandler, and Edith Jacobson, and it still persists today. In particular, there is a sometimes spoken, sometimes unspoken understanding or recognition among a number of psychoanalysts that Freud's development of psychoanalysis after he abandoned the seduction theory hampered rather than facilitated progress toward the goal he had set for his project, cultural analysis and interpretation. When it comes to social or cultural theory, in other words, Freud was doing better before the "breakthrough" than he was able to do afterwards, either in phylogenetic terms, or in terms of the ego psychology he introduced and others, notably Hartmann, Kris, and Anna Freud, subsequently elaborated. Freud's initial events and affects logic is not sufficient for a consistent, systematic sociological vantage point, but it was a better place to begin than the one Freud finally insisted upon.

Masson, who argued that Freud was wrong to have abandoned the seduction theory, cited a letter from Anna Freud to him in response to his argument. She wrote: "Keeping up the seduction theory would mean to abandon the Oedipus complex, and with it the whole importance of phantasy life, conscious or unconscious phantasy. In fact, I think there would have been no psychoanalysis afterwards."[119] This statement is worth taking another look at because it may not be entirely correct. Masson had a particular cause to promote, and he got into such hot water with his attack on Freud's character that the need to raise questions about the value to social or cultural theory of what Freud had done, and what the alternatives to Freud's version of psychoanalysis might have been, got lost. Still, not only are these questions worth raising, but psychoanalysts persist in raising them. For as Bennett Simon has pointed out, psychoanalysts from the beginning have been of two minds on the role of the external world and traumatic experience: they know they cannot exclude these issues, but they do not know how to fit them in either.[120]

Lest all this still appear too cryptic, let us follow the logic of one psychoanalyst, Joseph Sandler, as he has laid it out in a succession of papers.[121] To begin with, Sandler noted that "[f]rom a psychological point of view it is sufficient for us to take, as a basic unit, the *wish*."[122] Given Holt's declaration quoted earlier, "Drive is dead; long live wish!" and Holt's observation that Freud worked at least until 1905 without a drive theory, this is not an innocent observation. For as Holt went on to note, wish is the main motivational concept in the *The Interpretation of Dreams*. In addition, "[t]he main dynamic concept in *Studies in Hysteria*—affect-charged, repressed memories—has most of the major defining properties of wish: It is a cognitive-affective concept, framed in terms of meanings."[123]

Sandler's statement, then, should be taken as a signal, a cue, a reference to directions and prospects. Sandler also noted that "[t]he wish contains representations of self and object in interaction. One does not simply have a wish to exhibit oneself, for instance, but the hoped-for reaction of the audience is equally part of the wish." That is, the wish has social or cultural content and context, it emerges from real contacts or from a real relationship however construed on either side, meaning that the wishing person is a socialized person, and insofar as Sandler also notes that "[s]uch [socialized] relationships start early in life, and also exist in our wishful fantasy lives," the id cannot be conceived of as a chaos, a cauldron full of seething excitations. Rather the id—if one still wants to use Freud's structural language, and Sandler does not—must be conceived of as having structure.[124]

Sandler also argues that it is no longer tenable to claim that all wishes are derived from sexual or aggressive drive activity. "Just as the tension produced by drive stimuli may evoke wishes, so can other stimuli (e.g., external stimuli) call forth the wish. If, for some reason, there is a lessening of our background feeling of safety, appropriate wishes to do something that would restore that feeling of security are evoked." Sandler has emphasized that a psychoanalytic psychology of motivation that does not take instinctual drives into account is an impoverished one. But whatever value a concept of drives may still have for clinical practice, it is irrelevant to Freud's broader expectations for social and cultural analysis. In this broader context, the drive concept is not necessary within the social or cultural perspective that can be inferred from Sandler's work or from the work of others I have cited here, Holt, George S. Klein, or Kohut.[125]

In fact, Sandler's posture reminds one of Kohut's when Kohut was still claiming that the self psychology was complementary to and not independent of "mainstream" psychoanalysis, before it became clear that psychoanalysis could not absorb Kohut's work without important revisions.[126] By way of confirmation, Sandler offered an argument he had been making for over three decades on behalf of his own vantage point: "A psychoanalytic psychology of motivation related to the control of feeling states should, I believe, replace a psychology based on the idea of instinctual drive discharge."[127]

No wonder Loewenstein had warned Sandler that he was treading a dangerous path. The concept of drives in terms of particular aims was important to Freud's version of psychoanalysis for the same reason that money is important to any economist's version of the market place: some kind of energy directed at a goal is required to cause the system to begin to function and then to sustain it. However, once alternative motives for action are provided, for example, the "regulation of self-esteem, and the search for meaning" as a major adaptive strategy involving a feared loss of reality, or a feared inability to continue to organize experience or make sense of the world, drive theory as Freud understood it can be dropped.[128] Sandler emphasized that threats to feelings of safety, injuries to self-esteem, feelings of guilt and shame, threats from the social world, and anxieties of different sorts, all constitute highly important motives of clinical but also, by extension, sociological significance. Thus Sandler has also emphasized "that a large number of 'peremptory,' 'automatic,' 'urgent,' and 'compelling' tendencies arise within the apparatus *which are not drive motivated at the time*," and that "*[n]ot all unconscious wishes derive from the instinctual drives.*"[129]

In short, whatever comes after Sandler's reference to libidinal and aggressive drives as highly important motives is what counts for his perspective, at least in social terms. It is important to note that Sandler's paramount interest is adaptive and clinical, focused on genetic-developmental propositions in terms of the biological organism, the pleasure-unpleasure principle, and the dynamic unconscious. But insofar as his work is oriented to adaptive responses to events in the sense of society as a "background of safety" within which people can function to realize their own purposes, then it has sociological as well as clinical implications.[130]

There are more observations worth making here, but one in particular stands out, Sandler's reference to a well-known statement of Kris's from 1947. Kris's statement deserves to be recognized among the many challenges to Freud's version of psychoanalytic theory that appeared soon after the Second World War, that is, for all practical purposes very soon after Freud had died and as soon as the audience could again be reconstituted. "In 1926, in *Inhibitions, Symptoms, and Anxiety*, Freud reformulated a considerable set of his previous hypotheses. I am convinced that this reformulation reaches further than was realized at the time of publication, possibly by Freud himself."[131] In fact, Kris (with

Hartmann) eventually said even more, referring to *Inhibitions, Symptoms, and Anxiety* as "Freud's greatest contribution to the psychology of the ego."[132] These comments are best viewed, moreover, in the context of Robert White's statement that "it can no longer be claimed that the two instinctual drives are the sole driving forces of behavior and the ultimate cause of activity. *Inhibitions, Symptoms, and Anxiety* was a revolution which destroyed forever the psychodynamic special privileges of libido and aggression."[133]

This text of Freud's, also focused on separation, loss, and affect, was important to the work of the ego psychologists as it is also to the work of Sandler, who is critical of the ego psychologists. However, there has always been a problem locating this text in the body of Freud's work; it is not clear where it fits. James Strachey wrote in the editor's introduction of the *Standard Edition* that Freud continued to have trouble with it and that he "found an unusual difficulty in unifying the work." Rangell also wrote that "[i]t was Freud himself, who, in the fertile spurt of the late 20s and early 30s, contributed a major shift in the total theoretical position, resulting in new dimensions . . . and a new central orientation." Rangell went on to note that "it is well known . . . that Freud did not make this shift easily, nor was he able to reconcile completely the two quite different theories and approaches."[134]

The reason that Freud had difficulties with this work and the reason that other psychoanalysts had trouble fixing its location in the body of his work is that it too harks back to the period before the "breakthrough," to the period when psychoanalysis was based on the kind of events and affects logic referred to earlier. Given the fact that *Inhibitions, Symptoms, and Anxiety* fits most readily in this context, and that Freud always struggled mightily to preserve the integrity of his primary perspective, it is not hard to see why he had himself written that since he put forward the hypothesis "of the existence of two classes of instinct (Eros and the death instinct) (1920) and since I proposed a division of the mental personality into an ego, a super-ego and an id (1923), I have made no further decisive contributions to psycho-analysis: what I have written on the subject since then has been either unessential or would soon have been supplied by someone else."[135]

The statements of Kris and Rangell could not more obviously have contradicted Freud's.[136] In addition, Kris noted that "[i]f we turn to the ego as the psychic system that controls perception, achieves solutions, and directs actions, we have to insist on distinctions that seemed irrelevant when Freud first formulated his genetic propositions." Anna Freud had also written in *The Ego and the Mechanisms of Defense* (1936) that since the publication of *Inhibitions, Symptoms, and Anxiety*, "the term 'depth psychology' certainly does not cover the whole field of psychoanalytic research." She went on to define as the tasks of analysis, "to acquire the fullest possible knowledge of all the three institutions of which we believe the psychic personality to be constituted and to learn what are their relations to one another and to the outside world." Anna Freud indicated that in this well-known work she was merely summarizing what her father had already done, but in fact, like Kris, she had moved beyond what her father had done, she just chose not to say so at the time.[137]

This was one of those instances when a psychoanalyst felt obliged to disavow a change in perspective in order to protect the unity and integrity of Freud's work. Freud's ego psychology is generally more readily associated with *The Ego and the Id* (1923) than with *Inhibitions, Symptoms, and Anxiety*, but Kris referred to the latter work in the way that he did because it gives the individual an adaptive role in the face of real experience, whereas the earlier work suggested that people were passive recipients of a heteronomous morality.[138] The 1926 text shifted interest from drive to affect (as communication), and it facilitated focusing on the social world as opposed to the intrapsychic world. As Anna Freud went on to say, "The crucial point is that, whether it be dread of the outside world or dread of the superego, it is the anxiety which sets the defensive process going. The symptoms which enter consciousness as the ultimate result of this process do not enable us to determine which type of anxiety in the ego has produced them."[139] This point made a different orientation to the social world possible in terms of affective responses to threatened or actual loss, and it did so most importantly, although neither Anna Freud nor Kris commented on it or necessarily thought about it in terms of social change rather than in terms of the primary focus of *The Ego and the Id*, social stability.[140]

The anxiety book allowed the ego psychologists in the postwar period to offer sociological propositions on a better basis than that provided by *The Ego and the Id*. As Edith Jacobson observed with respect to Freud's 1926 work, his "emphasis on the causal role of reality events in the formation of mental life as such has once again focused attention on the role played by reality in emotional reaction patterns."[141] (Jacobson undoubtedly realized that this would lend added weight to Freud's observations from the period before the breakthrough, that is, before the single-minded emphasis on intrapsychic reality, contrary to Freud's wishes and his sense of what good theory entailed.)

Sandler contended with reference to his own work that psychoanalysis had reached a stage comparable to that which existed in the few years before the introduction of the structural theory in 1923.[142] But this is not entirely correct, for psychoanalysis then still included Freud's phylogenetic constructs, which were indispensable to him for both individual and social psychology. Besides, the emphasis on separation, loss, affect, wishfulness, safety, and self-preservation, vital elements of the basic logic of Freud's work before he abandoned the seduction theory, also suggests otherwise.[143] Given the persistence of certain critical themes, it is fair to argue that psychoanalysis in Sandler's work points back not to 1923 but to 1897, to the period before the "breakthrough."

Thus if one goes back to that early period of Freud's work and imagines where he might have gone with his theory before he decisively seized upon the primacy of intrapsychic reality, where the theory would have ended up if he had devoted time to the elaboration of the external "contingent" factors or the "events and affects" logic, one can imagine prospectively the anxiety book as a follow-up contribution, given Anna Freud's, Kris's, and Jacobson's glosses on it. And if one can then further project the development of this "events and affects" logic, one will get to Sandler, whose work is closer to the Freud of the affect theory than to the Freud of the drive theory. As Sandler indicated, Freud had made affects crucial to his theory before 1897 by relating the origin of affects to trauma and by making affects the source of symptomatic expression. Afterwards Freud began to neglect affects in favor of drive theory.[144]

By way of correcting the effects of this shift, Sandler claimed in 1968 that from a psychological point of view, feeling states in one form or another are the ultimate guiding or regulatory principle in adaptation and that to equate these with energic equilibrium or with drive equilibrium in particular may be misleading or incorrect. "From the point of view of the ego's functioning we are now in a position to say that the prime motivators are conscious or unconscious feeling-states; and that these are, in turn, associated with various forms of representational congruity or discrepancy. *The aim of all ego functioning is to reduce conscious or unconscious representational discrepancy and through this to attain or maintain a basic feeling state of well-being.*" If one goes back to the *Studies in Hysteria*, to the tale told, for example, by Frau Cäcilie, whose neuralgic facial tic Freud explained was a response her husband's insult which felt to her like "a slap in the face," one will find problems of representational congruity and discrepancy and a disrupted sense of a basic feeling state of well-being.[145] One will also find there an "exquisitely social" sense of the ego that strives to maintain "a benign connection with the interpersonal world," and hence also ample references to problems of loss, which Sandler had made a paramount issue in his revision of psychoanalysis.[146]

Consider also in this context the version of fantasy thinking Freud was wrestling with in the spring of 1897, before the breakthrough. This involved things seen, heard, or otherwise experienced that were too threatening or exciting, or too curiosity or anxiety provoking, to assimilate at the time, and for these reasons were imaginatively altered in the retelling to make them more readily acceptable in current cirumstances as conscious expression. This is approximately where Freud was before he began to conjure the prospect of endopsychic fantasy: *"Fantasies arise from an unconscious combination of things experienced and heard,* constructed for particular purposes." Freud goes on to describe the process by which fantasy thinking occurs (that is, "[a] fragment of a visual scene is then joined up to a fragment of an auditory one and made into a fantasy").[147] Such fantasy thinking, characterized by a particular language used to express and assimilate it, was a matter of emotional responses to subjectively perceived events that had or acquired a symbolic significance.

Thus the fantasy reports were both culturally and historically situated attempts to absorb behaviors that were difficult to understand or assimilate at the time they occurred. At this point in the spring of 1897 the notion of archaic heritage or phylogenetic inheritance did not figure in. Robert Wallerstein, in his accounting for Freud's abandonment of the seduction theory, wrote (and many others have written) that "Freud's shift in theory was predicated on his accumulating embarrassing and painful discoveries that the ubiquitous sexual seductions were so often fantasy elaborations, not facts of history."[148] But if there is no archaic heritage or phylogenetic inheritance, then the fantasy elaborations of Freud's patients *are* facts of history, whether the events, the seductions or abuse, had actually occurred as Freud had earlier believed, or whether they had not, as he subsequently insisted.[149]

That is, the question of whether Freud's patients were reporting real events or wish-fulfilling fantasy day-dreams is badly posed, for even the reports of traumatic events (and Freud never denied that some of his patients at least were molested or abused) could not have been veridical, a point that has been made many times, though it bears repeating.[150] The reports were altered, embellished, exaggerated, diminished, according to the needs of the individual at the moment. The relating of that kind of perception had to have a fantasy component in it. Still, even in that form, the reports reveal a lot about the privileged access of men to the social world and the employment of medical and religious ideologies to compel the subordination of women and children, and so on.

It is therefore not clear, as Morris Eagle, Jerome Kagan, and others have noted, that the strength of instincts as such is "naturally and inherently inimical to the welfare of the self," or that "what the panic patient fears is an id impulse."[151] In these terms, objective anxiety (fear of tarantulas in the example provided by Kagan) and moral anxiety are still relevant, the latter particularly insofar as wishful thinking or behavior might violate personal standards. "However, research points to a fourth source of anxiety which Freud seemed to ignore because . . . it did not fit well with his conception of the mechanism of anxiety . . . *the state produced by novel or unfamiliar events which cannot be assimilated or coped with immediately.*"[152] Included in this should be not only the personal experiences of his patients as reported by Freud, but all those normatively perceived events that constitute threatened or actual loss in a social sense, that is, of cultural orientations or authoritative leaders resulting from defeat in war, economic depression, or still lesser forms of change that nevertheless render cherished forms of belief and behavior dysfunctional or unavailable.

Thus if one acknowledges the persistent emphasis on loss among both scientific and hermeneutic critics (Bowlby and Ricoeur, respectively), on affective responses to loss and on the importance of affect as distinct from drive, and on the cognitive capacities of people who are compelled to scan the social world for ways of solving conflicts and dilemmas, particularly when the social world fails to sustain a "background of safety," then one must conclude that the position Freud had begun to develop before the breakthrough made better sense in terms of social change and social theory than anything that followed except perhaps the work on anxiety, which is what gives *Inhibitions, Symptoms, and Anxiety* its anomalous quality. The earlier Freud rooted in the "events and affect" logic, in fantasy representations of subjectively perceived social relationships viewed as a preliminary search for language and for authoritative figures able to help repair threatened or disrupted relationships, has more to recommend it as social theory than any of the other psychoanalytic terms Freud preferred.

There may be a strong temptation at this point to recall suspiciously Masson's critique of Freud, *The Assault on Truth*, and his comments on Freud's "suppression of the seduction theory" as a cowardly evasion of truth, but the temptation should be resisted. Masson's work is irrelevant in this respect; he just muddied the waters with his comments on Freud's abandonment of the seduction theory and his adoption of what ultimately became the drive theory, as if anyone could have invested forty years of painstaking labor, elaborating intricate theories of child development and adult conflict, theories that still retain a wide audience and have wide applicability for scholars in a dozen fields, on the strength of a cowardly evasion of the truth, or, more bluntly, on the strength of a lie.

However, there is, and there was before Masson, a hankering after the earlier version of psychoanalysis, an implicit acknowledgment that Freud gave up too much when he made that move. His famous discoveries could not take him where he wanted to go, as the work of Sandler and Kris suggests. By contrast, what he gave up could have brought him closer to where he wanted to go. It is important to recall, in addition to statements already referred to of Scott Dowling, Edith Jacobson, Martin Bergmann, and Bennett Simon, the many statements of Sandler's in this context. I refer particularly to his emphasis on conflicts that arise as a result of significantly discrepant self-representations, as distinct from conflicts that arise from the antagonism between impulse and social prohibitions. Moreover, as Jay Greenberg remarks, "Freud was on the right track early on," when he talked about ideas. "Ideas are constructed out of wishes, fears, experiences of the self and of others that are the residue of interpersonal exchanges, and a wide range of affective states. . . . It is useful to conceptualize mental contents as ideas or, in more contemporary terms, as representations . . . [which] are not passive renderings of the person's situation, but are the multiply determined creations of an active mind."[153] Greenberg's observation that "there was great wisdom in the early vision," confirms a statement of Edith Jacobson's made well before Masson launched his critique: "Freud's first theory of neurosis, which was, as it were, an affect theory, has never lost practical significance."[154]

Thus in this context too, it is not clear that Freud had no choice but to proceed as he did. But having done so, fragmentation in both clinical and theoretical realms will remain the likely fate of psychoanalysis for reasons I have given. It may be true that not all inferences or all clinical techniques are equally valid or correct, but there is no way of stopping the proliferation of vantage points because there is no way of discriminating better from worse among them as long as the only applicable criteria remain the traditionally accepted psychoanalytic criteria.[155] This probably does not matter for clinical purposes, but it matters a great deal for purposes of social theory and history.

CHAPTER 5

The Lessons for Social Theory

The fragmentation that affected psychoanalysis has affected the social sciences as well. According to Randall Collins, sociology has "lost all coherence as a discipline; we are breaking up into a conglomerate of specialties, each going its own way."[1] Similar observations have been made about economics, which is described as existing in a "fractious state," in which "a divisive fundamentalism seems rife." The dominant rational choice perspective is currently being challenged by behavioral and empirical perspectives, but a number of others can be identified as well.[2] Some thoughtful observers, in psychoanalysis and sociology at any rate, have claimed that this fragmentation (or "pluralism") is a good thing, but what it means is that the disciplines are lacking a cognitive consensus, an agreed-upon core of knowledge, a shared sense of direction or any reasonable prospect of deciding upon one.[3]

The social sciences resemble psychoanalysis in this respect because they share a number of problems in common. In particular, from the standpoints of correspondence (determining whether the conclusions that follow from a theory are confirmed by what can be observed empirically of the real world), and comprehensiveness (determining whether the theory is able to encompass all the known facts pertaining to the class of phenomena under study), none of the theories undergirding these disciplines has come close to providing the required explanatory power.[4] Weak theory precludes the possibility of justifiably foreclosing on alternatives, which are then constantly being produced.

Charles Lindblom and David K. Cohen explained two decades ago that what social scientists actually know is quite meager, and that the results of all social scientific inquiry have yielded but an insignificant quantity of findings of questionable value.[5] Their judgment remains valid because, simply put, no theory has proven sufficient to encompass the complex responses of people to events, in cognitive, moral, or wishful terms on one side, and in terms of the different social locations they inhabit on the other. The loyalties of heterogeneous populations have not remained constant or continuous over time,[6] because the changing situations people face always require them to reassess their sense of adequacy, which, pressed by successive and persistent challenges to a variety of material interests, moral perspectives, and wishful expectations, is also changing. Similar starting points do not lead to similar end points because while people may share a language to interpret expected or unexpected events, they do not share feelings about these events or a sense of adequacy in coping with them.

It is important to consider, too, that questions about commitments to authoritative leaders and cultural perspectives, as well as to the cognitive, moral, and wishful components of self, must be addressed anew in the context of the many social locations people occupy every time the stability of familiar relationships appears threatened. Even when situations can be anticipated, the outbreak of war, for example, it is impossible to predict with any degree of precision how people will assess their prospects when it actually occurs and equally impossible to predict which of the commitments (to party, class, family, religion, race, gender, or ethnic group) will prove paramount to them. And as the basis for decision making changes over time depending on the situation and on active assessments of prospects, so too do the numbers change, making it difficult to account even retrospectively for the shape of different instances of compliance or conflict.

The calculation of future relationships based on the knowledge of current or past relationships in any complex situation is therefore problematic. The ability to be cognitively and morally disciplined, or for certain purposes or under certain circumstances to be wishfully engaged, or the need to make choices, pursue alternatives, juggle primacies, discriminate instances, or discern prospects while coping with unexpected conditions and unexpected thoughts and feelings, makes heterogeneous and discontinuous responses a certainty and the development of a unified social theory in any conventional (or predictive) sense, except in the simplest of terms, unlikely.

The historical literature provides the best means of identifying the effects of the problems outlined here. There are many useful examples, but the history of the American revolution offers a particularly compelling one, a point that Gordon S. Wood has most persistently and effectively made. Indeed, one of the interesting ironies of Wood's many discussions of the concerns of the revolutionary leadership, particularly their concern for the potential effects of heterogeneous expressions of material interests and moral perspectives, is that in retrospect they proved to be better social observers than their European counterparts, who always viewed them as hopelessly naive because they were so oblivious to the ways in which "real" relationships are "structured" by unifying underlying realities and "masked" by lofty moral abstractions. The Europeans invented systematic social theory and developed many theories of social stability and change, but few of them understood with the clarity of those who crafted the American Constitution, whatever their motives were and however their plans and expectations were betrayed by what followed, that the outstanding problem of the society was how to orient a heterogeneous population to a common goal. As Wood explains, American society was even by then too fragmented in terms of interests, moral perspectives, and wishful expectations to be mobilized by a single perspective or explained by reference to a single vantage point like class, and if the Americans did not invent a structural conception intended to bypass the surface confusion by finding some unifying force underneath, seeking on that basis to impose a solution, that was just as well.

The best approach here is to let Wood speak for himself on the subjects of heterogeneous striving, historical discontinuities, and active constructions.

> Americans had begun the Revolution assuming that the people were a homogeneous entity in society set against the rulers. But such an assumption belied American experience, and it took only a few years of independence to convince the best American minds that distinctions in the society were "various and unavoidable," so much so that they could not be embodied in the government.[7]

> The blending of diverse views and clashing interests into the new federal system, Madison told Jefferson in October 1787, was nothing "less than a miracle." As Franklin observed, it was like a game of dice with so many players, "their ideas so different, their prejudices so strong and so various, and their particular interests, independent of the general, seeming so opposite, that not a move can be made that is not contested."[8]

> There were many diverse reasons in each state why men supported or opposed the Constitution that cut through any sort of class division. The Constitution was a single issue in a complicated situation, and its acceptance or rejection in many states was often dictated by peculiar circumstances . . . that defy generalization.[9]

> Antifederalists were saying, whether they realized it or not, that the people of America even in their several states were not homogeneous entities each with a basic similarity of interest for which an empathic elite could speak. Society was not an organic hierarchy composed of ranks and degrees indissolubly linked one to another; rather it was a heterogeneous mixture of "many different classes or orders of people, Merchants, Farmers, Planter Mechanics and Gentry or wealthy Men."[10]

> There were "rich and poor; creditors and debtors; a landed interest, a monied interest, a mercantile interest, a manufacturing interest," together with numerous subdivisions of these economic interests and

interests based on differing religious and political opinions. All of this heterogeneity, it had become increasingly evident, was responsible for the "instability" in the states.[11]

To explain how Americans, ten years after declaring independence from a far-removed and much-feared governmental authority, were prepared to create another such distant and astonishingly powerful government is in many ways even more difficult than explaining the coming of the Revolution itself. A powerful superintending national government like that embodied in the federal Constitution of 1787 was inconceivable to Americans in 1776.[12]

Given America's experience with central power, it is easy to see how the erection of a national government represented a political revolution as great as the revolution a decade earlier. . . . Only the profoundest disillusionment with the great hopes of the Revolution of 1776 could have led someone like Madison to make the extraordinary proposals he made to his Virginia correspondents in the spring of 1787.[13]

The Federalist defense of the Constitution "required no conscious wrenching and distortion of ideas, no hypocrisy, because so many piece-meal changes in thought had occurred in the decade since Independence that, without anyone's being fully aware of what was happening, the whole intellectual world of 1776 had become unraveled."[14] Finally, Wood also explained that in the 1750s and early 1760s, Benjamin Franklin was emotionally committed to the British Empire to an extent virtually unrivaled by anyone except perhaps William Pitt. "Few Englishmen were more proud of being English and few more devoted to the English monarchy. In the early 1760s it is hard to see any difference at all between Franklin and the man who eventually became the symbol to Americans of the arch-loyalist, Thomas Hutchinson of Mas-sachusetts. . . . In 1760 it would have been very hard to predict that the paths of Franklin and Hutchinson would so diverge. . . . In light of Franklin's identification with the Revolution and the American folk hero he would later become, it is embarrassing to read his correspon-dence of the 1750s and early 1760s."[15]

This historiographical example is just an immediately obvious one; I could have identified many others, including, especially from the standpoint of discontinuity, the interpretive literature on American cul-ture in the post–Second World War period, from Erich Fromm's *Man for Himself*, to Christopher Lasch's *The Culture of Narcissism*.[16] Any-one familiar with this literature must realize that no theoretical perspec-tive could connect the different character types described in William H. Whyte Jr.'s *The Organization Man* (1956), Charles Reich's *The Green-ing of America* (1969), and Christopher Lasch's *The Culture of Narcis-sism* (1979). Whyte had bemoaned the conformism imposed by American corporate culture, Reich heralded a forthcoming revolution in consciousness leading to the radical expansion of the American democracy, and not a decade later (1979) Lasch critically—and with considerable bitterness—commented on the way that modern capitalist society reinforces narcissistic traits and elevates narcissists to prominence. The best anyone can make of this literature is that the society was changing in the eyes of skilled observers faster than any conventional social theory could possibly have accounted for, apart from whatever else might have been happening with theory construction and deconstruction in other places or in other genres, notably fiction.[17]

I could also have commented on the considerable literature devoted to Nazism, especially, in this instance, in terms of the heterogeneity problem. The heterogeneous composition of the Nazi movement has been commented on many times, in psychoanalytic studies of Nazi elites, in sociological studies that made a deliberate effort to acquire relevant subjective data, such as the autobiographical statements collected by Theodore Abel in the 1930s, and in more numerate sociological studies.[18] Indeed, the authors of the most recent of study of the Nazi elite once again "failed to identify a homogeneous Nazi personality. In fact, the differences among the members of this group by far outweighed any similarities."[19]

These conclusions have serious implications for three conventional social science perspectives that I have referred to along the way, but that I want now to comment on more directly. One is based on categorical analysis, referring to class, gender, race, age, and the like. The strength of such analysis has historically derived from the unstated assumption that social location determines subjective experience (the interpretation of events, motives for behavior, in general, perceptions and feelings), without regard to the specifics of any situation. The implicit argument is that invariant interpretive rules for thinking, feeling, and behavior are embedded in the category and must prove decisive for the way that people respond.[20] But things do not work that way: people who share a particular social background do not share a sense of what is important about it, or how they feel about their ability to cope with the conflicts emerging from it. At the same time, they have critical obligations in a variety of social locations and it is always hard to know which of these obligations will prove decisive for them. Take these three statements of members of the German Social Democratic Party faced with the need to respond to the disintegrating political culture of the Weimar Republic:

> I am bitterly disappointed by the attitude of our [Social Democratic] leaders who show so little interest in class struggle at this point . . . . [I] have come to the conclusion that there can be no further progress under their direction. Under these circumstances I feel unable to follow the party line any longer.

I am and remain a "religious socialist." Under the pressure of circumstances the SPD, even against its will, will be pushed aside and into the
methods of left-wing radicalism. On the other hand, pressure from the
opposite side will grow. The only thing left for me to do in good conscience as a teacher, a Christian, and a German is to try to evade the
double pressure and . . . try to live for my job, my family, and my
books, without being a member of a party.

As a civil servant I have to make a choice. On the one hand, I see now
the tendency is growing on the part of my employer, the Reich, not to
tolerate those employees belonging to anti-government associations.
On the other hand, there is my loyalty to the [Social Democratic] Party.
Unfortunately, I see no other solution but to resign. The existence of
my family is at stake. If the fate of unemployment, which in my experience can be *very, very* hard, is unavoidable I need not reproach
myself for not having done everything in the interests of my wife and
child.[21]

Clearly, three individuals belonging to the same organization and faced
with the same bleak prospects arrived at the same decision from three
different vantage points.

The main problem of categorical analysis is that the attempts to
identify underlying unifying motives have always yielded a confound:
although some portion of a population may act consistently in terms of
class, gender, or age, some portion too great to be accounted for by accident or coincidence does not. The use of categories and the inferences
they permit are then linked to the actual composition of social movements by partial and statistical relationships, and the only way to make
a larger argument on the basis of these relationships is to take a part for
the whole (for example, to assume that class is such a dominant feature
that variations can also be explained in class terms without reference to
cases); or to violate scientific logic by multiplying theoretical entities as
a means of explaining the variation in response (explaining what one
group was doing in terms of class, and then explaining from a succession of other vantage points what all the other groups were doing at the
same time, contradicting the principle of parsimony).[22] This approach is
weak in its own terms, but it is weakest of all in explaining how diverse,
often competing and antagonistic groups are able to find each other and
pursue a common goal in the first place.

Social movements, in short, are invariably characterized by multiple
perspectives and by discontinuous degrees of support for the different
perspectives over time. There is not one kind of liberal or conservative,
or one kind of Nazi or Bolshevik, or one kind of participant in any
social movement. And because radical movements especially tend to
split apart, often in violent ways, it is more important to know how—

that is, the process by which—the variety was oriented to a common goal in the first place than it is to identify the persistence of statistical tendencies from one occasion to the next. Put another way, the question of how heterogeneous populations are mobilized in social movements and oriented to a common goal is more important than any question concerning the degree of unity that only imperfectly exists within such movements.[23] Moreover, and this cannot be emphasized too strongly, explanations of why such unity occurs will in any case prove to be too inferential, that is, based on unwarranted assumptions about the relationship of social location to mental outlook.

The categories are important, perhaps central to the organization of everyday life, but their significance to people is constructed from a variety of possible vantage points. People establish for themselves a hierarchy among the categories as a means of narrowing and focusing attention on particular problems of interest to them, but the primacies established within the hierarchy change over time, even in the course of a day, as situations change. Such interactive relationships are not fixed, nor is character in this sense fixed; they are rather a matter of constant negotiation with the wider social world, rendering responses to events, especially unexpected events, unpredictable.[24] Hence the salience of a recent comment by Patricia Williams, who explained that "[w]hile being black has been the powerful social attribution in my life, it is only one of a number of governing narratives or presiding fictions by which I am constantly reconfiguring my self in the world. Gender is another, along with ecology, pacifism, my peculiar brand of colloquial English, and Roxbury, Massachusetts. The complexity of role identification, the politics of sexuality, the inflections of professionalized discourse—all describe and impose boundary in my life, even as they confound one another in unfolding spirals of confrontation, deflection, and dream."[25]

The second perspective is rational choice (or rational actor) theory, still described by professionals as the best that especially economists have to offer, despite its widely recognized shortcomings.[26] It has already been observed that rationality as "a one-motive theory of human behavior," which has undergirded economic thinking for decades, is not persuasive "when we look, not at laboratory experiments on the axioms of choice, but at empirical studies of real economic behavior."[27] The reason is that the narrow or weak definition of rational choice theory focused on market activity requires that character (or mental processes as an element of economic activity) remain constant over time in violation of reported experience, and allows an unacceptably wide latitude of behavior to be construed as rational in terms of the self-interested maximization of utility ("subjective expected utility").[28] Thus if an unemployed teenager's girlfriend is pregnant, it is rational for him to abandon her on the grounds that the care of a young mother and child is more than he can manage, and it is rational not to abandon her because it is important to avoid social disapproval and censure. By the same token, if a teething baby cries beyond endurance, it is rational to walk away and let someone else take care of the problem and, on the same grounds as before, it is rational to stay and take care of it oneself. There are many other systematic objections to rational choice theory in addition to this one, "ranging from the recognition of the widespread use of 'data mining,' through the difficulty of replication of published empirical studies, and the problem of calibration and abuse of the rhetoric of 'significance,' to the fragility of the hypothesis-testing methodology itself."[29] Indeed, if the definition of rational choice is construed narrowly enough (calculated choice under conditions of resource constraints), Ahab's manipulation of his crew in the pursuit of the white whale is also rational, even though Ahab himself explained that "[a]ll my means are sane, my motive and my object mad."[30]

The narrow versions of rational choice theory fail because they cannot address the real complexity already known to exist. As Antonio Damasio explained, people cannot resort to the kind of behavior required by the standard conception of rational choice theory because at best decisions will take an unacceptably long time to make and at worst there may be no decision at all if the range of possible ramifications is taken into account. Moreover, "even if our reasoning strategies were perfectly tuned . . . they would not cope well with the uncertainty and complexity of personal and social problems. The fragile instruments of rationality need special assistance."[31] Then, too, "[e]motions and feelings, which are central to the view of rationality I am proposing, are a powerful manifestation of drives and instincts, part and parcel of their workings."[32] But once rational choice theory is expanded to cover the uncertainty and complexity of thought, especially to include a sense of moral obligation, wishful expectation, fear of social censure, or emotional responses to events, then the interpretive problems multiply as they do in all forms of social psychology, particularly because social problems and decisions taken in respect of them are more complex than the decision involved in whether or how to respond to a crying baby.[33]

These considerations have begun to affect even the thinking of mainline economists, as I noted earlier. Alan Greenspan's widely reported references to "irrational exuberance" and his explanation to Congress that "participants in financial markets are susceptible to waves of optimism" are just the most obvious indication of this.[34] Robert J. Shiller, whose opinions are well known to Greenspan, has explained that "one must look to behavioral considerations and to crowd psychology to explain the actual process of price determination in the stock market."[35] At the twenty-fifth anniversary of the social science division of the Institute for Advanced Study, Professors Gavin Wright (Stanford) and Kaushik Basu (Cornell) urged greater attention to cultural content in economic analyses. Basu "urged economists to attend explicitly to the role of norms and laws in shaping individual behavior," claiming that integrating the role of beliefs and rules in theory would add complexity to the models of individual rationality economists now typically employ.[36] Gregory Mankiw has stated that economic behaviorists have opened his eyes to alternative ways of thinking: "Maybe to fully understand market behavior we have to introduce some form of irrationality."[37]

But this is a much more complicated issue than it might at first appear to be. As some economists have already explained, it is important to take into account nonrational thinking in the sense of socially legitimate or moral forms of thinking not based on the kind of obligated cognitive and emotional constraints associated with rationality. As one economist explained, "Overall economic performance depends on transaction costs, and these reflect the level of trust in the economy. The level of trust depends in turn on culture. An effective culture has a strong moral content. Morality can overcome incentive problems that formal procedures—based on monitoring compliance with contracts—cannot."[38]

But it is also important to take into account wishful—or fantasy—thinking. The notion of wishful thinking obviously requires some clarification in social terms because as much as the cultural perspective so prominent in anthropology, sociology, history, and criticism has gone too far in diminishing the importance of the biological foundations of mind, Freud's biologically grounded concepts of instinct or drive and the implicit emphasis on endogenous rather than environmental origins of wishful thinking are irrelevant to the issue.[39] What must be emphasized rather is the way that people, codes, rules, objects, come to be represented in the mind, the way that these things come to constitute knowledge for people, and the different ways that people come to think and to feel about them.

Thus rather than conceive of wishful thinking in the familiar structural ("id") terms, as a determinative, undergirding, third sphere or realm of mental activity, along with ego and superego, it makes better heuristic sense to conceive of emotional commitments to mental representations of people and things based on real experiences in two culturally legitimate spheres, self-interested or material activity and moral activity, and to conceive of wishful thinking as occurring in either sphere, in terms of shifting primacies and priorities.[40] As I noted earlier, notions of self-interested behavior cast in terms of safe and dangerous, or in terms of advantage or disadvantage, are distinct from self-interested notions cast in terms of good and evil, as are the kinds of emotional and wishful expression involved in each.

Wishful (or fantasy) thinking as it affects contact with the social world refers here to an imagined omnipotent mastery and control of some portion of the world in pursuit of a goal that is beyond anyone else's capacity to obstruct, regardless of how their interests and moral perspectives are affected, so that whatever outcome one imagines for oneself is realized, because in wishful thinking there are no insurmountable obstacles.[41] Wishful thinking plays an important role in social relationships and should be valued similarly in social theory as well, because it is the originating source of novel forms of ideological expression and of authoritative leadership. Such thinking allows for experimenting (or playing) with different alternatives without needing to consider the possibility that the wished-for outcome will be thwarted by some resistance that cannot be overcome. It is therefore an important element in the ongoing construction of versions of the world, which are then refined—or constrained—in the process of negotiating outcomes with others. It is also a form of thinking that is beyond the power of the social order to inhibit.[42] There is always an element of subversion in wishful thinking, because it constantly evades rule governed behavior of every sort. The language and images of wishful thinking are borrowed from the surrounding world but are imaginatively deployed in ways that constantly transgress the boundaries of expected everyday behavior.

Wishful thinking, then, is used to imagine novel alternative practices all the time, and in this way (once the interests and moral perspectives of others are taken into account, as well as their likely objection to the undeviating pursuit of one's own) it can provide the basis for grappling with complex problems and ultimately for realistic appraisals of the world. As Albert Einstein wrote, "[w]hen I examine myself and my methods of thought, I come to the conclusion that the gift of fantasy has meant more to me than my talent for absorbing positive knowledge."[43] This capacity for wishful thinking undercuts such judgments as Pierre Bourdieu's, that the history of the individual is never anything other than a certain specification of the collective history of the group or class, "a structural variant" of all the other group or class habitus.[44] On the contrary, individuals are able constantly to elude culturally legitimate conceptions of past, present, and future, and if they can develop a coherent conception of an alternative vision oriented to real problems and conflicts, they may well affect the way people live in the world.

By the same token, however, if individuals cannot discriminate instances and they try to force the world into compliance with their wishful striving, they can prove to be dangerous to themselves and others. This has happened historically in all spheres of endeavor, including especially political and economic endeavor, as revealed by the ambitions and failures of the century's notorious dictatorships to establish a non-conflictual, harmonious, homogeneous world beyond division and strife.

Indeed, the development of psychoanalysis can itself be viewed in terms of the infiltration of scientific thinking by wishful ambitions. Freud's colleagues would not have put it so bluntly, but in their concern with his emphasis on the phylogenetic propositions they had clearly suggested as much. Moreover, Freud on his own testimony realized that he was often skirting the edge, if not going over it: "Without metapsychological speculation and theorizing—I had almost said 'fantasying'—we shall not get another step forward."[45] But he was not worried, because he thought he was right on principle and that subsequent research would provide the details to confirm this. He was also not worried because he trusted his intuition, and because he thought—as naive as this may sound—that if he offered his ideas in a rational manner they would be assessed by disciplined and discriminating individuals in a rational manner, so there could be no harm in it anyway. In the matter of his phylogenetic propositions, if not in other important matters, Freud proved to be right: those who followed him abandoned the phylogenetic propositions as soon as they could.

Wishful thinking is thus affected by but cannot be inferred from current social relationships and in a codified form may be conceived of as resembling what Marx referred to as utopian thinking or bourgeois idealism. In Marx's own social and material context, for example, there was no way for him to have known or even reasonably to have guessed that the bourgeois mode of production would be the last antagonistic mode of production. This conclusion of Marx's is a paramount example of wishful thinking, which was not just wrong in a retrospective sense but can be otherwise identified as having been wrong by the obvious lapse of logic (Marx always insisted that his perspective was rooted in concrete material conditions, although this crucial conclusion, which proved so compelling to people, could not have been rooted in such conditions). Wishful thinking can thus be identified by the presence of contradictions readily observable to others and sufficiently significant to compromise the logic of a vantage point, or by the failure of cognitive processes to bridge gaps in logic at any point in time, or to account for gaps between expectations and results that only expand over time.

As Jean-Paul Sartre pointed out, the contradictions in Marx's work can be resolved only if one interprets them as the expression of a process in which the subject and object of history, the proletariat, attempts to bring about a time when "history will have only one meaning, when it will tend to be dissolved in the concrete men who will make it common."[46] But this is precisely a form of moral wishfulness. It is not the empirically observable direction of any society, not excluding the well-reported attempts of even the most ruthless dictators to force behavioral compliance. There cannot be one meaning to history given the present state of knowledge; indeed, there is no certain knowledge available yet that would allow one to define the conditions necessary for such an outcome, let alone the state of knowledge current when Marx fashioned this prospect of a harmonious society beyond conflict. There is not even one meaning in Marx's own writing, or, for that matter, in anyone else's writing or experience.[47]

Thus it is easy to acknowledge the importance of nonrational thinking, but much more difficult to understand the process by which primacies among cognitive, moral, and wishful forms of thinking are affected by events. With respect to rational choice theory, this complexity is best explained in terms of Gerald Platt's summary of arguments against either narrow or expanded versions. According to Platt, experimental designs devised to examine narrow versions of rational conduct circumscribe action to the point of eliminating imagination and creativity, both of which are essential features of any form of rational action. Thus the narrow version cannot accommodate the testimony of many scientists who have claimed, contrary to the assumptions of the theory, that their work, heavily dependent upon the consolations of fantasy and affected by emotion, was guided as well by moral and esthetic considerations. I will just mention in this regard, in addition to the testimony of Albert Einstein, Max Planck, Werner Heisenberg, Paul Dirac, Erwin Schrödinger, Richard P. Feynman, Bertrand Russell, Linus Pauling, C. H. Anfinsen, Henri Poincaré, and F. A. Kekulé.[48] Then, too, rationality is retrospectively imputed to historical situations although it would have been impossible to say prospectively that rationality was the exclusive basis for action. At the same time, emotional components involved in decision making are eliminated from rational analysis because they are assumed to be antithetical to rational action, although, as we have seen, this assumption has never been demonstrated and indeed is being vigorously challenged even now.[49]

The third perspective involves a more traditional interpretive social psychology based on loyalties, moral obligations, identities, norms, emotional commitments, perceptions of transgression, and loss.[50] As I indicated earlier, this interpretive social psychology is now back in favor after two decades and more of social movement theory based on rationalist conceptions "within the instrumental, utilitarian natural science tradition," which placed "the weighing of costs and benefits rather than deprivation and grievances at the center of a theory of public goods."

The unresolved anomalies stemming from such issues as "values, grievances, ideology and collective identity" have compelled a reexamination of behavior in terms of this traditional social psychology, which is focused on the definition of the actor, the social construction of meaning, and the moral perspectives and cultural contents of movements.[51]

Robert Bellah had long before explained that "[t]he canons of empirical science apply primarily to symbols that express the feelings, values, and hopes of subjects, or that organize and regulate the flow of interaction between subjects and objects. . . . These symbols, too, express reality and are not reducible to empirical propositions."[52] This statement was intended to provide a way around the inadequacies of theories of class or similar forms of categorical analysis, and also of addressing aspects of reality that rational choice or rational actor theories failed to address. But as it rendered problematic the possibility of empirical demonstration, it thwarted the expectations of those who hoped still to create a science of society and who responded to this kind of observation by promoting a stricter adherence to scientific method.

However, the cost of this approach, the abandonment of the subjective side of human experience, along with the kind of cultural conversation characteristic of the classical social theorists, left a gap that many social scientists ultimately found unacceptable. Hence Jon Elster concluded in his reexamination of social theory, as Basu had too, that altruism, envy, and social norms interact with self-interest and contribute in complex ways to order, stability and cooperation. Elster noted that "social norms have a *grip on the mind* that is due to the strong emotions their violations can trigger. I believe that the emotive aspect of norms is a more fundamental feature than the more frequently cited cognitive aspects."[53]

Thus after a quarter century or more, social scientists, including economists, are again returning to a consideration of the symbolic and affective issues that Bellah had referred to. However, while it has not proved possible after all to ignore "feelings, values, and hopes," social scientists, like the contemporary cultural theorists, still have no better understanding of how to address these issues than they did before. Does this return to the earlier approach promise to enhance interpretive prospects, or are social scientists just going around in circles, uncertain about where to turn next?

The question is not an idle one. In 1951 Talcott Parsons addressed the "massive convergence of the fundamental insights of Freud and Durkheim" on the internalization of morality, which Parsons ranked as "one of the truly fundamental landmarks of the development of modern social science."[54] In 1981, Charles Tilly entitled one of the chapters in his book on sociology and history "Useless Durkheim," arguing that "key ideas in Durkheim are either circular or extraordinarily difficult to translate into verifiable propositions."[55] In 1989, Elster wrote that "I have come to believe that social norms provide an important kind of motivation for action that is irreducible to rationality or indeed to any other form of optimizing mechanism," a line that is right out of Durkheim.[56] This circle was closed by the publication in 1996 of a paper by Mustafa Emirbayer entitled, "Useful Durkheim."[57]

There is nothing inherently wrong with circles, but this one is problematic because Durkheim's answer to the classical question of how it is that societies do not dissolve into a series of struggles among competing, antagonistic self-seeking individuals and groups is that their members share a unified perspective on symbolic representations or on the value of a symbolic economy; they are oriented by common, internalized cognitive and moral assumptions about the world they live in that "predispose" them to certain outcomes. Durkheim believed that the kinds of structure, ritual expression, and authority characteristic of societies, provide the basis for unity and preclude their anomicization. But this view is again based on the empirically untenable notion that there is an underlying unity of motive, so that returning to Durkheim, or more generally to the preoccupations of the classical theorists, is not a sufficient response to the questions that persist. Max Weber's long-ago description of the social world as a "heterogeneous continuum," his perception of the chaotic flux of events that must somehow nevertheless be ordered and accounted for, underscored the persistence of problems caused by the surface confusion of everyday life but also the persistence of the wish for a parsimonious solution to the problems, made concrete in the work of social theorists like Durkheim, or more generally in the work of social, psychological, linguistic, and biological structuralists.

However, these structuralist perspectives, based on the inferences of theorists who typically claim to have discerned the "true order" of things beneath the confusion of the surface, were contradicted by the kinds of historical and comparative anomalies we have already identified: the persistently heterogeneous composition of groups that even the most ruthless dictatorships could neither absorb nor suppress; the idiosyncratic outcomes of personal conflict; and the discontinuity of events, reflected in the unexpected fate of different social movements and organizations. The point is that any psychosocial or sociological conception that implies a unity of motive, perception, or feeling, whether based on unconscious strivings or on "predispositions to behavior" fostered by particular socialization experiences ("authoritarian personality types" emerging from lower middle-class families), is bound to lead to unwarranted and unsupportable conclusions.[58]

The gap between the explanatory power of the three major interpretive approaches and the empirical problems they were meant to solve is too great to justify their continued conceptual status. The often reported sense of crisis in all disciplines results from their inability adequately to address empirical problems and therefore to resolve the resulting impasse. This is particularly the case with respect to the inability of these approaches to encompass the subjectivities of individuals as linked to the particularities of historical circumstances, apart from preconceived notions of the unity of unconscious motivations or predispositions to behavior. These fictional means used by observers to bypass the unexpectedly unruly circumstances of human behavior can no longer be justified.

It is important to understand the way in which these familiar approaches to theory resemble the tricks that, according to cognitive psychologists, the mind plays with memory: in both cases, the more remote from an event one is, the less situational and the more dispositional people's responses appear to have been.[59] The strategy undergirding these approaches needs to be abandoned in favor of one that can address the empirical dilemmas in a way that does not require any assumption of collective (in the sense of unified) identity, collective memory, unity of motive, fixity of character, "core personality," or continuity of response over time, based on theories of internalization, shared trauma, the structural features of language, class, or gender, and so on.

Given the historical and sociological data I have cited, the outcomes of clinical practice, especially the idiosyncratic and discontinuous resolutions (or attempted resolutions) to conflict, and the requirements of systematic theory as I have explained them, the best initial approach to the problem is also, ironically, the one remaining heuristically viable psychoanalytic perspective on the relationship of mind to society: D. W. Winnicott's concepts of transitional objects and transitional space. Winnicott's concepts are important because they connect the inner world of "wishes, feelings, memories, percepts, and symbols," to the outer world of cultural perspectives, social locations (for example, class, gender) authoritative figures, and concrete objects (money, property, sacred texts and sites, weapons) in a way that can absorb the heterogeneity of material, moral, and wishful motives.[60] The concepts are adequate to the situation because they do not obligate any sense of unity of unconscious motivation, of collective identity or memory, or of shared predispositions to behavior.[61]

Like Sandler's concept of the "background of safety," Winnicott's transitional concepts were intended to describe the interactions of infant and mother, but both are readily translated into terms useful for social theory. Winnicott discussed the "space" between infant and mother that is bridged by objects the infant finds to play with that are also invested with emotional significance. These objects then serve the infant as a means of maintaining the union between what he or she has come to perceive as two separate individuals. But in a broader sense, as a way of understanding how the interactions and relationships of everyday life come to be represented in minds, cultural perspectives, authoritative figures, social location, concrete objects, and the attachment to them may be conceived as occurring similarly in a "third," intermediate space between any individual's personal interests, moral outlook, and wishfulness and the cultural and structural demands of the social world. Winnicott related the use of this intermediate space to "the perpetual human task of keeping inner and outer reality separate yet interrelated."[62] Because, as he noted, no one is ever free of the strain of relating inner to outer reality, attachments to cultural perspectives, authoritative figures, and objects in this metaphoric sense persist through life, and there is a social and historical sense, as distinct from a developmental one, in which the concepts can be conceived.

Culturally available perspectives, figures, and objects are thus invested with special significance and used by perceiving, interpreting individuals for the sake of maintaining a personal sense of stability and adequacy and a sense of their social world as a "background of safety," a secure place within which they can pursue personal and group interests, even if this means investing people and things with an emotional significance far out of proportion to any intrinsic value they may possess. This interpretive elaboration of the world (or social construction of reality)[63] is an active process that, considering the vicissitudes of personal development, the variety of social locations that frame action, and the need sooner or later to cope with unanticipated events, helps account for the persistence of multiple, competing interests and perspectives, and for change over time.

These perspectives, figures, locations, and objects at the social level are correctly identified as transitional in the sense that individuals both find them in the world and construct subjectively relevant versions of their significance.[64] They are also transitional in an historical sense, as they have changed in form and content over time. And they remain important to people because they provide the space that allows them to orient themselves to the standards and expectations of a group, and to produce expected and appropriate forms of behavior, in terms they can live with. At the same time, the process I have described precludes any possibility of inferring unity of motivation from instances of concerted social activity.

It is in this sense that the struggle for individuation continues beyond the world established initially by parents for children, a struggle that people must engage to sustain themselves as perceiving, interpreting individuals. It is also in this sense that society serves as a "background of safety" for people, providing and maintaining the perspectives, structures, figures, and objects upon which any degree of autonomous behavior in stable circumstances is possible at all.[65] Finally, it is in this sense as well that individual perspectives on life, mediated by class, gender, race, or age, can readily be understood as negotiated and produced, not as fixed.

This is to say that social movements or organizations do not have a single or fixed meaning to the people who join or belong to them. The capacity of any movement to mobilize a following is related to its ability to recruit from among diverse populations, which happens because movement perspectives are abstract enough to allow all kinds of people to identify with them or to infer from them what they need to believe without threatening their sense of integration with the world; neither the social locations nor the content of cultural beliefs of movement members, which have been chosen for subjectively relevant reasons, can be assumed or inferred. Thus social movements of every sort are more diverse and precariously situated than might appear from the typical expressions of loyalty, the rallies, parades, banners, and slogans, which are intended to impress outsiders with their solidarity and unity.

I will provide one example involving the behavior of a single individual to illustrate how the process works. In the course of an interview psychoanalyst Arnold Goldberg referred to his mother as "a very smart man." When the interviewer noted the slip Goldberg replied, "My mentor, Heinz Kohut, used to say, 'When you make a slip of the tongue, it is a momentary disambulation of one's self.' It's just that. I don't make much of such slips." This psychoanalyst's explanation of the significance of a slip, so obviously different from Freud's and from many other versions of psychoanalysis, was an acceptable means of orienting himself to an unexpected situation. It is also an example of how the space provided by psychoanalysis is used in a transitional way. The abstract psychoanalytic perspective, the authoritative figure (in this case, Kohut), and the institutional setting all existed "out there," providing a means for this individual to cope with a potentially awkward moment by enabling him to manage an acceptable interpretive explanation of a faulty action.[66] People have used psychoanalysis this way since it was first proposed to them, proceeding along the way to invent a succession of versions that better conformed to their needs and interests than extant ones, including (as noted earlier) a host of private versions that we know little or nothing about.

Thus psychoanalysis continues to appeal to a broad range of people for subjectively relevant reasons, providing them with the perspectives and figures that allow for a sense of integration with the world, although what it means to them obviously cannot be assumed or inferred, it can only be established on a case by case basis. Needless to say, the same thing is true for religious, political, economic, and other cultural perspectives and organizations; they all serve a similar purpose and find themselves in a similar position. People can claim that they are Freudians, Protestants, Democrats, or Socialists, but it is always difficult to understand what they mean by the claim. The stability of all these movements and organizations is therefore always more uncertain and precarious than outside observers often imagine them to be.

One thing worth noting in this context, given the obvious latitude of answers to the question of what movement participation means, is that in terms of the perspectives, figures, and objects that people find "out there" and also evaluate in terms of their own interests and needs, the continued debate over whether there is such a thing as objective reality or whether there are only constructed versions of reality is pointless. Granted that there is an objective world of things, or a world in which events have occurred and are known to have occurred; it is still the case that things and events do not appear as they do in comic strips, with word-filled bubbles that reveal to everyone their "true" significance. On the contrary, people construct versions of their significance consistent with their own interests, moral perspectives, and wishful expectations, their own sense of adequacy and of self-esteem. People define for themselves the basis on which it is possible to continue to act in a way that links past, present, and future. Hence the persisting relevance of Winnicott's initial question: Did the baby find that bit of blanket or did he invent it? And the persisting relevance of the answer: "The baby creates the object, but the object was there waiting to be created."[67]

Of course it is still necessary to specify the ways in which the links between mind and society, or between organized mental activity and the organized social world, are facilitated and structured. We have already noted some of them, such as the various social locations like class or gender that serve to organize the space between individual striving and the social world. It must be emphasized, however, that participation in all such locations depends upon the effective conveyance of meaning and a common agreement as to the importance of situated actions. Such agreement is fostered by sociolinguistic features (or so-called "pragmatic contextual features") that allow people to use available narratives to construct versions of events consistent with their own interests, needs, and expectations. Such features include historical and communal memories of earlier triumphs when people were able to define their behavior as worthy, brave, and admirable, or, more generally, forms of knowledge and conceptions of social situations that may be shared in the sense of common agreement as to their importance, but not in the sense that they mean the same thing to all people or will continue to mean the same thing over a period of time.[68]

More important than social location, then, are the legitimating cultural perspectives, or the public culture, of societies or social organizations. These perspectives are of transcendent value in everyday life, viewed not as the causal or motivating factor in social activity (motives are as diverse as one can imagine in terms of all the idiosyncratic striving in the context of all the social locations that people inhabit), but as the paramount link between organized mental activity and the organized social world.[69] They establish the space within which people can construct versions of the world, providing the high and low level languages they require to rationalize the vicissitudes of life. Cultural cues and directive systems provide a way for people to explain to themselves and others all kinds of anticipated and unanticipated, favorable and unfavorable events.[70] They legitimate realistic social activity, focus heterogeneous cognitive, moral, and wishful ambitions on the completion of social tasks, define the range of appropriate or acceptable behaviors in terms of those tasks, and undergird the ability of leaders and the people they lead to use cultural perspectives in situated contexts as a way of integrating the varied interpretive responses to real circumstances.[71]

Cultural perspectives are thus associated with authoritative figures who actively promote interest in and loyalty to directive systems. While particular individuals may be capable of managing life without reference to such figures,[72] societies, even the most democratized among them, are not. The reason is in part efficiency, but more importantly, when "words fail" because of unexpected or threatening circumstances, or when cultural perspectives become unavailable or dysfunctional or can no longer be used to explain current circumstances, either the viability of the traditional language must be reconfirmed, or a new language substituted. People need to relate what they think and feel about the world as they perceive it to the language and structures available to them. The process of recovery or substitution is the defining function of authoritative figures. People are meaning seeking, but when their capacity to generate meaning is threatened they become object seeking, trying to find support from authoritative individuals as a way of remaining connected in an acceptable way to the social world.[73]

This use of leaders who appear able to repair disrupted situations, regardless of the domain in which they function, is well illustrated by the uses of Freud, or, as we have just seen, Kohut, in the history of psychoanalysis, keeping in mind Geertz's suggestion that such a charismatic figure can "arise in any realm of life that is sufficiently focused to seem vital—in science or art as readily as in religion or politics."[74] Moreover, this extends to the uses of the therapist in psychoanalytic practice itself. Regardless of the perspective of any individual psychoanalyst, people who cannot continue to match perception and conception or who cannot continue to use the culturally available language to account for their own conflicts, are able to seek out authoritative individuals, coming to rely in a very immediate way on this kind of cultural figure to help restore a sense of integration with the world.[75]

By the same token, however, this view of authority does not imply passive acceptance of a heteronomous morality, not in the political arena and not in the therapeutic one either. Indeed, when data permit the study of followers' attitudes to leaders, they do not uniformly reveal either their presumed unity of perspective or their passivity. On the contrary, followers are rather likely to be critical of policies, offering what they deem to be valuable assistance, making urgent recommendations, and otherwise taking an active, interpretive stance.[76] In Weber's original formulation, charisma is in the eyes of the beholder, and it is not legitimate to assume or infer that followers uncritically accept the orienting directives of leaders.

I have already referred to yet another important element in the link between mind and society, the ability of people to invent or reinvent versions of themselves, to survive and even thrive in novel surroundings, to scan the world for the purpose of avoiding conflict or finding possible solutions to conflict provoked by unexpected and unfamiliar conditions.[77] References to the ability of people to invent or reinvent themselves in different circumstance are hardly new.[78] Indeed, as both Bruner and Holt have reminded us, for Jean Piaget, "the drama was the child's reinvention of the world, a constant and recurring process achieved through action in the world in the present."[79] There are psychoanalytic references, too, in addition to those of Blos, Erikson, and others mentioned above, which suggest that in modern pluralized societies normative depictions of self and others are liable to change over time.[80]

Consider, for example, these statements by novelist Bharati Mukerjee, returning to the immigrant theme that she has often discussed, addressing the tension between her solution to the immigrant's problems and her sister's. She described their shared lives before coming to America and their divergent paths since: "I am an American citizen and she is not. . . . I was prepared for (and even welcomed) the emotional strain that came with marrying outside my ethnic community. . . . By choosing a husband who was not my father's selection, I was opting for fluidity, self-invention, blue jeans, and T-shirts, and renouncing 3000 years (at least) of caste observant, 'pure culture' marriage in the Mukherjee family."[81]

The point for the sisters, however, is that even traditional behaviors have changed over time, and both of them must be perceived as having used what they found in the environment to construct versions of themselves; they just took different paths and came to different conclusions. The behavior of both should be understood, to use Antonio Damasio's terms from a different context, as "live performances" rather than "rebroadcasts." What is played out in society is constructed anew, and in terms of motive, perception, expectation, or feeling is not a replica of anything that happened before.[82] As Erikson had before her, Mukherjee contemplated the immigrant-outsider experience in the United States, observing that "[p]erhaps it is this history-mandated training in seeing myself as 'the other' that now heaps on me a fluid set of identities denied to most of my mainstream American counterparts."[83] This idea of a fluid set of identities is not easily accommodated to conventional forms of social theory.

Whether the reference is to one individual (Freud), two (Mukherjee and her sister), or many (German citizens trying to manage the turmoil of the Weimar era), it is not difficult to demonstrate that people, from a variety of personal and social positions, do in fact engage in novel, discontinuous behaviors in an attempt to orient themselves to unexpected conditions. People, that is, have always used the space provided by ideological perspectives or public culture, including authoritative leaders, sacred texts and sites, and other valued objects like property and money, to invent versions of their significance for themselves, although the opportunities for doing so have expanded with the increasing differentiation of social organization, including psychoanalysis and other forms of psychotherapeutic intervention.[84]

In addition, emotion, cognition, and wishful thinking also figure importantly in the context of the multiple locations people occupy and the forms of public culture and authoritative leadership that make effective conveyance of meaning possible.[85] However, having discussed these factors at some length earlier, what I want to emphasize at this point is the inference that follows from the preceding discussions. Any network of explanatory perspectives, the authoritative figures identified with them, and the concrete objects that are especially represented and promoted by them, serve to define and sustain systematic cultural relationships.[86] Ties to abstract standards and expectations, concrete objects, and the people identified with them, however idiosyncratic or varied they may be, constitute a context of psychic support and allow meaning to be constructed or produced in everyday situations through social locations like class, gender, race, region, religion, and so on. Situations of psychic and social instability, as defined by the threatened or actual loss of these ties, or loss of everyday contexts for action and meaning, of the ability to act on moral standards or standards for achievement and for wishful expression, of the way that people evaluate, categorize, and feel about others, of the ability to assert or define identity in familiar and still cherished contexts, in short, of being able to continue to identify themselves as members of a community, are felt by people as threatening their hold on reality. However, rather than allow themselves to be thrust back on their own internal resources in the face of unexpected depths of emotion and unexpected and unwanted thoughts, they will scan the environment for perspectives and authoritative individuals who appear able either to restore still cherished standards or to provide new ones.

In sum, it is not simply that culture is historically and socially constructed but that it is constructed by idiosyncratic individuals who make subjective decisions about their needs and interests in the context of social locations that also have a subjective dimension. The perspectives or languages people use to frame their own perceptions and conceptions, even if their significance is not always manifest to them, provide an opportunity, a space, within which they can devise their own sense of what is important for them to do. Moreover, primacies change as situations change, which is why the numbers also change over time, although this precarious social arrangement is nevertheless capable of achieving a measure of stability on the basis of emotional commitments to variously understood or interpreted cultural orientations, figures, and objects.

The position I have outlined is consistent with available data and known results. Other positions are no doubt possible, but I am a strong advocate of this one because it justifies the integration of cultural and historical contexts in any conception of the process by which the construction of versions of things and events occurs, along with the reintegration into cognitive or learning theories of emotional commitments, moral perspectives, and wishful thinking. It also addresses problems raised by the idiosyncratic resolutions to personal development and the multiple subjective perspectives that flow from activity in multiple social locations, as well as from change over time. It can therefore account for the coherence or stability of culture in terms of the interpretive procedures for accommodating the different versions of reality that occur in a heterogeneous world, and it also accounts for the responses of people to unanticipated situations when interpretive procedures, viewed in terms of the ability to continue to use familiar language or produce familiar behaviors, become dysfunctional or unavailable. I refer to the search for codified language, authoritative leadership, and concrete things deemed capable of renewing a sense of adequacy and stability. It does not require us to maintain the fiction that everyone is attached to the same ideas and people or interested in the same things or events for the same reason, nor is it necessary to imagine a unified unconscious motive that, because there is no procedure for verification, fosters the constant proliferation of vantage points without providing any basis for discriminating better from worse among them.

I also advocate this position because it is consistent with established criteria for determining the potential validity of theoretical perspectives. What I have proposed provides a basis for integrating in a systematic way what Jerome Bruner has called the "paradigmatic mode" of causal explanation, and the "narrative mode" of explanation, that is, integrating the observer's view of events on one side and the subject's view on the other.[87] This is important because the only way to confirm assessments of the reasons people give for their behavior, or otherwise understand them, is to rely upon and use the subjective reporting that is available. This position also allows for the particularization of theory, that is, for explanations of the unique features of different historical events in a theoretical context.[88] In addition, what I have proposed also remains close to current research on cognitive processes, on the relationship of cognition to emotion, on the construction of memory, and on the capacity for actively reconstructing and inventing versions of self and world as an adaptive response to the demonstrated discontinuities of life.

There are two final points that need to be made concerning this or any social or cultural theory. First, it is important to keep in mind just how remote we still are from substantial knowledge of the process, the organizing rules, by which all of the different levels of activity get connected, and how little we know about how the world comes to be represented in the mind, how perceptual and mnemonic coding occurs, how information is processed and emotional and cognitive structures based on experience are built up. As Joseph LeDoux notes, "We don't fully understand how the human brain sizes up a situation, comes up with a set of potential courses of action, predicts possible outcomes of different actions, assigns priorities to possible actions, and chooses a particular action."[89] LeDoux and other students of brain and mind are only just beginning to understand the neural underpinnings of reason and emotion in terms of how thought processes work and how emotions and feelings are related to the reasoning process.

Thus it is still the case that most cognitive and social-psychological research involves narrowly defined experimental situations or laboratory tasks in which subjects passively receive stimulus information (static stimulus displays of geometric patterns, the linear ordering of objects, consonants from the alphabet, sequences of numbers, and simple hierarchies of propositions) very little of which is adequate to the diversity of structures, beliefs, and prospects potentially available to people in a social setting or to an account of how people manage life's problems day to day. The efforts of cognitive and social psychologists to solve problems of social cognition, their studies of unconscious processes that affect thought and behavior, and their use of a conceptual language of scripts, schemas, and stories, however relevant all of it may ultimately prove to be for understanding goal-oriented evaluative, judgmental, and behavioral decisions, are still at a simplistic level, barely related to the realities of social interactions in historical situations.[90]

One can then refer to active mastery of the environment, the capacity for and the impetus to gain control over events in the social world, but the best one can do empirically is point to modest studies of effectance pleasure in infants, or to recently discovered unexpected cognitive and emotional capacities in young children, or to the kinds of circumscribed laboratory studies described above.[91] One can refer to the social origins of memory, to the construction or reconstruction of versions of self and world, and to the ways that people struggle to remain cognitively focused, the ways they scan a troubled world in a search for leaders and perspectives, but given the current state of research, which is still remarkably deficient in important ways, all conclusions in this realm remain speculative by definition.[92]

The absence of any significant knowledge of the cognitive and social processes involved in controlling social change and conflict means that even the most fundamental question—how is social order possible—is still an open one. Still absent, too, is the ability to identify the sources of the ideological contents that have emerged historically to facilitate or help control social conflict (capitalism, socialism, liberalism, fascism). In fact, there is such a paucity of theory, that one or another version of psychoanalysis may justifiably serve as a heuristic source for social scientific and historical perspectives, while the more recent acknowledgment by psychoanalysts of the importance of academic developmental and cognitive psychology, learning theory, and studies devoted to the relationship of emotion, cognition, and memory to questions of human agency is bound also to be helpful.

Second, inventing languages and schemes to describe relationships is easy, but demonstrating a tangible connection to the social world is not. Morris Eagle, himself a psychoanalyst, complained of a familiar kind of psychoanalytic developmental construct that, to the extent one could decipher the jargon, amounted to a causal proposition regarding the effects of early experiences upon subsequent development, in the absence of any evidence.[93] But this kind of complaint can be made about any number of constructs in many different fields. How could so many economists have believed with such a strong sense of conviction that anything under 6 or even 7 percent unemployment in this society must lead to inflationary pressures? This position, actively promoted in the political arena for years by professional economists, affecting the lives of any number of people, has recently—and unexpectedly—become untenable.[94] The predicted relationship among unemployment, growth, and inflation more recently failed to materialize, as the jobless rate has dropped as low as 4.1 percent with little hint of inflationary pressures. Mainline economists never imagined and never provided any alternative perspectives on the problem; they were hastily obliged to reconsider what they had promoted for years as gospel, and they still have no way to account for what occurred. They were obviously unable in this instance, as they are still in many others, to distinguish the moral content of what they had been proposing from a "scientific" one.[95]

In any case, what kind of evidence did (and do) they have?[96] If a proposition as important as the one on wage and price pressures can be so unexpectedly contradicted with no way to account for what happened, what kind of theory do they have? No one knows why the predicted relationship of employment and growth to inflation did not materialize, although Greenspan has said that it is a far more complex process than was implied by the "natural rate" concept.[97] Greenspan has also explained that "the underlying structure of the economy is in a continuing state of flux," and computer models of the economy have proven unreliable "because they wrongly assume that past economic relationships will stay the same." Greenspan told reporters at a news conference in Tokyo, October 1992, that "[n]o models can explain the types of patterns we are having," and that the customary techniques for analyzing the economy were "simply failing."[98]

Then, too, Richard Hamilton noted of the presumed susceptibilities of lower-middle-class people in Weimar Germany to fascist solutions, probably the most often used hypothesis to explain German behavior in this period, that "the linkages between social structures and political responses are extremely loose, so loose, in fact, that one is led to wonder about the sources of the original assumption that they would be highly correlated." Having concluded that the initial premise, "is one of those 'things that never were,'" Hamilton wanted to know how scholars could have so thoroughly "misread the evidence and . . . sustained a consensus based on a pseudo fact."[99]

Hamilton's question was important enough for him to return to it many years later, emphasizing again the tendency among scholars to favor the internal integrity of theories they are committed to over available and accessible contradictory data. In this later work Hamilton returned to a discussion of the role of class in the rise of the Nazis to power, but he also discussed the discrepancies between theory and data in the work of Weber and Foucault as well. Hamilton then provided a variety of answers to his original question, How is it that these views are allowed to persist despite important evidence to the contrary?[100] Hamilton's work merits attention, and the reader is urged to take note of it. I just want to emphasize here by way of addressing this question that scholars constantly need to employ summary, codified language to account for the complexity of historical and contemporary situations and they are likely to use accepted and familiar arguments even when they are aware of data that render them problematic, rather than attempt to develop alternatives on their own or examine the significance of one or another available but competing alternative. In general, scholars are much more likely to invoke a widely accepted theory identified with an authoritative individual or tradition than to attempt to produce one of their own, no matter how substantial their knowledge may be.

Practically speaking, the important thing about the development of systematic interpretive theory, or the invention of codified language, is not the relationship to evidence, which hardly ever exists, but the degree to which authors are able to to instill hope by promising mastery through disciplined effort.[101] Also important, however, is the speed with which any author can turn out the work, thereby creating a perspective and possibly a school that others must acknowledge (or a market that others cannot stay out of). The famous language inventors could always do a number of things better than anyone else, particularly identifying patterns of behavior and devising novel language to explain their significance. But the one thing in particular these inventors do better than anyone else is produce it faster than anyone else, and while this is no small thing, their solutions do not necessarily address problems of evidence. Moreover, these perspectives are themselves typically so complex that it takes time to review empirically all the areas they cover, and because they often represent at least a partial, intuitive insight into social relationships, initial impressions can easily justify continued resort to them. After that, emotional issues—such as the need to demonstrate loyalty to a community, the reluctance to be critical of a venerated figure or tradition, and the difficulty of dealing with the prospect of having no ideologically compelling alternative vantage points available—prevail.

It is also important to emphasize that neither the systematic perspectives that elevate the interests and moral striving of those critical of the status quo, nor the perspectives of those who support it, are based on empirical considerations, much less are they based on the conclusions of value-free science. It is impossible to expect that future critical cultural conversations will be held in abeyance pending what the still radically deficient social and behavioral sciences might or might not produce; as Elster noted, if we wait for the kind of evidence that can provide unarguable conclusions, we will wait a long, long time. For this reason, however, it is necessary to pay attention to criteria that allow us to distinguish better from worse among different perspectives, and to devise new criteria, because it is important to guard against the implicit but widespread sense that in the absence of the ability to confirm specific interpretive conclusions by reference to evidence, one conclusion is as good as another. This is simply not the case.

NOTES

PREFACE

1. Jerome Bruner, *Acts of Meaning* (Cambridge, Mass.: Harvard University Press, 1990), xi. The "methodolatry" term was borrowed from Gordon Allport.

2. Richard Sennett, "Letter to the Editor," *The New York Review of Books* (May 25, 1995), 43.

3. Jerome Bruner, *Actual Minds, Possible Worlds* (Cambridge, Mass.: Harvard University Press, 1986), 139–47. Joseph LeDoux, *The Emotional Brain: The Mysterious Underpinnings of Emotional Life* (New York: Simon & Schuster, 1996), 227–46. Compare, for example, to Robert Wilcocks, *Maelzel's Chess Player: Sigmund Freud and the Rhetoric of Deceit* (Lanham, Md.: Rowman and Littlefield, 1994).

4. Lewis Thomas quoted in V. S. Ramachandran, "Anosognosia in Parietal Lobe Syndrome," *Cognition and Consciousness* 4 (1995): 22.

INTRODUCTION

1. Frederick C. Crews, *Skeptical Engagements* (New York: Oxford University Press, 1986); Frederick C. Crews et al., *The Memory Wars: Freud's Legacy in Dispute* (New York: New York Review of Books Press, 1995); Jeffrey Moussaieff Masson, *The Assault on Truth: Freud's Suppression of the Seduction Theory* (New York: Farrar, Strauss and Giroux, 1984); Frank J. Sulloway, *Freud, Biologist of the Mind: Beyond the Psychoanalytic Legend* (New York: Basic Books, 1983); Adolf Grünbaum, *The Foundations of Psychoanalysis: A Philosophical Critique* (Berkeley: University of California Press, 1984); Peter J. Swales, "Freud, His Teacher, and the Birth of Psychoanalysis," in *Freud: Appraisals and Reappraisals*, ed. P. E. Stepansky, 3 vols. (Hillsdale, N.J.: The Analytic Press, 1986–88, vol. 1, 1986), 3–82; Swales, "Freud, Katherina, and the First 'Wild Analysis,'" (ibid., vol. 3, 1988), 80–164.

2. Philip S. Holzman, "Psychoanalysis: Is the Therapy Destroying the Science?" *JAPA* 33 (1985): 727. Holzman offered various criteria as starting points for documenting his assertion.

3. Kenneth Eisold, "The Splitting of the New York Psychoanalytic Society and the Construction of Psychoanalytic Authority," *IJPA* 79 (1998): 881–82. On psychoanalysts' treatment of Freud's metapsychology see, for example, Wilma Bucci, *Psychoanalysis and Cognitive Science* (New York: The Guilford

Press, 1997), 2–3; Robert R. Holt, "The Current State of Psychoanalytic Theory," especially the section devoted to "The Decline and Fall of the Metapsychology," in *Freud Reappraised: A Fresh Look at Psychoanalytic Theory* (New York: The Guilford Press, 1989), 324–27. The economic and energy aspects of the metapsychology are in particular disfavor. Ibid., 326n20, 377; William I. Grossman, "Letters to the Editor," *JAPA* 34 (1986): 488–89; and the response by Darius Gray Ornston, *JAPA* 35 (1987): 489–91: "It is remarkable how much economic and regulatory considerations mattered twenty years ago and how little they mean today."

4. Malcolm Macmillan, *Freud Evaluated: The Completed Arc* (New York: North Holland Press, 1991), 603. Macmillan had already made this point, but it is worth emphasizing here again, because Macmillan's thorough, astute, but highly technical review has not gotten sufficient attention, and because my purposes, conclusions, and examples are different from his.

5. Fred Weinstein, *History and Theory after the Fall* (Chicago: University of Chicago Press, 1990), 92–116 and passim.

6. For an example of the interchangeable use of affect and emotion, see Edith Jacobson, *Depression: Comparative Studies of Normal, Neurotic, and Psychotic Conditions* (New York: International Universities Press, 1971), 6; or Peter H. Knapp, "Emotion and the Psychoanalytic Encounter," in *Affect: Psychoanalytic Perspectives*, ed. Theodore Shapiro and Robert N. Emde (Madison, Conn.: International Universities Press, 1992), 241. For an example of the distinctions among affects, emotions, feelings, moods, and so on, see Michael Franz Basch, "The Significance of a Theory of Affect for Psychoanalytic Technique," ibid., 298.

7. The importance of a theory of affects and the relation of affects to cognition is spelled out by Wilma Bucci, *Psychoanalysis and Cognitive Science*, passim. See also Antonio Damasio, *Descartes' Error: Emotion, Reason, and the Human Brain* (New York: G. P. Putnam's Sons, 1994), 158–59, 175, and passim. Sometimes Freud wrote as if there was a psychoanalytic theory of affects; for example, in "Group Psychology and the Analysis of the Ego" he wrote that "[l]ibido is an expression taken from the theory of emotions" (Freud, *SE* 18:90). But such a theory was never systematically developed; it did not exist. See Chapter 1 below.

8. As suggested by the more recent emphasis in history, sociology, anthropology, and other disciplines on the emotions. Peter N. Stearns and Carol Z. Stearns, "Emotionology: Clarifying the History of Emotions and Emotional Standards," *American Historical Review* 90 (1985): 813–36; Peter Stearns and Timothy Haggerty, "The Role of Fear: Transitions in American Emotional Standards for Children, 1850–1950," *American Historical Review* 96 (1991): 63–94. See also the symposium on the history of emotion, which includes papers by Carol Z. Stearns and Peter Stearns, Fred Weinstein, and John Toews, *The Psychohistory Review* 18 (1990); Randall Collins, "Is 1980's Sociology in the Doldrums?" *American Journal of Sociology* 91 (1986): 1347–49; Theodore D. Kemper, *A Social Interactional Theory of Emotions* (New York: Wiley, 1978); *Research Agendas in the Sociology of Emotions*, ed. Theodore D. Kemper (Albany: State University of New York Press, 1990); Richard A. Shweder, *Thinking through Cultures: Expeditions in Cultural Psychology* (Cambridge, Mass.: Harvard University Press, 1991), 241–65.

9. Michael Lewis, *Altering Fate: Why the Past Does Not Predict the Future* (New York: The Guilford Press, 1997), 177–78.

10. Richard Lazarus has argued that "although it is a daunting task, I believe we must . . . find effective ways of exploring what lies below the surface, how it relates to what is in awareness, and how it influences the entire emotion process." Quoted in Joseph LeDoux, *The Emotional Brain*, 67. LeDoux (68) also notes that both emotional and cognitive processing occurs unconsciously. It is important, however, to distinguish "dynamic" psychoanalytic conceptions of unconscious mental activity from cognitive conceptions of it. Cognitive conceptions typically relate to processes rather than contents, while interest in psychoanalytic conceptions typically relates to contents, and this is what I am referring to in my statement above. On the relationship of cognitive conceptions to psychoanalysis, see Wilma Bucci, *Psychoanalysis and Cognitive Science*, 8.

11. Most recently by Stanley A. Leavy, "Psychoanalysis as Askesis," *The Psychoanalytic Review* 86 (1999): 198.

12. Who now would accept Christopher Isherwood's characterization of himself as a camera with its shutter open, quite passive, recording, but not thinking. Jerome Bruner, *Actual Minds, Possible Worlds*, 98, 123, 130.

13. Morris N. Eagle, "The Psychoanalytic and the Cognitive Unconscious," in *Theories of the Unconscious and Theories of the Self*, ed. Raphael Stern (Hillsdale, N.J.: The Analytic Press, 1987), 164.

14. Freud, "The Question of Lay Analysis," *SE* 20: 248–49.

15. For example, George J. Makari, "The Seductions of History: Sexual Trauma in Freud's Theory and Historiography," *IJPA* 79 (1998): 857–69.

16. Freud then wrote in very "political" terms about the sexual abuse, describing the unequal conditions under which such abuse occurs, "conditions controlled by the adult who cannot escape his share in the mutual dependence necessarily entailed by a sexual relationship, and who is yet armed with complete authority and the right to punish, and can exchange the one role for the other to the uninhibited satisfaction of his moods, and on the other hand, the child who in his helplessness is at the mercy of this arbitrary will," and so on. "The Aetiology of Hysteria," *SE* 3:215.

17. Martin S. Bergmann, "Reflections on the History of Psychoanalysis, *JAPA* 41 (1993): 935.

18. Wilma Bucci, *Psychoanalysis and Cognitive Science*, 6.

19. Robert Wallerstein, "Psychoanalysis as a Science: A Response to New Challenges," *Psychoanalytic Quarterly* 55 (1986): 435. Ian Suttie had made this point with respect to Freud's version of psychoanalysis in 1935, in *The Origins of Love and Hate* (New York: The Julian Press, 1952), 218–19, 242–45. Psychoanalysts also refer to a break between developmental and clinical theories: the sequence of developmental phases cannot be inferred from the observations made in the clinical setting. Joseph Palumbo, "Bridging the Chasm between Developmental Theory and Clinical Theory," part I, *The Annual of Psychoanalysis* 19 (1991): 151–74. See also Elizabeth Lloyd Mayer, "Changes in Science and Changing Ideas about Knowledge and Authority in Psychoanalysis," *Psychoanalytic Quarterly* 65 (1996): 171.

20. Richard Lewontin, "Letter to the Editor," *The New York Review of Books* (May 25, 1995), 44.

21. It should be noted that for many psychoanalysts there is no source of data other than the clinical one, period.

22. David Sachs, "In Fairness to Freud: A Critical Notice of *The Foundations of Psychoanalysis*, by Adolph Grünbaum," in *The Cambridge Companion to Freud*, ed. Jerome Neu (New York: Cambridge University Press, 1991), 321–22. Sachs notes that Grünbaum slights Freud's reliance on symbolism because symbolism is not founded on clinical data. "To do so," Sachs claims, "is to give the go-by to one of the foundations of psychoanalysis" (322). But Grünbaum is right: the meaning of symbols is overdetermined, just as symbols have meaning at all levels of the personality (id, ego, superego, to use the structural language); an observer cannot ascribe a single meaning to them. Donald Spence, *The Freudian Metaphor: Toward Paradigm Change in Psychoanalysis* (New York: W. W. Norton, 1987), 47–48.

23. Freud, "Leonardo da Vinci and a Memory of His Childhood," *SE* 11:93; "Introductory Lectures on Psychoanalysis," *SE* 16:150. Robert R. Holt, "The Past and Future of Ego Psychology," in *Freud Reappraised*, 204.

24. Volney P. Gay, *Freud on Sublimation. Reconsiderations* (Albany: State University of New York Press, 1992), 87–88, 104, 110–11, 142.

25. E. H. Gombrich, *Meditations on a Hobby Horse*, 4th ed. (London: Phaidon, 1985), 31. Also, "Letters from Freud to Breton," *JAPA* 21 (1971): 128.

26. For example, Stanley A. Leavy, *The Psychoanalytic Dialogue* (New Haven, Conn.: Yale University Press, 1980), xiv. Leavy referred to Lacan as the most important contributor to psychoanalysis in recent times in these terms. However, Leavy is also quite critical of Lacan.

27. André Green, "Conceptions of Affect," *IJPA* 58 (1977): 146–49. Green, *Le Discours vivant: La Conception psychanalytique de l'affect* (Paris: Presses Universitaires de France, 1973); and "The Logic of Lacan's *objet a* and Freudian Theory," in *Interpreting Lacan*, ed. Joseph H. Smith and William Kerrigan (New Haven, Conn.: Yale University Press, 1983), 161–92. For another critical perspective on Lacan, see Joel Whitebook, "'A Scrap of Independence': On the Ego's Autonomy in Freud," *Psychoanalysis and Contemporary Thought* 16 (1993): 359–82. For other psychoanalytic perspectives on affects in clinical practice, see Steven H. Cooper, "Facts All Come with a Point of View," *IJPA* 77 (1996): 266–67.

28. No theoretical perspective has failed worse in this century than the structuralist perspective, whatever the vantage point, biological, psychological, social, or linguistic. See, by contrast, Hans Medick, "'Missionaries in the Row Boat?' Ethnological Ways of Knowing as a Challenge to Social History," *Comparative Studies in Society and History* 29 (1987): 88.

29. Craig Calhoun, "Social Theory and the Politics of Identity," in *Social Theory and the Politics of Identity*, ed. Calhoun (Cambridge, Mass.: Blackwell, 1991), 11–12, 33n6. Calhoun noted that a lot of recent social theory appears to be an unnecessary rehash of more familiar vocabularies; he could easily have made the same comment on the uses of psychoanalysis.

30. Elizabeth Lloyd Mayer, "Changes in Science and Changing Ideas about Knowledge and Authority in Psychoanalysis," *Psychoanalytic Quarterly* 65 (1996), 158–62.

31. Joseph LeDoux, *The Emotional Brain*, 33–34.

32. Thomas M. Ostrom, "Three Catechisms for Social Memory," David L, Hamilton, "Understanding Impression Formation," and Robert S. Wyer Jr., "Social Memory and Social Judgment," in *Memory: Interdisciplinary Approaches*, ed. Paul R. Solomon et al. (New York: Springer-Verlag, 1989), 201, 209–10, 212, 221, 223, 267. Subjective state, mood, and affect can only be understood by understanding the interplay between the cognitive system and social experience. By contrast with this level of complexity, researchers have only recently gotten their first glimpse of the physical activity underneath the creation of false memories, to give one example.

33. Joseph LeDoux, *The Emotional Brain*, 58–62.

34. "Pilgrims at Temples to Hash," *The New York Times* (June 23, 1993), C6. No author was cited for this article.

35. Molly O'Neill, "As Life Gets More Complex, Magic Casts a Wider Spell," *The New York Times* (June 13, 1994), A1, B7. Lionel Tiger is the social scientist quoted in this article.

36. Michiko Kakutani, "Horrors, or Why Monsters Are So Appealing," *The New York Times* (July 20, 1993), C19.

37. James Sterngold, "Does Japan Still Need Its Scary Monster?" *The New York Times* (July 23, 1995), sec. 4, p. 1.

38. This answer was provided by Douglas Noverr, described by *The New York Times* (May 28, 1992, C6) as a sports historian and professor of American thought and language at Michigan State University.

39. Karal Ann Marling, "City-Bashing through the Ages," *The New York Times Book Review* (May 10, 1992), 14 (hereafter, *NYTBR*).

40. Freud was obviously complicit in the formation and deployment of this familiar interpretive style that is intended to bypass the empirical problems raised by idiosyncratic outcomes. But he was by no means exclusively complicit; on the contrary, any structural vantage point that relies on a version of unconscious mental processes is complicit, and this is just one of the ways that psychoanalysis and the social sciences are linked in terms of outcomes.

41. Peter Berger, *Invitation to Sociology* (Garden City, N.Y.: Anchor Doubleday, 1964); "Sociology: A Disinvitation?" *Society* 30 (1992): 12–18.

42. Irving Louis Horowitz, *The Decomposition of Sociology* (New York: Oxford University Press, 1993), 4–5.

43. Stephen Cole, "Introduction: What's Wrong with Sociology?" *Sociological Forum* 9 (1994): 129. Irving Louis Horowitz, along with Berger, also pointed to the problems raised for a discipline that allows method to dictate approach. *The Decomposition of Sociology*, 5.

44. Clifford Geertz, *After the Fact: Two Countries, Four Decades, One Anthropologist* (Cambridge, Mass.: Harvard University Press, 1995). See the pages cited for the index entry, "Anthropology: Crisis of." See also the comments by Nancy Scheper-Hughes in her review of Geertz's book, "The End of Anthropology," *NYTBR* (May 7, 1995), 22.

45. Cited in Donald Spence, *The Rhetorical Voice of Psychoanalysis: The Displacement of Evidence by Theory* (Cambridge, Mass.: Harvard University Press, 1994), 85. The Skinner article referred to is "Whatever Happened to Psychology as a Science of Behavior?" *American Psychologist* 42 (1987): 784.

46. Kenneth Mark Colby and Robert J. Stoller, *Cognitive Science and Psychoanalysis* (Hillsdale, N.J.: Lawrence Erlbaum, 1988), 13.

47. Daniel Goleman, "Tough Call for Psychiatrists: Deciding Who Is Dangerous," *The New York Times* (July 13, 1986), A18. Earl Lane, "Predicting Lives of Crime," *Long Island Newsday* (June 4, 1985), 11.

48. John J. DiIulio, professor of political science and public affairs at Princeton University, quoted in Fox Butterfield, "Crime Fighting's About-Face," *The New York Times* (January 19, 1997) sec. 4, p. 1.

49. R. C. Lewontin, "Women versus the Biologists," *The New York Review of Books* (April 7, 1994), 32.

50. William D. Nordhaus, in his critical review of Joel E. Cohen's *How Many People Can the Earth Support?* noted that "after hundreds of pages of analysis and mathematics, we conclude that the number of humans the earth can durably support lies somewhere between one billion and one trillion; that the number changes over time and with technology; and that the factors determining the number are a complex and poorly understood interaction of land, water, social institutions and ingenuity." (*NYTBR* [January 14, 1996], 13).

51. Michael M. Weinstein, "Students Seek Some Reality amid the Math of Economics," *The New York Times* (September 18, 1998), B9, 11. Alan Blinder complained (B11) that what young scholars are writing now is "theoretical drivel, mathematically elegant but not about anything real."

52. Paul Krugman, *Peddling Prosperity: Economic Sense and Nonsense in the Age of Diminished Expectations* (New York: W. W. Norton, 1994), 9. See in general the preface and introduction, xi–xv, 3–19. Greg Mankiw quoted in John Cassidy, "The Decline of Economics," *The New Yorker* (December 2, 1996), 52.

53. Richard Thaler (then at Cornell, now at Chicago) is a leading "behavioral economist." Quoted in Peter Passell, *The New York Times* (April 12, 1994), A1, D10.

54. One example will have to suffice here: Robert Reich's recommendations as Secretary of Labor for raising the minimum wage were justified by the research of two Princeton economists, David Card (now at Berkeley) and Alan Krueger. Their research was vigorously criticized as sloppy by two other economists. According to Alan Blinder, a Princeton colleague defending the research of Card and Krueger in *The New York Times*, their critics used data provided by the Employment Policies Institute, "which is financed by manufacturers, restaurants and retailers and whose director has been a lobbyist for several fast food chains." The director of this institute, Richard Berman, came right back at Blinder in the same venue, once again attacking the research of Card and Krueger as sloppy (i.e., based on "real world" research and not on abstract mathematized theory). The comments by Card and Krueger on their research as reported in *The New York Times* are particularly interesting in a fantastical sort of way. See Sylvia Nasar, "Two Economists Catch Clinton's Eye by Bucking the

Common Wisdom," *The New York Times* (August 22, 1993), "News of the Week in Review," 6; and Nasar's earlier report on the subject, "Economics of Reality and Its Three Rising Stars," ibid. (June 29, 1992), D4. Interested readers can learn what the "reality" mentioned in the title refers to. Alan Blinder, "The $5.15 Question," ibid. (May 23, 1996), *op-ed* page. Richard Berman, "Letter to the Editor," ibid. (May 28, 1996), A16. See also Peter T. Kilborn, "A Minimal-Impact Minimum Wage," *The New York Times* (April 6, 1997), sec. 4, p. 5. Note particularly the comments of the Republican House Majority Leader, Richard K. Armey, himself a former professor of economics according to Kilborn, and completely wrong in his predictive assessments of the effects of the minimum wage bill. See also the comments on Card and Krueger by John Cassidy, "The Decline of Economics," 60.

55. Jon Elster, *The Cement of Society: A Study of Social Order* (New York: Cambridge University Press, 1989), viii. Nobel laureate Herbert Stein also noted that "Economists do not know very much," nor do their beliefs "provide a platform from which to make strong pronouncements about economics or economic policy." Quoted in Donald McCloskey, *Knowledge and Persuasion in Economics* (Cambridge, Mass.: Harvard University Press, 1994), 147, 218–19.

56. I have addressed this problem before in "Psychohistory and the Crisis of the Social Sciences," *History and Theory* 34 (1995): 299–319. Discussions of the heterogeneity problem go back a long way. See, for example, Ralph H. Turner and Lewis M. Killian, *Collective Behavior*, 2nd ed. (Englewood Cliffs, N.J.: Prentice Hall, 1972), 21–22, 25, 29, 259.

57. Borrowed with permission from Gerald M. Platt, "An Essay on the History and Epistemology of Weinstein's *History and Theory after the Fall*," in *The Psychohistory Review* 20 (1991): 3–20; see also *History and Theory after the Fall*, 68, 74–75, 153.

58. Lewontin, "Lettter to the Editor," *The New York Review of Books* (May 25, 1995), 44. Cognitive scientists who study human appraisal processes are for this reason challenged to find techniques that do not rely on verbal reports or on introspective commentary. Joseph LeDoux, *The Emotional Brain*, 67–68. It should be noted, however, that the processes by which particular contents achieve a primacy is only half the story. The other half is the source of the contents (liberalism, socialism, capitalism, and so on), which is an even tougher problem.

59. For example, Vicki Goldberg, "Photos That Lie—and Tell the Truth," *The New York Times* (March 16, 1997), sec. 2, pp. 1, 34.

60. Joseph D. Lichtenberg, "Listening, Understanding and Interpreting: Reflections on Complexity," *IJPA* 80 (1999): 719–20.

61. Paul Feyerabend, *Three Dialogues on Knowledge* (Oxford: Basil Blackwell, 1991), 41.

CHAPTER 1. LOSS AND AFFECT IN PSYCHOANALYSIS

1. Anna Freud, "Comments on Aggression," *IJPA* 53 (1972): 168. This harks back to her father's statement in *Civilization and Its Discontents* about

how mistaken he was to have overlooked the universality of nonerotic aggression. On the developmental (and theoretically problematic) switch from (childhood) aggression to (adult) sexuality that this perspective requires, see T. Wayne Downey, "Within the Pleasure Principle," *Ps St Chi* 39 (1984): 110–11. Elizabeth Young-Bruehl, "Anna Freud as a Historian of Psychoanalysis," ibid. 51 (1996): 66. On the preponderating influence of the sexual in Freud's work, Frank Sulloway noted that Freud made the claim so frequently that citing published examples is almost superfluous. *Freud: The Biologist of the Mind*, 376.

2. See, for example, the discussions of aggression in *The Freud-Klein Controversies, 1941–1945*, ed. Pearl King and Riccardo Steiner (London: Tavistock/Routledge, 1991), 442–43, 699–708, 828–31, and passim.

3. Others include Harry Guntrip, Henri Parens, Gregory Rochlin, Leon J. Saul, and Anthony Storr. Erich Fromm, *The Anatomy of Human Destructiveness* (New York: Holt, Rinehart, and Winston, 1973). On Erikson, see S. H. Foulkes, *IJPA* 33 (1952): 498. Henri Parens, "Development of Hostility," in *Affect: Psychoanalytic Perspectives*, ed. Shapiro and Emde, 81. Stephen J. Mitchell, *Hope and Dread in Psychoanalysis* (New York: Basic Books, 1993), 151–72.

4. Herbert Marcuse, *Eros and Civilization: A Philosophical Inquiry into Freud* (New York: Vintage Books, 1962), 149, 152–53. Also on narcissism as an independent vantage point, see Neville Symington, *Narcissism—A New Theory* (London: Karnac Books, 1993). Heinz Kohut, *The Analysis of the Self* (New York: International Universities Press, 1971); and Kohut, *The Restoration of the Self* (New York: International Universities Press, 1977). Annie Reich, *Psychoanalytic Contributions* (New York: International Universities Press, 1973).

5. Christopher Lasch, *The Culture of Narcissism. American Life in an Age of Diminishing Expectations* (New York: Warner Books, 1979), 22–23.

6. George Hagman, "Mourning: A Review and Reconsideration," *IJPA* 76 (1995): 909–24. Joseph Sandler, "Unconscious Wishes and Human Relationships," *Dimensions of Psychoanalysis*, ed. Joseph Sandler (Madison, Conn.: International Universities Press, 1989), 66. Peter Homans, *The Ability to Mourn: Disillusionment and the Social Origins of Psychoanalysis* (Chicago: University of Chicago Press, 1989), 221–31. Ian Suttie, *The Origins of Love and Hate* (New York: The Julian Press, 1952), 16, 205, 218–35.

7. On the experience of loss as the cultural source of psychoanalysis itself, see Peter Homans, *The Ability to Mourn*, 3–4 and passim; and Homans, "We (Not-So) Happy Few: Symbolic Loss and Mourning in Freud's Psychoanalytic Movement and the History of Psychoanalysis," *Psychoanalysis and History* 1 (1998): 69–85. Fred Weinstein and Gerald M. Platt, *Psychoanalytic Sociology. An Essay on the Interpretation of Historical Data and the Phenomena of Collective Behavior* (Baltimore: The Johns Hopkins University Press, 1973), 91–122. *Attachment Across the Life Cycle*, ed. Colin Murray Parkes et al. (London: Routledge, 1991). John Bowlby, *Attachment and Loss*, 3 vols. (London: Hogarth Press and the Institute for Psychoanalysis, 1969, 1973, 1980).

8. Peter Berger and Thomas Luckmann, *The Social Construction of Reality* (New York: Anchor Doubleday, 1966), 103. As the authors note, all social arrangements are precarious, all societies are constructions in the face of chaos.

9. Freud, "Civilization and Its Discontents," *SE* 21:108–9.

10. Fred Weinstein, *The Dynamics of Nazism* (New York: Academic Press, 1980), 118–21.

11. Michael Franz Basch, "The Concept of Affect: A Re-Examination," *JAPA* 24 (1976): 770, 774.

12. Humberto Nagera, "The Concepts of Structure and Structuralization," *Ps St Chi* 22 (1967): 98. See also Heinz Hartmann, *Ego Psychology and the Problem of Adaptation* (New York: International Universities Press, 1958), and *Essays on Ego Psychology: Selected Papers in Psychoanalytic Theory* (New York: International Universities Press, 1964). Walter Joffe and Joseph Sandler, "Adaptation, Affects, and the Representational World," in *From Safety to Superego*, ed. Joseph Sandler (New York: The Guilford Press, 1987), 221–34.

13. Peter Loewenberg, *Fantasy and Reality in History* (New York: Oxford University Press, 1995), 63.

14. André Green, "Has Sexuality Anything to Do with Psychoanalysis?" *IJPA* 76 (1996): 871–83.

15. For example, in terms of evolutionary psychobiology, Paul MacLean has argued that because the brain has been organized to encourage the creation of bonds and the avoidance of danger, our species is specially attuned to love and death and must suffer the pain of separation and loss. Noted by Winifred Gallagher, "Every Parent's Nightmare," *NYTBR* (June 2, 1996), 14.

16. See the series of papers by Harry T. Hardin, "On the Vicissitudes of Freud's Early Mothering," Part I, *Psychoanalytic Quarterly* 56 (1987): 628–44; part II, ibid., 57 (1988): 72–86; part III, ibid., 209–23. Characteristic for this literature, the papers are subtitled, respectively, "Early Environment and Loss," "Alienation from His Biological Mother," "Freiberg, Screen Memories and Loss." On the significance of loss to Freud, see also David Aberbach, *Surviving Trauma. Loss, Literature, and Psychoanalysis* (New Haven, Conn.: Yale University Press, 1989), 63–70.

17. Peter Homans, *The Ability to Mourn*, 1–28, 306, 221–31; Homans, "We (Not-So) Happy Few," 74–76. Philip Rieff, *The Triumph of the Therapeutic* (Chicago: University of Chicago Press, 1987), 2, 17, 21 (on "deconversion"). Ernest Gellner, "Psychoanalysis as a Social Institution," in *Freud in Exile*, ed. Edward Timms and Naomi Segal (London: Yale University Press, 1988), 223–29.

18. Bruce Mazlish, *A New Science* (New York: Oxford University Press, 1996). Robert Jay Lifton, *The Protean Self: Human Resilience in an Age of Fragmentation* (New York: Basic Books, 1993).

19. John Bowlby, *Charles Darwin* (London: Hutchinson, 1990), 53–79.

20. See note 16 above.

21. Stuart Feder, *Charles Ives: A Psychoanalytic Biography* (New Haven, Conn.: Yale University Press, 1992), 77, 129–30, 349–50. Edwin Haviland Miller, *Salem Is My Dwelling Place: A Life of Nathaniel Hawthorne* (Iowa City: University of Iowa Press, 1991), for example, pp. 25–26 (on the death of Nathaniel Hawthorne's father). Also on Nathaniel Hawthorne: T. Walter Herbert, *Dearest Beloved: The Hawthornes and the Making of the Middle-Class Family* (Berkeley: University of California Press, 1992). On Emily Dickinson, see

John Evangelist Walsh, *This Brief Tragedy: Unraveling the Todd-Dickinson Affair* (New York: Grove Weidenfeld, 1991), 97–100, particularly the references to *Wuthering Heights*; Judith Farr, *The Passion of Emily Dickinson* (Cambridge, Mass.: Harvard University Press, 1992), 126–28. Kenneth Silverman, *Edgar A. Poe, Mourning and Never-Ending Remembrance* (New York: HarperCollins, 1991), 76–78, 463–64 (bibliographic references to the psychoanalytic literature on death and mourning). See also Irving Howe, *The American Newness* (Cambridge, Mass.: Harvard University Press, 1986), 14, 65, 79. Wolf Lepenies, *Melancholy and Society*, trans. Jeremy Gaines and Doris Jones (Cambridge, Mass.: Harvard University Press, 1992). Lepenies refers as well to Judith Shklar, "The Political Theory of Utopia: From Melancholy to Nostalgia," *Daedalus: Journal of the American Academy of Arts and Sciences* (Spring 1965): 367.

22. Anthony Libby, "One Gives Us 'Happiness'; The Other 'Gluttony,'" *NYTBR* (January 15, 1995), 15.

23. Didier Anzieu, *Freud's Self-Analysis*, trans. Peter Graham (London: The Hogarth Press, 1986), 3–5. Homans, "We (Not-So) Happy Few," 71–74. William J. McGrath, *Freud's Discovery of Psychoanalysis: The Politics of Hysteria* (Ithaca, N.Y.: Cornell University Press, 1986), 173.

24. For example, Masson, *Letters*, 237 (letter of April 28, 1897).

25. Joan Raphael-Leff, "If Oedipus Was an Egyptian," *IRPA* 17 (1990): 325. Leff asserted that "the death of this baby [Freud's brother, Julius] was probably the most significant emotional event in Freud's entire life and remained encapsulated as an unprocessed wordless area of prehistoric deathly rivalry and identification." See also Carlo Bonomi, "Why Have We Ignored Freud the 'Paediatrician,'" in *100 Years of Analysis: Contributions to the History of Psychoanalysis*, ed. André Haynal and Ernst Falzeder (London: Karnac Books, 1994), 74–75. Bonomi also refers to the extraordinary influence of Julius's death, Freud's pathological mourning, and so on.

26. Peter Homans, *The Ability to Mourn*, passim. See also the papers of Harry T. Hardin cited in note 16; and Max Schur, *Freud: Living and Dying* (New York: International Universities Press, 1972), 124–25.

27. Helmut Thomä and Neil Chesire, "Freud's *Nachträglichkeit* and Strachey's 'Deferred Action': Trauma, Constructions and the Direction of Causality," *IRPA* 18 (1991): 410–11.

28. Ernest Becker, *The Denial of Death* (New York: Basic Books, 1973), 96. "*Consciousness of Death* is the primary repression, not sexuality" (italics in the original). J.-B. Pontalis was even more emphatic on this score. See *Frontiers in Psychoanalysis: Between the Dream and Psychic Pain*, trans. Catherine Cullen and Philip Cullen (New York: International Universities Press, 1981), 184. Richard A. Shweder, *Thinking through Cultures*, 244, 253–54.

29. William J. McGrath, *The Politics of Hysteria*, 170–71. Meynert had himself experienced a staggering succession of personal losses sufficient to destroy the morale of any human being, as Freud must have known. See Albert Hirschmüller, "Freud at Meynert's Clinic: The Paradoxical Influence of Psychiatry on the Development of Psychoanalysis," in *Understanding Freud: The Man and His Ideas*, ed. Emanuel E. Garcia (New York: New York University Press, 1992), 44–45.

30. Masson, *Letters*, 267–72.

31. Freud, *SE* 20:137.

32. A number of authors had earlier identified these experiences as traumatic, in addition to the many other references below. Suzanne Bernfeld, "Freud and Archeology," *American Imago* 8 (1951): 113. Bernfeld claimed that the move from Freiberg was a catastrophe that Freud spent his life trying to overcome. See Gregory Zilboorg, *Psychoanalysis and Religion* (New York: Farrar, Straus and Cudahy, 1962), 138, on Freud's lifelong difficulties with separation and loss.

33. Max Schur, *Freud: Living and Dying*, 124, 121–23. Schur was Freud's personal physician for the last decade of his life as well as a prominent psychoanalyst in his own right. In a footnote added to *The Interpretation of Dreams* in 1924, as discussed by Harry T. Hardin (Schur also referred to this footnote), Freud had dampened the significance of the emotional experience of separation and modified his recollection of its strength as he had described it earlier: "'I was crying my heart out' became transformed into a mild 'affect of disappointment' derived from 'the superficial motivation for the child's demand,' a wish for his mothers return." Harry T. Hardin, "On the Vicissitudes of Freud's Early Mothering," *Psychoanalytic Quarterly* 56 (1987): 630.

34. See Scott Dowling's comments in Lawrence B. Inderbitzen, Reporter, "Unconscious Fantasy," *JAPA* 37 (1989): 825; and Dowling's subsequent paper "Fantasy Formation: A Child Analyst's Perspective," *JAPA* 38 (1990): 95. Dowling notes that "[f]antasies of omnipotence and control are common efforts to assimilate these issues of helplessness."

35. Harry T. Hardin, "Freiberg, Screen Memories, and Loss," 212–14. Andrew Peto, "On Affect Control," *Psychoanalytic Study of the Child* 22 (1967): 36. Freud, "Screen Memories," *SE* 3:322. "Remembering, Repeating, and Working-Through," *SE* 12:148.

36. Freud, "Remembering, Repeating, and Working-Through," *SE* 12:148.

37. Edith Jacobson, *Depression*, 32.

38. Freud, "Totem and Taboo," *SE* 13:65.

39. Margaret S. Mahler, "On the First Three Subphases of the Separation-Individuation Process," in *The Selected Papers of Margaret S. Mahler*, 2 volumes in 1 (New York: Jason Aronson, 1982), 2:120 (paper originally published in 1972; italics in the original). It is useful to recall as well John Pratt's comments in the course of the Freud-Klein controversies of the 1940s: "Analysis is the accomplishment of mourning, the detachment of the libido from every infantile fixation point. . . . Our troubles start with reality, with separation." *The Freud-Klein Controversies, 1941–1945*, ed. King and Steiner, 338–39.

40. Paul Ricoeur, *Freud and Philosophy: An Essay on Interpretation*, trans. Denis Savage (New Haven, Conn.: Yale University Press, 1970), 372.

41. Joseph Sandler, "Reflections on Some Relations between Psychoanalytic Concepts and Psychoanalytic Practice," *IJPA* 64 (1983): 42. According to Sandler, psychoanalysts need to accept the proposition that "the latent content of a dream . . . can be an unconscious wish or fantasy created to deal with anxiety, pain, or any other unpleasant affect from any source. . . . *Not all unconscious wishes derive from the instinctual drives*" (italics in the original). See also San-

dler, "Reality and the Stabilizing Function of Unconscious Fantasy," *Bulletin of the Anna Freud Centre* 9 (1986): 177–94.

42. Joseph Sandler, "Unconscious Wishes and Human Relationships," in *Dimensions of Psychoanalysis*, 73 (italics in the original).

43. John Bowlby, *Personality and Mental Illness* (New York: Emerson Books, 1942), 146. On Bowlby and the emphasis among British psychoanalysts on loss, see N. Newcombe and J. Lerner, "Britain between the Wars: The Historical Context of Bowlby's Theory of Attachment," *Psychiatry* 44 (1981): 3–29.

44. On Marion Milner, see Michael Parsons, "Marion Milner's 'Answering Activity,'" *IRPA* 17 (1990): 418.

45. Erikson, *Young Man Luther* (New York: W. W. Norton, 1958), 261. David Aberbach, *Surviving Trauma*, 50.

46. Albert J. Solnit, "Youth and the Campus," *Ps St Chi* 27 (1972): 99. The paper of Anna Freud's is "Adolescence," in ibid., *Ps St Chi* 13 (1958): 255–78, referring to comments on 263.

47. Peter Blos, "Character Formation in Adolescence," *Ps St Chi* 23 (1968): 254.

48. Hans W. Loewald, "Ego and Reality," *IJPA* 32 (1951): 17.

49. Linda Joan Kaplan, "The Concept of Family Romance," *Psychoanalytic Review* 61 (1974): 171.

50. Didier Anzieu, *Freud's Self-Analysis*, 4–5.

51. Freud, "The Ego and the Id," *SE* 19:58.

52. Paul Ricoeur, *Freud and Philosophy: An Essay on Interpretation*, 369, 372. Margaret Mahler, "On the First Three Subphases of the Separation-Individuation Process," *IJPA* 53 (1972): 333.

53. Freud, "Beyond the Pleasure Principle," *SE* 18:14–15. See also "Three Essays on the Theory of Sexuality," *SE* 7:224: "Anxiety in children is originally nothing other than an expression of the fact that they are feeling the loss of a person they love"; and the passage cited earlier (p. 9) from "Inhibitions, Symptoms, and Anxiety," *SE* 20:137.

54. Freud, "Mourning and Melancholia," *SE* 14:243.

55. Freud, SE, "Types of Onset of Neurosis," *SE* 12:234.

56. Freud, "Group Psychology and the Analysis of the Ego," *SE* 18:118.

57. Freud "Moses and Monotheism," *SE* 23:60, 52.

58. Freud, ibid., 52. Ilse Grubrich-Simitis, *Freuds Moses-Studie als Tagtraum. Ein biographischer Essay* (Frankfurt: Verlag Internationale Psychoanalyse, 1991), 30–43.

59. The dream draws its title from Freud's slip, "non-vixit" ("he did not live"), in place of his intended "non-vivit" ("he is not alive"). Freud, ID, *SE* 5:422–23.

60. Freud, ID, *SE* 5:421–22, 480–84.

61. Freud, ID, *SE* 5:485, 423–24, 483.

62. See note 25. In addition, Richard P. Fox refers to passages in the Freud-Fliess correspondence that "seem to reveal a pining for a lost object." Fox also quotes a statement of Louis Stone's (1961), who suggested that "the psychoanalytic situation . . . tends to reproduce . . . the repetitive phases of the state of

relative separation from early objects." Richard P. Fox, "Towards a Revised Model of Psychoanalytic Technique: The Impact of Freud's Self-Analysis on Model Technique," *IRPA* 16 (1989): 478.

63. In addition to Harry T. Hardin, "On the Vicissitudes of Freud's Early Mothering: III, Freiberg, Screen Memories and Loss," 209–23, see also David Aberbach, *Surviving Trauma*, 66–69; Ruth Abraham, "Freud's Mother Conflict and the Formulation of the Oedipal Father," *Psychoanalytic Review* 69 (1982): 441–53; Jim Swan, "Mater and Nannie: Freud's Two Mothers and the Discovery of the Oedipus Complex," *American Imago* 31 (1974): 1–64; Samuel Slipp, *The Freudian Mystique* (New York: New York University Press, 1993), 80–90; Erich Fromm, *Sigmund Freud's Mission: An Analysis of His Personality and Influence* (New York: Harper and Brothers, 1959), 15; Philip Rieff, *The Mind of the Moralist* (New York: Doubleday, 1959), 203.

64. Ernest Jones, *The Life and Work of Sigmund Freud*, 3 vols. (New York: Basic Books, 1953), 1, 287. Kurt Eissler, "An Unknown Autobiographical letter by Freud and a Short Comment," *IJPA* 32 (1951): 322–23. Martin Bergmann, "Reflections on the History of Psychoanalysis," *JAPA* 41 (1993): 932–33. Octave Mannoni, "Psychoanalysis and the Decolonization of Mankind," in *Freud: The Man, His World, His Influence*, ed. Jonathan Miller, trans. Nicholas Fry (London: Weidenfeld and Nicolson, 1972), 93.

65. There has been some discussion of the problematic nature of Freud's concept of repression. On this see Morris N. Eagle, "The Psychoanalytic and the Cognitive Unconscious," in *Theories of the Unconscious and Theories of the Self*, ed. Raphael Stern (Hillsdale, N.J.: The Analytic Press, 1987), 179–80. V. S. Ramachandran, "Anosognosia in Parietal Lobe Syndrome," *Consciousness and Cognition* 4 (1995): 49.

66. Freud mentioned countertransference only four times in his career, and "he was clearly afraid to emphasize the analyst's reactions." From the introduction to *The Modern Freudians: Contemporary Psychoanalytic Technique*, ed. Carolyn S. Ellman et al. (Northvale, N.J.: Jason Aronson, 1998), xxv. Theodore J. Jacobs, "Countertransference Past and Present: A Review of the Concept," *IJPA* 80 (1999): 575–94.

67. Mark Kanzer, "Introduction: A Map of a Psychoanalytic Journey," in *Freud and His Self-Analysis* (Northvale, N.J.: Jason Aronson, 1979), 15. Referring to the tensions in Freud's relationship to Karl Abraham, Kanzer notes that "[s]elf-analysis found its limits here." On the "blind-spots" in the self-analysis, see Roberto Doria-Medina Jr., "On Freud and Monotheism," *IRPA* 18 (1991): 489. On resistances in the self-analysis, see Joan Raphael-Leff, "If Oedipus Was an Egyptian," *IRPA* 17 (1990): 309. Leff pointed out that there were instances of resistance in Freud's self-analysis that he would never have tolerated in anyone else. On Freud's failure to comprehend the significance of loss in his self-analysis, see Harry T. Hardin, "Freiberg, Screen Memories, and Loss," 214; and David Aberbach, *Surviving Trauma*, 67–69.

68. Masson, *Letters*, 281 (November 14, 1897).

69. *Sigmund Freud/Ludwig Binswanger. Briefwechsel 1908–1939*, ed. Gerhard Fichtner (Frankfurt am Main: S. Fischer Verlag, 1992), 80.

70. Nathan Hale, ed., *James Jackson Putnam and Psychoanalysis: Letters*

Between Putnam and Sigmund Freud, Ernest Jones, William James, Sandor Ferenczi, and Morton Prince, 1877–1917 (Cambridge, Mass.: Harvard University Press, 1971), letter of November 5, 1911, 133.

71. Freud, "The Subtleties of Faulty Action," *SE* 22:234.

72. Freud, "Analysis Terminable and Interminable," *SE* 23:248. The editors cite there still other references in Freud to the difficulties of self-analysis.

73. *The Freud/Jung Letters: The Correspondence Between Sigmund Freud and C. G. Jung*, ed. William McGuire, trans. Ralph Manheim and R. F. C. Hull (Cambridge, Mass.: Harvard University Press, 1988), Freud-Jung, November 29, 1912, 524; Jung-Freud, December 3, 1912, 525–26. On the fainting episodes noted there, see Max Schur, *Freud: Living and Dying*, 264–71. On Ferenczi, see Axel Hoffer, "Ferenczi's Search for Mutuality: Implications for the Free Association Method: An Introduction," in *100 Years of Analysis*, ed. Haynal and Falzeder, 199–201, 201n.

74. *The Freud/Jung Letters*, from Jung, December 3, 1912, 526; and Freud's response, December 5, 1912, 332.

75. Sandor Ferenczi, *The Clinical Diary of Sandor Ferenczi*, ed. Judith Dupont, trans. Michael Balint and Nicola Zarday Jackson (Cambridge, Mass.: Harvard University Press, 1988), 185–88, 92. *Correspondance Ferenczi-Groddeck* (Paris: Payot, 1982), 71–75.

76. Freud, "Leonardo da Vinci," *SE* 11:63.

77. Freud, "Inhibitions, Symptoms, and Anxiety," *SE* 20:136–37, 150.

78. Josef Breuer and Sigmund Freud, "Studies on Hysteria," *SE* 2:52.

79. As Jean G. Schimek has explained in detail, "Freud's conclusion that hysteria always requires the occurrence of sexual abuse in early childhood was not based directly on the patients' reports and conscious memories, but involved a great deal of selective interpretation and reconstruction." "Fact and Fantasy in the Seduction Theory: A Historical Review," *JAPA* 35 (1987): 938–39. George J. Makari, "The Seductions of History," *IJPA* 79 (1998): 680.

80. Masson, *Letters*, 430 (January 1, 1901). He also referred here to his deep loneliness.

81. Masson, *Letters*, 134 (July 24, 1895).

82. Sigmund Freud, *Briefe 1873–1939*, ed. Ernst L. Freud (Frankfurt am Main: S. Fischer Verlag, 1960), 72.

83. "I am so lonely" he wrote to Fliess. Masson, *Letters*, 172 (February 13, 1896). He had said as much to Fliess before.

84. Harry T. Hardin, "Early Mothering of Freud," II, 84. Michael Molnar, ed. and trans., *The Diary of Sigmund Freud, 1929–1939: A Record of the Final Decade* (New York: Charles Scribner's Sons, 1992), 82. Molnar also expressed surprise at this behavior of Freud's.

85. Harry T. Hardin makes this point as well, "Early Mothering of Freud," III, 222.

86. Freud, "An Autobiographical Study," *SE* 20:20.

87. Freud, "On the Psychical Mechanism of Hysterical Phenomena," *SE* 2:4. Sidney S. Furst, ed., *Psychic Trauma* (New York: Basic Books, 1967), 5.

88. Josef Breuer and Sigmund Freud, "Studies on Hysteria," *SE* 2:269. John Murray Cuddihy, *The Ordeal of Civility: Freud, Marx, Lévi-Strauss, and the*

Jewish Struggle with Modernity (New York: Basic Books, 1974), 28.

89. Israel Rosenfeld, *The Invention of Memory: A New View of the Brain* (New York: Basic Books, 1988), 6.

90. Freud, ID, *SE* 5:460–87.

91. Masson, *Letters*, 383 (November 7, 1899).

92. Freud, "Inhibitions, Symptoms, and Anxiety," *SE* 20:93–94.

93. On emotional resistance to psychoanalysis, "Introductory Lectures on Psychoanalysis," *SE* 15:23–24, *SE* 19:221. On biological aspects of affect, "Inhibitions, Symptoms, and Anxiety," *SE* 20:93–94. On affect and repression, "The Unconscious," *SE* 14:178. "Delusions and Dreams in Jensen's Gradiva," *SE* 9, 48–49.

94. For example, "Studies on Hysteria," *SE* 2:201–9.

95. Masson, *Letters*, 272.

96. Michael Franz Basch, "The Concept of Affect: A Re-Examination," *JAPA* 24 (1976): 774. Basch points out that affect had become a communication in the interest of adaptation rather than an indication of discharge—obviously by the time of *Inhibitions, Symptoms, and Anxiety*.

97. Nathaniel Ross, "Affect as Cognition: With Observations on the Meanings of Mystical States," *IRPA* 2 (1975): 79–93. Bjorn Killingmo, "Affirmation in Psychoanalysis," *IJPA* 76 (1995): 504–5.

98. Antonio Damasio, *Descartes' Error*, 171–72, 191. Jon Elster, "When Rationality Fails," in *The Limits of Rationality*, ed. K. S. Cook and M. Levi (Chicago: University of Chicago Press, 1990), 9–51. See also the special issue of *Political Psychology* 16.1 (March 1995).

99. Josef Breuer and Sigmund Freud, *Studies on Hysteria*, *SE* 2:4, 6 (italics in the original).

100. Bernard Penot, "Disavowal of Reality as an Act of Filial Piety, *IJPA* 79 (1998): 27.

101. Lawrence Friedman quoted in Richard P. Fox, "Towards a Revised Model of Psychoanalytic Technique," 477.

102. Freud, "The Question of Lay Analysis," *SE* 20:253–54.

103. Girard Franklin, "The Multiple Meanings of Neutrality," *JAPA* 38 (1990):200–1. Samuel Lipton, "The Advantage of Freud's Technique as Shown in 'The Rat Man,'" *IJPA* 58 (1977): 255–74.

104. Freud, "Recommendations to Physicians Practicing Psychoanalysis," *SE* 12:115–16.

105. Freud, "Remembering, Repeating, and Working-Through," *SE* 12:150.

106. On the significance of Dora's departure to Freud in these terms, Jules Glenn, "Freud, Dora, and the Maid: A Study of Countertransference," *JAPA* 34 (1986): 603–4. See also Axel Hoffer, "The Freud-Ferenczi Controversy—A Living Legacy," *IRPA* 18 (1991): 466–68. Hoffer explains Ferenczi's objections to Freud's therapeutic approach in these terms.

107. Wilfred R. Bion, *Cogitations* (London: Karnac Books, 1992), 365. Jerry Jennings, "The Revival of 'Dora': Advances in Psychoanalytic Theory and Technique," *JAPA* 34 (1986): 624.

108. See, for example, Freud/Binswanger, *Briefwechsel*, 86.

109. Colin Murray Parkes, *Bereavement: Studies of Grief in Adult Life* (London: Tavistock Publications, 1972), 74.

110. Freud, "Notes upon a Case of Obsessional Neurosis," *SE* 10:231–32. As Morris Eagle has noted, "[u]nawareness of a mental content (e.g., a wish) is only one means of disowning and only one possible symptom of failure of integration. Others are becoming intellectually and impersonally aware of an idea without the accompanying affect; experiencing generalized affects (moods) without connecting them to one's thoughts, wishes and expectations." As [George S.] Klein also emphasized, "failure to comprehend the personal significance of events or to make connections between them; failure to make a personal commitment to projects and aims pursued passively or symptomatically; or simply failure to experience certain sensations, goals, desires, emotions, wishes as familiar, characteristic of oneself, and one's own. All these means have in common a failure to acknowledge and integrate certain mental contents into one's self-organization." See Eagle, "The Psychoanalytic and the Cognitive Unconscious," 179–80.

111. Freud, "Letter to Frederick van Eeden," *SE* 14:301.

112. Freud, "Fragments of an Analysis of a Case of Hysteria," *SE* 7:77–78.

113. Schur, *Freud:Living and Dying*, 164.

114. See note 25.

115. Freud, ID, *SE* 5:485.

116. Joseph M. Jones, *Affects as Process: An Inquiry into the Centrality of Affect in Psychological Life* (Hillsdale, N.J.: The Analytic Press, 1995), 111–18.

117. Aaron Karush, "Instinct and Affect," in *Psychoanalysis: Toward the Second Century*, ed. Arnold Cooper et al., 85. Eric Gillett, "Revising Freud's Structural Theory," *Psychoanalysis and Contemporary Thought* 20 (1997): 495–96.

118. Bradd Shore, *Culture in Mind. Cognition, Culture, and the Problem of Meaning* (New York: Oxford University Press, 1996), 54–56. Stuart Clark, "French Historians and Early Modern Popular Culture," *Past and Present* 100 (August 1983): 91. For a version of the problem in a different domain, see Antonio Damasio, *Descartes' Error*, 243–44.

119. Christopher Lasch, *Haven in a Heartless World: The Family Beseiged* (New York: Basic Books, 1977), 60.

120. Take, for example, this contemporary psychoanalytic perspective on affects: as "the intertwined unit of drive-cognition-affect" dissolves, affect is provided with a developmental line of its own, and it plays "a far more prominent part in present-day psychoanalytic understanding than it did in the structural classical conception." Bjorn Killingmo, "Affirmation in Psychoanalysis," *IJPA* 76 (1995): 505.

121. Charles Spezzano, *Affect in Psychoanalysis: A Clinical Synthesis* (Hillsdale, N.J.: The Analytic Press, 1993), 62. See also Max Schur, "Affects and Cognition," *IJPA* 50 (1969): 650; and Peter Hartocollis, "Time as a Dimension of Affects," *JAPA* 20 (1972): 93.

122. Spezzano, *Affect in Psychoanalysis*, 62. George S. Klein, "The Vital Pleasures," in *Psychoanalytic Theory* I: *An Exploration of Essentials* (New York: International Universities Press, 1976), 210.

123. Jerome L. Singer, "Sampling Ongoing Consciousness and Emotional Experience: Implications for Health," in *Psychodynamics and Cognition*, ed. Mardi J. Horowitz (Chicago: University of Chicago Press, 1988), 299, 301. Mardi J. Horowitz, "Psychodynamic Phenomena and Their Explanation," ibid., 3–18.

124. See Nathaniel Ross's comments on Otto Fenichel's review of affect theory in psychoanalysis up to 1941, in "Affect as Cognition," 80.

125. There are other such instances, including especially Ferenczi's treatment of the clinical encounter, particularly his idea of "mutual analysis," which was understood for the longest time by psychoanalysts merely to have been a result of "the incomplete analysis he had with Freud"; there was no hint that Ferenczi could have had substantive reasons for his position, although these reasons are well argued now. Peter L. Rudnytsky et al., eds., *Ferenczi's Turn in Psychoanalysis* (New York: New York University Press, 1996). Martin S. Bergmann, "Reflections on the History of Psychoanalysis," 941.

126. Freud, "Civilization and Its Discontents," *SE* 21:65. For an overview of Freud's writings on affect, see Ruth Stein, *Psychoanalytic Theories of Affect* (New York: Praeger, 1991), 1–34. Hans Loewald, "Toward a Theory of Affects," in Pietro Castelnuovo-Tedesco, Panel Report, *JAPA* 22 (1974): 624. Note also the comments of Louis Kaywin (623) on the elusive quality of affect that prevents psychoanalysts from "achieving a more precise statement of its characteristics." Edward Joseph, too (615) underscored the private, subjective aspect of affective experience, which makes it difficult to describe and to theorize about.

127. Spezzano, *Affect in Psychoanalysis*, 53.

128. Richard P. Fox, "A Revised Model of Psychoanalytic Technique," 474.

129. Pietro Castelnuovo-Tedesco, "Toward a Theory of Affects," *JAPA* 22 (1974): 614.

130. Willard Gaylin, "Love and the Limits of Individualism," in *Passionate Attachments: Thinking about Love*, ed. Willard Gaylin and Ethel Person (New York: The Free Press, 1988), 53.

131. Frank M. Lachmann and Robert D. Stolorow, "The Developmental Significance of Affective States: Implications for Psychoanalytic Treatment," *The Annual of Psychoanalysis* 8 (1980): 215.

132. Henry Krystal, "The Hedonic Element in Affectivity," *The Annual of Psychoanalysis* 9 (1981): 94. On intellectualization, see also Pinchas Noy, ibid., 147–48.

133. Jones, *Affects as Process*, xxi. There are other instances of this approach as well. See Aaron Karush, "Instinct and Affect," in *Psychoanalysis: Toward the Second Century*, ed. Arnold Cooper et al., 133, 85.

134. Eugene F. Trunnell and William E. Holt, "The Concept of Denial or Disavowal," *JAPA* 22 (1974): 771.

135. Bernard D. Fine et al., *The Mechanism of Denial: The Manifest Content of the Dream*, Kris Study Group of the New York Psychoanalytic Institute (New York: International Universities Press, Monograph 3, 1969), 33. Charles M. Jaffe, "Disavowal: A Review of Applications in Recent Literature," *The Annual of Psychoanalysis* 16 (1988): 93–103.

136. On small signs, see Freud, "Leonardo da Vinci," *SE* 11:119.

137. Ruth Stein, *Psychoanalytic Theories of Affect*, xi.

138. Michael Franz Basch, "The Significance of a Theory of Affect," in *Affect: Psychoanalytic Perspectives*, ed. Shapiro and Emde, 295.

139. Charles Brenner, "On the Nature and Development of Affects: A Unified Theory," *Psychoanalytic Quarterly* 43 (1974): 533, 542, 544, 554.

140. Ethel Spector Person, "Romantic Love: At the Intersection of the Psyche and the Cultural Unconscious," in *Affect: Psychoanalytic Perspectives*, ed. Shapiro and Emde, 387.

141. Joseph Sandler, "Foreword," in Ruth Stein, *Psychoanalytic Theories of Affect*, vii. Spezzano, *Affect in Psychoanalysis*, 39. Henry Krystal, "The Hedonic Element in Affectivity," *The Annual of Psychoanalysis* 9 (1981): 95. Kurt Eissler wrote that "[f]rom 1900 on . . . Freud's creativity became immune to the vicissitudes of object relations. The quest for truth was maximally internalized, and Freud felt responsible to himself alone. He could rely on his conscience. . . . The responses of the outside world . . . did not count any longer, or else they took an inferior place." *Talent and Genius* (New York: Quadrangle Press, 1971), 297. This is the kind of idealization that would instantly have alerted Freud and made him wonder what kind of hostility such a mind could also harbor. Given Freud's high estimation of the power of unconscious mental activity, he would have been amused to learn that Eissler had arranged Jeffrey Masson's ill-fated and embarrassing appointment to the Freud Museum.

142. John Munder Ross, "A Psychoanalytic Essay on Romantic, Erotic Love," in *Affect: Psychoanalytic Perspectives*, ed. Shapiro and Emde, 453. On the relationship of cognition to affect, see, for example, Paul H. Seton, "The Psychotemporal Adaptation of Late Adolescence," *JAPA* 22 (1974): 802–3.

143. Ross, "A Psychoanalytic Essay on Romantic, Erotic Love," in *Affect: Psychoanalytic Perspectives*, ed. Shapiro and Emde, 451–52. Ethel Spector Person, "Romantic Love: At the Intersection of the Psyche and the Cultural Unconscious," ibid., 387. Willard Gaylin also asked "why in the fifty years of post-Freudian psychoanalysis a full blown attempt at consideration of love [sic] has not yet been attempted." "Love and the Limits of Individualism," in *Passionate Attachments*, 53. Evelyne A. Schwaber, "Reconstruction and Personal Experience: Further Thoughts on Psychoanalytic Listening," *JAPA* 34 (1986): 913. T. J. McLaughlin, "Transference, Psychic Reality, and Countertransference," *Psychoanalytic Quarterly* 50 (1981): 639–64.

144. Adrian Applegarth, "Psychic Energy Reconsidered," *JAPA* 25 (1977): 599–602. Adam Limentani, "Affects and the Psychoanalytic Situation," *IJPA* 58 (1977): 171–72.

145. Marjorie Brierly, "Affects in Theory and Practice," *Trends in Psychoanalysis* (London: The Hogarth Press, 1951 [1937]), 43–44 . Brierly's paper was effectively cited in *The Freud-Klein Controversies*, ed. Pearl King and Riccardo Steiner, 452. Brierly also cited a paper of Paul Federn's, "Zur Unterscheidung des gesunden und krafthaften Narcissimus," *Imago* 22, 5, which, she noted, contained the first systematic theory of affect in the literature.

146. Leo Rangell, "Psychoanalysis, Affects, and the 'Human Core,'" in *The Human Core*, 2 vols. (Madison, Conn.: International Universities Press, 1990), 1, 68.

147. Pietro Castelnuovo-Tedesco, "Toward a Theory of Affects," *JAPA* 22 (1974): 612, with reference also to statements by Arnold H. Modell and Burness Moore, as well as those already referred to, Loewald, Joseph, and Kaywin.

148. Leo Rangell, quoting Jacobson, ibid., 622. (Italics in Jacobson's original statement.)

149. Edith Jacobson, "Development of the Wish for a Child in Boys," *Ps St Chi* 5 (1950): 144. André Haynal made the same point in *Psychoanalysis and the Sciences: Epistemology-History*, trans. Elizabeth Holder (Berkeley: University of California Press, 1993), 59.

150. Edith Jacobson, *Depression*, viii, 3–4, 9, 12, 32, 36.

151. William W. Meissner, "Can Psychoanalysis Find Itself?" *JAPA* 34 (1986): 393.

152. The following references are meant to be illustrative, not exhaustive: Stuart Feder, "The Nostalgia of Charles Ives," *The Annual of Psychoanalysis* 10 (1982): 305–6. Feder quoted a statement of Glover's on the problem from 1938. David Rapaport, "On the Psychoanalytic Theory of Affects," *IJPA* 34 (1953): 177. This paper of Rapaport's is quoted more often on the subject than any other. Bertram D. Lewin, "Reflections on Affect," in *Drives, Affects, Behavior: Essays in Honor of Marie Bonaparte*, 2 vols. (New York: International Universities Press, 1965), 2:23. Lewin referred here to papers by Edith Jacobson and John Benjamin. Michael Radomisli, "Some Concepts in Search of a Theory," *Psychoanalytic Review* 60 (1973–74): 561-62. Ernst Kris explained that Freud had raised the issue of memory, the relationship of emotion to recollection, and the reorganization of thought in terms of memory and emotion, only to subordinate the series of problems and thoughts to the requirements of the drive theory. See the *Selected Papers of Ernst Kris*, "On Some Vicissitudes of Insight in Psychoanalysis," and "The Personal Myth: A Problem in Psychoanalytic Technique" (252–71 and 272–300, respectively). Arthur F. Valenstein, "On Attachment to Painful Feelings and the Negative Therapeutic Reaction," *Ps St Chi* 28 (1973): 370, 372. David Freedman quoted in Anthony Schmale, Reporter, "The Sensory Deprivations: An Approach to the Study of the Induction of Affects," *JAPA* 22 (1974): 626. Charles Brenner, "On the Nature and Development of Affects: A Unified Theory," *Psychoanalytic Quarterly* 43 (1974): 532–33. Vann Spruiell, "Theories of the Treatment of Narcissistic Personalities," *JAPA* 22 (1974): 276. Arnold H. Modell, "The Ego and the Id: Fifty Years Later," *IJPA* 56 (1975). André Green, "Conceptions of Affect," *IJPA* 58 (1977): 129. Jacob A. Arlow, "Affects and the Psychoanalytic Situation," in *Psychoanalysis: Clinical Theory and Practise* (Madison, Conn.: International Universities Press, 1991), 257. Pinchas Noy, "A Revision of the Psychoanalytic Theory of Affect," *The Annual of Psychoanalysis* 10 (1982): 139. Riccardo Steiner, "The Controversial Discussions," 12 (1985): 54. Peter H. Knapp, "Some Contemporary Contributions to the Study of Emotions," *JAPA* 34 (1986): 205–48. A. C. Garza-Guerrero, "The Superego Concept. part I: Historical Review; Object Relations Approach," *Psychoanalytic Review* 68 (1981): 321–42. See, for example, John

E. Gedo, "Kant's Way: The Psychoanalytic Contribution of David Rapaport," *Psychoanalytic Quarterly* 42 (1973): 416. Pinchas Noy, "Metapsychology as a Multi-Model System," *IRPA* 4 (1977): 8. Michael Franz Basch, "Empathic Understanding," *JAPA* 31 (1985): 106.

153. Stanley A. Leavy, "Psychoanalytic Interpretation," *Ps St Chi* 28 (1973): 326. See also Serge Viderman, "Interpretation in the Analytical Space," *IRPA* 1 (1974): 472. Warren S. Poland, "The Analyst's Word," *Psychoanalytic Quarterly* 55 (1986): 267–68, W. G. Joffe and Joseph Sandler, "Comments on the Psychoanalytic Psychology of Adaptation, with Special Reference to the Role of Affects and the Representational World," *IJPA* 49 (1968): 452. Charles Brenner, "Depressive Affect, Anxiety and Psychic Conflict in the Phallic-Oedipal Phase," *Psychoanalytic Quarterly* 48 (1979): 177–97. See also Mark Grunes, "The Therapeutic Object Relationship—II," in *The Modern Freudians*, ed. Carol S. Ellman et al., 132.

154. Rose Edgcumbe and Marion Burgner, "Some Problems in the Conceptualization of Early Object Relationships: Part I: The Concepts of Need Satisfaction and Need-Satisfying Relationships," *Ps St Chi* 27 (1972): 301.

155. Ross, "A Psychoanalytic Essay on Romantic, Erotic Love," 452.

156. On Freud's sense of the matter, in addition to the comment cited earlier from "Civilization and Its Discontents," see "Inhibitions, Symptoms, and Anxiety," *SE* 20:132.

157. Freud, "Beyond the Pleasure Principle," *SE* 18:51; "New Introductory Lectures on Psychoanalysis, *SE* 22:95; "Analysis Terminable and Interminable," *SE* 23:225.

158. "Within the universe of intersubjective meaning, we can only make the observation that . . . the formation of structures of meaning congruent with the structures of meaning in other persons, is at the same time an organization of affect." Stanley A. Leavy, "Psychoanalytic Interpretation," *Ps St Chi* 28 (1973): 326.

159. Robert N. Emde, "Moving Ahead: Integrating Influences of Affective Processes for Development and for Psychoanalysis," *IJPA* 80 (1999): 317–39.

160. On the psychoanalytic domain as Freud defined it, see the letter from Freud to Ferenczi, December 29, 1910, particularly Freud's statement that Jung was preoccupied with mythology but that hopefully he would return to the neuroses, "the motherland where we first have to secure our mastery against everything and everyone." *The Correspondence of Sigmund Freud and Sándor Ferenczi, 1908–1914*, ed. Eva Brabant, Ernst Falzeder, and Patrizia Giampieri-Deutsch (Cambridge, Mass.: Harvard University Press, 1993), 1:247. Frank Sulloway, *Freud*, 367. Leo Rangell, "Psychoanalysis, Affects, and the 'Human Core,'" 59, 61 (a comment on Heinz Hartmann's observation that psychoanalysis and the social sciences have two "different centers"). D. W. Winnicott, "The Location of Cultural Experience," in *Playing and Reality* (Hammondsworth, U.K.: Penguin, 1980 [1967]), 112–13.

161. Fausta Ferraro, "Trauma and Termination," *IJPA* 76 (1995): 62.

162. Freud, "New Introductory Lectures on Psychoanalysis," *SE* 22:179. Freud claimed here that psychology was chief among the social sciences; sociology was merely applied psychology.

163. On the status of the metapsychology, Robert R. Holt, "Death and Transfiguration of Metapsychology," in *Freud Reappraised*, 305–23. Wilma Bucci, *Psychoanalysis and Cognitive Science*, 2.

164. Leo Rangell, "Psychoanalysis, Affects, and the 'Human Core,'" 61–62.

165. Freud, "Introduction to 'Psychoanalysis and the War Neuroses,'" *SE* 17:207–10. "Inhibitions, Symptoms, and Anxiety," *SE* 20:129–30.

166. Freud, "Introduction to 'Psychoanalysis and the War Neuroses,'" *SE* 17:210 (207–10). "In traumatic neuroses and war neuroses the human ego is defending itself from a danger which threatens it from without or which is embodied in a shape assumed by the ego itself . . . [t]he ego is afraid of being damaged . . . by external violence." But see also "Inhibitions, Symptoms, and Anxiety," *SE* 20:129–30.

167. Freud, "Introductory Lectures on Psychoanalysis," *SE* 16:355, 432. Weinstein and Platt, *Psychoanalytic Sociology*, 37, for additional references.

168. Freud, "New Introductory Lectures on Psychoanalysis," *SE* 22:116. Freud pointed out here that psychoanalysis does not try to describe what a woman is, "but sets about enquiring how she comes into being."

169. For example, Freud worked hard to bring the war neuroses back to his preferred libidinal ground. "Inhibitions, Symptoms, and Anxiety," *SE* 20:129–30. Robert R. Holt, "Ego Autonomy and the Problem of Human Freedom," in *Freud Reappraised*, 222.

170. Freud, "Moses and Monotheism," *SE* 23:100. Max Schur, *Freud: Living and Dying*, 471–74. There is further discussion by Schur of this problem, including references to the criticism of Freud's position on the part of Jones, Kris, and Schur (473), and Schur's observation that Freud's stubbornness in the matter derived from unresolved neurotic conflict (474).

171. Leo Rangell, "Psychoanalysis, Affects, and the 'Human Core,'" 61. Of course individual psychoanalysts commented on various expressions of social conflict, but this was a personal concern and was not elevated in systematic theoretical terms.

172. Evelyne A. Schwaber, "Towards a Definition of the Term and Concept of Interaction," *IJPA* 76 (1995): 557.

173. Irving Steingart, "A Contemporary-Classical Freudian Views the Current Conceptual Scene," in *The Modern Freudians*, ed. Carolyn S. Ellman et al., 170.

174. This refers in particular to Erik Erikson. Robert Wallerstein, "Erikson's Concept of Ego Identity Reconsidered," *JAPA* 46 (1998): 229–46. Wallerstein explains that Erikson was never properly integrated into the psychoanalytic mainstream, but was marginalized instead.

175. Irving Z. Hoffman, "Discussion: Toward a Social-Constructivist View of the Psychoanalytic Situation," *Psychoanalytic Dialogue* 1 (1991): 74–105. Jay R. Greenberg, "Countertransference and Reality," ibid., 52–73, especially comments on Otto Kernberg and Roy Schafer, 58.

176. Irving Steingart, "The Current Conceptual Scene," in *The Modern Freudians*, ed. Carolyn S. Ellman et al., 164–72. As late as 1987 we still find references in the psychoanalytic literature to countertransference as a "neglected topic," and to "[t]he relatively sparse discussion of counter-transference" in the

literature. It was not until 1984 that "the term counter-transference ever appeared in the title of a program at the meetings of the American Psychoanalytic Association." Sidney J. Blatt and Rebecca Smith Bahrends, "Internalization, Separation-Individuation, and the Nature of Therapeutic Action," *IJPA* 68 (1987): 282. Jerry L Jennings, "The Revival of 'Dora': Advances in Psychoanalytic Theory and Technique," *JAPA* 34 (1986): 628. Jennings referred to the greatly expanded interest in countertransference as a "revolutionary change in attitude," noting also that it remains a controversial topic. Sander M. Abend, "Countertransference, Empathy, and the Analytic Ideal: The Impact of Life Stresses on Analytic Capability," *Psychoanalytic Quarterly* 55 (1986): 566. Shula H. Gray, "Countertransference and Hate," *Bulletin of the Menninger Clinic* 47 (1983): 15–35.

177. Michael Franz Basch has stated specifically that psychoanalysts must resort to extra-analytic disciplines for adequate perspectives on affect and cognition. See his comments on this and on Silvan S. Tomkins, in "The Significance of a Theory of Affects," in *Affect: Psychoanalytic Perspectives*, ed. Shapiro and Emde, 295–98. Martin Leichtman, "Developmental Psychology and Psychoanalysis: I. The Context for a Revolution in Psychoanalysis," *JAPA* 38 (1990): 915–50. Eric Gillett, "Learning Theory and Intrapsychic Conflict," *IJPA* (77, 1996): 689–706. Ruth Stein, *Psychoanalytic Theories of Affect*, chap. 8, 137–58. Wilma Bucci, *Psychoanalysis and Cognitive Science*. On neuroscience, see Richard C. Simons, "Our Analytic Heritage: Ideals and Idealizations," *JAPA* 38 (1990): 26.

178. Richard Lasky, "The 'More Difficult' Patient," in *The Modern Freudians*, ed. Carolyn S. Ellman et al., 205.

179. Edith Jacobson, *Depression*, 12.

180. Roy Schafer, "In the Wake of Heinz Hartmann," *IJPA* 76 (1995): 227. Martin Bergmann, "Asking for Freud's Blessing," in *The Modern Freudians*, ed. Carolyn Ellman et al., 290; idem, "Reflections on the History of Psychoanalysis," 951.

181. Dale Meers, "Contributions of a Ghetto Culture to Symptom Formation," *Ps St Chi* 25 (1970): 209–10, 213, 217. Ralph R. Greenson and Milton Wexler, "The Non-Transference Relationship in the Psychoanalytic Situation," *IJPA* 50 (1969): 32: "There is always the possibility that we, rather than the patient, are unrealistic about the external world, including the patient's world."

182. See by contrast, Adam Limentani, "On the Psychodynamics of Drug Dependence," in *Between Freud and Klein* (London: Free Association Books, 1989). After explaining the role of social and environmental factors in drug abuse (216–17), Limentani nevertheless insisted, by contrast with Zinberg, on the primacy of intrapsychic conflict (222).

183. Norman E. Zinberg, "Addiction and Ego Function," *Ps St Chi* 30 (1975): 567, 569, 571–72. Steven Maran, "Psychoanalysis on the Beat," ibid., 51 (1996): 522–23. The damaging effects of the persistent environmental threats characteristic of a war zone were astutely described by Sandor Ferenczi many years earlier, in terms of what later came to be called "cumulative trauma." "Über zwei Typen der Kriegsneurosen," *International Zeitschrift für ärtzliche Psychoanalyse* 4 (1916–17): 135. See also S. Freud, "Introduction to 'Psychoanalysis and the War Neuroses,'" *SE* 17:207.

184. This is no longer as true; see n. 177, this chapter.

185. For example, Nasir Ilahi, "Panel Report, The Psychoanalytic Status of Social Reality," *IJPA* 77 (1996): 53. Paul Williams, "Panel Report, Psychic Reality: Theoretical Concepts," ibid., 80. Roy Schafer, "Problems in Freud's Psychology of Women," in *Retelling a Life: Narration and Dialogue in Psychoanalysis* (New York: Basic Books, 1992), 59–60.

186. Erik Erikson, "Reality and Actuality," *JAPA* 10 (1962): 452–53.

187. Robert R. Holt, "Drive or Wish?" in *Freud Reappraised*, 194.

188. On the details of publication in *JAPA*: Kenneth T. Calder, Reporter, "Psychoanalytic Knowledge of Group Phenomena," 27 (1979): 146. Peter Gay recently noted that Burness Moore, after chairing the session of the American Psychoanalytic Association in 1977 on "Psychoanalytic Knowledge of Group Processes," expressed the hope that from then on psychoanalysts would discuss group processes more often than every twenty-one years (referring to the last time the problem had been raised). Of course they did not, leading Gay to conclude that the issue is even more urgent now than it was then. "From Couch to Culture," *The Psychohistory Review* 26 (1997): 11.

189. Lawrence B. Inderbitzen and Steven T. Levy, "On Grist for the Mill: External Reality as Defence," *JAPA* 42 (1994): 767.

190. Charles Brenner, "A Psychoanalytic Theory of Affects," in *Affects: Psychoanalytic Perspectives*, ed. Shapiro and Emde, 305. Others have made the same point with respect to countertransference. Theodore Jacobs, "Countertransference Past and Present," *IJPA* 80 (1999): 580.

191. There are other instances in which this happened. As Bennett Simon has written, "*The study of actual incest and its ramifications definitely moved out of the center of Freud's interests after the early 1900s and thus also was not a central interest of other psychoanalysts*" ("An Error in Psychoanalysis," 963 [italics in the original]).

192. This is not an example of "a community of disavowal." Bernard Penot, "Disavowal of Reality as an Act of Filial Piety," *IJPA* 79 (1998): 27–28.

193. The problems presented by different definitions of disorders, competing or alternative diagnoses, and the uncertainty as to whether some symptom is new or just recently emphasized as a result of changing focus among practitioners, should have given rise to a cultural or social analysis to account for them. But obviously this kind of analysis is difficult for psychoanalysts to accomplish, even when the need is clear. Jay Greenberg, *Oedipus and Beyond*, 179.

194. On traumatic experience, for example, Ethel Spector Person and Howard Klar, "Establishing Trauma," *JAPA* 42 (1994): 1068–69. The authors point out that Freud never completely denied the significance of traumatic experience, which is obviously true, but it never again had for him the salience that it did earlier or that it does for others now.

195. Robert Wallerstein, "Erikson's Concept of Ego Identity Reconsidered," 229–31. Stanley J. Coen, "The Passions and Perils of Interpretation (of Dreams and Texts): An Appreciation of Erik Erikson's Dream Specimen Paper," *IJPA* 787 (1996): 537. The work of Robert Jay Lifton deserves reexamination in this context as well.

196. Erikson, *Childhood and Society*, 278.

197. There is a significant bibliography on the issue of psychoanalysis as a natural as distinct from a hermeneutic science. But see Adolf Grünbaum, *The Foundations of Psychoanalysis: A Philosophical Critique* (Berkeley: University of California Press, 1984).

198. Riccardo Steiner, "The Controversial Discussion," *IRPA* 12 (1985): 54. "Affects, anxieties and defenses are the objects of research and yet at the same time are part of the personal experience of the researcher."

199. Many psychoanalysts have by now challenged the objective or "neutral" posture of the psychoanalyst, and the "scientific" position on which it rests. Irwin Z. Hoffman, "The Intimate and Ironic Authority of the Psychoanalyst's Presence," *Psychoanalytic Quarterly* 65 (1996): 103–4; Nancy J. Chodorow, "Reflections on the Authority of the Past in Psychoanalytic Thinking," ibid., 32–51. Owen Renick, "Analytic Interactions: Conceptualizing Technique in the Light of the Analyst's Irreducible Subjectivity," *Psychoanalytic Quarterly* 62 (1993): 585–91; and Renick, "The Ideal of the Anonymous Analyst and the Problem of Self-Disclosure," ibid. 64 (1995): 466–95.

200. "Robert Waelder on Psychoanalytic Technique: Five Lectures," ed. Samuel A. Guttman, *Psychoanalytic Quarterly* 56 (1987): 1-67, specifically, 18, 30, 31.

201. Maxwell Gitelson, "Therapeutic Problems in the Analysis of the 'Normal' Candidate," *IJPA* 35 (1954): 176. If Kohut's theoretical orientation served analysts who wanted to interact with their patients and who welcomed the justification from an authoritative source, how far-fetched is it to argue that the classical theory appealed to those who suffered from dampened affect who were not analyzed for this problem because it is so useful in the clinical situation, a problem that could well have characterized the supervising analyst too.

202. Theodore J. Jacobs, "Posture, Gesture, and Movement in the Analyst: Cues to Interpretation and Countertransference," *JAPA* 21 (1975): 77–92.

203. See note 190.

204. Freud, "Recommendations to Physicians Practising Psychoanalysis," *SE* 12:115.

205. John Klauber, *IJPA* 53 (1972): 389.

206. Adam Limentani, "Affects and the Psychoanalytic Situation," 172.

207. E. Victor Wolfenstein, "Mental Functioning in Theory and Practise," *IJPA* 66 (1985): 79. The "memory and desire" reference is to T. S. Eliot, "The Wasteland," from the first section, "The Burial of the Dead," quoted here.

208. Ernest Becker, *The Denial of Death* (New York: Basic Books, 1973), 195n.

209. Robert Zajonc "Feeling and Thinking Preferences Need No Inferences," *American Psychologist* 35 (1980): 153. See the comments on Zajonc and on David R. Heise, *Understanding Events: Affect and the Construction of Social Action*, in Harold L. Rausch's review in *Psychiatry* 44 (1981): 87. Silvan S. Tomkins, "The Quest for Primary Motives: Biography and Autobiography of an Idea," *Journal of Personality and Social Psychology* 14 (1981): 306. (See also Tomkins's two-volume work, *Affect, Imagery, Consciousness* (New York: Springer, 1962, 1963). In sociology, see Randall Collins, "Is 1980's Sociology in the Doldrums?" *American Journal of Sociology* 91 (May 1986): 1336, 1341. In

anthropology, see *Culture Theory: Essays on Mind, Self, and Emotion*, ed. Richard Shweder and Robert Levine (Cambridge: Cambridge University Press, 1984), including essays by Michelle Z. Rosaldo, 137–59, Robert I. Levy, 214–37, and Robert C. Solomon, 238–54. In history, see for example, Peter N. Stearns and Carol Z. Stearns, *Anger: The Struggle for Emotional Control in American History* (Chicago: University of Chicago Press, 1986); and *An Emotional History of the United States*, ed. Peter N. Stearns and Jan Lewis (New York: New York University Press, 1998).

210. Donald P. Spence, *The Rhetorical Voice of Psychoanalysis*, 103–4. See note 67 above.

CHAPTER 2. COGNITIVE ISSUES IN PSYCHOANALYSIS

1. Masson, *Letters*, 264; and the Fliess reference, 146 (October 20, 1895).

2. Masson, *Letters*, 264, 272.

3. Masson, *Letters*, 148 (October 31, 1895); 325 (August 31, 1898).

4. Masson, *Letters*, 237. Freud was able immediately to qualify this statement as he reported to his friend the appearance the day before of a new patient who had "brought a fresh confirmation of paternal etiology."

5. Didier Anzieu, *Freud's Self-Analysis*, 222. Masson, *Letters*, 239, 249.

6. Ernst Kris referred to the earlier version of psychoanalysis as the "seduction theory." See Henrika C. Halberstadt-Freud, "*Studies on Hysteria* One Hundred Years On: A Century of Psychoanalysis," *IJPA* 77 (1996): 985–86.

7. For example, Marianne Krüll, *Freud and His Father*, trans. Arnold J. Pomerans (London: Hutchinson, 1987). Marie Balmary, *Psychoanalyzing Psychoanalysis: Freud and the Hidden Fault of the Father*, trans. Ned Lukacher (Baltimore, Md.: Johns Hopkins University Press, 1982); Madelon Sprengnether, *The Spectral Mother: Freud, Feminism, and Psychoanalysis* (Ithaca, N.Y.: Cornell University Press, 1990); Donald P. Spence, *The Rhetorical Voice of Psychoanalysis: Displacement of Evidence by Theory* (Cambridge, Mass.: Harvard University Press, 1994), 19–20.

8. For example, Donald P. Spence, *The Rhetorical Voice of Psychoanalysis*, 18–19. Fred Weinstein and Gerald M. Platt, *Psychoanalytic Sociology: An Essay on the Interpretation of Historical Data and the Phenomena of Collective Behavior* (Baltimore, Md.: Johns Hopkins University Press, 1973), 102–14.

9. Erik Erikson, *Life History and the Historical Moment*, 58–79.

10. André Haynal, "Freud's Relation to Philosophy and Biology as Reflected in His Letters," in *100 Years of Psychoanalysis*, ed. André Haynal and Ernst Falzeder, 151–67. George J. Makari, "The Seductions of History," *IJPA* 79 (1998): 857–69.

11. Masson, *Letters*, 379.

12. Frank J. Sulloway, *Freud: The Biologist of the Mind*, 208–9.

13. Eric Gillett, "Learning Theory and Intrapsychic Conflict," *IJPA* 77 (1996): 703.

14. Masson, *The Assault on Truth*, 188.

15. Frank Sulloway, *Freud: The Biologist of the Mind*, 358.

16. Masson, *Letters*, 239; 144 (October 15, 1895).

17. Masson, *Letters*, 246–47, 249.

18. Masson, *Letters*, 252.

19. Masson, *Letters*, 261.

20. Masson, *Letters*, 259–60, 264–67, 270–73.

21. Masson, *Letters*, 184 (April 26, 1896); 147 (October 31, 1895).

22. Freud, "Three Essays on a Theory of Sexuality," *SE* 7:190–91,190–91n; "My Views on the Part Played by Sexuality in the Aetiology of the Neuroses," *SE* 7:274–75; "An Autobiographical Study," *SE* 20:36.

23. Freud wrote to Fliess, "Of course I shall not tell it in Dan, nor speak of it in Askelon, in the land of the Philistines." Freud erred here, as Kurt Eissler, among many others, has pointed out. "Freud referred here to II Samuel 1:20, where it says, 'Tell it not in Gath, publish it not in the streets of Askelon.' Why did he confuse Gath and Dan?" Eissler went on to explain this slip in great detail. K. R. Eissler, "An Interpretation of Four of Freud's Letters," in *Understanding Freud*, ed. Emanuel E. Garcia (New York: New York University Press, 1992), 89–92.

24. Masson, *Letters*, 265–66 (September 21, 1897).

25. Masson, *Letters*, 265 (September 21, 1897).

26. Freud, ID, *SE* 5:499.

27. Masson, *Letters*, 249, 269, 274, 284, 285 (May 31, 1897; October 3, 1897; October 27, 1897; December 3, 1897).

28. Masson, 283–84 (November 18, 1897).

29. Masson, *Letters*, 379, 404 (October 11, 1899; March 23, 1900).

30. See the discussion in Patrick Mahoney, "Psychoanalysis—The Writing Cure," in *100 Years of Psychoanalysis*, ed. Haynal and Falzeder, 110.

31. Breuer and Freud, "Studies in Hysteria," *SE* 2:295–96.

32. Freud, ID, *SE* 4:138n (italics added). In "The Psychopathology of Everyday Life," Freud also pointed out that he had committed a series of "historical errors" in *The Interpretation of Dreams* that had eluded him even though he had carefully proofread the text three times. Freud also ascribed these errors to an unsuccesssful attempt to conceal certain thoughts. *SE* 6:217–21.

33. Masson, *Letters*, 276 (October 31, 1897).

34. Sigmund Freud and Lou Andreas-Salomé, *Letters*, ed. Ernst Pfeiffer, trans. William and Elaine Robson-Scott (London: The Hogarth Press, 1972), 45 (May 25, 1916).

35. Freud, ID, *SE* 5:499. Letter to Felix Deutsch, quoted in Schur, *Freud: Living and Dying*, 357.

36. *A Psychoanalytic Dialogue: The Letters of Sigmund Freud and Karl Abraham*, ed. Hilda C. Abraham and Ernst L. Freud, trans. Bernard Marsh and Hilda C. Abraham (New York: Basic Books, 1965), 345 (February 15, 1924).

37. Masson, *Letters*, 274, 281 (October 27, 1897; November 14, 1897).

38. Freud, "Introductory Lectures," *SE* 16:288. "On Beginning the Treatment," *SE* 12:135n1.

39. Freud, "Creative Writers and Day-Dreaming," *SE* 9:146, 147–48.

40. *The Correspondence of Sigmund Freud and Sandor Ferenczi, 1914–1919*, 2:43 (January 11, 1915).

41. Freud, "Leonardo da Vinci," *SE* 11:80, 74, 77–78.

42. Freud, "The Ego and the Id," *SE* 19:44–45. Weinstein and Platt, *Psychoanalytic Sociology*, 50–51.

43. Joseph M. Jones, *Affects as Process*, 142–43. As Jones noted, mastery is difficult to fit within the framework of psychoanalytic theory, although this is changing. The major effort to establish a theoretical basis for competence/mastery as a motivational system was begun with Robert White's 1959 paper, "Motivation Reconsidered: The Concept of Competence," *Psychological Review* 66 (1959): 297–333; White also pointed out that Freud's *Inhibitions, Symptoms, and Anxiety* undercut the privileged position of libido and aggression in psychoanalysis. See also Eric A. Plaut, "Ego Instincts," *Ps St Chi* 39 (1984): 240.

44. Robert Waelder, "Opening Remarks to the Panel Discussion 'Neurotic Ego Distortion,'" *IJPA* 39 (1958): 243.

45. Kurt Eissler wrote, "The heroism—one is inclined to describe it so—that was necessary to carry out such an undertaking has not yet been sufficiently appreciated." *Talent and Genius: The Fictitious Case of Tausk contra Freud* (New York: Quadrangle Books, 1971), 279–80. There is more here of the same.

46. Eric Gillett, "Learning Theory and Intrapsychic Conflict," *IJPA* 77 (1996): 703.

47. Masson, *Letters*, 417 (June 12, 1900).

48. Masson, *Letters*, 147–48 (October 31, 1895); 332 (October 23, 1898).

49. Masson, *Letters*, 392 (December 21, 1899).

50. Schur, *Freud: Living and Dying*, 139. The incorrectness of this assessment is underscored by the two famous fainting episodes, and also by Freud's problems with Fliess and with Adler as "a little Fliess redivivus." See on Fliess, *The Freud/Jung Letters*, ed. William McGuire, trans. Ralph Mannheim and R. F. C. Hull (Cambridge, Mass.: Harvard University Press, 1988), 379–80 (letter to Jung of December 18, 1910).

51. Freud and Lou Andreas-Salomé, *Letters*, 206–7 (dated mid-January 1935). Sigmund Freud, Lou Andreas-Salomé, *Briefwechsel*, ed. Ernst Pfeiffer (Frankfurt am Main: S. Fischer, 1966), 226–27. On Lou Andreas-Salomé's relationship to Freud, see Biddy Martin, *Woman and Modernity: The (Life) Styles of Lou Andreas-Salomé* (Ithaca, N.Y.: Cornell University Press, 1991), 195–229.

52. Freud, "The Ego and the Id," *SE* 19:44, 27.

53. Freud, "Inhibitions, Symptoms, and Anxiety," *SE* 20:128.

54. See Erich Fromm's discussion of Freud in this context as a rebel and not a revolutionary. According to Fromm, a revolutionary, as distinct from a rebel, overcomes his ambivalence toward authority because he frees himself from attachment to authority and from the wish to dominate others, which, on his view, Freud had not done. *Sigmund Freud's Mission*, 60.

55. Freud, "On Narcissism: An Introduction," *SE* 14:94, 100–2.

56. Freud, "Future Prospects of Psychoanalysis," *SE* 11:147.

57. Anzieu, *Freud's Self-Analysis*, 1–2.

58. See, for example, Sidney J. Blatt and Rebecca Smith Behrends, "The Nature of Therapeutic Action," *IJPA* 68 (1987), 282.

59. Masson, *Letters*, 265 (September 21, 1897).

60. Carlo Bonomi, "Why Have We Ignored Freud the 'Paediatrician,'" in *100 Years of Psychoanalysis*, ed. Haynal and Falzeder, 55–99.

61. Freud, ID, *SE* 5:517.

62. Margo Jefferson, "Importance of Being Modern," *The New York Times* (May 12, 1997), C11, 13. J. E. Chamberlin, "From High Decadence to High Modernism," *Queens Quarterly* 87 (1980): 592, quoting Oscar Wilde: "One should so live that one becomes a form of fiction. . . . To be a fact is to be a failure."

63. Freud, ID, *SE* 5:467.

64. Freud, ID, *SE* 4:173.

65. Freud, ID, *SE* 5:434.

66. Freud, ID, *SE* 5:438 (italics in the original).

67. Masson, *Letters*, 74 (May 21, 1894).

68. Freud, ID, *SE* 4:260–63.

69. Peter Blos, "The Epigenesis of the Adult Neurosis," *Ps St Chi* 27 (1972): 107–10, and 109n3, references to Heinz Hartmann and to Freud's "Future of an Illusion," *SE* 21:3–56. Blos quoted Anna Freud's *Normality and Pathology in Childhood* (New York: International Universities Press, 1965), 151–52.

70. Bernice Neugarten, in Irving Sternschein, Reporter, "The Experience of Separation-Individuation in Infancy and Its Reverberations throughout the Course of Life," *JAPA* 21 (1973): 638.

71. Gerald M. Platt, "The Sociological Endeavor and Psychoanalytic Thought," in *Psycho/History: Readings in the Method of Psychology, Psychoanalysis, and History*, ed. Geoffrey Cocks and Travis L. Crosby (New Haven, Conn.: Yale University Press, 1987), 241–42. Richard A. Shweder, *Thinking Through Cultures*, 270, 284–86. The authors together have provided the necessary bibliography. See also S. Fisher and R. P. Greenberg, *The Scientific Credibility of Freud's Theories and Therapy* (New York: Basic Books, 1977), for example, 146.

72. Bennett Simon, "Is the Oedipus Complex Still the Cornerstone of Psychoanalysis? Three Obstacles to Answering the Question," *JAPA* 39 (1991): 662–63.

73. See remarks by Emmy Sylvester in Robert Gilman, Reporter, "Genetic, Dynamic, and Adaptive Aspects of Dissent," *JAPA* 19 (1971): 124–25. As Gilman noted in this report with respect to the radical behavior of the contemporary youth, "Early childhood experience is only an initial influence among many factors that shape dissident behavior" (125). Kenneth Keniston, also on this panel, stated that it was necessary for psychoanalysts to appreciate how sociocultural and historical events affected personality.

74. John Bowlby, *Personality and Mental Illness* (New York: Emerson Books, 1942), 188 (italics in the original).

75. Erik Erikson, *Young Man Luther: A Study in Psychoanalysis and History* (New York: W. W. Norton, 1962), 18. Peter Blos, "Character Formation in Adolescence," *Ps St Ch* 23 (1968): 246–47. Peter Blos, "The Epigenesis of the Adult Neurosis," *Ps St Chi* 27 (1972): 110.

76. Peter Blos, "The Epigenesis of the Adult Neurosis," 109. Here, once again, Blos claimed that it is "by now a generally accepted opinion" that the

"neurotic illness of the adult did not pre-exist in an immutable form from the prelatency years up to the time when it irrupts in the form of an adult neurosis."

77. Eva Rosenfeld, "Dream and Vision," *IJPA* 37 (1956): 100.

78. Erik Erikson, *Life History and the Historical Moment* (New York: W. W. Norton, 1975), 78.

79. Ibid., 78. Freud, "Moses and Monotheism," *SE* 23:12. As Freud often pointed out in this historical fiction (15, 28, n. 2, p. 28, 31, 89), no one could say where Moses actually came from or what his background was. A more obviously autobiographical comment is found in "The Moses of Michelangelo," *SE* 13:233: The highest mental achievement possible in a man is to struggle successfully against an inward passion for the sake of a cause to which he has devoted himself.

80. Freud, "Moses and Monotheism," *SE* 23:28.

81. Ibid., 23:12.

82. Freud, "An Autobiographical Study," *SE* 20:9. "Address to the Society of B'nai B'rith," *SE* 20:274.

83. Freud, "Leonardo da Vinci," *SE* 11:122–23. Freud referred to Leonardo's researches in the same terms that he referred to his own, that is, Leonardo was "engrossed in fathoming the great riddles of nature." Ibid., 124.

84. Ibid., 91–92, 99, 117, 121.

85. Erikson, *Life History and the Historical Moment*, 164.

86. Paul Roazen, *Freud and His Followers* (New York: New American Library, 1974), 420–21.

87. Jeanne Lampl-De Groot, "Some Thoughts on Adaptation and Conformism," in *Psychoanalysis—A General Psychology: Essays in Honor of Heinz Hartmann*, ed. Rudolph M. Loewenstein et al. (New York: International Universities Press, 1966), 340–41. Lampl-De Groot's statement on Michelangelo's guilt is a standard but unwarranted inference.

88. Freud, "Leonardo da Vinci," *SE* 11:75–76. On Freud's identification with Leonardo, Alan C. Elms, "Freud as Leonardo: Why the First Psychobiography Went Wrong," *Journal of Personality* 56 (1988): 24. Elms cites an often-quoted statement of Ernest Jones (*The Life and Work of Sigmund Freud*, 3 vols. [New York: Basic Books, 1953–1957], 2:432, 78), but he refers as well to J. D. Lichtenberg, Harry Trosman, and E. R. Wallace on the subject. On Freud's identification with Moses and Michelangelo, see Harold P. Blum, "Freud and the Figure of Moses: The Moses of Freud," in *Reading Freud's Reading*, ed. Sander L. Gilman et al. (New York: New York University Press, 1994), 113. (Blum, like Elms, provides other bibliography.)

89. See Freud's well-known statement on the liberation of individuals from the authority of parents as they grow up, "Family Romances," *SE* 9:237: "It is quite essential that that liberation should occur and it may be presumed that it has been to some extent achieved by everyone who has reached a normal state. Indeed, the whole progress of society rests upon the opposition between successive generations. On the other hand, there is a class of neurotics whose condition is recognizably determined by their having failed in this task."

90. Freud's father had wanted him to stay in England and join his brothers in business there. Freud, "Screen Memories," *SE* 3:314.

91. Eric Gillett, "Learning Theory and Intrapsychic Conflict," 703. Volney Gay, *Freud on Sublimation: Reconsiderations* (Albany: State University of New York Press, 1992), 88, 142.

92. Pierre Bourdieu, *Outline of a Theory of Practise*, trans. Richard Nice (Cambridge: Cambridge University Press, 1977), 86. Herbert Marcuse, *One-Dimensional Man* (Boston: Beacon Press, 1968), 6, 32.

93. I will return to the larger social implications of this position in chapter 5.

94. Charles Rycroft, *Imagination and Reality* (New York: International Universities Press, 1968), 102–3.

95. Masson, *Letters*, 207 (December 6, 1896).

96. Masson, *Letters*, 239 (May 2, 1897) and Draft L, 240.

97. Helmut Thomä and Neil Chesire, "Freud's *Nachträglichkeit* and Strachey's 'Deferred Action': Trauma, Constructions and the Direction of Causality," *IRPA* 18 (1991): 411.

98. Masson, *Letters*, 74 (May 21, 1894).

99. "All I was trying to do was to explain defense, but just try to explain something from the very core of nature!" Masson, *Letters*, 136 (August 16, 1895). See also the 1954 edition, *The Origins of Psycho-Analysis: Letters to Wilhelm Fliess, Drafts and Notes, 1887–1902*, ed. Marie Bonaparte, Anna Freud, and Ernst Kris (New York: Basic Books, 1954), 123; and the original text, *Briefe an Wilhelm Fliess*, ed. Jeffrey Moussaieff Masson (Frankfurt am Main: S. Fischer, 1986), 139.

100. For example, Freud, "On Beginning the Treatment," *SE* 12:131. The analyst "can point out that money matters are treated by civilized people in the same way as sexual matters—with the same inconsistency, prudishness, and hypocrisy. The analyst is therefore determined not to fall in with this attitude, but, in his dealings with his patients, to treat of money matters with the same matter-of-course frankness to which he wishes to educate them in things relating to sexual life."

101. Masson, *Letters*, 155 (December 8, 1895); Freud, ID, *SE* 4:103.

102. Ruth Thomas et al., "Comments on Some Aspects of Self and Object Representation in a Group of Psychotic Children," *Ps St Chi* 21 (1966): 557n10.

103. Freud, ID, *SE* 5:621. See the story told by Ernest Jones, *The Life and Work of Sigmund Freud*, 2:13–14.

104. It should be noted, too, that Ernst Kris had explained that Freud had raised the issue of memory, the relationship of emotion to recollection, and the reorganization of thought in terms of memory and emotion, only to subordinate the series of problems and thoughts to the requirements of the drive theory. *The Selected Papers of Ernst Kris*, "On Some Vicissitudes of Insight in Psychoanalysis," and "The Personal Myth: a problem in Psychoanalytic Technique," 252–71 and 272–300, respectively.

105. Peter Fonagy, "Memory and Therapeutic Action," *IJPA* 80 (1999): 218.

106. Robert R. Holt, "Drive or Wish," in *Freud Reappraised*, 179.

107. Evelyne Schwaber, "A Particular Perspective on Impasses in the Clinical Situation: Further Reflections on Psychoanalytic Listening," *IJPA* 76 (1995): 720. Schwaber, like Fonagy referred to in note 105, has adopted one of

several possible perspectives on psychoanalytic therapy. See Stephen A. Mitchell, *Hope and Dread in Psychoanalysis*, 51–53.

108. Peter Fonagy has argued, for example, that the recovery of memory is not part of the therapeutic action of the treatment, and there is no evidence that it is. "Memory and Therapeutic Action," 215–19.

109. Freud, "Analysis Terminable and Interminable," *SE* 23:227–28.

110. Patrick J. Mahoney, *Freud and the Rat Man* (New Haven, Conn.: Yale University Press, 1986), 213.

111. *The Correspondence of Sigmund Freud and Sandor Ferenczi*, 2 vols., ed. Ernst Falzeder and Eve Brabant, trans. Peter Hoffer (Cambridge, Mass.: The Belknap Press of Harvard University Press, 1996), 2:305 (October 27, 1918, italics in the original).

112. See in this vein, S. Freud, "Introduction to 'Psychoanalysis and the War Neuroses,'" *SE* 17:210 (207–10). But also "Inhibitions, Symptoms, and Anxiety," *SE* 20:129–30; and Meyer S. Gunther, "Freud as Expert Witness; Wagner-Jauregg and the Problem of the War Neuroses," *The Annual of Psychoanalysis* 2 (1975): 14.

113. Quoted in Ernest Jones, *The Life and Work of Sigmund Freud*, 3:464.

114. Anzieu, *Freud's Self-Analysis*, 1–2.

115. Freud, *The Letters of Sigmund Freud to Eduard Silberstein, 1871–1881*, ed. Walter Boehlich, trans. Arnold J. Pomerans (Cambridge, Mass.: The Belknap Press of Harvard University Press, 1990), 17–18 (September 4, 1872).

116. Freud, "Some Early Unpublished Letters," trans. Ilse Scheier, *IJPA* 50 (1969): 420. See the entry on Meseritch in Ignaz Bernstein, *Jüdische Sprichwörter und Redensarten* (Warsaw: for J. Kauffmann, Frankfurt am Main, 1908), 163. Bernstein related there one of the *schnorrer* (beggar) jokes Freud was so fond of.

117. Freud, *The Letters of Sigmund Freud to Eduard Silberstein, 1871–1881*, 121, and n. 4 (June 28, 1875).

118. Martin Freud, "Who was Freud?" in *The Jews of Austria: Essays on Their Life, History, and Destruction*, ed. Josef Fraenkel (London: Vallentine, Mitchell, 1970), 202. Sander L. Gilman, *Freud, Race, and Gender* (Princeton, N.J.: Princeton University Press, 1993), 165. See also the extraordinary statement, considering when it was written, by Arthur J. May *The Hapsburg Monarchy, 1867–1914* (New York: W. W. Norton, 1968), 179.

119. Sander Gilman, *Freud, Race, and Gender*, 15.

120. For example, Arthur Schnitzler, *The Road to the Open*, trans. Horace Samuel (Evanston, Ill.: Northwestern University Press, 1991), 382.

121. Masson, *Letters*, 268 (October 3, 1897). On Reik, see Erika Freeman, *Insights; Conversations with Theodor Reik* (Englewood Cliffs, N.J.: Prentice Hall, 1971), 80, 84–89. See also Sander Gilman, "Freud's Dora," in *Freud under Analysis: Essays in Honor of Paul Roazen*, ed. Todd Dufresne (Northvale, N.J.: Jason Aronson, 1997), 5, 8 (and 14, on *Mauscheln*, the speaking of German with a Yiddish accent, intonation, or vocabulary, as the language of Freud's mother).

122. Freud, ID, *SE* 5:467.

123. Ernest Jones, *The Life and Work of Sigmund Freud*, 1:178–79.

124. Freud, *The Letters of Sigmund Freud to Eduard Silberstein*, 126–27 (September 9, 1875).

125. McGrath, *Freud's Discovery of Psychoanalysis*, 63.

126. Freud, "Family Romances," *SE* 9:238–39.

127. Freud, "Some Reflections on Schoolboy Psychology," *SE* 13:244.

128. Freud and Lou Andreas-Salomé, *Letters*, 17 (June 29, 1914). "I was only able to carry out this inescapable task [of writing "On the History of the Psycho-Analytical Movement"] by writing as if I myself were the sole arbiter involved and by concerning myself as little as possible with a jury to whose favor I might have been appealing."

129. Freud, "Some Reflections on Schoolboy Psychology," *SE* 13:244. ID, *SE* 5:435. "The authority wielded by a father provokes criticism from his children at an early age, and the severity of the demands he makes upon them leads them, for their own relief, to keep their eyes open to any weakness of their father's."

130. Freud, ID, *SE* 4:197.

131. *Letters of Sigmund Freud*, ed. Ernst L. Freud, 26–27, 49 (August 18, 1882; August 28, 1883) .

132. Freud, ID, *SE* 5:437 (italics in the original).

133. Freud, ID, *SE* 5:435. Commenting on a dream, Freud noted that "it evidently meant to say: 'This is a *topsy-turvy* world and a *crazy* society; the person who deserves something doesn't get it, and the person who doesn't care about something *does* get it.'"

134. *Letters of Sigmund Freud*, ed. Ernst Freud, 302 (July 9, 1913). (Also in *The Correspondence of Sigmund Freud and Sandor Ferenczi*, ed. Eva Brabant et al., 1:500.)

135. *Letters of Sigmund Freud*, ed. Ernst L. Freud, 86–87 (January 10, 1884).

136. Masson, *Letters*, 374 (September 21, 1899).

137. Ibid., 266 (September 21, 1897). Freud, ID, *SE* 4:173.

138. Masson, *Letters*, 315, on "the *Dalles*" (June 9, 1898), and the quoted passage, 321 (July 30, 1898).

139. Masson, *Letters*, 392 (December 21, 1899) .

140. *Letters of Sigmund Freud*, ed. Ernst Freud, 27 (August 18, 1882).

141. *The Freud/Jung Letters: The Correspondence between Sigmund Freud and C. G. Jung*, ed. William McGuire, 210 (March 9, 1909; December 29, 1906). Jung had earlier pointed out that his wife was rich (14); and Fliess's wife had money as well. The circumstances of these colleagues did not make Freud feel any better.

142. *A Psycho-analytic Dialogue: The Letters of Sigmund Freud and Karl Abraham, 1907–1926*, ed. Hilda C. Abraham and Ernst L. Freud, 208. Ernest Becker, *The Denial of Death*, 115.

143. Freud, "An Autobiographical Study," *SE* 20:10–11.

144. Ibid., 11.

145. Freud's angry feelings about his indebtedness to Breuer are expressed, for example, in a letter to Fliess. Masson, *Letters*, 294 (January 16, 1898). Also

see on the subject, *Letters of Sigmund Freud,* ed. Ernst Freud, 116, 137–38 (June 29, 1884; March 10, 1885).

146. Freud, ID, *SE* 4:173.

147. Ibid., *SE* 5:434.

148. David Meghnagi, "Jewish Humor on Psychoanalysis," *IRPA* 18 (1991): 225.

149. John Martin, "Inventing Sincerity, Refashioning Prudence," *American Historical Review* 102 (1997): 1339. Martin offers a much more extensive and differentiated explanation including widely diffused humanist educational practice, evolving child-rearing theories, a developing model of companionate marriage, Protestant sermons that emphasized plain speaking, the diffusion of books, new practices of reading, and so on.

150. *The Letters of Sigmund Freud,* ed. Ernst Freud, 140–41 (April 28, 1885).

151. Joseph M. Jones, among others, has pointed out that Freud found it much easier to deal with guilt than with shame, so even if he thought about the implications of what he had done there is not much chance that he would have commented on it. *Affects as Process,* 140–41.

152. Freud, ID, *SE* 4:216–17.

153. Freud, "Moses and Monotheism," *SE* 23:12.

154. Peter Berger, *Invitation to Sociology,* 57–60. Hannah Arendt, *The Jew as Pariah: Jewish Identity and Politics in the Modern Age,* ed. Ron H. Feldman (New York: Grove Press, 1978), 43, 68.

155. Freud, ID, *SE* 4 (preface to the 2nd Edition), xxvi.

156. Masson, *Letters,* 202 (November 2, 1896).

157. Freud, "A Disturbance of Memory on the Acropolis," *SE* 22:247–48, 311–12 (italics in the original).

158. See by contrast Mark Kanzer, "Sigmund and Alexander Freud on the Acropolis," in *Freud and His Self-Analysis,* ed. Mark Kanzer and Jules Glenn (Northvale, N.J.: Jason Aronson, 1979), 259–84.

159. M. Masud R. Khan, *The Long Wait and Other Psychoanalytic Narratives* (New York: Summit Books, 1989), 62.

160. John E. Toews, "Historicizing Psychoanalysis: Freud in His Time and for Our Time," *Journal of Modern History* 63 (1991): 525.

161. Jacqueline Amati-Mehler et al., *The Babel of the Unconscious: Mother Tongue and Foreign Languages in the Psychoanalytic Dimension* (Madison, Conn.: International Universities Press, 1993), 67–71, 49–54. Ernest Jones, *The Life and Work of Sigmund Freud,* 1:3–4. "From his father Freud inherited his sense of humor, his shrewd skepticism about the uncertain vicissitudes of life, his custom of pointing a moral by quoting a Jewish anecdote, his liberalism and free thinking, and perhaps his uxoriousness. From his mother came, according to him, his 'sentimentality.' This word, still more ambiguous in German, should probably be taken to mean his temperament, with the passionate emotions of which he was capable."

162. Of course, Freud's outlook on life was derived from many cultural sources, but his family background was surely one of them.

163. *The Clinical Diary of Sandor Ferenczi,* ed. Judith Dupont, trans. M.

Balint and N. Zarday-Jackson (Cambridge, Mass.: Harvard University Press, 1990), 56, 93; see also 185–89 and Judith Dupont's "Introduction."

164. M. Masud R. Khan, *The Long Wait*, 200.

165. On the difference between Freud's approach and Ferenczi's, see Axel Holder, "The Freud-Ferenczi Controversy—a Living Legacy," *IRPA* 18 (1991): 465–71, especially 466.

166. Herbert Marcuse, *Eros and Civilization*, 227; on the difference between Freud's and Ferenczi's (and Fromm's) approach to therapy, based on the rejection of the "patricentric-authoritarian" and neutral posture of the therapist, as distinct from a nurturant posture, 222–23. Freud, *Briefe 1873–1939*, ed. Ernst L. Freud (Frankfurt am Main: S. Fischer, 1960), 52 (September 4, 1883). *The Letters of Sigmund Freud*, ed. Ernst L. Freud, 54.

167. Joseph Wortis, *Fragments of an Analysis with Freud* (New York: J. Aronson, 1984), 144–46.

168. Judith Heller, "Freud's Mother and Father," in *Freud as We Knew Him*, ed. Hendrick Ruitenbeek (Detroit: Wayne State University Press, 1973), 337–39.

169. In Josef Fraenkel, *The Jews of Austria*, 203–7.

170. Freud, "The Question of Lay Analysis," *SE* 20:253.

CHAPTER 3. OBSTACLES TO
THEORY AND PRACTICE IN PSYCHOANALYSIS

1. Erik H. Erikson and Huey P. Newton, *In Search of Common Ground. Conversations with Erik H. Erikson and Huey P. Newton*, ed. Kai T. Erikson (New York: W. W. Norton, 1973), 84–85 (italics in the original).

2. Clifford Geertz, "Ideology as a Cultural System," in *Interpretation of Cultures* (New York: Basic Books, 1973), 207.

3. Morris Eagle refers to an "integrated self structure" that includes "all the cognitive and affective contents, desires, plans, evaluative schemas,'rules,' representations, predispositions, and schemas that are part of one's overall personality." "The Psychoanalytic and the Cognitive Unconscious," in *Theories of the Unconscious and Theories of the Self*, ed. Raphael Stern (Hillsdale, N.J.: The Analytic Press, 1987), 180–81, 163, 165, 168.

4. George S. Klein, "On Hearing One's Own Voice," in *Drives, Affects, Behaviors*, ed. Max Schur, 1:90. Klein's position is still consistent with contemporary cognitive psychology and its emphasis on unconscious mental processes rather than on contents. On this, see Morris N. Eagle, "The Psychoanalytic and the Cognitive Unconscious," 155–90.

5. Jerome Bruner, *Actual Minds, Possible Worlds*, 117–18. Max Schur, "Affects and Cognition," *IJPA* 50 (1969): 647–53; and Michael Franz Basch, "The Concept of Affect: A Re-Examination," *JAPA* 24 (1976): 759–77.

6. H. Leventhal, quoted in Jeremy D. Safran and Leslie S. Greenberg, "Affect and the Unconscious: A Cognitive Perspective," in *Theories of the Unconscious and Theories of the Self*, ed. Raphael Stern, 206.

7. I have addressed the importance of emotions in this context before, in

Weinstein and Platt, *Psychoanalytic Sociology*, 91–93, 113–16. See also Weinstein, *The Dynamics of Nazism*, 54.

8. Jerome Bruner, *Actual Minds, Possible Worlds*, 117.

9. Jean Piaget, *Intelligence and Affectivity* (Palo Alto, Calif.: Stanford University Press, 1954), 5. Eric Gillett, "Revising Freud's Structural Theory," 491–95. Gillett provides additional relevant bibliography.

10. Jerome Bruner, *Actual Minds, Possible Worlds*, 117–18, 103–4, 110. Bruner also discusses in this context Nelson Goodman and Howard Gardner.

11. Jerome L Singer, "Sampling Ongoing Consciousness and Emotional Experience: Implications for Health," 299.

12. Antonio Damasio, *Descartes' Error*, 160. "What are the neural processes by which we *feel* an emotional state. . . . I do not know precisely; I think I have the beginning of an answer, but I am not certain about the ending."

13. Ibid., 159 (italics in the original), 124, 166.

14. Ibid., 175, 179. Raphael Stern also argues that "[e]motions are highly cognitive, value-bearing items that are best viewed as fitting and shaping interventions to one another. Since 'fitting' and 'shaping' are tasks of rationality, the emotions may be viewed as 'agents' of rationality." "Emotions and the Self," in *Theories of the Unconscious and Theories of the Self*, ed. Raphael Stern, 110.

15. Robert N. Emde, "Moving Ahead: Integrating Influence of Affective Processes," *IJPA* 80 (1999): 317–39.

16. Joseph D. Lichtenberg, "Listening, Understanding and Interpreting," *IJPA* 80 (1999): 719–20. Joseph M. Jones, *Affects as Process*, xxi–ii.

17. Harold Bloom, "Freud, The Greatest Modern Writer," *NYTBR* (March 23, 1986), 26.

18. Nelson Pichardo, "New Social Movements: A Critical Review," *Annual Review of Sociology* 23 (1997): 418.

19. Eve K. Sedgwick, *Epistemology of the Closet* (Berkeley, Calif.: University of California Press, 1990), 25.

20. Leo Rangell, "On the Cacophony of Human Relations," *Psychoanalytic Quarterly* 42 (1973): 343–44. Maxwell Gitelson, "On Ego Distortion," *IJPA* 39 (1958): 246. George Gero, "An Equivalent of Depression: Anorexia," in *Affective Disorders*, ed. Phyllis Greenacre, 138. Ernst A. Ticho, "The Development of Superego Autonomy," *The Psychoanalytic Review* 59 (1972): 221. John A. Lindon, "A Psychoanalytic View of the Family: A Study of Family Member Interaction," *The Psychoanalytic Forum* 3 (1969): 18–19. Stanley A. Leavy, "Psychoanalytic Interpretation," *Ps St Chi* 28 (1973): 324. Ralph R. Greenson, "The Problem of Working Through," in *Drives, Affects, Behavior*, ed. Max Schur, 2:278. Ava Siegler, "The Oedipus Myth and the Oedipus Complex: Intersecting Realms, Shared Structures," *IRPA* 10 (1983): 211. In an earlier work, *History and Theory after the Fall*, I provided a number of other examples of psychoanalytic reporting on the idiosyncratic results of therapy (25 and 173, notes 62–67).

21. Charles Brenner, "Countertransference as Compromise Formation," in *Countertransference*, ed. Edmund Slatker (Northvale, N.J.: Jason Aronson, 1987), 45.

22. Harold P. Blum, "The Position and Value of Extratransference Interpretation," *JAPA* 31 (1983): 590.

23. Philip S. Holzman, "Psychoanalysis: Is the Therapy Destroying the Science?" *JAPA* 33 (1985): 741.

24. Mortimer Ostow, Letter to the Editor, "The Unknown Freud: An Exchange," *The New York Review of Books* 41 (February 3, 1994): 37. There are many expressions of this point: Michael Rustin, "Social Organization of Secrets," *IRPA* 12 (1985): 144–45. Charles Brenner, "On the Nature and Development of Affects: A Unified Theory," *Psychoanalytic Quarterly* 63 (1973): 545.

25. Oliver Sacks, "Making up the Mind," *The New York Review of Books* 40 (April 8, 1993): 49.

26. Weinstein and Platt, *The Wish to Be Free*, 139. Weinstein, *History and Theory after the Fall*, 24–28.

27. Michael Parsons, "Marion Milner's 'Answering Activity,'" *IRPA* 17 (1990): 420–21, on Otto Fenichel, who thought that the patient gets taken by surprise, not the analyst, who has heard it all before.

28. Marshall Edelson, *Hypothesis and Evidence in Psychoanalysis* (Chicago: University of Chicago Press, 1984), 136–37. Theodor Reik raised this issue at the International meetings (Wiesbaden), 1933, stressing that genuine insight occurs as a surprise to both analyst and analysand. Harvey A. Kaplan, "The Theodor Reik Memorial Lecture," *NPAP News and Reviews* (Fall 1995), 1. Hartmann, Kris, and Loewenstein also addressed the issue of surprise, "The Function of Theory in Psychoanalysis," 120. See Donald P. Spence, *The Freudian Metaphor*, 119, 148.

29. See the many references in Henry F. Smith, "Analytic Listening and the Experience of Surprise," *IJPA* 76 (1995): 69.

30. Jay Greenberg (*Oedipus and Beyond*, 127) describes the Dora case as "a thriving cottage industry devoted to detailing what Freud should have discovered, but didn't." On the games people play: Maria Ramas, "Freud's Dora, Dora's Hysteria," *In Dora's Case. Freud—Hysteria—Feminism*, ed. Charles Bernheimer and Claire Kahane (New York: Columbia University Press, 1985), 168.

31. Masson, *Letters*, Draft E, 79 (June 1894). Ed. Masson, *Briefe an Wilhelm Fliess*, 72–73.

32. In *Minutes of the Vienna Psychoanalytic Society*, 4 vols., ed. H. Nunberg and E. Federn (New York: International Universities Press, 1962–76), 1:172.

33. Freud, "Inhibitions, Symptoms and Anxiety," *SE* 20:82, 65. No single event is the originator and no single form is characteristic of anxiety. There are various forms of phase-appropriate anxiety, the conditions of which are internalized as all the possible situations of threat, loss of the object, of the object's love, castration, and dread of superego persist in the mind. Any of them can become determinative of behavior again depending upon how people evaluate their ability to cope, especially with unexpected situations.

34. Freud to Else Voigtlander, in *Letters of Sigmund Freud*, ed. Ernst Freud, trans.Tania and James Stern (New York: Basic Books, 1960), 284–85 (October 1, 1911); (italics in the original).

35. Freud, "Types of Onset of Neurosis," *SE* 12:237; "Three Essays on the

Theory of Sexuality," *SE* 7:131; "Analysis Terminable and Interminable," *SE* 23:235.

36. Freud, "On Beginning the Treatment," *SE* 12:123.

37. Harold P. Blum, "The Transference in Psychoanalysis and Psychotherapy," *The Annual of Psychoanalysis* 10 (1982): 120. Sidney E. Pulver, "Can Affects be Unconscious?" *IJPA* 52 (1971): 347–54.

38. Masson, *Letters*, 286 (December 12, 1897). Freud made many statements on the subject, in "The Psychopathology of Everyday Life," *SE* 6:258–59, and *A Psychoanalytic Dialogue: The Letters of Sigmund Freud and Karl Abraham, 1907–1926*, ed. Hilda C. Abraham and Ernst L. Freud, trans. Bernard Marsh and Hilda C. Abraham (New York: Basic Books, 1965), 261–62. Weinstein, *History and Theory after the Fall*, 105–6.

39. On phylogenetic propositions as an embarrassment to psychoanalysts, see the citations in Malcolm Macmillan, *Freud Evaluated*, 541–42. Estelle Roith, *The Riddle of Freud: Jewish Influences on His Theory of Female Sexuality* (London: Tavistock Publications, 1987), 122. Thöma and Chesire, "Freud's *Nachträglichkeit* and Strachey's 'Deferred Action,'" 417.

40. Schur, *Freud: Living and Dying*, 313, and Jones, *The Life and Work of Sigmund Freud*, 3:310–13. Jones refers to his "obstinate adherence" to the discredited Lamarckian doctrine (311).

41. Freud, "An Outline of Psychoanalysis," 1940 [1938], *SE* 23:188.

42. Schur, *Freud, Living and Dying*, 472.

43. Morris N. Eagle, *Recent Developments in Psychoanalysis* (New York: McGraw-Hill, 1984), 30.

44. O. H. D. Bloomfield, "Anna Freud: Creativity, Compassion, Discipline," *IRPA* 18 (1991): 41.

45. Joseph Sandler, "The Id—or the Child Within?" in *Dimensions of Psychoanalysis*, 238.

46. Joseph Sandler, "Reflections on Some Relations between Psychoanalytic Concepts and Psychoanalytic Practice," *IJPA* 64 (1983): 37 (italics in the original); or Sandler, "The Id—or the Child Within?" in *Dimensions of Psychoanalysis*, 228.

47. On "absolute time," Masson, *Letters*, 268 (October 3, 1897). See the opposed arguments of John Toews ("Consuming Freud in Consumer Culture: Historicizing the Empty Self") and Eli Zaretsky ("The Problem of the Relation of 'Self' and 'Society' in Writing the History of Psychotherapy") in *The Psychohistory Review* 24 (1995): 21, 38.

48. Freud claimed, for example, that external forms of compulsion had become internal over time as the dependence on external authority in the regulation of impulse diminished. Weinstein, *History and Theory after the Fall*, 103–5.

49. Israel Rosenfeld, *The Invention of Memory*, 83, 159. See also Antonio Damasio, *Descartes' Error*, 240, 226–27. Damasio claims that "[a]t each moment the state of self is constructed, from the ground up. It is an evanescent reference state, so continuously and consistently *reconstructed* that the owner never knows it is being *remade* unless something goes wrong with the remaking." In Damasio's terms (158) we should think of behavior in terms of "live

performances" rather than as "rebroadcasts" (italics in the original).

50. Robert Waelder, "The Principle of Multiple Function: Observations on Over-determination," *Psychoanalytic Quarterly* 5 (1936): 5–62.

51. Heinz Hartmann, Ernst Kris, and Rudolph M. Loewenstein, "Some Comments on 'Culture and Personality,'" in *Papers on Psychoanalytic Psychology*, 110.

52. Anna Freud, quoted from Bennett Simon, "Can There Be a Psychoanalysis without a Political Analysis?" in *Genocide, War, and Human Survival*, ed. Charles Strozier and Michael Flynn (Lanham, Md.: Rowman and Littlefield, 1996), 292. William I. Grossman, "Psychological Vicissitudes of Theory in Clinical Work," *IJPA* 76 (1995): 889.

53. Charles Brenner, "Countertransference as Compromise Formation," 47–48.

54. Roy Schafer, "Ideals, the Ego Ideal, and the Ideal Self," in *Motives and Thought: Psychoanalytic Essays in Honor of David Rapaport*, ed. Robert R. Holt, Psychological Issues, Monograph 18/19 (New York: International Universities Press, 1967), 141. Mardi Horowitz et al., "Person Schemas and Emotion," in *Affect: Psychoanalytic Perspectives*, ed. Shapiro and Emde, 195. Elio J. Frattardi, *IRPA* 17 (1990): 275.

55. Peter McHugh, *Defining the Situation. The Organization of Meaning in Social Interaction* (New York: Bobbs-Merrill, 1968), 35–45, on emergence and relativity.

56. Erik Erikson, "The Problem of Ego Identity," in *Identity and the Life Cycle*, Psychological Issues (1, 1, 1959), 101. On Otto Fenichel, see Russell Jacoby, *The Repression of Psychoanalysis* (Chicago: University of Chicago Press, 1983), 102. Arnold H. Modell, "The 'Holding Environment' and Therapeutic Action of Psychoanalysis," *JAPA* 24 (1976): 361. Anna Freud, "The Mutual Influences of the Ego and the Id," *Ps St Chi* 7 (1952): 50. Jeanne Lampl-De Groot, "Re-evaluation of the Role of the Oedipus Complex," *IJPA* 33 (1952): 336; and Maxwell Gitelson, under the same title, ibid., 351, 354.

57. Barbara R. Easser and Stanley R. Lesser, "Hysterical Personality: A Reevaluation," *Psychoanalytic Quarterly* 34 (1965): 390.

58. Arnold H. Modell, quoted in Samuel Abrams, "Panel Report, "Models of the Psychic Apparatus," *JAPA* 19 (1971): 135. John Schimel et al., "Changing Styles in Psychiatric Syndromes, A Symposium," *The American Journal of Psychiatry* 130 (1973): 149.

59. On this point see, for example, Maxwell Gitelson, "Therapeutic Problems in the Analysis of the 'Normal' Candidate," *IJPA* 35 (1954): 175; Gitelson, "On Ego Distortion," *IJPA* 39 (1958): 246–47. Because of his emphasis on narcissism, Christopher Lasch also had a particular interest in this point. See *The Culture of Narcissism*, 87–90, 356–57, 390–91 (and the relevant footnotes for further bibliography). Weinstein and Platt, *The Wish to Be Free*, 286–87n28.

60. Joseph Sandler and Anne-Marie Sandler, "The Past Unconscious, the Present Unconscious, and Interpretation of the Transference," *Psychoanalytic Inquiry* 4 (1984): 385.

61. Ethel Spector Person, "The Crucial Role of Mentalism in an Era of Neurobiology," in *Psychoanalysis: Toward the Second Century*, ed. Cooper et al.,196–97. Damasio, *Descartes' Error*, 112.

62. Freud, "Screen Memories," *SE* 3:322.

63. Hans Loewald, "Hypnoid State, Repression, Abreaction and Recollection," *JAPA* 3 (1955): 210.

64. Ernst Kris, "The Recovery of Childhood Memories in Psychoanalysis," *Ps St Chi* 11 (1956): 54–88.

65. Freud "The Ego and the Id," *SE* 18:56; Holt, "Ego Autonomy and the Problem of Human Freedom," in *Freud Reappraised*, 219.

66. Humberto Nagera, "The Concepts of Structure and Structuralization," *Ps St Chi* 22 (1967): 95, 99, and passim.

67. Gilbert Rose, *The Power of Form: A Psychoanalytic Approach to Aesthetic Form* (New York: International Universities Press, 1980), 24–26, 91.

68. Jay Greenberg, *Oedipus and Beyond*, 137.

69. Daniel L. Schacter, *Searching for Memory*, 173–75. Ellie Ragland-Sullivan, *Jacques Lacan and the Philosophy of Psychoanalysis* (Urbana: University of Illinois Press, 1986), 22–24.

70. Irving Z. Hoffman, "The Intimate and Ironic Authority of the Psychoanalyst's Presence," *Psychoanalytic Quarterly* 65 (1996): 116–17. Peter Fonagy, "Memory and Therapeutic Action," *IJPA* 80 (1999): 218.

71. Eric Gillett, "Learning Theory and Intrapsychic Conflict," *IJPA* 77 (1996): 694.

72. Nancy J. Chodorow, "Reflections on the Authority of the Past in Psychoanalytic Thinking," *Psychoanalytic Quarterly* 65 (1996): 33, 40, 45–47. See Peter McHugh *Defining the Situation*, 31, for a definition of emergence. By contrast with Chodorow's standpoint, see Judith Hughes, *Emotion and High Politics: Personal Relations at the Summit in Late Nineteenth Century Britain and Germany* (Berkeley, Calif.: 1983), 10. Hughes writes: "Though one would hesitate to regard the emotional balance—or imbalance—achieved in childhood as fixed, one cannot help stressing the limited extent to which it is likely to change."

73. Irwin Z. Hoffman, "Toward a Social-Constructivist View of the Psychoanalytic Situation," *Psychoanalytic Dialogue* 1 (1991): 91.

74. Jay Greenberg, *Oedipus and Beyond*, 173 (italics in the original).

75. Richard Gartner et al., Letter to the Editor ("Victims of Memory: An Exchange"), *The New York Review of Books* (January 12, 1995): 42.

76. Irwin Z. Hoffman, "The Intimate and Ironic Authority of the Psychoanalyst's Presence," *Psychoanalytic Quarterly* 65 (1996): 116–17; and Hoffman,"Toward a Social-Constructivist View of the Psychoanalytic Situation," 94–95.

77. Neville Symington, *The Analytic Experience: Lectures from Tavistock* (London: Free Association Press, 1986), 19.

78. Janine Puget, cited in "Panel Report, Psychic Reality: Theoretical Concepts," *IJPA* 77 (1996): 80.

79. Roy Schafer, "In the Wake of Heinz Hartmann," *IJPA* 76 (1995): 229.

80. See Irwin Z. Hoffman, "Toward a Social-Constructivist View," 74. Robert S. Wallerstein, "Erikson's Concept of Ego Identity Reconsidered," *JAPA* 46 (1998): 240.

81. Roy Schafer, "Narratives of the Self," in *Retelling a Life. Narration and*

Dialogue in Psychoanalysis (New York: Basic Books, 1992), 23. W. W. Meissner, "Self-as-Agent in Psychoanalysis," *Psychoanalysis and Contemporary Thought* 16 (1993): 459–95.

82. In a technical sense the perspective has sources in phenomenological sociology, symbolic interactionism, ethnomethodology, reflexive sociology, philosophy, and cultural anthropology.

83. Helmut Thomä and Neil Chesire, "Freud's *Nachträglichkeit* and Strachey's 'Deferred Action': Trauma, Constructions and the Direction of Causality," 407–24. Masson, *Letters*, 207 (December 6, 1896). "As you know, I am working on the assumption that our psychic mechanism has come into being by a process of stratification: the material present in the form of memory traces being subjected from time to time to a *rearrangement* in accordance with fresh circumstances—to a *retranscription*" (italics in the original).

84. Arnold H. Modell, *Other Times, Other Realities: Toward a Theory of Psychoanalytic Treatment* (Cambridge, Mass.: Harvard University Press, 1990), 18–19. Israel Rosenfeld, *The Invention of Memory: A New View of the Brain,*192–93.

85. Quoted in Daniel L. Schacter, *Searching for Memory*, 106.

86. Israel Rosenfeld, *The Invention of Memory*, 75–80, 83, 156–59. See also, from a different perspective, Wilma Bucci, *Psychoanalysis and Cognitive Science,*105–6, and passim.

87. Daniel L Schacter, *Searching for Memory*, 91, 56, 266.

88. Hans W. Loewald, *Sublimation: Inquiries into Theoretical Psychoanalysis* (New Haven, Conn.: Yale University Press, 1988), 76. Loewald argued the matter somewhat differently, but he too explained how the infant/mother "invents the mouth-breast 'combination,' which comes into existence in the manner of a newly invented instrumentality."

89. Oliver Sacks, "Making up the Mind," *The New York Review of Books* 49 (1993): 44, 48. Sacks notes that Daniel Stern's *The Interpersonal World of the Infant: A View from Psychoanalysis and Developmental Psychology* (New York: Basic Books, 1985) is close to this position. Sacks (47) also refers to Esther Thelen ("Dynamical Systems and the Generation of Individual Differences," in *Individual Differences in Infancy: Reliability, Stability and Prediction*, ed. J. Colombo and J. W. Fagen [Hillsdale, N.J.: Lawrence Erlbaum, 1990]), noting that "[e]ach child . . . explores a rich range of possible ways to reach for an object and selects its own path, without the benefit of any blueprint or program. The child is forced to be original, to create its own solutions." This is the context for John Kotre's recent popularization of the topic, *White Gloves*, which is subtitled *How We Create Ourselves through Memory* (New York: The Free Press, 1995).

90. Antonio Imbasciati, "A Psychoanalytic Model of Cognitive Processes," *IRPA* 16 (1989): 225. Eric Gillett, "Learning Theory and Intrapsychic Conflict," 703. Joseph Sandler, "Psychoanalytic Psychology and Learning Theory," in *From Safety to Superego*, 256.

91. Quoting Jerome Bruner, *Acts of Meaning*, 105 (italics in the original). See Gerald M. Platt and Michael R. Fraser, "Race and Gender Discourse Strategies: Creating Solidarity and Framing the Civil Rights Movement," *Social Prob-*

lems 45 (1998): 175–76, with reference to the need to situate action, citing in addition Robert Benford, Clifford Geertz, C. Wright Mills, Michelle Rosaldo, and Alfred Schutz.

92. Weinstein and Platt, *Psychoanalytic Sociology*, 91–122.

93. Michiko Kakutani, "Art is Easier the Second Time Around," *The New York Times* (October 30, 1994), D4. See also the the following day's reference to the movie director John Dahl in William Grimes, "Film Noir of Open Spaces, not Mean Streets," *The New York Times* (October 31, 1994), C13.

94. James Wolcott, "Beyond the Values of the Supervixens: Two Washington Insiders Reinvent Themselves on the Spiritual Plane," *The New Yorker* (February 13, 1995), 91.

95. Quoted from Richard D. Lyons' obituary of Ralph Ellison, *The New York Times* (April 17, 1994), B38. Lifton too refers to Ellison in this context, *Protean Man*, 33.

96. Peter J. Boyer, "The Rise of Kweisi Mfume," *The New Yorker* (August 1, 1994), 29.

97. Robert Jay Lifton, "Protean Man," *Partisan Review* 35 (1968): 1–27; "Protean Man," *Archive of General Psychiatry* 24 (1971): 298–304. On the relationship of Erikson to Lifton in this connection, Lawrence J. Freidman, "Erik Erikson and Robert Lifton: The Pattern of a Relationship," in *Trauma and Self*, ed. Charles B. Strozier and Michael Flynn, 131–50.

98. Kai T. Erikson, *In Search of Common Ground*, 121–22, 129.

99. For a psychoanalytic discussion of the invention or reinvention of self that remains within the traditional domain, see Stephen Rittenberg and L. Noah Shaw, "On Fantasies of Self-Creation," *Ps St Chi* 46 (1991): 217–35.

100. Robert Jay Lifton, *The Protean Self*, 3. Lifton indicated that the process "can be traced back to the Enlightenment and even the Renaissance in the West, and to at least the Meiji Restoration of the nineteenth century in Japan." Lifton included among the historical influences the dislocations of rapid historical change, the mass media revolution, and the threat of human extinction.

101. Robert Jay Lifton, *The Protean Self*, 10, 33, 50. Lifton has also continued to elaborate a concept of "multiple selves," a much more inclusive characterological shift that he sees emerging in everyday life as a way of addressing novel conditions in an ever changing society. Erikson in 1971 had trouble with the concept (*In Search of Common Ground*, 122), but I doubt that he would now. Robert Jay Lifton, "The Protean Man," *Partisan Review* (Winter 1968): 13–27; *The Protean Self*, 1–34. On Lifton's role in psychohistory, see Philip Pomper, *The Structure of Mind in History: Five Major Figures in Psychohistory* (New York: Columbia University Press, 1985), 156–58, 164–65.

102. Stephen Greenblatt, *Renaissance Self-Fashioning: From Moore to Shakespeare* (Chicago: University of Chicago Press, 1980), 2–3. The ability to invent or reinvent versions of oneself is never independent of the larger culture from whence comes the language necessary for the project. See, however, the astute critique of Greenblatt (and Michel Foucault), by John Martin, "Inventing Sincerity, Refashioning Prudence: The Discovery of the Individual in Renaissance Europe," *American Historical Review* 102 (December 1977): 1316–17, 1335, 1337–40. See also Stephen Greenblatt, "Fiction and Friction," and

Natalie Zemon Davis, "Boundaries and the Sense of Self in Sixteenth-Century France," in *Reconstructing Individualism. Autonomy, Individuality and the Self in Western Thought*, ed.Thomas Heller et al. (Stanford, Calif.: Stanford Univesity Press, 1986), 30–52, 53–63.

103. Nelson A. Pichardo, "New Social Movements: A Critical Review," *Annual Review of Sociology* 23 (1997): 411–30. Weinstein and Platt, *Psychoanalytic Sociology*, 72–73.

104. Peter Blos, "Character Formation in Adolescence," *Ps St Chi* 23 (1968): 246–47.

105. Gerald M. Platt and Stephen J. Lilley, "Multiple Images of a Charismatic: Constructing Martin Luther King Jr.'s Leadership," in *Self, Collective Behavior and Society*, ed. Gerald M. Platt and Chad Gordon (Greenwich, Conn.: JAI Press, 1995).

106. Weinstein and Platt, *Psychoanalytic Sociology*, 72.

107. Peter Blos, "Character Formation in Adolescence," 246–47.

108. Nancy J. Chodorow, "Reflections on the Authority of the Past in Psychoanalytic Thinking," 33–34, 41, 44–47.

109. On this see Peter McHugh, *Defining the Situation*, passim.

110. Erikson, *Childhood and Society*, 279–83, 295 (on discontinuity); see below on active constructions.

111. Erikson, *Life History and the Historical Moment* (New York: W. W. Norton, 1975), 205–6. For Erikson's relationship to Lifton in these terms, see Lawrence J. Friedman, "Erik Erikson and Robert Lifton: The Pattern of a Relationship," in *Trauma and Self*, ed. Charles Strozier and Michael Flynn (Lanham, Md.: Rowman and Littlefield, 1996), 131–50. Note particularly the reference to two papers (149) by Lifton, "Protean Man," *Partisan Review* 35 (1968): 1–27; and "Protean Man," *Archives of General Psychiatry* 24 (1971): 298–304.

112. *In Search of Common Ground: Conversations with Erik H. Erikson and Huey P. Newton*, ed. Kai T. Erikson, 89–90 (italics added).

113. *In Search of Common Ground*, 121–22.

114. Ibid., 134.

115. See the recent discussions of Erikson's contributions in the psychoanalytic literature: Robert S. Wallerstein, "Erikson's Concept of Ego Identity Reconsidered," *JAPA* 46 (1998): 229–47; Stanley J. Coen, "The Passions and Perils of Interpretation (of Dreams and Texts): An Appreciation of Erik Erikson's Dream Specimen Paper," *IJPA* 77 (1996): 537–47.

116. See, for example, Erikson's comments on Freud and Marx, *In Search of Common Ground*, 104. "In historical perspective, the young Marx and the young Freud were much less far apart from each other than was the case when they became Marx and Freud."

117. Veikko Takha, "The Early Formation of the Mind," *IJPA* 68 (1987): 241. Allan Compton, "The Current Status of the Psychoanalytic Theory of Instinctual Drives," *Psychoanalytic Quarterly* 52 (1983): 365. Instinctual drive "to be understood as a demand for work made by the body upon the mind in itself is without quality." Jean G. Schimek, "A Critical Re-examination of Freud's Concept of Unconscious Mental Representation," *IRPA* 2 (1975):

179–80; and Schimek, "The Interpretation of the Past: Childhood Trauma, Psychical Reality, and Historical Truth," *JAPA* 23 (1975): 854.

118. Veikko Takha, "The Early Formation of the Mind," *IJPA*, 241. Takha also explains Freud's contradictory position on drives, a quantitative force without qualities and something that is mentally represented, that is, having content and qualities. Freud wrote "Totem and Taboo" to get around the problem, but psychoanalysts are unable to accept his explanation.

119. This version of Freud's notion of fantasy appeared, curiously, in a letter to the editor, *The New York Times*, "Letters" (August 11, 1992), A18, letter of Victor Schwartz, described by the *Times* as clinical assistant professor of psychiatry at New York University and chief psychiatrist of the university counseling service.

120. Freud, ID, *SE* 4:318.

121. Robert R. Holt, "The Current Status of Psychoanalytic Theory," in *Freud Reappraised*, 331, 338–39.

122. John E. Gedo, *Psychoanalysis and Its Discontents* (New York: The Guilford Press, 1984), 180. Douglas Kirsner, "Is There a Future for American Psychoanalysis?" *Psychoanalytic Review* 77 (1990): 183. For the radical perspective, see Russell Jacoby, *Social Amnesia: A Critique of Conformist Psychology from Adler to Laing* (Boston: Beacon Press, 1975).

123. Philip S. Holzman, "Psychoanalysis: Is the Therapy Destroying the Science?" 760.

124. Joseph Sandler was the principal editor of the *International Journal of Psychoanalysis* when Wallerstein was the American editor and for a long time editor as well of the *International Review of Psychoanalysis* (1969–78, 1974–78, respectively).

125. Robert Wallerstein, "One Psychoanalysis or Many?" *IJPA* 69 (1988): 16–17. Reprinted in *The Common Ground of Psychoanalysis*, ed. Robert S. Wallerstein (Northvale, N.J.: Jason Aronson, 1992), 51, 56–57.

126. Freud, "The Question of Lay Analysis," *SE* 20:254; his statement that he was not a "therapeutic enthusiast" occurs in the "New Introductory Lectures," *SE* 22:151. On the fear that the therapy might destroy the science, see Freud's letter to Paul Federn, in E. Federn, "How Freudian Are the Freudians? Some Remarks on an Unpublished Letter," *Journal of the History of the Behavioral Sciences* 3 (1967): 270.

127. George S. Klein, "Two Theories or One?" in *Psychoanalytic Theory: An Exploration of Essentials* (New York: International Universities Press, 1976), 41-71. See Wallerstein's reference to Klein, in "One Psychoanalysis or Many?" *The Common Ground of Psychoanalysis*, 52.

128. Robert S. Wallerstein, "Psychoanalysis: The Common Ground," in *The Common Ground of Psychoanalysis*, ed. Wallerstein, 223–24. See also Jacob Arlow, "The Dynamics of Interpretation," 69–70.

129. Robert R. Holt, "The Current Status of Psychoanalytic Theory," in *Freud Reappraised*, 327–44. Donald Spence, *The Rhetorical Voice of Psychoanalysis*, 199.

130. Cecilio Paniagua, "Common Ground, Uncommon Methods," *IJPA* 76 (1995): 359.

131. Theodore Shapiro, Panel, "Clinical Aspects of Language," *JAPA* 34 (1986): 694.

132. Arnold Goldberg, "Psychoanalysis and Negotiation," *Psychoanalytic Quarterly* 56 (1987): 122.

133. Joseph Sandler, "Psychoanalytic Concepts and Practice," 38.

134. Cited in Arnold D. Richard, "The Search for Common Ground," 260–61. On the concept of defense, see Steven H. Cooper, "Facts All Come with a Point of View," *IJPA* 77 (1996): 262–63.

135. Stanley Grand, "On the Place of Self-Reflection in the Psychoanalytic Process," in *The Modern Freudians*, ed. Carolyn S. Ellman et al., 100–1. Grand cites a number of other commentaries on this problem.

136. Bennett Simon, "Is the Oedipus Complex Still the Cornerstone of Psychoanalysis?" 661. See also Wallerstein, "Psychoanalysis as Science: A Response to New Challenges," *Psychoanalytic Quarterly* 55 (1986). Wallerstein wrote some years earlier that "it behooves us to turn in an intensified way to the systematic testing of our propositions within the crucible of the data derived from our consulting rooms, and in ways that are consonant with the requirements of empirical science."

137. See, for example, Robert Wallerstein, "Psychoanalysis as a Science: A Response to New Challenges," *Psychoanalytic Quarterly* 55 (1986): 416, on multiple interpretations. Wallerstein also cited Edward Glover and David Rapaport on the absence of any established canon in psychoanalysis for interpreting clinical observations (415). Donald Spence, *The Rhetorical Voice of Psychoanalysis*, 185; and Lawrence Friedman, "How Real is the Realistic Ego in Psychotherapy," *Archives of General Psychiatry* 28 (1973): 378. On the longitudinal problem, see Bennett Simon, "Is the Oedipus Complex Still the Cornerstone of Psychoanalysis?" 662–63. On neglect of the confirmation problem, see Rosemarie Sand, "Confirmation in the Dora Case," *IRPA* 10 (1983): 336; and Jay Greenberg, *Oedipus and Beyond*, 109–12. Greenberg cites here well-known statements of Robert Holt and Benjamin Rubenstein. On the absence of outcome data, see Arnold Cooper, "Limitations of Therapeutic Effectiveness," *Psychoanalytic Quarterly* 55 (1986): 588–89.

138. In the more familiar and extensive conception of 1922 (1923), Freud was much more emphatic: "The assumption that there are unconscious mental processes, the recognition of the theory of resistance and repression, the appreciation of the importance of sexuality and of the Oedipus complex—these constitute the principal subject-matter of psychoanalysis and the formulations of its theory. No one who cannot accept them all should count himself a psychoanalyst." Freud, "On the History of the Psychoanalytic Movement," *SE* 14:16, and "Two Encyclopedia Articles," *SE* 18:77. For an overview of the problem see Arnold M. Cooper, "Psychoanalysis at One Hundred," *JAPA* 32 (1984): 253–54.

139. Arnold D. Richards, "The Search for Common Ground," 246. On the political content of this tactical approach, see ibid., 261. Wallerstein, for example, resorts to Freud's earlier and narrower conception of psychoanalysis (1914). "One Psychoanalysis or Many?" in *The Common Ground of Psychoanalysis*, 29–30, 44, 52.

140. See Arnold D. Richards, "The Search for Common Ground," 261–62.

141. Joseph Sandler, "The Id— or the Child Within?" 237. On John Gedo, *Beyond Interpretation* (New York: International Universities Press, 1979), 9. Morris Eagle, *Recent Developments in Psychoanalysis: A Critical Evaluation*, 4–5, 9. Eric Gillett, "Revising Freud's Structural Theory," 492–96. Gillett argues that the structural theory retains its primacy only by default, because there is apparently nothing better at the moment. Martin Leichtman, "Developmental Psychology and Psychoanalysis: I. the Context for a Revolution in Psychoanalysis," *JAPA* 38 (1990): 939, 942–43. Freud expressed to Joan Riviere in 1923 his anticipation that the structural theory would be obsolete in thirty years. Cited in Harry Guntrip, *Psychoanalytic Theory: Therapy and the Self* (New York: Basic Books, 1971), 23. In any event, if id has structure and therefore a history, as Otto Kernberg has claimed, there is no point in continuing with Freud's structural model. See Richard Kuhns on Otto Kernberg, "Governing of the Self," in *Theories of the Unconscious and Theories of the Self*, ed. Raphael Stern, 51; and Morris Eagle, "The Psychoanalytic and the Cognitive Unconscious," in ibid., 177–78.

142. Bennett Simon, "'Incest—See under Oedipus Complex': The History of an Error in Psychoanalysis," *JAPA* 40 (1992): 957, 966.

143. Ann Hulbert, "Fifty Years of Dr. Spock," *The New Yorker* (May 20, 1996), 89.

CHAPTER 4. THE FRAGMENTATION OF PSYCHOANALYSIS

1. Robert R. Holt, "The Manifest and Latent Meanings of Metapsychology," in *Freud Reappraised*, 15.

2. Freud, "The Future of an Illusion," *SE* 21:6; "Civilization and Its Discontents" *SE* 21:95, 97.

3. Anna Freud, "The Past Revisited," *The Annual of Psychoanalysis* 10 (1982): 260.

4. See the discussion in Malcolm Macmillan, *Freud Evaluated*, 425–28. The gap between psychoanalytic theories of aggression and libido persists. Sidney S. Furst, "A Psychoanalytic Study of Aggression," *Ps St Chi* 53 (1998): 161.

5. Ruben Blanck and Gertrude Blanck, "The Transference Object and the Real Object," *IJPA* 58 (1977): 33. Henri Parens, "Development of Hostility," in *Affect: Psychoanalytic Perspectives*, ed. Shapiro and Emde, 81. Michael Franz Basch, "Selfobject and Selfobject Transference," in *Kohut's Legacy: Contributions to Self Psychology*, ed. Paul E. Stepansky and Arnold Goldberg (Hillsdale, N.J.: The Analytic Press, 1984), 32. Eric Gillett, "Revising Freud's Structural Theory," *Psychoanalysis and Contemporary Thought* 20 (1997): 496.

6. Leo Rangell, "Transference to Theory: The Relationship of Psychoanalytic Education to the Analyst's Relationship to Psychoanalysis," *The Annual of Psychoanalysis* 10 (1982): 52–53, 39. Nathan G. Hale Jr., *The Rise and Crisis of Psychoanalysis in the United States: Freud and the Americans, 1917–1985*, 2 vols. (New York: Oxford University Press, 1995), 2:377.

7. Thomas H. Ogden, "Reconsidering Three Aspects of Psychoanalytic Technique," *IJPA* 77 (1996): 883, 889–90 (on the fundamental rule). Owen Renik, "Analytic Interaction: Conceptualizing Technique in the Light of the Analyst's Irreducible Subjectivity," *Psychoanalytic Quarterly* 62 (1993): 585–91; and Renik, "The Ideal of the Anonymous Analyst and the Problem of Self-Disclosure," ibid., 64 (1995): 466–95 (on abstinence, neutrality, and objectivity). Peter Fonagy, "Memory and Therapeutic Action," *IJPA* 80 (1999): 218 (on Freud's notion of the lifting of repression).

8. Heinz Kohut, *The Restoration of the Self* (New York: International Universities Press, 1977), chapter 5, 220–48. Hans W. Loewald, "The Waning of the Oedipus Complex," *JAPA* 27 (1979): 768–69. Van Spruell, "Narcissism: Theories of Treatment," *JAPA* 22 (1974): 273.

9. Bennett Simon, "Is the Oedipus Complex Still the Cornerstone of Psychoanalysis? Three Obstacles to Answering the Question," *JAPA* 39 (1991): 641–68; Bennett Simon, "'Incest: See under Oedipus Complex': The History of an Error in Psychoanalysis," *JAPA* 40 (1992): 955–88.

10. Freud, "Three Essays on the Theory of Sexuality," *SE* 7:226 (1905, note added in 1920).

11. On the identification of all the relevant figures as initiators of action in clinical experience, that is, Oedipus, Laius, and Jocasta, see Leo Rangell, "Aggression, Oedipus and Historical Perspective," *IJPA* 53 (1972): 7–8; or Bennett Simon, "Is the Oedipus Complex Still the Cornerstone of Psychoanalysis?" 655–59, on "the Counteroedipal." The literature on this subject is far too extensive to be listed here. Examples include *The Oedipus Papers*, ed. George H. Pollock and John Munder Ross (Madison, Conn.: International Universities Press, 1988); or John Munder Ross, "Oedipus Revisited. Laius and the Laius Complex," *Ps St Chi* 37 (1982): 189–93. On Laius too, see M. Balmary, *Psychoanalyzing Psychoanalysis: Freud and the Hidden Fault of the Father*, trans. with an introduction by N. Lukacher (Baltimore, Md.: Johns Hopkins University Press, 1982), 74. On Jocasta, see Estelle Roith, *The Riddle of Freud* (London: Tavistock Publications, 1987), 166–67; Desmond J. Drinkwater, "The Problem of Jocasta—A Theory of Adult Culpability," *Adolescence* 7 (1972): 77–94, especially 84–87; Matthew Besdine, "The Jocasta Complex, Mothering and Genius," *Psychoanalytic Review* 55 (1968): 259–77. See also Yosef Hayim Yerushalmi, *Freud's Moses: Judaism Terminable and Interminable* (New Haven, Conn.: Yale University Press, 1991), 92. Yerushalmi asks why Freud concentrated so exclusively on patricide, why not a Cain complex? Of course the primacy of the Oedipus complex is still defended. Leo Rangell, for example, claimed that he could not imagine psychoanalysis without it. "Transference to Theory," *The Annual of Psychoanalysis* 10 (1982): 39, or *The Human Core*, 2:839.

12. Axel Hoffer, "Ferenczi's Search for Mutuality: Implications for the Free Association Method," in *100 Years of Psychoanalysis*, ed. Haynal and Falzeder, 199. This obviously contradicts the position cited earlier on the fundamental rule.

13. Wilma Bucci, *Psychoanalysis and Cognitive Science*, 24, 28–29.

14. John Bowlby, *Maternal Care and Mental Health* (Geneva: World

Health Organization, 1951). Bowlby cited 158 multilingual bibliographic items on maternal care and mental health of which five dated from the period 1924–29, 22 from 1930–39, and 131 from 1940–51. See Sylvia Brody, *Patterns of Mothering* (New York: International Universities Press, 1956).

15. Erik H. Erikson, *Childhood and Society*, 277–83. Michael Franz Basch, "Selfobject Theory of Motivation and the History of Psychoanalysis," in *Kohut's Legacy*, ed. Stepansky and Goldberg, 12.

16. Hans W. Loewald, "Ego and Reality," *IJPA* 32 (1951), the quote is on 13, references to father and mother figures, 14–16. Note particularly Loewald's judgment that what the ego defends itself against primarily is the loss of reality, of integration with the world.

17. Loewald, "Ego and Reality," 17. Michael Balint also observed the changing focus of psychoanalysis, "Changing Therapeutic Aims and Techniques in Psychoanalysis," *IJPA* 31 (1950): 121.

18. *The Freud-Klein Controversies, 1941–1945*, ed. Pearl King and Riccardo Steiner, 710–29.

19. D. W. Winnicott, "Transitional Objects and Transitional Phenomena," in *Playing and Reality* (London: Tavistock Publications, 1971 [1953]), 1–10.

20. Hans W. Loewald, "Instinct Theory, Object Relations and Psychic Structure Formation," *JAPA* 26 (1978): 493–506; or Loewald, *Sublimation: Inquiries into Theoretical Psychoanalysis* (New Haven, Conn.: Yale University Press, 1988), 32.

21. Otto Kernberg, "Object Relations Theory and Transference," *Psychoanalytic Quarterly* 56 (1987): 198. The major influences include Melanie Klein, Winnicott, Erikson, Mahler, Jacobson, and Sandler.

22. Otto Kernberg, ibid., 198. For a brief but useful overview of Kernberg's perspective, see Ruth Stein, *Psychoanalytic Theories of Affect*, 113–22.

23. Joseph Sandler and Walter G. Joffe, "Toward a Basic Psychoanalytic Model," *IJPA* 50 (1969): 80. Walter G. Joffe and Joseph Sandler, "Comments on the Psychoanalytic Psychology of Adaptation, with Special Reference to the Role of Affects and the Representational World," *IJPA* 49 (1968): 447. The papers should be read together. For a brief overview of Sandler's work in this vein, see Ruth Stein, *Psychoanalytic Theories of Affect*, 103–12.

24. Joseph D. Lichtenberg, "Foreword," in Joseph M. Jones, *Affects as Process: An Inquiry into the Centrality of Affect in Psychological Life* (Hillsdale, N.J.: The Analytic Press, 1995), xiv–xv. Robert D. Stolorow, "Varieties of Selfobject Experience—Discussion," in *Kohut's Legacy*, ed. Stepansky and Goldberg, 46.

25. Robert Holt, "The Development of the Primary Process: A Structural View," in *Freud Reappraised*, 264–65.

26. I. Peter Glauber, "Federn's Annotation of Freud's Theory of Anxiety," *JAPA* 11 (1963): 91. Robert Holt, "The Development of the Primary Process: A Structural View," in *Freud Reappraised*, 264–65. Pinchas Noy, "A Revision of the Psychoanalytic Theory of the Primary Process," *IJPA* 50 (1969): 155–78, especially 176–77. Noy's point here is that as the secondary processes have to become more impersonal and objective, the primary process also "has to improve its ability to deal with these personal meanings, i.e., become more and

more *subjective*. So, each one has to develop in a different direction—*but of course to the same degree.*" The bibliography on this topic is also too extensive to note here.

27. Talcott Parsons, *Social Structure and Personality* (Glencoe, Ill.: The Free Press, 1965), 25. Parsons went on to note that "[t]his may be felt to be a relatively radical conclusion—namely, that emotions, or affect on the normal human adult level, should be regarded as a *symbolically generalized* system, that it is never 'id-impulse' as such" (*Social Structure and Personality*, 31 [italics in the original]). Parsons's judgment was initially ignored by psychoanalysts, but see Neville Symington, "The Analyst's Act of Freedom as Agent of Therapeutic Change," *IRPA* 10 (1983): 287; and W. W. Meissner, "Can Psychoanalysis Find Its Self?" *JAPA* 34 (1987): 394.

28. See the several papers by Anna Freud, Heinz Hartmann, and Willi Hoffer, in *Ps St Chi* 7 (1952), particularly Hoffer's "The Mutual Influences in the Development of the Ego and the Id," 32.

29. See for example Max Schur, *The Id and the Regulatory Principle of Mental Functioning* (New York: International Universities Press, 1966), 199–202.

30. Robert R. Holt, "Drive or Wish? A Reconsideration of the Psychoanalytic Theory of Motivation," in *Freud Reappraised*, 196. For further useful discussion of the clinical theory, see ibid., 174; and George S. Klein, "Two Theories or One?" in *Psychoanalytic Theory, an Exploration of Essentials*, 41–71.

31. Freud, "The Dynamics of Transference," *SE* 12:106, on the patient's "final independence." And "Introductory Lectures," *SE* 16:453, where Freud claimed that when the transference is resolved therapeutic success appears not as a result of suggestion but of internal resistances overcome. Also on demystification of the world, Rudolph M. Loewenstein, "Developments in the Theory of Transference in the Last Fifty Years," *IJPA* 50 (1969): 587.

32. Transference replaced dreams as the royal road to the unconscious. Dreams and dream theory still present problems psychoanalysts continue to explore, and there are still papers written on the subject, but it is no longer as significant as it was or that it may still be in popular imagination. Phillip McCaffrey, *Freud and Dora: The Artful Dream* (New Brunswick, N.J.: Rutgers University Press, 1984), 1-5. There is a significant reference to the literature on dreams in note 9, p. 142. See also note 11, 143, with reference to the minimal role of the dream work in Anna Freud's *The Ego and the Mechanisms of Defense* and Heinz Hartmann's *Ego Psychology and the Problem of Adaptation*.

33. Stephen K. Firestein refers to Rudolph Ekstein, Anna Freud, and other psychoanalysts who have raised this question. "Termination of Psychoanalysis of Adults: A Review of the Literature," *JAPA* 22 (1974): 881, 877. A number of authors have also explained that there is not much to be learned in object relational terms from the transference situation because it does not resemble real interactions in routine social encounters. Phyllis Greenacre, "The Role of Transference," *JAPA* 2 (1954): 684; Nicole Berry-Bertrand, "From Fantasy to Reality in the Transference (or the Double Aspect of the Psychoanalyst)," *IJPA* 55 (1974): 471-77.

34. Edward Glover, "Research Methods in Psycho-Analysis," *IJPA* 33 (1952): 403. See also Frank Sulloway, "Reassessing Freud's Case Histories: The Social Construction of Analysis," *Isis* 82 (June 1991): 274.

35. Adam Limentani, "Presidential Address: Variations on Some Freudian Themes," *IJPA* 67 (1986): 241.

36. Otto F. Kernberg, "Institutional Problems of Psychoanalytic Education," *JAPA* 34 (1986): 800. Victor Calef and Edward M. Weinshel referred in turn to the cultist quality of Kernberg's following, "The New Psychoanalysis and Psychoanalytic Revisionism," *Psychoanalytic Quarterly* 48 (1979): 471.

37. Jacob Arlow, "Psychoanalytic Education: A Psychoanalytic Perspective," *The Annual of Psychoanalysis* 10 (1982): 12–13.

38. Helen H. Tartakoff, "The Normal Personality in Our Culture and the Nobel Prize Complex," in *Psychoanalysis as a General Psychology: Essays in Honor of Heinz Hartmann*, ed. Rudolph M. Loewenstein et al., 233.

39. Erich Simenauer, "Some Aspects of Training Analysis," *IRPA* 10 (1983): 147. See, for example, Shelly Orgel, "The Impact of Training Analysis," in *The Identity of the Psychoanalyst*, ed. Edward D. Joseph and Daniel Widlöcher (New York: International Universities Press, 1983), 225–41.

40. According to Eagle, "[t]he same considerations apply to both." *NPAP News and Reviews* (Spring 1997): 3. See also Leo Rangell, "The Analyst's Relationship to Psychoanalysis," *The Annual of Psychoanalysis* 10 (1982): 50.

41. On the treatment of psychotics, D. W. Winnicott, "Hate in the Countertransference," *IJPA* 30 (1949): 69–74. Gerald Adler, "Issues in the Treatment of the Borderline Patient," in *Kohut's Legacy*, 125–33. Nathan G. Hale, Jr., *The Rise and Crisis of Psychoanalysis in the United States: Freud and the Americans, 1917–1985*, 2:160, 270. Schur, *The Id and the Regulatory Principles of Mental Functioning*, 21. Schur quotes here from a well known letter of Freud's to Istvan Hollos: "Ultimately I had to confess to myself that . . . I do not care for these patients [psychotics], that they annoy me, and that I find them alien to me and to everything human." Freud believed that psychoanalysis had no role to play in situations in which ego functions had failed. Martin S. Bergmann, "Reflections on the History of Psychoanalysis," 937.

42. Samuel Lipton, "The Advantages of Freud's Technique as Shown in his Analysis of the Rat Man," *IJPA* 58 (1977): 255–73.

43. On the history of the concept, see Theodore J. Jacobs, "Countertransference Past and Present," *IJPA* 80 (1999): 575–94. Jerry L. Jennings refers to the revolutionary change in attitude toward countertransference, in "The Revival of 'Dora': Advances in Psychoanalytic Theory and Technique," *JAPA* 34 (1986): 624–28. Aso on Dora, see Jules Glenn, "Freud, Dora, and the Maid: A Study of Countertransference," ibid., 591–606. Frieda Fromm-Reichmann, *Principles of Intensive Psychotherapy* (Chicago: University of Chicago Press, 1950), 5–6.

44. Bennett Simon, "Is the Oedipus Complex Still the Cornerstone of Psychoanalysis?" 661. Morris Eagle, *NPAP News and Reviews* (Spring 1997), 3.

45. Joseph Sandler, "The Id—or the Child Within?" in *Dimensions of Psychoanalysis*, 229. Balint was an object relations theorist who would have denied the possibility of primary narcissism, a period in life when the individual is not object seeking.

46. James William Anderson, "Henry A. Murray's Early Career: A Psychobiographical Exploration," *Journal of Personality* 56 (1988): 157. Murray recalled that in the Boston Psychoanalytic Society, Ives Hendrick and M. Ralph Kaufman "fought like dragon flies."

47. Peter Loewenberg, "The Creation of a Scientific Community," 63–64. Robert Wallerstein has noted that "if the Jungian viewpoint had arisen today, it would be accommodated within the body of psychoanalysis the way Kohut has been, rather than the Jungians feeling they had to leave." Virginia Hunter, *Psychoanalysts Talk* (New York: The Guilford Press, 1994), 333. However, Wallerstein makes the absorption of Kohut's perspectives appear more amicable than it was. See Michael Franz Basch, "Selfobject Theory and Psychoanalytic History," 3–17. See in brief on Lacan's equally bitter experiences, Jeanine Parisier Plottel, "Jacques Lacan: Psychoanalytic, Surrealist, and Mystic," in *Beyond Freud: A Study of Modern Psychoanalytic Theories*, ed. Joseph Reppen (Hillsdale, N.J.: The Analytic Press, 1985), 333–52.

48. *Ferenczi's Turn in Psychoanalysis*, ed. Peter Rudnystsky et al. (New York: New York University Press, 1996), 4. Judith Dupont,"The Notion of Trauma According to Ferenczi: Progress or Regression in Psychoanalytic Theory," in *100 Years of Psychoanalysis. Contributions to the History of Psychoanalysis*, ed. André Haynal and Ernst Falzeder, 206.

49. This despite Freud's admonition that whoever appeals to authority in the matter of conflicting opinions is relying on his memory rather than his reason. "Leonard da Vinci," *SE* 11:122.

50. John D. Sutherland, "The British Object Relations Theorists: Balint, Winnicott, Fairbairn, Guntrip," *JAPA* 28 (1980): 842. Sutherland notes that Winnicott tried to tone down Fairbairn's critique of Freud, which Guntrip pointed out was no way to advance a science (830). Adam Limentani, "Presidential Address: Variations on Some Freudian Themes," 235.

51. Robert S. Wallerstein, "Reflections," in *The Identity of the Psychoanalyst*, ed. Edward D. Joseph and Daniel Widlöcher, 271–72. The first part of this comment appears also in "One Psychoanalysis or Many," *The Common Ground of Psychoanalysis*, 36. Robert Wallertein refers here to similar statements by Robert Knight. Linda Joan Kaplan, "The Concept of the Family Romance," *Psychoanalytic Review* 61 (1974): 198. Kaplan referred to the idealization of Freud among analysts, and others have as well.

52. Ruth Mack Brunswick, "The Pre-Oedipal Phase of Libido Development," *Psychoanalytic Quarterly* 9 (1940): 293–94. Bennett Simon, "'Incest—See under Oedipus Complex,'" 980–81. Michael Balint, "Changing Therapeutical Aims and Techniques in Psycho-Analysis," 121. James William Anderson, "Henry Murray's Early Career," 157–58.

53. By contrast, Erikson's connection of the identity concept to Freud's work was minimal, although Erikson was also reluctant to be as critical as he could have been. Erik Erikson, *Identity and the Life Cycle*, Psychological Issues (monograph 1, 1959), 101–2. See also Erikson's statements in *Childhood and Society* (New York: W. W. Norton, 1963, 2nd edition), 281; "The Dream Specimen of Psychoanalysis," *JAPA* 2 (1954): 53.

54. On Melanie Klein's comment, see *The Complete Correspondence of*

Sigmund Freud and Ernest Jones, 1908–1939, ed. R. Andrew Paskauskas (Cambridge, Mass.: The Belknap Press of Harvard University Press, 1993), 624. On the slow progress of theory that results from these antagonisms, see Robert R. Holt, "The Death and Transfiguration of Metapsychology," in *Freud Reappraised*, 305–6. On the religious content of psychoanalysis, see the comments of Max Graf, the father of "Little Hans," on the Wednesday meetings of the Vienna Psychoanalytic Society, in "Reminiscences of Professor Sigmund Freud," *Psychoanalytic Quarterly* 11 (1942): 474–75; see also Erikson's comment on this in Nathan G. Hale Jr., *The Rise and Crisis of Psychoanalysis in the United States*, 2:30; and Henry Murray's comments in James William Anderson, "Henry A. Murray's Early Career," 157–58.

55. Robert R. Holt, "The Death and Transfiguration of Metapsychology," *IRPA* 8 (1981): 129; *Freud Reappraised*, 305–6.

56. Samuel Weber, *Return to Freud. Jacques Lacan's Dislocation of Psychoanalysis*, trans. Michael Levine (New York: Cambridge University Press, 1991), 120. Stanley A. Leavy, *The Psychoanalytic Dialogue*, x, n2.

57. Martin S. Bergmann, "Reflections on the History of Psychoanalysis," *JAPA* 41 (1993): 930. "A typical strategy for a modifier is to claim that his or her modification is implicit."

58. Charles Spezzano, *Affects in Psychoanalysis*, 61.

59. Herbert Marcuse, *Eros and Civilization* (New York: Vintage Books, 1962), 186, 200, 211. Marcuse later abandoned his utopian expectations of freedom, arguing in his own turn that society penetrates all levels of the mind including the id. See *One Dimensional Man* (Boston: Beacon Press, 1964) 6, 32.

60. On Wilhelm Reich's radicalism, see Russell Jacoby, *The Repression of Psychoanalysis: Otto Fenichel and the Political Freudians* (Chicago: University of Chicago Press, 1986), 83.

61. Margaret Mahler, "Thoughts about Development and Individuation," *Ps St Chi* 18 (1963): 307. Reprinted in *The Selected Papers of Margaret S. Mahler*, 2 vols. in 1 (New York: Jason Aronson, 1982), 3. Irving B. Harrison, "On Freud's View of the Infant-Mother Relationship," *JAPA* 27 (1979): 402.

62. Martin Wangh, "The Genetic Sources of Freud's Differences with Romain Rolland on the Matter of Religious Feelings," in *Fantasy, Myth, and Reality: Essays in Honor of Jacob A. Arlow*, ed. Harold Blum et al. (Madison, Conn.: International Universities Press, 1988), 259–86.

63. Irving B. Harrison, "On Freud's View of the Infant-Mother Relationship," 402. Reuben Fine, *The Development of Freud's Thought* (Northvale, N.J.: Jason Aronson, 1987), 243.

64. Roy Schafer, "The Idea of Resistance," *IJPA* 54 (1973): 278.

65. George S. Klein, "Freud's Two Theories of Sexuality," in *Clinical-Cognitive Psychology, Models and Integrations*, ed. Louis Breger (Englewood Cliffs, N.J.: Prentice-Hall, 1969), 136–37.

66. Heinz Kohut, "Thoughts on Narcissism and Narcissistic Rage," *Ps St Chi* 27 (1972): 366–67.

67. Pinchas Noy "Metapsychology as Multi-Model System," *IRPA* 4 (1977): 10.

68. Jay Greenberg, *Oedipus and Beyond*, 45–46. Note the comments on

David Rapaport's treatment of drive theory, which brought him closer to C. G. Jung than to Freud.

69. As noted earlier, Freud then had insisted only on "the facts of transference and resistance. Any line of investigation which recognizes these two facts and takes them as the starting point of its work has a right to call itself psychoanalysis, even though it arrives at results other than my own." James Strachey had pointed out that Freud's later, more focused definition of psychoanalysis would have been stultifying to progress. Cited in Phyllis Grosskurth, *Melanie Klein: Her World and Her Work* (New York: Alfred A. Knopf, 1986), 335.

70. *Minutes of the Vienna Psychoanalytic Society*, ed. H. Nunberg and E. Federn, trans. M. Nunberg and H. Collins, 4 vols. (New York: International Universities Press, 1962), 1:234.

71. Freud, "From the History of an Infantile Neurosis," *SE* 17:86, 97, 119.

72. Samuel Ritvo and Albert J. Solnit, "Influences of Early Mother-Child Interaction on Identification Processes," *Ps St Chi* 13 (1958), and Discussion, Anna Freud, "Child Observation and Prediction of Development," 96.

73. Charles Brenner, "The Psychoanalytic Concept of Aggression," *IJPA* 52 (1971): 141. Anna Freud, "The Mutual Influences in the Development of the Ego and the Id," *Ps St Chi* 7 (1952): 42–50.

74. Melanie Klein, *The Psychoanalysis of Children* (New York: The Grove Press, 1960), passim. *The Complete Correspondence of Sigmund Freud and Ernest Jones, 1908–1939*, 640–41 (February 22, 1928); see also 690 (January 23, 1932). Of course, any number of psychoanalysts, including Bowlby, Sandler, Winnicott, and Kernberg, have acknowledged their indebtedness to Klein's work.

75. Herbert Marcuse, *Eros and Civilization*, 231 (italics in the original).

76. *The Writings of Anna Freud*, 7:145. "Opening Discussion on Problems of Pathogenesis," *Ps St Chi* 38 (1983): 383. Hans W. Loewald, "Waning of the Oedipus Complex," *JAPA* 27 (1979): 768. David Rapaport referred famously to this Kleinian perspective as an "id mythology." Jay Greenberg, *Oedipus and Beyond*, 177n. D. W. Winnicott, "Ego Distortion or the True and False Self," in *The Maturation Processes and the Facilitating Environment* (New York: International Universities Press, 1965), 145.

77. Michael Balint, *The Basic Fault* (London: Tavistock, 1968); John Bowlby, *A Secure Base: Parent Child Attachment and Healthy Human Development* (New York: Basic Books, 1988); David Stern, *The Interpersonal World of the Infant: A View from Psychoanalysis and Developmental Psychology* (New York: Basic Books, 1985); D. W. Winnicott, *The Family and Individual Development* (London: Tavistock, 1965). John Bowlby, "Psychoanalysis as a Natural Science," *IRPA* 8 (1981): 249. Bowlby wrote that psychoanalysis is a developmental discipline, but it is nowhere weaker than in its concept of development. See Peter Wolff, "The Irrelevance of Infant Observation for Psychoanalysis," *JAPA* 44 (1996): 369–87, and the discussions that follow.

78. On Heinz Kohut, *The Analysis of the Self* and *The Restoration of the Self* (New York: International Universities Press, 1971, 1978, respectively). For an overview of Kohut's work, see Stephen A. Mitchell, "Twilight of the Idols. Change and Preservation in the Writings of Heinz Kohut," *Contemporary Psy-*

choanalysis 15 (1979): 170–89. On incompatible theories of motivation and the problems raised by that situation, John E. Gedo, "Theories of Object Relations: A Metapsychological Assessment," *JAPA* 27 (1979): 363–64.

79. Robert R. Holt, "Drive or Wish?" in *Freud Reappraised*, 179.

80. George S. Klein, "On Hearing One's Own Voice," in *Drives, Affects, Behavior*, ed. Max Schur, 2:90.

81. Stephen A. Reid, "A Psychoanalytic Reading of 'Troilus and Cressida,' and 'Measure for Measure,'" *Psychoanalytic Review* 57 (1970): 279.

82. Cited in Joseph M. Jones, *Affects as Process*, 67.

83. Ian Suttie, *The Origins of Love and Hate*, 203.

84. J.-B. Pontalis, *Frontiers in Psychoanalysis: Between the Dream and Psychic Pain*, trans. Catherine Cullen and Philip Cullen (New York: International Universities Press, 1981), 184.

85. On Heinz Hartmann and the ego psychology, see *Essays on Ego Psychology* (New York: International Universities Press, 1964). Marjorie Brierly, "'Hardy Perennials' and Psychoanalysis," *IJPA* 50 (1969): 450. Brierly (451) claimed that psychoanalysts like Hartmann and Harry Guntrip only "offer balm to the human pride so badly wounded by the findings of Freud."

86. Paul Ricoeur, *Freud and Philosophy*, 286.

87. Ethel Spector Person, "Romantic Love: At the Intersection of the Psyche and the Cultural Unconscious," in *Affect: Psychoanalytic Perspectives*, ed. Shapiro and Emde, 397.

88. Edward Bibring, "The Mechanism of Depression," in *Affective Disorders*, ed. Phyllis Greenacre (New York: International Universities Press, 1953), 24, 27. Margaret Mahler, "On Sadness and Grief in Infancy and Childhood: Loss and Restoration of the Symbiotic Love Object," in *The Selected Papers*, 1:272. The paper was originally published in 1961.

89. Anna Freud, "Comments on Aggression," *IJPA* 53 (1972): 163–71.

90. Jay Greenberg, *Oedipus and Beyond*, 131–38.

91. *Ferenczi's Turn in Psychoanalysis*, ed. Peter L. Rudnytsky et al. (New York: New York University Press, 1996). Axel Hoffer, "The Freud-Ferenczi Controversy—A Living Legend," *IRPA* 18 (1991): 465–71. Bennett Simon, "An Error in Psychoanalysis," 971–78. Simon asks (974): "How did Ferenczi manage to see what other analysts then were unable to see and that many analysts now can and do see?" Michael Parsons, "Marion Milner's 'Answering Activity,'" *IRPA* 17 (1990): 418–20.

92. Freud, "Recommendations to Physicians Practicing Psycho-analysis," *SE* 12:115. Jacob A. Arlow, "The Dynamics of Interpretation," *Psychoanalytic Quarterly* 56 (1987): 68–69. Ralph Greenson, "Loving, Hating, and Indifference toward the Patient," *IRPA* 1 (1974): 263. Heinz Kohut, "The Psychoanalytic Treatment of Narcissistic Personality Disorders," *Ps St Chi* 23 (1968): 105.

93. Elisabeth Young-Bruehl, *Anna Freud* (New York: Summit Books, 1988), 440. See also Charles Hanley, "A Problem of Theory Testing," *IRPA* 10 (1983): 393; and Michael Franz Basch, "A Comparison of Freud and Kohut: Apostasy or Synergy," in *Self Psychology: Comparisons and Contrasts* (Hillsdale, N.J.: The Analytic Press, 1989), 20–21.

94. On Winnicott, see also T. Wayne Downey, "Transitional Phenomena in

Adolescent Analysis," *Ps St Chi* 33 (1978): 24; Adam Limentani, "Presidential Address. Variations on some Freudian Themes," *IJPA* 67 (1986): 242.

95. Michael Franz Basch, "The Selfobject Theory of Motivation and the History of Psychoanalysis," in *Kohut's Legacy*, ed. Stepansky and Goldberg, 4. Joseph Sandler and Anne-Marie Sandler, "The Past Unconscious, the Present Unconscious, and Interpretation of the Transference," *Psychoanalytic Inquiry* 4 (1984): 385.

96. Freud, quoted in *The Diary of Sigmund Freud, 1929–1939: A Record of the Final Decade*, trans. with an introduction by Michael Molnar (New York: Charles Scribner's Sons, 1992), xxv. Hartmann's expectation for psychoanalysis, that the contribution of analysis to prevention many one day become even more essential than to therapy, does not appear in reach either. Hartmann also referred to "theories of analysis which lead to generalization and objectivation beyond immediate experience, and in turn to hypotheses which are accessible to testing." Hartmann, "Comments on the Scientific Aspects of Psychoanalysis," *Ps St Chi* 13 (1958): 122, 138. By constrast Christopher Lasch more recently referred to "the probable collapse of the whole psychoanalytic enterprise." "For Shame," *The New Republic* (August 10, 1992), 30.

97. Anna Freud said that she and Hartmann shared the same father, but as often happens with siblings, they did not always agree. "Links between Hartmann's Ego Psychology and the Child Analyst's thinking," *Psychoanalysis—A General Psychology: Essays in Honor of Heinz Hartmann*, ed. Rudolph M. Loewenstein et al., 18. Joseph Sandler, "The Id— or the Child Within?" 225–26. Erikson wrote, in reference to Hartmann's notion of conflict-free spheres of the ego, that "[c]onflict free is a miserly way of characterizing our access . . . to the world of deeds." "Reality and Actuality," *JAPA* 10 (1962): 470.

98. Note, for example, the critiques of Erik Erikson: John E. Gedo, "Kant's Way: The Psychoanalytic Contribution of David Rapaport," *Psychoanalytic Quarterly* 42 (1973): 428. Gedo described Erikson as a peripheral figure for psychoanalysis, noting that Rapaport's espousal of his psychosocial vantage point was a strange historical misjudgment. See also Charles K. Hofling and Robert W. Meyers, "Recent Discoveries in Psychoanalysis: A Study of Opinion," *Archives of General Psychiatry* 26 (June 1972): 518–23; Roy Schafer, "Concepts of Self and Identity and the Experience of Separation-Individuation in Adolescence," *Psychoanalytic Quarterly* 42 (1973): 55. Edith Jacobson, *The Self and the Object World* (London: Hogarth Press, 1965), 28, 140.

99. On Erikson, see Daniel Yankelovich and William Barrett, *Ego and Instinct* (New York: Random House, 1970), 120–21, 152–53. On Balint's reluctance to become a psychoanalytic heretic, see Stephen J. Morse, "Structure and Reconstruction: A Critical Comparison of Michael Balint and D. W. Winnicott," *IJPA* 53 (1972): 498. On Winnicott's attempt to constrain the criticism of W. R. D. Fairbairn (M. Masud R. Khan and Harry Guntrip were also involved on different sides—although Khan himself later made some cutting comments on Freud's hold over his career and how relieved he was to be out from under that influence): John D. Sutherland, "The British Object Relations Theorists:

Balint, Winnicott, Fairbairn, Guntrip," *JAPA* 28 (1980): 829–30. There were many others who could have said more than they did.

100. Gerald Weissmann, *They All Laughed at Christopher Columbus: Tales of Medicine and the Art of Discovery* (New York: Times Books, 1987), 159.

101. Arnold Goldberg, "Translation between Psychoanalytic Theories," *Annual of Psychoanalysis* 12/13 (1985): 129–30. Ricardo Bernardi and Beatriz de León de Bernardi, "Does Our Self-Analysis Take into Consideration Our Assumptions?" in *Self-Analysis: Critical Inquiries, Personal Visions*, ed. James W. Barron (Hillsdale, N.J.: The Analytic Press, 1993), 43.

102. Michael Franz Basch, "Selfobject Theory of Motivation and the History of Psychoanalysis," in *Kohut's Legacy*, ed. Stepansky and Goldberg, 15.

103. Donald Spence, *The Freudian Metaphor*, 71–83.

104. See the exchange between John Bowlby, "Grief and Mourning in Infancy and Early Childhood," and Anna Freud, "Discussion of Dr. John Bowlby's Paper," in *Ps St Chi* 15 (1960): 9–52, 53–62.

105. Joseph Sandler, "Toward a Reconsideration of the Psychoanalytic Theory of Motivation," in *Psychoanalysis: Toward the Second Century*, ed. Arnold Cooper et al. (New Haven, Conn.: Yale University Press, 1989), 98–99. Aaron Karush, "Instinct and Affect," ibid., 85.

106. *Translating Freud*, ed. Darius Gray Ornston Jr. (New Haven, Conn.: Yale University Press, 1992).

107. Robert Wallerstein, "Psychoanalysis: The Common Ground," in *The Common Ground of Psychoanalysis*, 204. Martin S. Bergmann, "Reflections on the History of Psychoanalysis," 944.

108. Freud, "Analysis of a Phobia in a Five-Year-Old Boy," *SE* 10:140. Freud wrote with respect to an observation of Adler's, "I cannot bring myself to assume the existence of a special aggressive instinct alongside of the familiar instincts of self-preservation and of sex, and on an equal footing with them." Later, in *Civilization and Its Discontents*, he reversed himself.

109. Robert Wallerstein, "One Psychoanalysis or Many?" refers to aspects of Adler's work that have been reincorporated into the main body of psychoanalysis, including Adler's emphasis on ego, adaptation, and the motive power of aggression. On Erikson and Jung, see "Ego Development and Historical Change," *Identity and the Life Cycle*, 31n. On Adler again, Joseph Sandler, "On the Concept of Superego," *Ps St Chi* 15 (1960): 157. According to Jay Greenberg (*Oedipus and Beyond*, 45–46), Rapaport's notion of drive theory more closely resembles Jung's than Freud's. See also Leo Rangell on Ernest Jones's comments on the problem of anxiety, "A Further Attempt to Resolve the Problem of Anxiety," in *The Human Core*, 1:277.

110. Peter Loewenberg, "The Creation of a Scientific Community: The Burghölzli, 1902–1914," in *Fantasy and Reality in History*, 63–64. Other psychoanalysts have recognized this as well, for example, John Klauber, "On the Dual Use of Historical and Scientific Method in Psychoanalysis," *IJPA* 49 (1968): 87.

111. Weinstein and Platt, *Psychoanalytic Sociology*, 91–122; Peter Homans, *The Inability to Mourn*; Gregory Rochlin, "The Dread of Abandonment. A Contribution to the Etiology of the Loss Complex and to Depression," *Ps St Chi* 16 (1961): 451–70.

112. Joseph Sandler, "Introduction," and "The Id—or the Child Within?" in Sandler, ed., *Dimensions of Psychoanalysis*, 11, 229. Anne Hayman, "Some Thoughts on the Inner World and the Environment: Setting the Scene," *IRPA* 17 (1990): 73–79.

113. *The Complete Correspondence of Sigmund Freud and Ernest Jones*, 703 (June 17, 1932).

114. For example, Sandor Ferenczi and Otto Rank, *The Development of Psychoanalysis*, trans. C. Newton (New York: Nervous and Mental Disease Publishing, 1925).

115. Joseph Sandler et al., "An Approach to Conceptual Research in Psychoanalysis illustrated by a Consideration of Psychic Trauma," *IRPA* 18 (1991): 133. Joseph Sandler, "The Id—or the Child Within?" 229.

116. See Arnold D. Richards, "The Search for Common Ground," 258, 263–64.

117. Rose Edgcumbe and Marion Burgner, "Some Problems in the Conceptualization of Early Object Relationships," part I, *Ps St Chi* 27 (1972): 301.

118. Anna Freud quoted in *Defense and Resistance*, ed. Harold Blum (New York: International Universities Press, 1985), 90. On the successive versions of the seduction theory, see Rachel B. Blass and Bennett Simon, "The Value of the Historical Perspective to Contemporary Psychoanalysis," *IJPA* 75 (1994): 677–94.

119. Jeffrey Masson, *The Assault on Truth*, 113.

120. Bennett Simon, "'Incest—See under Oedipus Complex': The History of an Error in Psychoanalysis," 962, 957, 965–66.

121. Many of these papers have been collected in a volume edited by Sandler, *From Safety to Superego* (New York: Guilford Press, 1987).

122. Joseph Sandler, "Unconscious Wishes and Human Relationships," *Dimensions of Psychoanalysis*, 68; also 5–6 (italics in the original).

123. Robert R. Holt, "Drive or Wish?" in *Freud Reappraised*, 186. Charles Brenner, "The Components of Psychic Conflict and Its Consequences in Mental Life," *Psychoanalytic Quarterly* 48 (1979): 547–67.

124. Hence the title of Sandler's paper, "The Id—or the Child Within?" in *Dimensions of Psychoanalysis*, 219–39, especially 232, 234–36. "I hope . . . that I have made a convincing case for considering unconscious mental conflict as involving peremptory urges that cannot simply be equated with an instinctual 'id.'" See also Jay Greenberg on the shortcomings of the structural model, *Oedipus and Beyond*, 160–66; and Eric Gillett, "Revising Freud's Structural Theory," 490–96.

125. See also Ethel Spector Person, "Romantic Love: At the Intersection of the Psyche and the Cultural Unconscious," in *Affect: Psychoanalytic Perspectives*, ed. Shapiro and Emde, 397–98. Person explains why drive theory is inadequate to an explanation of romantic love, not unexpectedly referring to Sandler's position on psychic pain as an example of an alternative motive force.

126. Charles Hanley, "A Problem of Theory Testing," *IRPA* 10 (1983): 393. Robert Ehrlich, "The Social Dimensions of Heinz Kohut's Psychology of the Self," *Psychoanalysis and Contemporary Science* 8 (1985): 336. John E. Gedo, "Theories of Object Relations: A Metapsychological Assessment," *JAPA* 27 (1979): 363–64.

127. This brief overview of Sandler's work is adapted from two papers, "Unconscious Wishes and Human Relationships," in Sandler, ed., *Dimensions of Psychoanalysis*, particularly 73–74; and "Toward a Reconsideration of the Psychoanalytic Theory of Motivation," in Cooper, ed., *Psychoanalysis: Toward the Second Century*, particularly 106–7. Relevant bibliography is provided in these two works.

128. The quotation is from Ethel Spector Person, "Romantic Love," in *Affect: Psychoanalytic Perspectives*, 400. Many psychoanalysts never accepted Freud's death instinct, many others never accepted or do not now accept his premise of aggression as a primary nonerotic drive, as indicated earlier. Edward Glover noted in 1931 that "the old Freudian classification of instincts was in some respects more convenient than the recent antithesis of death and life instincts." "Sublimation, Substitution and Social Anxiety," *IJPA* 12 (1931): 249. In any event, it is questionable whether Freud's assumption of wish-fulfilling endopsychic fantasies requires a theory of drives, which cannot account for the content of the fantasies as they are recalled. The same is true for Freud's notion of defense and for other important notions, the sexual and emotional turmoil of children, the reality of the unconscious (i.e., in terms of the memory of affecting but disavowed experience that is still recallable), the way that acting out serves people as a substitute for memory, and so on.

129. First quotation, in Joseph Sandler, "Psychological Conflict and the Structural Model: Some Clinical and Theoretical Implications," *IJPA* 55 (1974): 58 (italics in the original). Second quotation, Joseph Sandler, "Reflections on Some Relations between Psychoanalytic Concepts and Psychoanalytic Practise," *IJPA* 64 (1983): 42 (italics in the original).See also Joseph Sandler, "Reality and the Stabilizing Function of Unconscious Fantasy," *Bulletin of the Anna Freud Center* 9 (1986): 186.

130. Joseph and Anne-Marie Sandler distinguish between a "past unconscious" and a "present unconscious." The former includes internalized childhood relationships and conflicts, while the latter is oriented to the here and now; in terms of cultural analysis, the latter is of greater theoretical interest than the former. "The 'Second Censorship,' the 'Three Box Model,' and some Technical Implications," *IJPA* 64 (1983): 413–25.

131. Joseph Sandler, "The Id—or the Child Within?" in *Dimensions of Psychoanalysis*, 221, referred to again in "Toward a Reconsideration of the Psychoanalytic Theory of Motivation," 106. On the importance of this text to the ego psychologists, see Heinz Hartmann, Ernst Kris, and Rudolph M. Loewenstein, "Comments on the Formation of Psychic Structure," in *Papers on Psychoanalytic Psychology*, Psychological Issues 4 (1964): 28. The original Kris statement that Sandler quoted is from "Discussion of Problems in Clinical Research," Round Table, *American Journal of Orthopsychiatry* 17 (1947): 210–14.

132. Heinz Hartmann and Ernst Kris, "The Genetic Approach in Psychoanalysis," in *Papers on Psychoanalytic Psychology*, ed. Hartmann, Kris, and Loewenstein, 20.

133. Robert W. White, *Ego and Reality in Psychoanalytic Theory*, Monograph 11, Psychological Issues (New York: International Universities Press,

1963), 156. In *Affects as Process* (142–43) Joseph M. Jones noted Robert White's contribution to the issue of competence/mastery as a motivational system (from "Motivation Reconsidered: The Concept of Competence," *Psychological Review* 66 [1959]: 297–333). White wanted to separate the instinct for mastery from aggression. Earlier, Ives Hendrick, "The Discussion of 'the Instinct to Master,'" *Psychoanalytic Quarterly* 11 (1943): 564, wanted to separate it from sadism. See also Eric A. Plaut, "Ego Instincts," *Ps St Chi* 39 (1984): 240.

134. Leo Rangell, "A Further Attempt to Resolve the 'Problem of Anxiety,'" in *The Human Core*, 1:277–78. Rangell refers to Strachey's comments on *Inhibitions, Symptoms, and Anxiety*, 278–79, concluding that Freud never really fused the two lines of thinking on anxiety in a way satisfactory to himself or to others. See also, for example, Martin S. Bergmann, *The Anatomy of Loving: The Story of Man's Quest to Know What Love Is* (New York: Columbia University Press, 1987), 173n.

135. Freud, "An Autobiographical Study," *SE* 20:72 (Postscript, 1935).

136. Holt, "The Past and Future of Ego Psychology," in *Freud Reappraised*, 212–13.

137. Subsequently she did say so. Joseph Sandler with Anna Freud, *The Analysis of the Defense: The Ego and the Mechanisms of Defense Revisited* (New York: International Universities Press, 1985), 264. Paul Gray, *The Ego and Analysis of Defense* (Northvale, N.J.: Jason Aronson, 1994), xviii.

138. Charles Spezzano, *Affect in Psychoanalysis*, 61. Peter Barglow and Leo Sadow, "Visual Perception: Its Development and Maturation from Birth to Adulthood," *JAPA* 19 (1971): 435.

139. Anna Freud, *The Ego and the Mechanisms of Defense*, *The Writings of Anna Freud*, 2:57.

140. John Bowlby, "Separation Anxiety: A Critical Review of the Literature," *Journal of Child Psychology and Psychiatry* 1 (1961): 251-69.

141. Edith Jacobson, *Depression*, 9.

142. Joseph Sandler, "The Id—or the Child Within?" 237.

143. Joseph Sandler, "Reality and the Stabilizing Function of Unconscious Fantasy," 186, 191.

144. Joseph Sandler, "The Role of Affects in Psychoanalyitc Theory," in *From Safety to Superego*, 285–97. Aaron Karush, "Instinct and Affect," in *Psychoanalysis: Toward the Second Century*, ed. Arnold Cooper, 83.

145. W. G. Joffe and Joseph Sandler, "Comments on the Psychoanalytic Psychology of Adaptation with Special Reference to the Role of Affects and the Representational World," *IJPA* 49 (1968): 447, 450–51 (italics in the original). Sandler notes that he and Joffe prefer the language of "feelings states," rather than "affect" because the term "affect" in a technical sense implies bodily changes as well as feeling states, which is more than they want to imply. See Sandler and Joffe, "Toward a Basic Psychoanalytic Model," *IJPA* 50 (1969): 79–90. Joseph Sandler, "Reality and the Stabilizing Function of Unconscious Fantasy," 191.

146. The quotations are from Jay Greenberg, *Oedipus and Beyond*, 162. Greenberg's work is in good part derived from Sandler's.

147. Masson, *Letters*, Draft M, 247 (May 25, 1897; italics added).

148. Robert Wallerstein, "Psychoanalysis as a Science," *Psychoanalytic Quarterly* 55 (1986): 432.

149. See Donald P. Spence, *The Rhetorical Voice of Psychoanalysis*, 3–4.

150. Daniel L. Schacter, *Searching for Memory*, 217, 266. Holt, *Freud Reappraised*, 285–86. Edgar Levenson, *The Ambiguity of Change* (New York: Basic Books, 1983), 14–17.

151. The first quotation is from Morris Eagle, *Recent Developments in Psychoanalysis: A Critical Evaluation* (Cambridge, Mass.: Harvard University Press, 1984), 110–11; the second is from Jerome Kagan, "A Conceptual Analysis of the Affects," in *Affect: Psychoanalytic Perspectives*, ed. Shapiro and Emde, 126. Kagan acknowledges his reliance on Eagle in his own discussion of the problem.

152. Jerome Kagan, "A Conceptual Analysis of the Affects," 126 (italics added).

153. Jay Greenberg, *Oedipus and Beyond*, 147, 166, 170.

154. Edith Jacobson, *Depression*, 3, 9.

155. See Cecilio Paniagua, "Common Ground, Uncommon Methods," *IJPA* 76 (1995): 359, 366–67. Paniagua addresses the problems of inference and technique, but his solution does not appear promising.

CHAPTER 5. THE LESSONS FOR SOCIAL THEORY

1. Quoted in Irving Louis Horowitz, *The Decomposition of Sociology*, 9.

2. "There are the old advocates of neoclassical synthesis, monetarists, new classicals, neo- and post-Keynesians, neo-institutionalists, supply-siders and several variant Marxists." Richard Parker, "The Momentary Science," *NYTBR* (January 28, 1996), 29. "To the uninitiated, it can be startling to discover how much disagreement there is at the top." Peter Engel, "What Science Can't Tell Us," *NYTBR* (October 28, 1992), 12.

3. Arthur L. Stinchcombe, "Disintegrated Discipline and the Future of Sociology," *Sociological Forum* 9 (1994): 280, 290. Roy Schafer, cited in Arnold D. Richards, "The Search for Common Ground," in *The Common Ground of Psychoanalysis*, ed. Robert Wallerstein, 262. Donald McCloskey, *Knowledge and Persuasion in Economics*, 27–37, 75.

4. These terms are adapted from Alfred S. Eichner, "Why Economics Is Not Yet a Science," in *Why Economics Is Not Yet a Science*, ed. Alfred S. Eichner (Armonk, N.Y.: M. E. Sharpe, 1983), 207–8.

5. Charles E. Lindblom and David K. Cohen, *Usable Knowledge: Social Science and Social Problem Solving* (New Haven, Conn.: Yale University Press, 1979), 6, 10, 15–16. For a contrasting point of view, see Robert Bellah et al., *Habits of the Heart: Individualism and Commitment in American Life* (New York: Harper & Row, 1985), 298.

6. To cite a recent example, Vladimir Zhirinovsky received 24 percent of the Russian vote in the elections of December 1993, and 6 percent of the vote in the elections of June 1996. William R. Meyers et al., "Jean Marie Le Pen, Vladimir Zhirinovsky, and the World Press," paper read at the meetings of the

International Society of Political Psychology," Montreal, Canada, July 13, 1998. See Richard F. Hamilton's critique of Thomas Childers in *The Social Misconstruction of Reality: Validity and Verification in the Scholarly Community* (New Haven, Conn.: Yale University Press, 1996), 258n40, and the discussions on 112–13, 126–27, and 251n7. But see also Childers's comments on the heterogeneous composition of the Nazi Party in *The Nazi Voter: The Social Foundations of Fascism in Germany, 1919–1933* (Chapel Hill: University of North Carolina Press, 1983), 118, 127, 268; and in "The Social Language of Politics in Germany," *American Historical Review* 95 (1990): 354–57. Whatever the problems with Childers's work, his basic question, how a heterogeneous population was oriented to a common goal, is the correct one. Barrington Moore Jr., *Injustice: The Social Basis of Obedience and Revolt* (White Plains, N.Y.: M. E. Sharpe, 1978), 409–11.

7. Gordon S. Wood, *The Creation of the American Republic, 1776–1787* (New York: W. W. Norton, 1972), 606, 449.

8. Ibid., 593, 389. See also Wood, *The Radicalism of the American Revolution* (New York: Knopf, 1994), 247.

9. Gordon S. Wood, *The Creation of the American Republic*, 484.

10. Ibid., 491–92, 499. This point was repeated in *The Radicalism of the American Revolution*, 258; see also 294.

11. Gordon S. Wood, *The Creation of the American Republic*, 502.

12. Gordon S. Wood, "Star-Spangled History," (a review of Robert Middlekauff's *The Glorious Cause: The American Revolution, 1763–1789*), *The New York Review of Books* (August 12, 1982), 8. Wood, "Ideology and the Origins of Liberal America," *William and Mary Quarterly* 44 (July 1987): 633.

13. Gordon S. Wood, *The Creation of the American Republic*, 472; *The Radicalism of the American Revolution*, 255, 363–67; and "Ideology and the Liberal Origins of America," 635, 638.

14. Gordon S. Wood, *The Creation of the American Republic*, 524. "Indeed the entire Revolution could be summed up by the radical transformation Americans made in their understanding of property." *The Radicalism of the American Revolution*, 269–70, 229.

15. Gordon S. Wood, "Not So Poor Richard," (a review of Robert Middlekauff's *Benjamin Franklin and His Enemies*, and David T. Morgan's *The Devious Dr. Franklin, Colonial Agent*), *The New York Review of Books* (June 6, 1996), 48–49.

16. The Chicago school of sociology developed around the question raised by Madison, namely, how could the claims of many self-interested, competing groups be reconciled? Berenice M. Fisher and Anselm L. Strauss, "Interactionism," in *A History of Sociological Analysis*, ed. Tom Bottomore and Robert Nisbet (New York: Basic Books, 1978), 461–62.

17. The literature includes Erich Fromm, *Man for Himself* (New York: Holt, Rinehart and Winston, 1947); David Riesman et al., *The Lonely Crowd* (Garden City, N.Y.: Anchor Doubleday, 1950); William H. Whyte Jr., *The Organization Man* (New York: Simon & Shuster, 1956); Kenneth Keniston, *The Uncommitted: Alienated Youth in American Society* (New York: Harcourt, Brace and World, 1965), and *Young Radicals: Notes on Committed Youth* (New York:

Harcourt, Brace and World, 1968); Charles A. Reich, *The Greening of America* (New York: Bantam Books, 1970); Christopher Lasch, *The Culture of Narcissism* (New York: Warner Books, 1979). Specific references include Reich, *The Greening of America*, 2–4, 416–19; and Lasch, *The Culture of Narcissism*, 391. Lasch's solution to the confound (127–28) was to claim that the others had it wrong from the beginning and that narcissism had been the real issue all along.

18. See the references cited in note 6. In addition, see Richard F. Hamilton, *Who Voted for Hitler?* (Princeton, N.J.: Princeton University Press, 1982), 375, 383–85, 391–92, 413–17, 426–27. 435, 448, and 451, 420–21. Michael Kater, *The Nazi Party: A Social Profile of Members and Leaders, 1919–1945* (Cambridge, Mass.: Harvard University Press, 1983), 287, 155 (on the heterogeneous composition of the Nazi Party). I addressed the heterogeneity and discontinuity problems in *The Dynamics of Nazism* (New York: Academic Press, 1980), 17–32. See notes 68–70, 45–46 for the relevant bibliography, including the Theodore Abel reference.

19. Eric A. Sillmer et al., *The Quest for the Nazi Personality. A Psychological Investigation of Nazi War Criminals* (Hillsdale, N.J.: Lawrence Erlbaum Associates, 1995), 99. The authors cite instances of opposed conclusions but their conclusion, based on their own research and that of other observers, is clear: "The most important overall statement regarding these [Nuremberg] defendants, however, is the degree to which each of these individual records contained idiosyncratic features, and the wide response variability in members of this group" (96).

20. Gerald M. Platt has explained in detail the deficiencies of this approach in "Thoughts on a Theory of Collective Action," *New Diretions in Psychohistory*, ed. Mel Albin (Lexington, Mass.: D. C. Heath, 1980), 75.

21. *Das Ende der Parteien, 1933*, ed. Erich Matthias and Rudolf Morsey (Düsseldorf: Droste Verlag, 1960), 234, 239–40.

22. Platt, "Thoughts on a Theory of Collective," 69–94.

23. Alberto Melucci, "Getting Involved: Identity and Mobilization in Social Movements," in *From Structure to Action: Comparing Social Movements Research Across Cultures*, ed. Bert Klandermans, Hanspeter Kriesi, and Sidney Tarrow (Greenwich, Conn.: JAI Press, 1988), 329–48. Gerald M. Platt, "Thoughts on a Theory of Collective Action," 78–82.

24. Seymour Martin Lipset, *Political Man: The Social Bases of Politics* (Garden City, N.Y.: Anchor Doubleday, 1960), 129, 137, 148n29. Lipset claimed a fairly logical relationship in Weimar Germany between ideology and social base, noting that "[t]he Socialist left derives its strength from manual workers and the poorer rural strata," while the democratic center derives its strength from "the middle classes, especially small businessmen, white-collar workers, and the anti-clerical sections of the professional classes." However, having analyzed the vote in 1930, Lipset was obliged to point out that an estimated 40 percent of Socialist Party voters were not manual workers; rather the party was backed in 1930 by 25 percent of the white-collar workers, 33 percent of the lower civil servants, and 25 percent of the self-employed in artisan shops and retail business. There was no way that a conventional social science could survive numbers like that.

25. Patricia J. Williams, *The Alchemy of Race and Rights* (Cambridge, Mass.: Harvard University Press, 1991), 256.

26. Michael Hechter, "Through Thick and Thin. How Far Can Theory Predict Behavior?" *Times Literary Supplement* (March 29, 1996), 15. Donald P. Green and Ian Shapiro, *Pathologies of Rational Choice Theory: A Critique of Applications in Political Science* (New Haven, Conn.: Yale University Press, 1994), 189.

27. On the critique in economics of rationality as the one motive for behavior, see Adrian Furnham and Alan Lewis, *The Economic Mind: The Social Psychology of Economic Behavior* (New York: St. Martin's Press, 1986), 10–12. See also *New Directions in Economic Psychology: Theory, Experiment and Application*, ed. Stephen E. G. Lea et al. (Aldershot, England: Edward Elgar, 1992), 4. For a critique of Milton Friedman and the reliance on a theory of rationality, see ibid., 4–10.

28. Green and Shapiro, *Pathologies of Rational Choice Theory*, 18.

29. Robert Heilbroner and William Milberg, *The Crisis of Vision in Modern Economic Thought* (New York: Cambridge University Press, 1995), 92–93. The authors note that the flexibility of rational choice theory would be a strength "if *empirical* inquiry could satisfactorily sort out the valid from the invalid insight of rational decision making. But this has not been the case" (italics in the original). Green and Shapiro, *Pathologies of Rational Choice Theory*, 186–97. John L. Casti, *Searching for Certainty* (New York: William Morrow & Co., 1990), 249, 251. Casti was still looking for a deterministic rule or mechanism that governs the price generation process, apart from the subjective intentions of people.

30. Herman Melville, *Moby-Dick*, ed. Harrison Hayford and Hershel Parker (New York: W. W. Norton, 1967), 160–61, 184. Ahab thinks of his crew (183–84) that "[t]hey may scorn cash now; but let some months go by, and no perspective promise of it to them, and then this same quiescent cash all at once mutinying in them, this same cash would soon cashier Ahab." This is an excellent example of rational calculation of means and ends. J. Ron Stanfield, "Institutional Analysis: Toward Progress in Economic Science," in *Why Economics Is Not Yet a Science*, ed. Alfred S. Eichner, 190.

31. On Antonio Damasio's depiction of weaknesses in "rational thinking," *Descartes' Error*, 165–75, especially 172, 174, 191.

32. Ibid., 115.

33. Hechter ("Through Thick and Thin: How Far Can Theory Predict Behaviour?" 15), and Green and Shapiro (*Pathologies of Rational Choice Theory*, 17–18) discuss thick and thin models of rational choice theory. Thick models, as Hechter notes, are often just plain wrong, and thin models can be used to account for anything, they are "substantively empty."

34. Leslie Eaton, "The Bulls and Bears and the Little Pigs," *The New York Times* (March 2, 1997), sec. 4, p. 4. "Psychology may be as important as reality [sic] in determining what happens to the economy and inflation."

35. Jonathan Feuerbringer, "Why Both Bulls and Bears Can Act So Bird-Brained," *The New York Times* (March 30, 1997), sec. 3, pp. 1, 6. Feuerbringer claims that the economics establishment has come a long way in understanding

behavioral about-faces and unexpected responses. This is consistent with Donald McCloskey's observation that "economics cannot supply the social engineering it promises, so it had better learn the stories." "Introduction," *Second Thoughts*, 5. One of the behavioral considerations worth examining here too is loss. See, for example, Adrian Furnham and Alan Lewis, *The Economic Mind*, 128 (with references to Colin Parkes, *Bereavement: Studies of Grief in Adult Life*, and John Bowlby, *Attachment and Loss*).

36. "25 Years: Social Science and Social Change," *The Institute Letter* (Princeton, N.J., Spring 1997), 1 (no author cited).

37. Jonathan Fuerbringer, "Why Both Bulls and Bears Can Act So Bird-Brained," 1, 6. See also Robert A. Johnson, "What Asia's Financial Crisis Portends," *The New York Times* (December 29, 1997), A19. Johnson, chief economist of the Senate Banking Committee in 1987–88 and a former managing director at Soros Fund Management, noted that responses to the recent Asian crisis are "a matter of subjective psychology."

38. Mark Casson, "Moral Constraints on Strategic Behaviour," in *New Directions in Economic Psychology*, ed. Stephen E. G. Lea et al., 66. Casson emphasizes the relevance of culture to economics. See also Kenneth Boulding, "Economics as a Moral Science," *American Economic Review* 59 (1969): 1–12; and Donald McCloskey, *Knowledge and Persuasion in Economics*, 95, 101. For the record, Heinz Hartmann wrote almost fifty years ago that "Social Science no doubt falls short of its aims as long as it bases its interpretation of human behavior exclusively on the model of the interest-directed . . . utilitarian type of action." "Comments on the Psychoanalytic Theory of the Ego," *Ps St Chi* 5 (1950): 91. See also Alberto Melucci, "Getting Involved: Identity and Mobilization in Social Movements," 329–48.

39. Antonio Imbasciati, "A Psychoanalytic Model of Cognitive Processes," 225. In his interesting work on the First World War, *Rites of Spring*, Modris Ecksteins refers many times to fantasy thinking without ever indicating what he means by the term. (New York: Black Swan Press, 1990), 104, 131, 133, 136, 145, 221, 239, 265, 267. For a survey of the role of fantasy thinking in psychoanalysis see Ethel S. Person, *By Force of Fantasy. How We Make Our Lives* (New York: Basic Books, 1995).

40. A number of psychoanalysts have noted that the structural theory is outmoded (Eric Gillett, "Revising Freud's Structural Theory," 495–96), and retains its primacy only by default, because there is apparently nothing better at the moment (Martin Leichtman, "Developmental Psychology and Psychoanalysis," 939). If the id has structure and therefore a history, as Otto Kernberg and others have claimed, there is no point in continuing with the structural model. See Richard Kuhns on Otto Kernberg, "Governing of the Self," in *Theories of the Unconscious and Theories of the Self*, ed. Raphael Stern, 51; and Morris Eagle, "The Psychoanalytic and the Cognitive Unconscious," ibid., 177–78.

41. Thomas H. Ogden, "On Potential Space," *IJPA* 66 (1985): 129–41. Reality refers to that which is experienced as outside the realm of the subject's omnipotence (135). It is in this sense that "[e]very psychic reality awaits an objective challenge." "Panel Report, Psychic Reality: Theoretical Concepts," Reporter, Paul Williams, *IJPA* 77 (1997): 80. On different views on fantasy

thinking, in addition to Person, *By Force of Fantasy*, see Joseph Sandler and Humberto Nagera, "Aspects of the Metapsychology of Fantasy," *Ps St Chi* 18 (1963), especially 163.

42. Cecily de Monchaux, "Thinking and Negative Hallucination," *IJPA* 43 (1962): 314.

43. Quoted in Stephen M. Rittenberg's review of Ethel Spector Person's *By Force of Fantasy*, *IJPA* 77 (1996): 1047.

44. Pierre Bourdieu, *Outline of a Theory of Practice*, 86.

45. Freud, "Analysis Terminable and Interminable," *SE* 23:225.

46. Jean Paul Sartre, *Search for a Method* (New York: Vintage Books, 1968), 90.

47. Fred Weinstein, *History and Theory after the Fall*, 89–90, on Marx, 89–111, on wishful thinking in general and among Marxists in particular.

48. See the discussion in Gilbert J. Rose, *The Power of Form: A Psychoanalytic Approach to Aesthetic Form*, 28–32. See also Donald Spence, "Momentary Forgetting: an Alternative Formulation," in *Psychodynamics and Cognition*, ed. Mardi J. Horowitz, 256. Spence tried to explain how this kind of thinking might work.

49. Gerald M. Platt and Chad Gordon, "Introduction," *Self, Collective Behavior, and Society: Essays Honoring the Contributions of Ralph H. Turner*, ed. Platt and Gordon (Greenwich, Conn.: JAI Press, 1994), 1–16. See also Antonio Damasio on "somatic markers," in *Descartes' Error*, 174. Joseph LeDoux, *The Emotional Brain*, passim. Jerome L. Singer, "Sampling Ongoing Consciousness and Emotional Experience: Implications for Health," in *Psychodynamics and Cognition*, ed. Mardi J. Horowitz, 299–300. Kristin R. Monroe, "Psychology and Rational Actor Theory," *Political Psychology* 16 (March 1995): 6–15. Donald McCloskey cites the relevant literature on the failure of rational choice theory in *Knowledge and Persuasion in Economics*, 88–89, 209.

50. Benjamin Nelson, "Cultural Cues and Directive Systems," in *On the Roads to Modernity: Selected Writings by Benjamin Nelson*, ed. Toby E. Huff (Totowa, N.J.: Rowman and Littlefield, 1981), 17–33, 5. See also *Social Movements and Culture*, ed. Hank Johnston and Bert Klandermans (Minneapolis: University of Minnesota Press, 1995), and *New Social Movements: From Ideology to Identity*, ed. Enrique LaRana, Hank Johnston, and Joseph Gusfield (Philadelphia, Pa.: Temple University Press, 1994).

51. Carol McClurg Mueller, "Building Social Movement Theory," in *Frontiers in Social Movement Theory*, ed. Aldon Morris and Carol McClurg Mueller (New Haven, Conn.: Yale University Press, 1992), 3–22; for the specific references here, 3–5. Alberto Melucci, "The Process of Collective Identity," in *Social Movements and Culture*, ed. Hank Johnston and Bert Klandermans, 41–63.

52. Robert N. Bellah, *Beyond Belief: Essays on Religion in a Post-Traditional World* (New York: Harper & Row, 1970), 252.

53. Jon Elster, *Cement of Society*, 287; the quotation is from 100 (italics in the original). This reverses Elster's earlier arguments on behalf of rational choice theory. See Green and Shapiro, *Pathologies of Rational Choice Theory*, 186–87.

54. Talcott Parsons, "Superego and the Theory of Social Systems," in *Social Structure and Personality*, 19.

55. Charles Tilly, *As Sociology Meets History* (New York: Academic Press, 1981), 95–108 (the quoted passage is on page 108).

56. Jon Elster, *The Cement of Society*, 15, 104–5. At one point Elster even made some brief references to the work of Sigmund Freud and Otto Fenichel, although none of the names (i.e., Durkheim, Freud, Fenichel), appear in the index. With respect to Elster's statements and the references to economic behavior made earlier, Emile Durkheim had long since pointed out that rational adherence to contractual obligations implies a moral commitment that is of a higher order than the rational performance obligated by the commitment.

57. Mustafa Emirbayer, "Useful Durkheim," *Sociological Theory* 14 (1996): 109–30.

58. Richard F. Hamilton, *Who Voted for Hitler?* (Princeton, N.J.: Princeton University Press, 1982), 426–27, 435, 448. Kevin Durrheim, "Theoretical Conundrum: The Politics and Science of Theorizing Authoritarian Cognition," *Political Psychology* 18 (1997): 626. Durrheim points out that ideologically driven "scientific" studies have variously concluded that irrational cognitive functioning is associated with conservatism, liberalism, communism, fascism, radicalism, extremism, and moderatism. Durrheim provides the bibliography for each instance.

59. David C. Riccio et al., "Memory: When Less Is More," *American Psychologist* 49 (1994): 917.

60. See Joseph Sandler, "Psychoanalytic Psychology and Learning Theory," in *From Safety to Superego*, 257–58.

61. For a summary explanation of why Winnicott can serve and Lacan, for example, cannot, see Jane Flax, *Thinking Fragments: Psychoanalysis, Feminism, and Post-Modernism in the Contemporary West* (Berkeley: University of California Press, 1990), 84–132.

62. D. W. Winnicott, "Transitional Objects and Transitional Phenomena," in *Collected Papers* (London: Tavistock, 1958), 230.

63. Peter L. Berger and Thomas Luckmann, *The Social Construction of Reality* (New York: Anchor Books, 1967), 102–3.

64. On subjective relevance, note Elias Canetti's observation of a particular German experience in the Weimar and Nazi eras: "Prohibition of the army was like prohibition of religion, of specific and sacrosanct practices without which life could not be imagined—and this resulted in unlimited recruitment to the Nazis from within the nation." *Crowds and Power* (London: Gollancz, 1962), 181.

65. Fred Weinstein, *History and Theory after the Fall*, 115.

66. Virginia Hunter, *Psychoanalysts Talk* (New York: The Guilford Press, 1994), 225. See also Morris Eagle, "The Psychoanalytic and the Cognitive Unconscious," 179–80, on unintegrated, unobserved, or disowned mental contents; and Donald Spence,"Momentary Forgetting: An Alternative Formulation," 254–58.

67. D. W. Winnicott, "Transitional Objects and Transitional Phenomena," in *Playing and Reality*, ed. Winnicott (London: Tavistock Publications, 1971), 89.

68. It bears emphasizing that "common agreement" on the importance of events and of narrative tales of past triumphs and virtuous responses does not

imply that events are perceived by people in the same way or that they mean the same things to them.

69. Clifford Geertz, "Ideology as a Social System," in *The Interpretation of Culture*, 193–233. Fred Weinstein, *The Dynamics of Nazism*, 118–19. Gordon S. Wood, "Ideology and the Origins of Liberal America," 629–31.

70. Benjamin Nelson, "Cultural Cues and Directive Systems," in *On the Roads to Modernity*, ed. Toby Huff, 17–33.

71. Gerald M. Platt, "Thoughts on a Theory of Collective Action," 78–82. See also Antonio Damasio, *Descartes' Error*, passim.

72. Some sociologists have claimed that informal local organizations pursuing expressive—as distinct from instrumental—goals can function in the absence of authoritative leadership because flexibility, small size, and shared values are conducive to such expressive goals. Manisha Desai, "Informal Organizations as Agents of Change: Notes from the Contemporary Women's Movement in India," *Mobilization* 1 (1996): 159–73. Belinda Robnett, *How Long? How Long? African-American Women in the Struggle for Civil Rights* (New York: Oxford University Press, 1997).

73. Hence they have always vacillated between dependence and independence, in the extreme, between surrender and rebellion, a result of inevitable discrepancies between cultural ideals and real levels of attainment.

74. Clifford Geertz, *Local Knowledge: Further Essays in Interpretive Anthropology* (New York: Basic Books, 1983), 122–23. Geertz discussed charismatic authority as it is related to "the active centers of the social order," referring, in his explanation of emotional and even idealized commitments, to "concentrated loci of serious acts," the "point or points in a society where its leading ideas come together with its leading institutions to create an arena in which the events that most vitally affect its members' lives take place."

75. As W. R. D. Fairbairn put it, "You can go on analyzing forever and get nowhere. It's the personal relation that is therapeutic." In other words, the "cure" is in the relationship, not in the interpretations. In Harry Guntrip, "My Experience of Analysis with Fairbairn and Winnicott," *IRPA* 2 (1975): 145.

76. Gerald M. Platt and Stephen J. Lilly, "Multiple Images of a Charismatic: An Interpretive Conception of Martin Luther King Jr.'s Leadership," in *Self, Collective Behavior and Society*, ed. Platt and Gordon, 55–74. In the therapeutic situation it would be hard to find a patient who does not make decisions about what to tell and when to tell it.

77. Charles Rycroft, *Imagination and Reality* (New York: International Universities Press, 1968), 102–3.

78. See the references to Luigi Pirandello and F. Scott Fitzgerald in Stephen Rittenberg and L. Noah Shaw, "On Fantasies of Self-Creation," *Ps St Chi* 46 (1991): 220–24.

79. Bruner, *Actual Minds, Possible Worlds*, 141. Holt, "Present Status of the Primary Process," in *Freud Reappraised*, 285.

80. Roy Schafer, *Aspects of Internalization* (New York: International Universities Press, 1968), 132, 135. Note also W. R. D. Fairbairn's comment that "[e]motion can be drained out of the old patterns by new experience." Harry Guntrip, "My Experience in Analysis with Fairbairn and Winnicott," 145. Paul

A. Dewald, "Transference Regression and Real Experience in the Psychoanalytic Process," *Psychoanalytic Quarterly* 45 (1976): 216–17.

81. Bharati Mukherjee, "Two Ways to Belong in America," *The New York Times* (September 22, 1996), E13.

82. Antonio Damasio, *Descartes' Error*, 158. Hans W. Loewald also referred to "repetition as recreation," as distinct from "repetition as reproduction," in "Some Considerations on Repetition and Repetition Compulsion," *IJPA* 52 (1971): 60.

83. Bharati Mukherjee, "Immigrant Writing: Give Us Your Maximalists!" *NYTBR* (August 28, 1988), 29. Mukherjee addressed this issue more formally in her own *Jasmine* (New York: Grove Weidenfeld, 1989), 85, 215.

84. As a reminder, Peter Fonagy has written, "Psychoanalysis is more than the creation of a narrative, it is the active construction of a new way of experiencing self with others." "Memory and Therapeutic Action," *IJPA* 80 (1999): 218.

85. Jerome Bruner, *Actual Minds, Possible Worlds*, 117–18.

86. Of course these things are also represented in the mind.

87. Jerome Bruner, *Acts of Meaning*, e.g., 33–65. Idem., *Actual Minds, Possible Worlds*, 11–43, especially 13.

88. Friedrich Engels tried to explain the need to particularize Marx's theory in a letter to Joseph Bloch that has been publicly available for some time. See Howard Selsam et al., *Dynamics of Social Change* (New York: International Publishers, 1975), 76–77.

89. Joseph Le Doux, *The Emotional Brain*, 177.

90. Ibid., 63. Note especially the references to the work of social psychologist John Bargh. Thomas M. Ostrom, "Three Catechisms for Social Memory," 203–4, 207. On scripts, schemas, and stories, see Bradd Shore, *Culture in Mind: Cognition, Culture, and the Problem of Meaning* (New York: Oxford University Press, 1996), 343–72; Mardi J. Horowitz, "Psychodynamic Phenomena and Their Explanation," in *Psychodynamics and Cognition*, 13–17; and Jerome L. Singer, "Sampling Ongoing Consciousness and Emotional Experience: Implications for Health," ibid., 327–32. See the Singer paper as well for the kinds of experimental studies that I am referring to; or Jerome Bruner, *Actual Minds, Possible Worlds*, 89–92.

91. Richard A. Shweder, *Thinking through Cultures*, 259–60, 279–80. On effectance pleasure, Joseph M. Jones, *Affect as Process*, 144.

92. Thomas M. Ostrom, "Three Catechisms for Social Memory," 205, 209–9, 211 ("Despite the prominent role of language in social interaction, social psychologists have stubbornly resisted the study of language."). Of course, language is studied in many other contexts. On collective memory, see Maurice Halbwachs, *La Mémoire collective* (Paris: Presses Universitaires de France, 1950, 2nd edition, 1968); English edition, *The Collective Memory* (New York: Harper & Row, 1980). Ostrom notes (213) that Halbwach's work on the social distribution of memory is fully congruent with contemporary information-processing concepts. But it is easier to write on collective memory (or collective identity) than to show how it happens. See also Susan A. Crane, "Writing the Individual Back into Collective Memory," and Alon Confino, "Collective Mem-

ory and Cultural History: Problems of Method," *American Historical Review* 102 (1997): 1371–1403.

93. Morris Eagle, *Recent Developments in Psychoanalysis*, 138.

94. "The American economy may be capable of generating more production and prosperity—without inflation—than either the statistics or conventional theory acknowledge. . . . This deviation from economic dogma produces puzzling statistics. . . . Inevitably, economists are debating the accuracy of their assumptions." Louis Uchitelle, "New Economy Dashes Old Notions of Growth," *The New York Times* (November 27, 1994), sec. 4, p. 5.

95. Their predictive theory on inflation failed, but the policies they had promoted on the basis of the theory protected the well-being of one group over others. The policies they had recommended on the basis of a failed theory were certainly not the only ones possible; other possible policies would have favored other groups.

96. Claudia Golden, who teaches economic history at Harvard, probably had some question like this in mind when she noted that "[e]xplanations for why the stock market went up or down . . . belong on the funny pages." Quoted in Peter Passell, "Trends Are Down, Yet the Market's Up," *The New York Times* (May 7, 1995), sec. 4, p. 6. The explanations for market activity that belong on the funny page include "seasonal fluctuations," "profit-taking," "market correction," and the more recent "rolling correction."

97. Richard W. Stevenson, "Joblessness Is Down. Prices Aren't Up. Go Figure," *The New York Times* (April 11, 1999), sec. 4, p. 18.

98. Quoted in Keith Bradsher "Greenspan Says the Fed Uses Anecdotal Guides," *The New York Times* (August 11, 1994), D2; and Alfred L. Malabre Jr., *Lost Prophets: An Insider's History of the Modern Economists* (Boston, Mass.: Harvard Business School Press, 1994), 216.

99. Richard F. Hamilton, *Who Voted for Hitler?* 463, 451, 420–21.

100. Richard F. Hamilton, *The Social Misconstruction of Reality*, 165–67, 197–223.

101. Harold N. Boris, "On Hope: Its Nature and Psychotherapy," *IRPA* 3 (1976): 145.

INDEX